Pre-publication praise for
Without a Prayer

John Robbins is as stalwart a defender of a free society as I have known. His love of freedom—religious, political, and economic—motivated him to write *Without a Prayer,* a brilliantly insightful analysis of Ayn Rand's influential philosophy. *Without a Prayer* deserves to be read by everyone who loves freedom— everyone who wants to advocate freedom with arguments that cannot be refuted. Robbins furnishes the indispensable ideas— the intellectual ammunition—required to defend freedom successfully.

> —Ron Paul (R-TX)
> U. S. House of Representatives
> Washington, D. C.

Dr. Robbins is a Christian scholar, an indefatigable researcher, and a brillant logician. . . . There are no *ad hominem* tactics in this book, no debater's tricks; just straight-forward reasoning at a high level. A well structured argument is a work of art; to follow this one is an exhilarating experience.

> –Edmund A. Opitz
> Foundation for Economic Education
> New York

This is a powerful book—a book of strong reasoning, sound apologetics, passionate persuasion, and brilliant logic—all aimed at dismantling the error with which Ayn Rand mesmerized perhaps a generation or two.

Dr. Robbins removes, with surgical accuracy, the attractive outer layer of Rand's lethal philosophy to reveal the familiar underlying corruption of humanism and atheism. Some may find his attack too aggressive, too inclusive, too uncompromising. But the influence on a nation's spirituality left by Ayn Rand requires the counter-blow of a giant intellect in order to move at least one wrong from the throne to the scaffold.

—D. James Kennedy
Coral Ridge Presbyterian Church
Ft. Lauderdale, Florida

John Robbins has performed a salutary service by making a critical analysis of Objectivism. . . . Robbins demonstrates at length that Rand's thought was derivative, that she was a child of her age and was greatly influenced by 19th and early 20th century thought, that of materialists and atheists . . . Friedrich Nietzsche, Karl Marx, Friedrich Engels. . . .

—Clarence B. Carson
American Historian
Alabama

By careful, minute argumentation John Robbins refutes the Objectivist position of atheist Ayn Rand and her followers. . . . His chapters on epistemology and on values are worth the price of the book.

—Jay E. Adams
Best-selling Christian Author
South Carolina

Fallacies, falsehoods, question-beggings, stolen concepts and evil masquerading as good—these are but some of the failings in Ayn Rand's system, which have been brought to light by John Robbins' penetrating and cogent analysis. No matter what they might have said before, the Objectivists no longer have any excuses. I say this as a Christian Objectivist myself.

—Michael Bauman
Professor of Theology and Culture
Hillsdale College
Hillsdale, Michigan

WITHOUT A PRAYER

AYN RAND AND THE CLOSE OF HER SYSTEM

WITHOUT A PRAYER

AYN RAND

AND THE

CLOSE OF HER SYSTEM

John W. Robbins

The Trinity Foundation

Without a Prayer: Ayn Rand and the Close of Her System
Copyright ©1997 John W. Robbins
Published by The Trinity Foundation

ISBN: 0-940931-50-8

CONTENTS

Acknowledgments viii
The Atheist's Creed ix
Foreword xi

Chapter 1. The Objectivist Canon 1

Chapter 2. The Meanings of *Reason* 6

Rand's Humanism 8
The Autonomy of Reason 10
Reason and Force 14
The Plan of the Book 18

Chapter 3. Imagining Truth: Objectivist Epistemology 25

The Primacy of Epistemology 25
The Meanings of "Reason" 27
The Tabula Rasa Contradiction 29
Ignoring the Problem of the Senses 31
Skepticism and Empiricism 31
The Mystics of Muscle 36
The Senses 37
Introduction to Objectivist Epistemology 38
Measurement and Science 47
Popper on Science 52
Russell on Induction 55
Concept Formation 56
Abstraction 68
Ostensive Definition 72
Open-ended Concepts 74

v

Implicit Concepts 76
What Is Truth? 77
Essences 78
Axiomatic Concepts 81
Open-ended Concepts 94
Volitional Consciousness 96
Causality 102
The Self 104
A Confession of Epistemic Failure 106

Chapter 4. Imagining Gods: Objectivist Theology 108

A Childish Atheism 108
Excursus on Rand's Attacks on Christian Doctrine 112
The Traditional Proofs for God 115
Objectivism's First God 119
Objectivism's Second God 123
Anthem 128
The War of the Gods 137

Chapter 5. Imagining Values: Objectivist Ethics 144

Definitions 145
The Alternative 147
Suicide 150
Pleasure and Pain 156
Plants, Animals, and Men 159
Epistemology and Ethics 160
Volitional Consciousness 162
Free Will and Determinism 165
Man Qua Man 172
Excursus on Good and Evil 176
Conclusion 177

Chapter 6. Imagining Justice, Peace, and Freedom:
          Objectivist Politics 180

The Incoherence of Natural Rights 181

Contents

The Initiation of Force 186
Retaliation and Self Defense 188
Excursus on the Initiation of Force in the Welfare State 190
The Crime of Punishment 192
The Consent of the Governed 193
The Depravity of Men 194
Taxation and Government Finance 200
Totalitarianism and the Doctrine of Forfeiture 203
Eating Babies for Breakfast 205
Life Unworthy of Living 209
Animal Rights 212

Chapter 7. Ayn Rand and the Close of Her System 215

The Perennial Failure of Secular Philosophy 217
The Promise of Christianity 219
Solving the Epistemological Problem 222
Conclusion 225

Appendices

A. *The Ominous Parallels* by Leonard Peikoff 229
B. *Objectivism: The Philosophy of Ayn Rand*
    by Leonard Peikoff 232
C. *The Evidence of the Senses* by David Kelley 255
D. God and Logic 277
E. Science and Truth 290
F. Kant and Old Testament Ethics 300
G. Christ and Civilization 309
H. An Introduction to Gordon H. Clark 332

Bibliography 350
Index 355
The Crisis of Our Time 383
Intellectual Ammunition 390

ACKNOWLEDGMENTS

There are several theological and philosophical debts I might acknowledge, but I shall mention only one here: that owed to the late Gordon H. Clark, Professor of Philosophy and Chairman of the Department at Butler University. Dr. Clark generously consented to read and comment upon a draft of my first book on Ayn Rand, *Answer to Ayn Rand*, and he thereby saved me from a number of errors. For his help, not only in his criticism of my work, but in his voluminous and unparalleled work in philosophy, most of which has yet to receive its proper recognition, I wish to thank Dr. Clark publicly.

I would also like to thank the Board of Trustees of The Trinity Foundation for making this book possible.

THE ATHEIST'S CREED

That Man is the product of causes which had no prevision of the end they were achieving;

That his origin, his growth, his hopes and fears, his loves and his beliefs are but the outcome of accidental collocations of atoms;

That no fire, no heroism, no intensity of thought and feeling can preserve an individual life beyond the grave;

That all the labours of the ages, all the devotion, all the inspiration, all the noonday brightness of human genius are destined to extinction in the vast death of the solar system, and the whole temple of Man's achievement must inevitably be buried beneath the debris of a universe in ruins—

All these things, if not quite beyond dispute, are yet so nearly certain, that no philosophy which rejects them can hope to stand.

Only within the scaffolding of these truths, only on the firm foundation of unyielding despair, can the soul's habitation henceforth be safely built. . . .

Brief and powerless is Man's life; on him and all his race the slow, sure doom falls pitiless and dark.

Blind to good and evil, reckless of destruction, omnipotent matter rolls on its relentless way; for Man, condemned today to lose his dearest, tomorrow himself to pass through the gate of darkness, it remains only to cherish, ere yet the blow falls, the lofty thoughts that ennoble his little day; . . . proudly defiant of the irresistible forces that tolerate, for a moment, his knowledge and his condemnation, to sustain alone, a weary but unyielding Atlas, the world that his own ideals have fashioned despite the trampling march of unconscious power.

Bertrand Russell
Mysticism and Logic

One misty winter day [near the end of her life], she [Ayn Rand] stood in front of her living room window, gazing silently at the city veiled in fog. Wearily, she said, "What was it all for?"

Barbara Branden
The Passion of Ayn Rand

FOREWORD

This is a book about ideas. It is not about personalities or movements; it is neither biographical nor sociological. Since I last wrote about Ayn Rand more than twenty years ago, Rand has died and gone to her eternal reward; two of her closest disciples have published revealing and unflattering (to them, to Rand, and to her movement) memoirs; and collections of her essays, letters, and early works have appeared, apparently with more to come. Although Rand herself is dead, her ideas, expressed in the thirty million books sold over the past 50 years, live on.

The perennial attractiveness of Rand, especially to young people of high school and college age, may be explained, not only by her ability to construct plots, but by her uncompromising vision, expressed primarily in her fiction, of how the world might be and ought to be—a vision that appeals to the idealism of youth. That was its appeal to me when I read *The Fountainhead* in my freshman year in college.

Already an individualist (because I was already a Christian), I admired Rand's portrayals of rational, creative, and intransigent individuals. After reading *The Fountainhead*, I read all that Rand published, and knew that she was a first rate novelist of ideas, or, as she herself had put it in the 1940's: a competent propagandist.[1] She was, however, more than a novelist, an entertainer, or a propagandist; she was entitled to the title philosopher, a title some academics still wish to deny her, despite her non-fiction work.

---

[1] "I'm the chief living writer of propaganda fiction, I think—at least I think I'm the only one who knows how to do it properly . . ." (*Letters of Ayn Rand*, 157).

xi

Rand's vision was particularly appealing to the lost generations of twentieth century America, the young people who had abandoned the religions of their grandfathers and great-grandfathers. She appealed to the children of those who professed Christianity but didn't believe it; to the children of those who professed Judaism, but thought the Torah an old book full of myths, fables, and foolishness. Her appeal was a religious appeal to a post-Christian America. She wrote to Channing Pollock in 1941: "We will give people a *faith*—a positive, clear and consistent system of belief."[2] And Rand did so, without the help of others.

Rand, too, rejected the Bible, but she provided a way for people to be religious without being religious. Hers was an ersatz religion, a secular religion. Like many other Jews, Rand could not accept Jesus of Nazareth as the Messiah, so she sought the Messiah elsewhere. Unlike many secular and religious Jews of the twentieth century, who thought the State of Israel was messiah, Rand found her messiah in her imagination, and expressed it in her fiction. Her messiah was not living; she imagined him: John Galt.[3] In the nineteenth and early twentieth centuries idealistic young people, rejecting the empty religious formalism of their parents and looking for a vision, were attracted to Karl Marx and his vision of Heaven on Earth, brought about by the absolute predestination of historical and material forces; in the late twentieth century, the same disaffected were attracted to Ayn Rand and her vision of Heaven on Earth.

This book is an analysis and refutation of the ideas that Rand set forth so persuasively in both her fiction and non-fiction works. Ideas, for better or for worse, rule the men who hold them, and through them, they rule the world. When a generation is presented

---

[2] *Letters of Ayn Rand,* 54.

[3] Howard Roark was Rand's first attempt at creating a messiah: "Howard Roark represents my conception of man as god, of the absolute human ideal." In the same letter to Frank Lloyd Wright in 1944, Rand referred to Roark as "my own god" (*Letters of Ayn Rand,* 113). She signed many of her letters to Wright, who was the model for Roark, "Reverently yours."

with such a lethal system of ideas so attractively packaged, someone must take the time to suggest that all is not as it appears to be, that Rand's system is really a Trojan thoroughbred.

This book is very critical of Rand's philosophy. In the succeeding chapters I explain in detail why her philosophy is false. But I want to point out to my readers here at the start that there are some conclusions for which Rand argues with which I agree, and which are, in truth, correct. Her praise of purpose and productive work, her condemnation of laziness, her enthusiasm for private property, her advocacy of laissez-faire capitalism and limited government, her attacks on altruism, her support of egoism, and her vigorous defense of logic are some of the major ideas for which she cannot be faulted. But anyone who has read a history of philosophy and philosophers—or anyone who has merely read Rand's own letters— knows that philosophers, like ordinary mortals, come up with their conclusions first, and then later construct arguments to support those conclusions. It is not primarily her *conclusions* (though some are flagrantly wrong, such as her atheism and empiricism) but with her *arguments* that I deal, for her arguments cannot and do not logically support her conclusions. Rand was in some ways (certainly not with regard to her metaphysics, nor her epistemology) *right for the wrong reasons.* She did not offer a logically competent defense of capitalism and a free society, as I demonstrate in the following pages, nor a logically competent defense of egoism, ethics, nor any other laudable conclusion. Therefore, anyone who relies on her arguments for those points of view must ultimately be disappointed. Where Rand was right in her conclusions, her arguments were invalid, and anyone who relies on her arguments in an intellectual engagement will lose the battle.

Moreover, those ideas that Rand espoused that are correct are set within a context of error. Because she saw her philosophy as a system, a package deal that must be accepted entire or rejected entire, we must reject her entire philosophy. We are not at liberty— Rand herself forbade it—of accepting part and rejecting the rest. The situation, to borrow a metaphor, is this: Rand offered us a glass of freshly squeezed orange juice—laced with strychnine. At first glance it looks delicious; it appears healthful; it tastes good; but upon analysis, it become clear that it is deadly poison. Deadly, not only so far as this life here on Earth is concerned, but deadly for the life to come, as well. Rand, despite her repeated claims, did not offer a code of values for living on Earth as opposed to one for living elsewhere. She offered an argument that is not valid anywhere, either now or later, either temporally or eternally. The choice is not values for living on Earth or values for living in Heaven; that is a false alternative. The only choice is values for living on Earth *and* in Heaven, or no values at all. Rand, as I demonstrate, offered no values at all. Her arguments are specious; her conclusions unwarranted.

What has given impetus to Rand's views is not so much her logic—she was not nearly logical enough—but her powerful rhetoric. In the course of a novel, rigorous argumentation plays a relatively small part in persuasion. It is but one of many tools at the disposal of the novelist, and not a very important one at that. It is no accident that Rand first presented her fictitious philosophy in the form of fiction. It is no accident that she continually confused her characters with living people. The rhetorical apparatus—the plots, the characters, the scenes, the humor, sarcasm, and figures of speech—all are persuasive. Many are the readers of *Atlas Shrugged* who have read every word except Galt's speech. They liked the story, but they disliked or were bored by the lecture. I shall not attempt to match Rand's obvious talent for writing fiction; but I am more than willing to match her attempts—or her disciples' attempts—at logical argumentation. She was fond of quoting Aristotle's dictum that fiction was more important than history, for fiction could provide a picture of what might be and ought to be. Truth and logic, however, are more important than either fiction or history. It is logic, not rhetoric, that in the long run will carry the day.

Because this is a book about ideas, I will not be presenting a biography of Rand, except for some incidentals that are relevant to the intellectual story (it is reported that an "authorized" biography is forthcoming—authorized by whom, I do not know, since

Rand has been dead for 15 years); nor will I be rehashing the scandalous biographical accounts presented by her disciples. In any polemic, one should not indulge either in abusive *ad hominem* attacks or commit logical fallacies, even though in doing so one may score debating points, for such tactics weaken one's own argument and ultimately destroy one's own integrity, honesty, and credibility. Rather, I will attempt to face Rand's arguments squarely, without misrepresentation or exaggeration. When I am through, I hope the reader will agree that my conclusions about Rand's philosophy are both important and accurate, and that the methods by which I reached those conclusions have been fair and valid.

I have held Rand to a strict standard: my standard and hers: logical consistency. If any reader thinks that my arguments against her philosophy are too detailed, he must disagree with Rand herself, who wrote, "[P]hilosophers, above all, must be as meticulously precise as it is possible to be, and I am in favor of the most rigorous 'hairsplitting,' where necessary—I hold that philosophy should be more precise than the strictest legal document, because much more is at stake. . . . I never think or speak of anything except as a philosopher."[4] That, of course, is the only proper standard for philosophy. My principal criticism of Rand, illustrated over and over again in the pages that follow, is her failure to be logical in her argumentation and precise in her definition.

I write from a perspective that is almost unknown in this century: Christianity. What? you say, this century is crawling with Christians, from Mother Teresa to Robert Schuller, from Martin Luther King to Pope John Paul! Well, those are four of the reasons why I say that Christianity is almost unknown in this century. The objection has proved my point. I ask the reader to consider that he himself may not know what Christianity is: If he has obtained his information about Christianity from any church with a membership over 2,000, or from any book (except an accurate translation of the Bible) which has sold more than 5,000 copies a year, he almost certainly does not know what Christianity is. Like the phi-

---

[4] *Letters of Ayn Rand*, 503, 506.

losophers, those who profess to be Christians in the twentieth century have either imbibed large amount of irrationalism with their sermons, or they have been dispensers of large amounts of irrationalism in their sermons and books. I hope that my readers will take the trouble to find out what Christianity is. The list of books at the end of this book, most of them written by Gordon Clark, is an excellent place to start. Some of my comments in this book may seem odd, if the reader assumes that when I use the word *Christian* I mean what the word has come to mean in the twentieth century. Rand herself did not understand Christianity: Her family was (secular) Jewish, and her cultural background was Russian Orthodoxy, neither of which has much to do with Christianity. She was familiar with parts of the Bible, but she seems to have read it in the course of doing what those in politics call "opposition research." Like most Americans, Rand simply did not know what Christianity is. Perhaps my next book should be titled *Christianity: The Unknown Ideal*.

When my earlier book, *Answer to Ayn Rand*, appeared in 1974, Rand was still on Earth—an Earth that she loved inordinately, for she could spend only a short time here, and she knew it, but deliberately refused to think about it[5]—and she was still very much in control of her faculties. Nevertheless, to my knowledge, she never made any attempt to respond to the criticisms of her philosophy made in that book. Nor, I might add, have any of her disciples, at least not explicitly. Imitating Rand's rodomontade, her disciples continue to write as if there were no serious problems in her philosophy—and that anyone who dares to suggest there might be a problem is a whim-worshiping mystic. Rand's silence—and her disciples' silence—should cause anyone interested in these mat-

---

[5] Rand realized her mortality, but she deliberately evaded that knowledge all her life: "I don't think about it [death] at all—although I have definite philosophical reasons why one should not think about it. I have given it that much thought, and no more. . . . I think so much of this life that I am not interested in what comes after, if anything" (*Letters of Ayn Rand*, 341). Although she castigated and ridiculed others who "blanked out" facts, blanking out the fact of mortality was essential to Rand's philosophy.

ters to ask why. The Objectivist first string did not deal with my earlier book. I doubt the Objectivist second string will deal with this one.

At the conclusion of this book I discuss three books written by two of Rand's disciples—Leonard Peikoff and David Kelley. I included discussions of these books, even though this book is about Ayn Rand's philosophy, because some readers may believe that Kelley and Peikoff, as second generation Objectivists, have solved at least some of the problems in Objectivism. They have not. In fact, by venturing into areas of philosophy where Rand herself feared to tread, her disciples have complicated things by introducing errors of their own. Two centuries after Plato died, his Academy was Skeptical; his philosophy had been supplanted by the sophists. What the Objectivist school will look like in the future is anybody's guess. But that is not what Rand meant by *Objectivism,* nor is it what I mean. Just as Plato's writings alone define Platonism, so Rand's writings alone define Objectivism, and it is at her works that I direct my criticism. The reader himself must decide whether it is accurate.

As far as we know, Rand was born in Russia in 1905 (as Alissa Zinovievna Rosenbaum) and died in New York in 1982. At the end of her life her hatred for Christianity was so intense that she was repulsed by anyone who even smelled of it, no matter how rarefied his religion. One of those people was Ronald Reagan. In the mid-1970s she had expressed her wish to die if Ronald Reagan was elected President.[6] He was inaugurated in 1981; she died in 1982. One should be careful what one wishes for: One just might get it. Even an atheist.

---

[6] As cited in Sciabarra, *Ayn Rand The Russian Radical,* 349. In an excerpt from his biography written by Edward Ellis, "Not Yours to Give," Congressman Davy Crockett expressed a similar wish: "If I ever vote for another unconstitutional law, I wish I may be shot." Well, Crockett was shot at the Alamo, so he may have voted for another unconstitutional law.

1

THE OBJECTIVIST CANON

A ny philosophy, especially any philosophy that claims to be a coherent system,[1] must have a reasonably well defined canon. For example, the Westminster Confession of Faith (1645) clearly defines the canon of Christianity in its first chapter by listing the sixty-six books of the Old and New Testaments, "all of which are given by inspiration of God to be the rule of faith and life," and excluding "the books commonly called Apocrypha." The Confession furnishes a denotative definition of the canon of Christianity. Any critique of Christianity that includes the Koran, the Book of Mormon, the Apocrypha, Martin Luther King's "Letter from Birmingham Jail," papal encyclicals, or any other document within its scope would miss the mark, for such works do not belong to the canon of Christianity.

So it is with Objectivism. A critic of that philosophy must first attempt to isolate its canon, that is, the works which are proper statements of the philosophy. This is not difficult, although some

---

[1] "Objectivism is a philosophical system. One cannot regard any single, out-of-context statement or action as an 'example' of a philosophical system" (*The Objectivist*, March 1967, 13). "Since Objectivism is not a loose body of ideas, but a philosophical system originated by me and publicly associated with my name . . ." (June 1968, 7). See Sciabarra for Rand's endorsement of Objectivism as a system (105) and Peikoff's hostility to systems (141).

1

of Objectivism's critics have ignored Rand's own words. Ayn Rand established Objectivism's canon herself. She wrote in 1968:

> I want, therefore, formally to state that the only authentic sources of information on Objectivism are: my own works (books, articles, lectures), the articles appearing in and the pamphlets reprinted by this magazine (*The Objectivist*, as well as *The Objectivist Newsletter*), books by other authors which will be endorsed in this magazine as specifically Objectivist literature, and such individual lectures or lecture courses as may be so endorsed. (This list includes also the book *Who Is Ayn Rand?* by Nathaniel Branden and Barbara Branden, as well as the articles by these two authors which have appeared in this magazine in the past, but does not include their future works.)[2]

She further stated that "Mr. and Mrs. Branden's writings and lectures up to this time were valid and consonant with Objectivism."[3]

Although this definition of the Objectivist canon is not entirely unambiguous, nor does it appear to be final,[4] it is certainly clear enough to enable a critic to engage in criticism without fear that he is basing them upon unrecognized writings. This critic has, wherever possible, sought to restrict the works used to those written by Rand herself, but has also occasionally used the writings of the Brandens or Leonard Peikoff that have appeared in Rand's newsletters and books. This criticism is based not at all on lectures, for

---

[2] *The Objectivist*, June 1968, 7.

[3] *The Objectivist*, May 1968, 5.

[4] An earlier canon was mentioned by Nathaniel Branden in *The Objectivist Newsletter*, April 1965, 17: "In her *Los Angeles Times* column (8/26/62), Ayn Rand stated: 'Please take the following as an official "Public Notice." The only authentic sources of information about Objectivism are: My own works. *Who Is Ayn Rand?* by Nathaniel Branden ... *The Objectivist Newsletter* ... and the publications of that Institute.' ... No group, organization, newsletter, magazine, book or other publication—with the exception of those named above—is endorsed or recognized by us as a qualified spokesman for Objectivism.' "

such lectures are rather fleeting sources when compared to the written word. I also believe that the reader should be spared the expense of acquiring expensive taped lectures in order to judge whether various criticisms have been justly leveled against Objectivist ideas. The written word affords the most accessible, least expensive, and the only truly public source of Objectivist philosophy.[5]

Since Rand's death in March 1982, some new books by her and her disciples have appeared. Some of these books, such as *The Early Ayn Rand* and *Philosophy: Who Needs It?* do not contribute significantly to our understanding of Objectivism. Other, more significant books by both Rand and her disciples are discussed in the appendixes. One of them, *Objectivism* by Leonard Peikoff, claims to be the written version of his many audiotapes. But the criticisms I make of Rand will be based on her writings, not that of her disciples. The criticisms I make of Peikoff and Kelley will be made of their writings. I will try to keep Rand distinct from her followers, just as she wished. Whatever one thinks of Rand's attempts to close the canon of Objectivism—and apparently one reason for the split

---

[5] One reviewer of *Answer to Ayn Rand* wrote: ". . . a large measure of the alleged 'proofs' of Objectivism's theses exist [*sic*] only on tape. Thus, what is the point of discussing the Objectivist theory of knowledge without reference to Branden's lectures on 'The Nature of Reason,' 'Logic and Mysticism,' or even Peikoff's ten lectures on Objectivism's theory of knowledge? What is the point of discussing the Objectivist ethics without tracking down Leonard Peikoff's lecture on 'The Objectivist Meta-ethics,' or even referring to Nathaniel Branden's five or six lectures on the subject in 'The Basic Principles of Objectivism'? This kind of gall, coming from a serious thinker, boggles the mind."

The proper and devastating response to this criticism is the reviewer's own words: "Part of the fault lies with the principals of the philosophy itself, who do not ever seem to have understood that serious philosophy cannot be done in taped lectures, that this procedure precludes serious investigation by scholars and, hence, fundamental debate over key or subtle points and insights" (Roy A. Childs, *Libertarian Review*, November/December 1976). Reviewer Childs proceeded to mention a few points on which he thought I had misunderstood Objectivism, but he failed to quote a single word, phrase, or sentence from any taped lecture substantiating a single misunderstanding. If the tapes were such an important source, he should have done so.

3

in the ranks of those who call themselves Objectivists is this issue —one must agree that Rand's philosophy is what Rand wrote or approved as canonical, not what Leonard Peikoff or David Kelley published after her death. Just as Platonism is what Plato wrote, and not necessarily what the teachers in the Academy taught; just as Hegelianism is what Hegel wrote; and just as Christianity is what the Bible says, and not necessarily what teachers in churches teach, so Objectivism is what Rand wrote. She was concerned to maintain a distinction between herself and her followers, whom she called "students of Objectivism." I shall respect that distinction, because it is entirely reasonable to do so. There can be no serious objection to Rand's attempt to close the Objectivist canon. She was merely and explicitly doing for herself what scholars do for other philosophers.

Not only is this the only proper way for a critic of Objectivism to proceed, it is the only practical way to proceed. Rand herself recognized the difficulty in criticizing philosophers:

> Within a few years of the [philosophy] book's publication, commentators will begin to fill libraries with works analyzing, "clarifying" and interpreting its mysteries. . . .
> Within a generation, the number of commentaries will have grown to such proportions that the original book will be accepted as a subject of philosophical specialization, requiring a lifetime of study—and any refutation of the book's theory will be ignored or rejected, if unaccompanied by a full discussion of the theories of all the commentators, a task which no one will be able to undertake.
> This is the process by which Kant and Hegel acquired their dominance.[6]

---

[6] *Philosophy: Who Needs It?* 142-143. Rand herself, it seems, read very little philosophy after leaving the University of Petrograd. Nathaniel Branden reports: ". . . she was not a conscientious scholar of the history of philosophy; far from it; in the eighteen years of our relationship I cannot recall a single book on philosophy that she read from cover to cover. She skimmed; she read summaries

Ironically, it may also be the process by which Rand will acquire her academic respectability, if not her dominance. But this writer has no intention of dealing with all the commentators on her work; rather we will look directly at her own writings and refute them.

---

and distillations; and she depended on the reports of her associates, such as Leonard [Peikoff], Barbara [Branden], and myself; progressively, Leonard became her primary resource" (*Judgment Day*, 282). Branden's account is confirmed by John Hospers: "I realized that Ayn read almost no philosophy at all. And I was amazed how much philosophy she could generate 'on her own steam,' without consulting any sources ("Conversations with Ayn Rand," *Liberty*, September 1990, 47). Oddly, Leonard Peikoff reports: "I learned more about philosophy listening to her than I did from ten years in graduate school getting a Ph.D. in the subject" (*The Early Ayn Rand*, ix). Rand's failure to read philosophy is apparent in her own works: She does not even seem to notice problems in epistemology, for example, which would have been called to her attention had she seriously read philosophy.

2

THE MEANINGS OF *REASON*

Every one of them [philosophers] pretends that he has
discovered and reached his opinions through the self-de-
velopment of cold, pure, divinely untroubled dialectic . . .
whereas, at bottom, a pre-conceived dogma, a notion, an
"institution," or mostly a heart's desire, made abstract and
refined, is defended by them with arguments sought after
the fact. They are all of them lawyers . . . and for the most
part quite sly defenders of their prejudices which they chris-
ten "truths."

Friedrich Nietzsche
Beyond Good and Evil

It has been 40 years since *Atlas Shrugged* was first published in
1957. Several books which are "nonfiction footnotes" to the
massive novel have appeared since then.[1] Rand's books demand

---

[1] Rand's works since 1957 include: *For the New Intellectual*, 1961; *The Virtue
of Selfishness*, 1964; *Capitalism: The Unknown Ideal*, 1967; *Introduction to
Objectivist Epistemology*, 1967, second edition, 1990; *The Romantic Manifesto*,
1971; *The New Left: The Anti-Industrial Revolution*, 1971; *Night of January
16th*, 1971; *Philosophy: Who Needs It?* 1982; *The Early Ayn Rand*, 1984; *The
Voice of Reason*, 1989; *The Ayn Rand Column*, 1991; *Letters of Ayn Rand*, 1995.

an answer, for they continue to influence millions of people—mostly young people, if one may judge by their sales. While Rand's promised treatise on Objectivism[2] never appeared, catechization of the faithful proceeded apace under the tutelage of Leonard Peikoff, who replaced Nathaniel Branden as the heir of Rand's literary corpus.[3] For decades, taped lectures by Nathaniel Branden and later Leonard Peikoff were the primary vehicle for catechization, a method that by its nature effectively precludes both serious discussion and adverse criticism of the theories expounded. Apparently the purpose of such a procedure was to indoctrinate the followers before the appearance of any philosophical treatise, thus guaranteeing: (1) profitable publication, and (2) a hard-core of Objectivists impervious to reasonable criticism and disdainful of any who dare to express disagreement.[4]

In addition, Leonard Peikoff, Harry Binswanger, David Kelley, and Michael Berliner have published booklets and books. An Ayn Rand Institute and an Institute for Objectivist Studies have been established, and the Objectivist movement seems to have split into two or more factions. One of the more useful books is a Rand chrestomathy edited and compiled by Harry Binswanger: *The Ayn Rand Lexicon*, published in 1986.

[2] Promised in *For the New Intellectual*, vii, and in *Introduction to Objectivist Epistemology*, 7, *inter alia*. All page numbers of Rand's books, with the exception of *Atlas Shrugged*, refer to paperback editions, when available.

[3] Peikoff published an Objectivist catechism consisting of a series of questions followed by references to Objectivist literature for the answers: *An Examination Study-Guide to the Ethics of Objectivism*. Nathaniel Branden began catechization of the Objectivists through live and taped lectures, a procedure that several other Objectivists chose to follow. Peikoff published *Objectivism* in 1991, and we shall discuss that book in an appendix. He sees his book as fulfilling Rand's promise.

[4] "Mr. Branden's stated long-range goal in regard to NBI [Nathaniel Branden Institute] was to create a philosophically educated group of Objectivist intellectuals who would apply the principles of Objectivism to their own professions, and who would serve as a hard-core audience for the future works of young Objectivist writers . . . a goal of which I thoroughly approved" (Ayn Rand, *The Objectivist*, May 1968, 2).

Without a Prayer: Ayn Rand and the Close of Her System

Rand's Humanism

One of the greatest dangers to human beings is humanist thought. Humanism is neither humane nor humanitarian, concepts with which it is frequently confused. The main assumption of all humanist thought is the autonomy of reason; that is, all humanist philosophers claim that their philosophies are independent of religious presuppositions.[5] This claim is quite explicit in Rand, for throughout her work she has drawn a hard and fast line between "reason" and "faith," maintaining that her philosophy, and hers alone, is based on reason. "Reason," she wrote, "is the faculty that perceives, identifies, and integrates the material provided by his senses."[6] All other philosophies (with the possible exception of Aristotle's, to the degree that he agrees with Rand) are based on faith. "Faith," she wrote, "is the commitment of one's consciousness to beliefs for which one has no sensory evidence or rational proof."[7] Objectivism is the only completely and consistently rational philosophy; all others are irrational. Indeed, "rational philosophy" is redundant; only philosophy can be rational; if a system of thought is not based upon and governed by reason, it is irrational, mystical, and religious.[8] It

[5] Brand Blanshard, whose work we shall call upon in the next chapter, confesses at the end of *The Nature of Thought*: "That theory [Blanshard's own], as any informed reader will have seen, only restates with variations an ancient doctrine of 'the great tradition,' of what Professor Urban has been persuasively urging as *philosophia perpetua* or *perennis*, the doctrine of the autonomy and objectivity of reason . . ." (II, 519).

[6] "Man cannot survive except by gaining knowledge, and reason is his only means to gain it. Reason is the faculty that perceives, identifies and integrates the material provided by his senses. The task of his senses is to give him the evidence of existence, but the task of identifying it belongs to his reason; his senses tell him only that something is, but what it is must be learned by his mind" (*Atlas Shrugged*, 1016).

[7] Nathaniel Branden, "Mental Health Versus Mysticism and Self-Sacrifice," *The Virtue of Selfishness*, 37. "The alleged short-cut to knowledge, which is faith, is only a short-circuit destroying the mind . . ." (*Atlas Shrugged*, 1018).

[8] Rand does at times concede that "Religion is a primitive form of philosophy—an attempt to offer a comprehensive view of reality . . ." (*The Objectivist*, February 1966, 1). This is merely a minor inconsistency on her part.

8

follows logically from this that the label "philosophy" may be assigned only to Objectivism, while all other systems are religious, that is, mystical.[9] Nathaniel Branden made this logical consequence of the Objectivist distinction between "reason" and "faith" explicit in his book *The Psychology of Self-Esteem*:

> Indeed, for many years, when lecturing on my psychological theories, it was my practice to designate my system as "Objectivist Psychology." I knew, however, that this was only a temporary designation—a working title. . . . It is, of course, an indication that a science is at an early stage of development when that science is still divided into schools, each with its own name. . . . And, in truth, in my own mind I do not call what I am doing Biocentric Psychology. I call it psychology.[10]

If Rand had been as consistent as Branden on this point she would not have called her system Objectivism, but simply Philosophy, thereby implicitly denying that status to any other system of thought. If what Rand did is based on reason, and all other systems are either partially or wholly based on faith, then the label "philosophy" correctly belongs only to those thoughts and theories that Rand approved.[11] To the extent that others disagreed with her, Rand denied that they were rational, or that they used reason. Dissidents to Objectivism are "mystics" and "altruists," terms uttered with abhorrence and disgust by Objectivists.

[9] "Reason is the faculty which perceives, identifies, and integrates the material provided by man's senses. Mysticism is the claim to a non-sensory means of knowledge" (Ayn Rand, "Faith and Force," 6).

[10] Nathaniel Branden, *The Psychology of Self-Esteem*, ix-x.

[11] Of course, when Branden labeled his theories "psychology," he was simply committing what Rand described as the fallacy of the frozen abstraction: "It revealed a fallacy which may be termed 'the fallacy of the frozen abstraction' and which consists of substituting some one particular concrete for the wider abstract class to which it belongs–in this case, substituting a specific ethics (altruism) for the wider abstraction of 'ethics' " (*The Virtue of Selfishness*, 81).

Without a Prayer: Ayn Rand and the Close of Her System

The Autonomy of Reason

Being committed to the autonomy of humanist thought, Rand shared a dogma common to many non-Christian philosophies: that "reason" is independent of and prior to any presuppositions. In accepting this common notion, Rand failed to offer a radical break with past philosophies, despite her claim to be challenging the philosophical and cultural tradition of two and a half thousand years.[12] Rand's failure to challenge 2,500 years of humanist thought is one of the reasons why this book is necessary: Objectivism represents one of the newest versions of humanism that has appeared in the twentieth century.[13] While it purports to be a radical break with the past, Objectivism includes many dogmas that characterize secular thought. If the reader is genuinely interested in a philosophy that challenges 2,500 years of secular philosophy, he should read the books of Gordon H. Clark.

In her philosophy of Objectivism, Rand is compelled to insist upon the autonomy of reason, that is, its independence of religious ideas or presuppositions, more vigorously than many contempo-

---

[12] Ayn Rand in *Who Is Ayn Rand?* 1.

[13] "Objectivism—which, following the publication of Rand's major philosophical novel, *Atlas Shrugged*, in 1957, quickly became a kind of New Marxism of the Right. A generation earlier, the same converts now flocking to her would just as enthusiastically have joined the Marxist bandwagon tearing down the rocky road of the thirties" (Jerome Tuccille, *It Usually Begins with Ayn Rand*, 16).

Rand seems to say as much when she writes: "As an advocate of reason, freedom, individualism and capitalism, I seek to address myself to the men of the intellect . . . and I believe that more of them may be found among the former 'liberals' than among the present 'conservatives' " ("The Intellectual Bankruptcy of Our Age," 3-4). Earlier in the same essay Rand had written: "For many decades, the 'liberals' had been the representatives of the intellect in America, if not in the content of their ideas, then at least in form, method and professed epistemology. They claimed that their views were based on reason, logic, science; and, even though they were glorifying collectivism, they projected a manner of confident, distinguished intellectuality—while most of the so-called 'conservatives,' allegedly devoted to the defense of individualism and capitalism, went about apologetically projecting such a cracker-barrel sort of folksiness that Li'l Abner would have found it embarrassing . . ." (3).

10

rary philosophers. She even requested that the word *Reason* be engraved on her tombstone.[14] Other philosophers have been influenced or overwhelmed by depth psychologies, by radical historicism, or by Existentialism, and have questioned the traditional certitudes of secular thought, including the presupposition of autonomy. It was Rand's purpose to reaffirm the autonomy of reason "as the ultimate judge in matters of truth and falsehood,"[15] on pain of skepticism. Rand is a modern champion of reason against the philosophical skeptics and the religious mystics.

---

[14] As reported in *Comment!* May 2, 1971, 6 [transcript of NBC talk show]. The bodies of Rand and her husband Charles Francis (Frank) O'Connor are buried in Kensico Cemetery in Valhalla, New York, along with those of many other famous men. The *Guide* distributed by the Cemetery says this about Rand:

"Ayn Rand was born in St. Petersburg, Russia in 1905 as Alice Rosenbaum [actually Alissa Zinovievna Rosenbaum]. She was a passionate capitalist who hated her country's communist government. After graduating from the University of Petrograd, she accepted an invitation to visit relatives in Chicago and happily left her homeland, never to return.

"In 1926, the young immigrant changed her name to Ayn Rand, taking her new last name from her Remington Rand typewriter. With several screenplays tucked beneath her arm, she headed to Hollywood.

"After a series of rejections, Rand finally sold her first story, 'Red Pawn,' to Universal Pictures in 1932. Although the movie was never produced, the sale enabled Rand to quit her job as an extra at the Cecil B. DeMille studios and pursue her writing career full-time.

"Rand's first novel, 'We, the Living,' was published in 1936 followed by 'Anthem' in 1938 and two bestsellers, 'The Fountainhead' in 1943 and 'Atlas Shrugged' in 1957. Rand's books reflected her deep political philosophy of objectivism which embraced the pursuit of self-interest without regard to common good. She promoted her controversial views through lectures and newsletters.

"When she died in 1982, Rand was laid out in a coffin next to a six-foot dollar sign, her favorite symbol. She is buried beside her husband, Frank O'Connor, an aspiring actor whom she had married during her early years in Hollywood." When the author visited the cemetery in 1992, there was no six foot dollar sign visible, only a simple, elegant stone.

[15] Herman Dooyeweerd, *In the Twilight of Western Thought*, 2. Rand belongs to the Enlightenment: "The eighteenth century is imbued with a belief in the unity and immutability of reason" (Ernst Cassirer, *The Philosophy of the Enlightenment*, 6).

11

But "reason" is simply a cue word that has been used by all varieties of philosophers since the world began. Its cognates—*reasonable, unreasonable, rational* and *irrational*—are the necessary verbiage of all statist legal systems, which are established to eliminate "unreasonable risks" to citizens or establish "reasonable standards" for their behavior. The word "reason" is a great empty vessel into which any and all meanings may be and have been poured; without it or its equivalent it is inconceivable that humanist thought and society could exist.[16]

In the history of philosophy, "reason" has had as many meanings as there have been philosophers. For David Hume, "reason" meant sense experience. For Spinoza and Hegel, "reason" meant logic. For Thomas Aquinas, reason was a combination of sense experience and ratiocination. Rand seemed to use the word, as many atheists have done, to mean "non-revelational," referring to sense experience, introspection, discussion, logic, or to all four, as the context requires. One must not assume that Rand herself used the word univocally or unambiguously.

One consequence of this equivocation on the meaning of "reason" is that it disguises the irreconcilable conflict that necessarily exists between different schools of philosophy. Disagreement between adherents of different secular schools cannot be overcome by an appeal to reason, for each school has a different notion of "reason." One of the ways in which systems of thought differ is over epistemic authority. The logical empiricist Herbert Feigl understood this very well:

> Probably the most decisive division among philosophical attitudes is the one between the worldly and the otherworldly types of thought. Profound differences in person-

---

[16] "We can scarcely use this word [reason] any longer without being conscious of its history; and time and again we see how great a change of meaning the term has undergone. This circumstance constantly reminds us how little meaning the terms 'reason' and 'rationalism' still retain, even in the sense of purely historical characteristics" (Ernst Cassirer, *The Philosophy of the Enlightenment*, 6).

ality and temperament express themselves in the ever changing forms these two kinds of outlook assume. Very likely there is here an irreconcilable divergence. It goes deeper than disagreement in doctrine; at bottom it is a difference in basic aim and interest.[17]

Axioms, presuppositions, assumptions—I am using the terms interchangeably—govern all philosophers and philosophies, including those who claim that they have no axioms, make no assumptions, and are completely unbiased. Plato, Aristotle, Descartes, Hobbes, Hume, Kant, Hegel, and Ayn Rand have all been champions of reason.[18] There is no word more meaningless nor more eagerly used by philosophers than the word "reason."[19] Once philosophers define the word, however, the irreconcilable disagreements begin. One suspects that the reason Rand refused debate,[20] and John Galt delivers a lengthy monologue in *Atlas Shrugged*, is the realization that debate and dialogue would emphasize the irreconcilable clashes among non-Christian philosophers, many of whom accept "reason," and few of whom are "mystics." Proscription of debate and dialogue is desirable if one wishes to proclaim autonomous reason as the standard in epistemology. If reason is the source of knowledge, it must of necessity speak with one voice.

[17] *Logical Empiricism*, Iowa: Littlefield, Adams, 1956, 325. Of course, differences in basic aims and interests are differences in doctrine. Nothing is deeper than thought.

[18] "As soon as we seek to penetrate to the root of these fundamentally different conceptions, we are confronted with a fundamental difference in presuppositions. ... In the last analysis these very presuppositions determine the meaning ascribed to this autonomy" (Dooyeweerd, *In the Twilight of Western Thought*, 2-3).

[19] This in no way, of course, implies that any philosopher's use of the word "reason" is meaningless. Indeed, it is the variety of meanings and the definiteness of the various meanings that forms the problem for anyone wishing to base epistemology on "reason."

[20] This is not to say that there are no good reasons to eschew public debate; it is simply to say that Rand's avoidance of debate may be for reasons other than the descent to trickery and grandstanding that nearly all public debate involves.

Rand also claimed reason is the indispensable means of reconciling disagreement.[21] The solution is itself the problem, because reasonable men differ on what reason is, just as Plato, Aristotle, Descartes, Hobbes, Kant, Hume, Hegel, and Ayn Rand did. Rather than being a solution to the problem of disagreement, "reason" in its many meanings is a source of disagreement. Men cannot solve their problems and disagreements by an appeal to an autonomous, objective reason, for there are as many autonomous reasons as there are schools of philosophy.[22] Rand herself wrote that the man she took as her arch-enemy, Immanuel Kant, "announced himself as a champion of reason—of 'pure' reason."[23] Yet Rand regarded Kant as a "mystic" *par excellence*.[24] Could Kant be given equal time, he would no doubt reply in the same vein as he is criticized, and the two champions of "reason" would be irreconcilably opposed.

Reason and Force

Despite this situation, Rand insisted that reason is the solution to disagreements:

I have said that faith and force are corollaries, and that mysticism will always lead to the rule of brutality. The cause of it is contained in the very nature of mysticism. Reason [whose?] is the only objective means of communi-

---

[21] "Reason is the only objective means of communication and of understanding among men; when men deal with one another by means of reason, reality is their objective standard and frame of reference" ("Faith and Force," 11).

[22] "... philosophy (or let us translate the word properly: 'the love of his own wisdom')!" (Nietzsche, *Beyond Good and Evil*, I. 5).

[23] "Faith and Force," 7. Rand even speaks of "the Kantian version of reason ..." (11). On top of all this, she apparently misunderstood Kant, who wrote a *critique* of pure reason, and whose philosophy occupies a middling position.

[24] "It is a known historical fact that Kant's interest and purpose in philosophy was to save the morality of altruism, which could not survive without a mystic base. His metaphysics and his epistemology were devised for that purpose. He did not, of course, announce himself as a mystic ..." ("Faith and Force," 7).

cation and of understanding among men. . . .[25] But when
men claim to possess supernatural means of knowledge, no
persuasion, communication or understanding are possible.
Why do we kill wild animals in the jungle? Because no
other way of dealing with them is open to us. And that is
the state to which mysticism reduces mankind—a state
where, in case of disagreements, men have no recourse except to physical violence.[26]

In saying that reason is the proper means of settling disputes among
men, and force is an improper means, Rand equivocated on the
meaning of "reason." Now if Rand wished to give the word a certain meaning, to stipulate its definition, we could not quarrel with
her procedure. In fact, we insist on precise definitions. If she then
used the word in a sense different from what she herself stipulated,
we must point out her equivocation. Rand had defined "reason" as
"the faculty that identifies and integrates the material provided by
man's senses."[27] Then she used "reason" in the sense of "conversation," "discussion" or "persuasion."[28] Her entire argument in

[25] "The most depraved sentence you can now utter is to ask: Whose reason? The
answer is: Yours. . . . Your mind is your only judge of truth—and if others dissent from your verdict, reality is the court of final appeal" *(Atlas Shrugged,* 1017).
With her reply, "Yours . . . ," Rand abdicated her position on the objectivity of
reason, and accepted the purest subjectivism, for no longer is there a Reason to
which disputants can appeal, there is only "reality," that is, force.

[26] "Faith and Force," 11. As Cassirer has pointed out: "The same line of reasoning is to be found in Lamettrie's *Man A Machine.* The world will never be happy
so long as it does not decide to become atheistic. When the belief in God van-
ishes, all theological disputes and religious wars will cease too: 'nature hitherto
infected with a sacred poison, would resume its rights and purity' " *(The Philosophy of the Enlightenment,* 70-71; Lamettrie, *L'homme machine,* 111).

[27] *The Virtue of Selfishness,* 20. See also *The Objectivist Newsletter,* March
1962, 11; January 1962, 3, etc.

[28] "The precondition of a civilized society is the barring of physical force from
social relationships—thus establishing the principle that if men wish to deal with
one another, they may do so only by means of reason: by discussion, persuasion
and voluntary, uncoerced agreement" *(The Virtue of Selfishness,* 108).

15

"Faith and Force," and much of her argument in the initial essay in *For the New Intellectual* rests on the second meaning of reason, not the first.

It is the presuppositions or axioms of all philosophies that lead to their irreconcilable conflict. It would be no more unusual for a Roman Catholic prelate to use force against a Christian than for a Randian to use force against a Kantian, both of them championing the cause of reason. Ironically, Rand did not eschew all use of force, even though faith and force are "corollaries." Rand's argument on this correlation lacks both validity and plausibility.

Rand offered twentieth-century political systems as examples of the necessary connection between faith and force. She apparently overlooked the historical fact that it is scientific socialism that reduced half the world to the level of a prison camp in the twentieth century, and that it was the "reasonable" men, those whom Rand herself viewed as the men of reason, the liberals, who guided the remaining half to its near collapse. It is these men who, as Rand noted in her writings,[29] have always been more open to "reason" than the conservatives, who achieved precisely the state of affairs that Rand most angrily denounced. Rand adopted the position that reason is the means of communication and reconciliation; then she refused debate and dialogue with many people; and then she reprimanded the men of reason, the liberals, for their efforts to open communication, dialogue, and seek reconciliation with the scientific socialists. The adoption of these positions should demonstrate that "reason" has no univocal sense for "reasonable" men or even for Ayn Rand, and thus reason cannot serve as a solution to their problems or as the means of achieving a solution.[30] "Reason" had no univocal meaning, not even for Rand herself.

[29] See footnote 13.

[30] "The Kantian or Hegelian will show as little understanding for this typical scholastic striving after accommodation [of "reason" and "faith"] as would have been the case with Aristotle himself, had he been acquainted with Thomism. Thus the dogma concerning the autonomy of theoretical thought can never account for the fundamentally different conceptions of it. Thereby it loses its right to serve as an unproblematic starting-point of philosophy" (Dooyeweerd, *A New Critique of Theoretical Thought*, I, 36).

The Meanings of Reason

It follows from this that force and brutality are no more corollaries of faith than they are of reason: It is the scientific socialists and the atheistic materialists who have slaughtered more people in the twentieth century than any "mystic" group Rand might name.

Humanism—which is a polite word for the more crude and plebeian *atheism*—is the ideological underpinning of the French Revolution, Marxism, and Objectivism,[31] and there is reason to fear that the practical results of the last will be similar to those of the former, should an Objectivist government ever come to power.

Should a reader object that the Communists are really not scientific and that the liberals are really not reasonable, he must be reminded that such objections are in principle no different from one "mystic" insisting that another "mystic" is mistaken.[32] All such disagreements are fundamental and irreconcilable.

[31] "We saw how the French philosophers of the eighteenth century, the forerunners of the Revolution, appealed to reason as the sole judge of all that is. A rational government, rational society, were to be founded; everything that ran counter to eternal reason was to be remorselessly done away with" (Friedrich Engels, *Socialism: Utopian and Scientific*, 30-31).

[32] After all, on Rand's own terms, it is only *your* reason that tells you so. The Communist's reason tells him differently. And the "final court of appeal" in such disagreements is "reality," which can only mean force, in this context. Rand deals with Communists as men deal with rabid animals. Interestingly, Karl Marx shared Rand's optimistic view of reason:

> The most stubborn form of the opposition between Jew and Christian is the religious opposition. How is an opposition resolved? By making it impossible. And how is religious opposition made impossible? By abolishing religion. As soon as Jew and Christian come to see in their respective religions nothing more than stages in the development of the human mind [Rand refers to religion as a primitive form of philosophy] . . . they will no longer find themselves in religious opposition, but in a purely critical, scientific and human relationship. Science will then constitute their unity. But scientific oppositions are resolved by science itself (*Early Writings*, Bottomore, 5).

Lenin shared Rand's view of "reality" as the ultimate authority: "My sensation is subjective, but its foundation [*Grund*] is objective" (*Materialism and Empirio-Criticism*, 195). Lenin is quoting Feuerbach with approbation. "Metaphysically, the only authority is reality; epistemologically—one's own mind. The first is the ultimate arbiter of the second" (Ayn Rand, *The Objectivist Newsletter*, February 1965, 7).

If all philosophical currents that pretend to choose their starting points in theoretical reason alone, had, indeed, no deeper presuppositions, it should be possible to settle every philosophical argument between them in a purely theoretical way. But the factual situation is quite different. A debate between philosophical trends which are fundamentally opposed to each other usually results in a reasoning at cross-purposes, because they are not able to find a way to penetrate to each other's true starting points.[33]

The Plan of the Book

I have shown that Rand insisted on the autonomy of reason; hence her alternative philosophy is not a radical departure from perennial philosophy at all, despite her boasting. In the remaining chapters of this book I hope to show that her alternative, Objectivism, is neither full nor consistent. The most important topics in epistemology, to cite but one example, Rand did not address, and the areas in which her discussions are relatively extensive are riddled with ambiguities, inconsistencies, and contradictions.

Our examination of Objectivism will attempt to expose primarily the internal contradictions in the philosophy. Some Objectivist theories will be shown to be in hopeless conflict with others; the conclusions in conflict with the premises. Disproof will consist of a series of *reductiones ad absurdum*. Because I cannot ask Ayn Rand (nor anyone else) to demonstrate her axioms,[34] the only method of argument remaining is the apagogic. If deductions from her axioms result in contradictions, her axioms must be rejected as false.

This apagogic method of argumentation has been chosen because no other method is available: Christianity and Objectivism

---

[33] Dooyeweerd, *In The Twilight of Western Thought*, 3.

[34] "Every system is based on indemonstrable axioms, and . . . to insist that all propositions be demonstrable is an unreasonable, indeed an irrational, demand . . ." (Gordon H. Clark, *Karl Barth's Theological Method*, 71). "Unreasonable" here means illogical.

have no presuppositions or propositions in common. They have no common ground. The argument of this book will be destructive; it will attempt to demonstrate that Objectivism is self-contradictory, that its epistemology must lead to skepticism, its metaphysics to indestructible matter, its ethics to hedonism, and its politics to anarchy and totalitarianism. Of course, along the way we will point out other difficulties in Objectivism besides contradictions, but it is the demonstration of internal contradictions that requires the conclusion that the philosophical system of Objectivism is false.

The philosophical situation is further complicated—and misunderstanding made more likely—by the fact that two opposing systems—both of which claim to be true, such as Objectivism and Christianity—cannot have any propositions in common; but that two individuals, if at least one is inconsistent, may share certain propositions. Ayn Rand, for example, believed both the law of contradiction (which she pedantically called the law of non-contradiction) and limited government, but her system entitled her to believe in neither. The structure of knowledge that she erected, in which metaphysics depends on epistemology, ethics on both, and politics on all three—her structure eliminated the possibility of both limited government and the laws of logic. She smuggled those ideas in from Christianity, whose structure, whose systematic philosophy, she rejected.

To deal with this difficulty—that is, the difference between systems and persons—I have endeavored to point out the specific ideas to which Rand has no philosophical right but has smuggled into Objectivism from another system, Christianity. It is only because Rand was inconsistent with her fundamental principles that her philosophy has gained the attention it has, and it is because of her inconsistency that the apagogic argument can succeed. In short, her system contains both truth(s) and error(s). If it were totally error (assuming that that were possible) it would never have attracted the attention of anyone outside of Bedlam; if it were totally true, apagogic argument would be futile, and this book a waste of time. The contradictions appear largely in the conflict between truth and error. I shall maintain that the truths have been smuggled into Objectivism from Christianity, and that the errors are indigenous.

In some cases in which Rand's views are obviously at odds with her systematic philosophy—such as her belief that women should not be President—her disciples have rejected her views and labeled them as her "personal" views, as though her philosophy was not her personal views.[35] In such cases—a woman President, her belief that homosexuality is immoral and disgusting, her doubts about the theory of evolution, for example—her disciples have tended to reject those ideas that are smuggled into Objectivism from Christianity, and to take the humanist view of Albert Ellis, one of Rand's early critics: Homosexuality, for example, is at worst a mild disorder, or there is nothing wrong with it at all; rather, it is those who do not love homosexuals who suffer from a disorder.

Perhaps a word about Christianity is in order here. If the reader comes from a Roman Catholic, conventional Protestant, or Jewish background, he may be surprised to learn what Christianity is. It is not what those religious movements and organizations teach; in fact, it is almost the opposite. It has nothing to do with rituals, spiritual encounters, eating the physical body and blood of Christ, hierarchies, lowerarchies, contemporary miracles, cathedrals, mystical feelings, or ethical altruism. Kant's notion that an action is moral only if done out of a sense of duty rather than hope of reward or fear of punishment is about as far removed from Christian ethics as possible.[36] Christ's words, "What shall it profit a man if he should gain the whole world but lose his own soul?" are not those of a proto-Kantian. Christ appealed to genuine self-interest—his words are properly translated by the English word *profit*—not to a sense of unrewarded duty. For an accurate explanation of Christianity, the reader should study the books of Gordon Clark.

---

[35] In his essay, "My Thirty Years with Ayn Rand," Leonard Peikoff repeatedly distinguishes between Ayn Rand as a mind and Ayn Rand as a person, as though a person were not a mind. This is a hint of the irrationalism that appears in *Objectivism*.

[36] See Appendix F, Gordon H. Clark, "Kant and Old Testament Ethics" (1935), from *Essays on Ethics and Politics*.

The Meanings of Reason

Epistemology has been chosen as the first subject for investigation, for it furnishes the basis for all other branches of philosophy, including metaphysics. Epistemology is the foundation on which the structure of knowledge is built. While one may insist (and Rand undoubtedly would) that "reality" is more basic than "consciousness," that is, that metaphysics is in some sense prior to epistemology, it does not follow that metaphysics may be investigated prior to epistemology. If a person claims that the universe is made of indestructible atoms, or of ineffable essences, or of individual "things," these assertions must be answered by the question: "How do you know?" If the person cannot provide a coherent account of his claim to know, if a person cannot furnish a logical defense of his assertions about "reality," then his assertions are without foundation and deserve no further attention. In the enterprise of philosophy, epistemology is the first inquiry; all other inquiries are secondary. "It is the task of epistemology to provide the answer to the question, How do you know?—which then enables the special sciences to provide the answers to the What?"[37]

Rand failed to make clear that metaphysics is a "special science" in the sense used here, for it answers the question "What?" The priority of epistemology to metaphysics must be emphasized, because Rand continually stressed the priority of "existence" to "consciousness" and castigated those who posit "consciousness" before "existence."[38] This is not the place to discuss the merits of the two orders of "existence" and "consciousness": They will be discussed in chapter three. But in philosophy, epistemology is first; it is the most basic of all investigations.[39]

[37] *Introduction to Objectivist Epistemology*, 70-77. ". . . the principles of epistemology, that crucial branch of philosophy which studies man's means of knowledge and makes all other sciences possible" (*For the New Intellectual*, 26). See also *Who Is Ayn Rand?* 190.

[38] She attacked those who hold to " 'the prior certainty of consciousness,' the belief that the existence of an external world is not self-evident . . ." (*For the New Intellectual*, 28).

[39] Peikoff seems to agree: "Method is fundamental; it is that which underlies and shapes content . . . in every field" ("My Thirty Years with Ayn Rand: An Intellectual Memoir," *The Voice of Reason*, 334).

The order of the remaining chapters is not accidental either. From epistemology, we logically move to metaphysics, and the capstone of metaphysics is theology, just as in Aristotle's works. Some readers may find it peculiar to include a chapter on Objectivist theology, since Rand was an atheist. The peculiarity disappears when one realizes that the concept "atheism" is applicable in our culture to only one God, the God of the Bible. A person who disbelieves in this God may quite correctly be labeled an atheist. Atheism, however, in the sense of disbelieving in any and all gods is a logical impossibility. Every philosopher believes in some sort of supreme being, and Rand was no exception. It is quite true that most philosophers believe in a false god; they "suppress the truth [which they are aware of] in unrighteousness," that is, in futile philosophical speculations (Romans 1:18). Knowing that God the Creator exists and that they are the creatures of this God and owe him obedience, they suppress this knowledge. Unable to obliterate this knowledge, they pervert it into an idol: the demiurge, the pure Form, the Regulative Idea, the Prime Mover, the Ground of Being, the Universe, etc. Some philosophers are monotheistic and some are polytheistic. None is atheistic. They can be anti-theistic, that is, opposed to the God of the Bible; the history of philosophy is largely the history of such anti-theism.

One of the greatest misinterpretations of the history of philosophy is that contained in the statement that the Renaissance was the period in which reason cast off the chains of faith (or theology) and ceased to be faith's handmaid. Reason can never cease to be the handmaid of faith: All thought must start somewhere, and that initial postulate is unproved, by definition. What the Renaissance represents is not the liberation of reason from bondage of faith, but the exchange of faiths—the adoption of new axioms—in the minds of men. Reason is and must always be the handmaid of faith. The only question that remains is, Which faith—which axiom—shall reason serve?

Chapters 5 and 6 deal respectively with ethical and political philosophy. As with the preceding inquiry, theology, ethics and politics depend on epistemology. If the solution to the problem of knowledge is poor or no solution at all, the subsequent inquiries can be no better, for they have no foundation on which to rest. In addition, ethics and politics build upon metaphysics, and politics upon ethics. If any link in this chain of argument is weak or broken, the entire subsequent argument collapses. Rand's political philosophy is, therefore, the most fragile of all her sub-philosophies, yet it is this branch of her philosophy which forms the dominant theme of her works. It is politics, man versus the state in Spencerian terms, that forms the theme of *Anthem, We, the Living, The Fountainhead, Capitalism: The Unknown Ideal, The New Left,* and *Atlas Shrugged.* Epistemology was the last of the disciplines studied by Rand. It is in politics and ethics—not in metaphysics or epistemology—that the consequences of one's fundamental beliefs become obvious.

My desire is to furnish a defensible philosophical foundation for a free society—not to undermine any such foundation. The author believes that Rand failed to provide either a coherent foundation for a free society or a coherent description of a free society. What she did was to rely on her literary ability—her narrative power, her eloquence, and her rhetoric—to cover the leaps, blunders, and contradictions in her arguments, hoping that her readers would be inclined to follow, because of their emotional commitment to freedom. The degree of her success is a tribute to her literary talent, for novels are not arguments, they are discourses in which all persuasive forces, not merely logic, are brought to play. Rhetoric is not an adequate substitute for logic, and no matter how entertaining Rand's novels may be, their philosophy will not withstand serious criticism. Should Rand's arguments in favor of a free society be generally accepted, they will offer no defense against the onslaughts of freedom's opponents, for her arguments are self-contradictory and inconsistent. Acceptance of such arguments will leave a society defenseless against critics who use logic in their attack on Objectivism. Objectivism does not furnish a logically competent defense of freedom.

The purposes of this book are, therefore, complex. One purpose is to demonstrate the errors of Objectivism. The errors are numerous, important, and appear in all branches of Rand's philosophy. A second purpose is to reply to Ayn Rand in the name of Jesus Christ, who was and is the Man that Rand, following her Jewish family, denied he was, the Messiah. A third purpose is to point the reader to the only logically competent defense of truth and freedom, Christian philosophy. Finally, I want to urge those young people who are perennially attracted to Rand by her novels —as this writer was when he was in college—to continue to study philosophy, especially the works of Gordon Clark, for in them they will find what Rand only promises: a full, consistent, and radical alternative to the reigning philosophies of the world. Of the two books published in 1957, Rand's fictional *Atlas Shrugged* and Clark's non-fiction history of philosophy, *Thales to Dewey*, it is Clark's book, not Rand's, that challenges 2,500 years of philosophy.

3

IMAGINING KNOWLEDGE
OBJECTIVIST EPISTEMOLOGY

The heirs of Greek thought find it repugnant to accept information revealed by God; they insist on discovering truth by their own resources; and if this cannot be done in any case, they would rather go without the truth than to receive it as a gift from God.

> Gordon H. Clark
> *Thales to Dewey: A History of Philosophy*, 1957

An error made on your own is safer than ten truths accepted on faith. . . .

> Ayn Rand
> *Atlas Shrugged*, 1957

The Primacy of Epistemology

According to Rand, epistemology is the most important branch of philosophy: "Philosophy is the foundation of science; epistemology is the foundation of philosophy. It is with a new approach to epistemology that the rebirth of philosophy has to begin."[1] In her notes for a major work on epistemology Rand wrote:

> The real crux of this issue is that philosophy is primarily epistemology—the science of the means, the rules, and the methods of human knowledge. It is the base of all other sciences and the one necessary for man because man is a being of volitional consciousness—a being who has to discover, not only the content of his knowledge, but also the means by which he is to acquire knowledge. . . . All the fantastic irrationalities of philosophical metaphysics have been the result of epistemological errors, fallacies, or corruptions.[2]

With these statements in mind, it would be a mistake to understand her reply to a book salesman who asked her to present her philosophy while standing on one foot as an indication of the order of the disciplines in Rand's philosophy:

1. Metaphysics: Objective Reality
2. Epistemology: Reason
3. Ethics: Self-interest
4. Politics: Capitalism[3]

Using a medieval distinction, Rand's off-balance and impromptu reply to the salesman might refer to the order of being (*ordo essendi*), and her more deliberate order of disciplines might refer

---

[1] *Introduction to Objectivist Epistemology* (first edition), 66. "The philosophical and historical importance of the ethical system presented and dramatized in *Atlas Shrugged* does not consist only of the specific conclusions advocated, but of their manner of derivation—the epistemological and metaphysical foundation, the starting point, the place at which the system begins, and the method of development" (Nathaniel Branden, *Who Is Ayn Rand?* 21).

[2] Quoted in Barbara Branden, *The Passion of Ayn Rand*, 322-323.

[3] *The Objectivist Newsletter*, August 1962, 35.

to the order of knowing (*ordo cognoscendi*). Epistemology is first and fundamental. No metaphysical assertion can be taken seriously until one has explained how he knows.

The Meanings of "Reason"

Rand defined *reason* as "the faculty which identifies and integrates the material provided by man's senses."[4]

Reason, then, is a *faculty* distinct from the senses. Reason identifies and integrates the material—whatever that material is—provided by the senses. In another place, Rand wrote: "Reason integrates man's perceptions by means of forming abstractions or conceptions, thus raising man's knowledge from the perceptual level, which he shares with animals, to the conceptual level, which he alone can reach."[5]

However, Rand also told us that reason is "man's only means of perceiving reality, his only source of knowledge, his only guide to action, and his basic means of survival." If reason is "man's *only* means of *perceiving* reality,"[6] it would seem that reason *is* the senses.

Third, Rand also told us that reason is something else, or at least has another function besides perceiving, identifying, and integrating: *"Reason* is the only *objective* means of communication and of understanding among men. . . ."[7] Here reason is not a faculty of each individual, nor is it the senses, but it is an *objective* means of communication. It would appear that Rand has offered us more than one definition of *reason*.[8] This multiplicity of defini-

---

[4] *The Virtue of Selfishness*, 20.

[5] *Philosophy: Who Needs It?* 75.

[6] *The Objectivist Newsletter*, August 1962, 35.

[7] *Philosophy: Who Needs It?* 85.

[8] *Reason* is not the only term that has multiple definitions in Objectivism. *Pride*, one of Objectivism's three cardinal virtues, has no less than eight. (See Ronald E. Merrill, *The Ideas of Ayn Rand*, 120.)

tions of a fundamental term indicates serious problems in the philosophy.

Furthermore, reason is to be distinguished from emotion or feelings, which "are not tools of cognition,"[9] and from faith, which is "the acceptance of an idea without evidence or proof, or in spite of evidence to the contrary."[10] The first part ("without evidence or proof") of this Objectivist distinction between faith and reason seems almost Thomistic, with the exception, of course, that Rand, unlike Thomas, allowed no role for "faith." The second part ("in spite of evidence to the contrary") seems to be the view that "faith is believing what you know isn't so." Now that might be the meaning of faith in some modern theologies (I am thinking of the theologies of Soren Kierkegaard and Rudolf Bultmann, as two examples), or even in the medieval theory of two-fold truth, but it is not the sense in which Christianity uses the word *faith*.

Rand explained her use of the terms:

> Reason is the faculty that identifies and integrates the material provided by the senses. Faith is the acceptance of ideas or allegations without sensory evidence or rational demonstration. "Faith in reason" is a contradiction in terms. "Faith" is a concept that possesses meaning only in contra-

---

[9] *The Objectivist Newsletter*, January 1962, 3. Despite Rand's epistemological distinction between emotion and reason, she places great emphasis on the importance of emotions in one's life. In fact, she seems to think that emotions can, in fact, be tools of cognition: "Just as the pain-pleasure mechanism of man's body is an automatic indicator of his body's welfare or injury, a barometer of its basic alternative, life or death—so the emotional mechanism of man's consciousness is geared to perform the same function . . . by means of two basic emotions: joy or suffering. Emotions are automatic results of man's value judgments integrated by his subconscious; emotions are estimates of that which furthers man's values or threatens them . . . lightning calculators giving him the sum of his profit or loss. . . . Man is born with an emotional mechanism, just as he is born with a cognitive mechanism; but, at birth, both are tabula rasa" (*The Virtue of Selfishness*, 27).

[10] Barbara Branden, *The Objectivist Newsletter*, March 1962, 11.

distinction to reason. The concept of "faith" cannot antecede reason, it cannot provide the grounds for the acceptance of reason—it is the revolt against reason.[11]

Reason is accepted while "Faith—instinct—intuition—revelation—feeling—taste—urge—wish—whim"[12] are rejected.

The Tabula Rasa *Contradiction*

Yet reason, we must not forget, is only half the Objectivist epistemological story: Reason acts only on the "material provided by the senses." The gathering or reception of this "material" and its combination into a form usable by the faculty called "reason" is the first and primary step in gaining knowledge. Man's mind, according to Objectivism, is a *tabula rasa* at birth, that is, all his knowledge comes through the senses:

> At birth, a child's mind is *tabula rasa*; he has the potential of awareness—the mechanism of a human consciousness—but no content. Speaking metaphorically, he has a camera with an extremely sensitive, unexposed film (his conscious mind), and an extremely complex computer waiting to be programmed (his subconscious). Both are blank. He knows nothing of the external world.[13]

Now this assertion that man's mind is a *tabula rasa* is important to Rand's philosophy, as it is to all varieties of empiricism. Notice that it is not a conclusion for which arguments are presented; it is simply asserted. Of course, it is required by Rand's assumption that all our knowledge comes through the senses. If there were something already in the mind, then all our knowledge would not come through the senses. But Rand does not bother to prove that

[11] Nathaniel Branden, *The Objectivist Newsletter*, January 1963, 4.

[12] Ayn Rand, *The Virtue of Selfishness*, 15.

[13] *The New Left*, 155-156.

man's mind is *tabula rasa*; she simply asserts it as a corollary of her empiricism.

Now this notion leads to some peculiar difficulties. The question immediately arises: How could Rand speak of the child's *conscious* mind if that mind is "unexposed" and the child "knows *nothing* of the external [i.e., external to the child] world"? If the child's mind is like a camera, and its film is unexposed, what is the child *conscious* of? Rand's words imply that he is conscious of nothing. But to be conscious of nothing, as Rand elsewhere argued, is not to be conscious:

> . . .a consciousness with nothing to be conscious of is a contradiction in terms. . . ."[14]

> It is only in relation to the external world that the various actions of a consciousness can be experienced, grasped, defined or communicated. Awareness is awareness of something. A content-less state of consciousness is a contradiction in terms.[15]

But it is precisely a "content-less state of consciousness" that is the original state of man's mind. *Tabula rasa* means content-less. Therefore, a *tabula rasa* mind is a contradiction in terms.

Rand maintained that the child—every child—knows nothing, his mind is "unexposed," and yet he has a conscious mind. The contradiction is inherent in the notion of a *tabula rasa* mind. A mind that is *tabula rasa* is simply not a mind. A consciousness conscious of nothing is simply not a consciousness. A mind that is empty is not a mind, any more than a geometrical figure that has no sides is a geometrical figure. This egregious contradiction lies at the foundation of Rand's epistemology[16]—not only Rand's, but

---

[14] *Atlas Shrugged*, 1016. Galt's rodomontade.

[15] *Introduction to Objectivist Epistemology*, 37.

[16] Rand seemed to be misled by her machine metaphors (if indeed they were merely metaphors). Elsewhere she wrote: "Nothing is given to man on earth except a potential and the material on which to actualize it. The potential is a superlative machine: his consciousness . . ." (*The Virtue of Selfishness*, 22).

at the base of all empirical philosophies, including those of John Locke, Thomas Aquinas, and Aristotle.

Ignoring the Problem of the Senses

This contradiction would seem to make a discussion of the role of the senses the first and most important part of empiricist epistemology, yet it is not the senses that are discussed in *Introduction to Objectivist Epistemology*. Rather, Rand's *Introduction* discusses the conceptual faculty. Rand was concerned with the "problem of universals" (it is "philosophy's central issue"), because "the validity of man's knowledge depends on the validity of concepts."[17]

Now the problem of universals is extremely important. Without solving it, no one can give a coherent account of thought. Yet neither Rand, nor any other empirical philosopher, has been able to solve it. The problem is insoluble if one does not start one's epistemology with propositions, rather than with sensations or perceptions. Rand herself, as we shall see shortly, smuggled universals and even propositions into sensation and perception. But the relevant issue at this point in our analysis of her epistemology is that she jumped into the middle of things. Universals are not the first problem a sensate philosopher must solve. They are not the sort of problem one would expect to see discussed in an "introduction" to epistemology. The first problem is the one Rand studiously avoided: sensation itself. What is sensation? Can it even be defined? Does it occur? How do sensations become perceptions? And so on. Rand discusses none of these questions. They are a continuing embarrassment to empiricists, ever since Aristotle failed to provide an intelligible answer to these questions 2,400 years ago.

Skepticism and Empiricism

Throughout her writings, Rand was adamant that knowledge is possible to man, that, in fact, man actually possesses knowledge.

---

[17] *Introduction to Objectivist Epistemology*, 7.

She never tired of repeating that those who claim man can know nothing claim to know something—and therefore refute themselves; that those who say there are no absolutes are uttering an absolute—and therefore contradict themselves; that those who maintain that there is no truth, maintain a truth—and therefore show themselves to be liars. All of this is quite in order. Yet Rand seemed peculiarly susceptible to the idea that the self-refutation of skepticism and relativism is in itself a theory of knowledge: It is not. Skepticism is inadmissible precisely because it is absurd, that is, internally contradictory. But to make such a statement is not to show *how* knowledge is possible to man, only *that* it is possible.

There lurks a great danger here for readers of Rand, especially young readers impressed by her demonstration that knowledge must be possible to man because of the absurdity of skepticism. Unfamiliar with the problems of epistemology, such readers might thoughtlessly accept what Rand maintained was the source of knowledge: sensation plus abstraction. In view of the fact that Rand never presented any theory, let alone a logically coherent theory, of how knowledge is gained through the senses, the leap from an anti-skeptical position to an empirical position is not only unwarranted, but is no more "self-evident" than the closely related conclusion that knowledge is gained through feelings or mystical experiences. Those who believe otherwise are merely expressing their personal preference for the word *reason* rather than the word *emotion* or the word *intuition*. The lack of a substantiating theory of sensation and perception reduces one's choice of a means of cognition to what Rand professed to abhor: whim.

The logical chasm between these two ideas—(1) that knowledge is possible to man, and (2) that knowledge is gained only by means of the senses—is the chasm that Rand never bridged, nor even attempted to bridge. She was not alone, of course. For two thousand years the world has been waiting for the empiricists to furnish an explanation of how sensation—whatever that is—becomes propositional truth. That explanation still has not appeared. Will it appear in the next two thousand years? If Aristotle failed to provide the explanation, is Leonard Peikoff likely to succeed?

The chasm between sensation and truth is not bridged by *ad hominem* arguments, nor by castigating others as "mystics." By the lack of evidence and argument, Rand *by her own definition of faith*, posited faith in the senses. In the foreword to *Introduction to Objectivist Epistemology* she wrote:

> I do not include here a discussion of the validity of man's senses—since the arguments of those who attack the senses are merely variants of the fallacy of the "stolen concept." (That fallacy consists of "the act of using a concept while ignoring, contradicting, or denying the validity of the concepts on which it logically and genetically depends.")
> ... For the purposes of this series, the validity of the senses must be taken for granted . . . .[18]

But this writer, heeding Rand's own warnings about faith, refuses to take it for granted. If Rand had been logically consistent, she also would have refused.

Echoing Rand, Nathaniel Branden wrote, "It is rational to ask: 'How can man achieve knowledge?' It is not rational to ask: Can man achieve knowledge?"[19] This, of course, is quite correct: It is merely the self-refutation of skepticism stated another way. But Branden (and he is the source to which Rand refers in *Introduction to Objectivist Epistemology*) went on to say: "It is rational to ask: 'How do the senses enable man to perceive reality?' It is not rational to ask: 'Do the senses enable man to perceive reality?' " Empiricism does not follow from the absurdity of skepticism. Both Rand and Branden begged the question. They assumed what they should have proved, and they did it loudly, arrogantly, and repeatedly, hoping to intimidate both followers and critics into not noticing their *petitio*. The unwarranted leap from the possibility of knowledge to the certainty that knowledge is possible only through the senses is quite obvious in their works. Branden, for example, wrote:

[18] *Introduction to Objectivist Epistemology*, 9.

[19] *The Objectivist Newsletter*, January 1963, 2.

"If they [the senses] do not [enable man to perceive reality], by what means did the speaker acquire his knowledge of the senses, of perception, of man, and of reality?"

Apparently Branden (and Rand) thought his sophomoric query devastating to all anti-empirical views. Does knowledge of unicorns, atoms, or dreams require us to have sensations of unicorns, atoms, or dreams? By which sense are dreams or justice or love known? Smell? Well, something smells fishy in Objectivism. Rand and Branden were brazenly begging the epistemological question. By asserting that these things had to be learned through the senses (they never tell us how such learning is possible), they were asserting what in fact they are required to demonstrate. Statements such as Branden's that arguments opposing the "validity" of the senses commit the fallacy of the "stolen concept" are quite simply gigantic *petitiones principii*: They assume what they should prove.

Because of this Objectivist sleight-of-argument, it must be emphasized that the question is not: "Can man know anything?" That question, this writer insists, must be answered in the affirmative, on pain of contradiction. Augustine, whom the Objectivists despise, made that very point sixteen centuries ago. There is nothing original in the Objectivist argument against skepticism. The relevant question is: "*How* can man know anything?" Instead of showing *how* knowledge is possible through the senses, Rand simply asserted *that* it is possible. This, of course, is properly a conclusion to a long and detailed argument, not the premise. As a premise, it begs the whole epistemological question. It assumes that the problem of how knowledge is achieved through the senses is solved by saying that it is. The question "by what means [does a man] acquire his knowledge of the senses, of perception, of man and of reality?" is answered by an asseveration: by the senses. Arguments challenging such an asseveration are dismissed as "merely variants of the fallacy of the 'stolen concept.' "[20]

In one sense, a trivial sense, the question, "Are the senses the source of knowledge for man?" does logically presuppose, as Branden says, "knowledge of [or at least acquaintance with the ideas

---

[20] *Introduction to Objectivist Epistemology*, 9.

of] the senses, of perception, of man, and of reality."[21] But the question does not logically presuppose that such knowledge is gained through the senses. If it did, Branden (and Rand) would have scored a legitimate point. The cognitive reliability of the senses is what they are required to demonstrate, not to asseverate. The question presupposes only that knowledge is possible to man and possessed by man; that is, that skepticism is absurd. To maintain that the question "Are the senses valid?" does presuppose the validity of the senses is to assume without evidence: (1) that the senses are the source of knowledge, which is the proposition requiring demonstration; and (2) that there is no other source of knowledge, which also must be demonstrated. Rand's and Branden's position rests upon these two assumptions, assumptions made quite without warrant or argumentation.

Let me repeat this point to make it clear: Questioning the "validity" of the senses ("accuracy" or "cognitive reliability" might be better terms) presupposes only awareness of the ideas of the senses, of perception, of man, and of reality. Such questioning does not "logically or genetically" presuppose that knowledge can be gained only through the senses—nor has Rand or Branden ever shown that such questioning makes this latter presupposition. Just as talking about unicorns, dreams, minds, square roots, or justice does not presuppose that our knowledge of them came through the senses, so speaking of reality and the senses does not presuppose our knowledge of them came through the senses. The Objectivist position rests on unwarranted, undefended, and indefensible assumptions about the means of cognition. To say, therefore, that attacks on the validity of the senses are fallacious is untrue. Where lies the fallacy? Objectivism assumes what it should prove: that the senses give us knowledge.[22]

---

[21] *The Objectivist Newsletter*, January 1963, 4.

[22] "No one in the history of philosophy has made a more determined effort than Aristotle to build knowledge on sensation. Surely Locke is no better; and contemporary phenomenalism with its experience that is neither mental nor physical is as meaningless and unverifiable as Spinoza's substance that is both. It is for this reason that [my] first Wheaton lecture used Aristotle as the exponent of empiricism. Therefore until my destructive analysis of Aristotle . . . is overturned, an appeal to sensation is a *petitio principii*" (Gordon Clark, *The Philosophy of Gordon H. Clark*, 446-447).

Perhaps Rand and Branden meant to grant the status of an axiom to the reliability of the senses. In that case, the axiom must be rejected because it leads to contradictory results: The axiom that the senses are reliable logically leads to the conclusion that the senses are unreliable. I shall speak more of the unreliability of the senses later.

The Mystics of Muscle

Rand misrepresented the epistemology of the Communists (whom she self-servingly called "mystics of muscle") when she wrote: "The mystics of muscle do not bother to assert any claim to extrasensory perception: they merely declare that your senses are not valid, and that their wisdom consists of perceiving your blindness by some manner of unspecified means."[23] As a matter of fact, no more vigorous defenders of the "validity" of man's senses can be found than Ludwig Feuerbach, Karl Marx, Friedrich Engels, and V. I. Lenin. For example, Lenin wrote:

> Acceptance or rejection of the concept matter is a question of the confidence man places in the evidence of his sense-organs, a question of the source of our knowledge, a question which has been asked and debated from the very inception of philosophy, which may be disguised in a thousand different garbs, by professorial clowns, but which can no more become antiquated than the question whether the source of human cognition is sight and touch, hearing, and smell. To regard our sensations as images of the external world, to recognize objective truth, to hold the materialist theory of knowledge—these are all one and the same thing.[24]

For every scientist who has not been led astray by professorial philosophy, as well as for every materialist, sen-

---

[23] *Atlas Shrugged*, 1034-1035.

[24] *Materialism and Empirio-Criticism*, 128-129.

sation is indeed the direct connection between consciousness and the external world; it is the transformation of the
energy of external excitation into a state of consciousness.[25]

Feuerbach wrote: "How banal to deny that sensation is the evan-
gel, the gospel (*Verkundung*) of an objective saviour."[26]

Marx wrote: "Sense experience . . . must be the basis of all
science. Science is only genuine science when it proceeds from
sense experience, in the two forms of sense perception and sensu-
ous need; i.e. only when it proceeds from nature."[27]

Rand called the Communists "mystics of muscle" because she
would not and perhaps could not admit that the greatest totalitar-
ians the world has ever known were empiricists whose epistemology and metaphysics were her own. By abusing them as mystics,
Rand avoided acknowledging their common ideas. Rand was educated in the Soviet Union. She physically escaped from the Communists in 1924. She never escaped from the Communists intellectually.

The Senses

Although Rand's epistemology requires a full and complete vindication of the senses, she nowhere provided one, or even attempted

---

[25] *Materialism and Empirio-Criticism*, 44. David Kelley's words in *The Evidence
of the Senses* are an unwitting echo of Lenin: "We live our lives bathed in streams
of physical energy: sound waves, electromagnetic fields, mechanical forces of
every kind. Much of this energy passes us by, leaving behind no discernible
trace. But some of it, at every moment, sets off reactions in the cells we call
sense receptors, and these in turn set off electrical impulses that reverberate
through the physical structure we call the nervous system. Like radios, we are
tuned to a portion of the energy that eddies around us" (1). In this passage, one
can see how easily Communist materialism slides into the mysticism of new age
occultism. Kelley is a radio receiver channeling omnipresent energy.

[26] *Samtliche Werke*, x, 194-195.

[27] *Early Writings*, 164.

to provide one.[28] She simply took the cognitive reliability and accuracy of the senses for granted. In *The Romantic Manifesto*, she wrote of "man's five cognitive senses, two of which provide him with a direct awareness of entities: sight and touch. The other three senses—hearing, taste, and smell—give him an awareness of some of an entity's attributes . . . but in order to perceive something, he needs sight and/or touch."[29]

Now this formulation is quite incorrect. Sight cannot provide direct awareness of an entity; it too, at best, provides only an awareness of some attributes. Sight perceives only patches of color. One cannot see a tree, for a tree is, presumably, more than patches of color. Rand's statement about touch is even more problematic. Empiricists cannot decide how many senses touch actually is.[30] There is no small disagreement about how many human senses there are, with some opinions ranging up to seventeen. (In addition to human senses, there are many more forms of animal senses: infrared, magnetic, electric, to mention a few.) In any case, touch does not give direct awareness of entities, as Rand asserts, but only of texture, or resistance, or temperature. Presumably a gold dollar sign is not merely hard and cold. Touch cannot tell us what more it is. It, too, yields an awareness only of attributes. No sense yields an awareness of entities.

Introduction to Objectivist Epistemology

Having noted these initial problems, problems to which we shall return later, we may now begin an examination of Rand's monograph on epistemology, *Introduction to Objectivist Epistemology*. The first edition of this book appeared in 1967; the second edition, edited by Leonard Peikoff and Harry Binswanger, appeared after Rand's death, in 1990. The second edition contains Peikoff's pre-

[28] I examine David Kelley's *The Evidence of the Senses* in Appendix C.

[29] *The Romantic Manifesto*, 46.

[30] See, for example, *Deciphering the Senses,* Rivlin and Gravelle. Simon and Schuster, 1984.

viously published essay, "The Analytic-Synthetic Dichotomy," as well as a long appendix of "Excerpts from the Epistemology Workshops." These excerpts have been edited from tapes made of these conversations with Rand. Those conversations, despite the best efforts of Peikoff and Binswanger, display much of the confusion in Rand's thought in the area of epistemology.

Her opening statement of the book is, "Consciousness, as a state of awareness, is not a passive state, but an active process that consists of two essentials: differentiation and integration."[31] These processes of differentiation and integration are performed by two apparently different entities: the brain and the mind: "A percept is a group of sensations automatically retained and integrated by the brain of a living organism." "A concept is a mental integration of two or more units which are isolated according to a specific characteristic(s) and united by a specific definition."[32] Rand believed that "Chronologically, man's consciousness develops in three stages: the stage of sensations, the perceptual, the conceptual . . . [but that] . . . epistemologically, the base of all man's knowledge is the perceptual stage."[33]

This is a curious position for an empiricist to take, namely, that perceptions, not sensations (which are the indispensable components, the *sine qua non* of perceptions), are the "base of all man's knowledge." Why did Rand take such a position? Ostensibly, because "Sensations, as such, are not retained in man's memory, *nor*

---

[31] *Introduction to Objectivist Epistemology*, first edition, 11.

[32] *Introduction to Objectivist Epistemology*, 15.

[33] *Introduction to Objectivist Epistemology*, 11. This statement is logically at odds with others, for Rand proposed to base all man's knowledge on the senses, on sensations. This statement seems to indicate that she also wanted to evade the insoluble epistemological problems involved in the passage from "sensation" to "perception" by declaring epistemology to be unconcerned with the relationship between sensation and perception or even with establishment of the fact that sensation occurs. Rand admitted that pure sensations can neither be experienced nor remembered. Therefore, sensation is not a sound foundation for her epistemology.

is man able to experience a pure isolated sensation."[34] "As far as can be ascertained, an infant's sensory experience is an undifferentiated chaos." Note the tentative language, "As far as can be ascertained." If sensation, which cannot be experienced, remembered, or organized, is the basis of Rand's epistemology, then her claim to provide us with knowledge is ludicrous. Her theory of knowledge collapses on page one. "A mind's cognitive development involves a continual process of automatization. For example, you cannot perceive a table as an infant perceives it. . . ."[35] If that is so, one must ask, then whose perception is correct, yours or the infant's?

This point should be kept in mind: At the basis of Rand's epistemology stands sensation, which cannot be experienced in its "pure" form, cannot be remembered, and is undifferentiated experiential chaos. It is the brain which somehow transforms (retains, differentiates, and integrates) this chaos of unexperienced, unremembered sensations into "percepts." How this feat is accomplished, we are not told. That it is accomplished, we are told; and that it is accomplished properly, that is, in accordance with "reality," we are told emphatically. No account, explanation, or argument is given to show how the brain retains, differentiates, and integrates chaotic sensations accurately, that is, in accordance with "reality." We are to take all this "for granted."

I do not grant it. On pain of accepting "ideas or allegations without sensory evidence or rational demonstration"[36] and thereby being guilty of the sin of "faith," I must refuse to take this for granted. Yet to present "sensory evidence or rational demonstra-

---

[34] On the other hand, "Single musical tones are not percepts, but pure sensations; they become percepts only when integrated. Sensations are man's first contact with reality; when integrated into percepts, they are the given, the self-evident, the not-to-be-doubted" (*The Romantic Manifesto*, 59). So, according to Rand's own statements, man both can and cannot experience pure sensation; and perception is indubitable. Rand repeats this view in *Introduction to Objectivist Epistemology*, 321.

[35] *The New Left*, 157.

[36] Nathaniel Branden, *The Objectivist Newsletter*, January 1963, 4.

tion" for the statement that the brain works correctly is impossible on empirical grounds: One would have to know "reality" by means other than his brain and mind in order to compare "reality" with the "percepts" constructed by the brain. The position that the percepts accurately correspond to "reality" is not open to verification or falsification; it must be an act of faith in the cognitive reliability of the brain. We must have faith in ("take for granted") not only the infallibility of the senses, but also the infallibility of the brain before we may arrive at the subject of Rand's "introduction" to epistemology, the formation of concepts by the mind.

In *For the New Intellectual*, however, Rand takes a conflicting position. There she despises the idea that reality is exactly as it is perceived. That is regarded as the epistemology of the mystic or animal.

> An animal has no critical faculty; he has no control over the function of his brain and no power to question its content. [Presumably Rand does not mean the content of his *brain,* but the content of his *mind.* His brain's "contents" are chemicals, electricity, and tissue.] To an animal, whatever strikes his awareness is an absolute that corresponds to reality . . . ; reality, to him, is whatever he senses or feels. And this is the [mystic's] epistemological ideal. . . .[37]

Despite these sentences about mystics and animals, it seems to be Rand's position that what is given in the senses is in absolute correspondence to reality, so much so, that when she was hallucinating in the hospital, she attacked Joan Blumenthal for suggesting that her perceptions were not accurate.

> One day, after Ayn had received a heavy dose of pain medication, she said that she could see the branches of a tree waving across the window pane. How could it reach so high, wasn't she on the ninth floor?—she asked, disturbed

[37] *The Ayn Rand Lexicon*, 322-323.

by the mystery. Joan [Blumenthal] realized she was seeing a reflection of the pole holding her intravenous equipment. She explained it to Ayn, adding that it was not uncommon to have mild hallucinatory experiences under heavy medication. Ayn refused to believe it. She continued to insist that it was a tree, she knew it was a tree. . . . "A number of months later," Joan recalled, "she called me in to discuss what she said was a serious matter. When I arrived, she shouted at me over the issue of the tree. How could I have tried to make her doubt her mind?—she demanded. How could I have attempted to undermine her rationality?"[38]

In *Introduction,* Rand wrote, "The building-block of man's knowledge is the concept of an 'existent'—of something that exists. . . ."[39] Notice that Rand here wrote that a concept—not a percept, not a sensation—is *the* building block of man's knowledge. Not only are concepts apparently grasped perceptually in Rand's chaotic epistemology, they may even be grasped at the level of sensation: "It may be supposed that the concept 'existent' is implicit even on the level of sensation. . . ."[40] This concept is *implicit* in every percept and sensation, she maintained, since "to perceive a thing is to perceive that it exists. . . ."[41] This *implicit concept*

---

[38] *The Passion of Ayn Rand,* 383. Rand clearly believed in the infallibility of the senses. See *Introduction to Objectivist Epistemology,* 228.

[39] *Introduction to Objectivist Epistemology,* 11.

[40] *Introduction to Objectivist Epistemology,* 11.

[41] The philosophical problems ignored by Rand in making this statement are gigantic. To suggest a few, I quote from George Berkeley:

> The table I write on I say exists, that is, I see and feel it; and if I were out of my study I should say it existed—meaning thereby that if I was in my study I might perceive it. . . . There was an odor, that is, it was smelt; there was a sound, that is, it was heard; a color or figure, and it was perceived by sight or touch. This is all that I can understand by these and the like expressions. For as to what is said of the absolute existence of unthinking things without any relation to their being per-

"undergoes three stages of development in man's mind": (1) entity; (2) identity; and (3) unit. By the phrase "implicit concept entity," Rand meant, as far as we can tell, what a child is aware of. She wrote: "The first stage is a child's awareness of objects, of things. . . ."[42] By the phrase, "implicit concept identity," Rand meant "the awareness of specific, particular things which he [the child] can recognize and distinguish from the rest of his perceptual field—which represents the (implicit) concept *'identity.'*" These words do not make clear what the distinction between entity and identity is, nor how one can have (or know) an entity without an identity. By the phrase, "implicit concept unit," Rand meant "an existent regarded as a separate member of a group of two or more similar members."[43] We are to understand that these three stages

---

ceived, that seems perfectly unintelligible. Their *esse* is *percipi*, nor is it possible they should have any existence out of the minds or thinking things which perceive them (*A Treatise Concerning the Principles of Human Knowledge*, 30-31).

Rand would be insulted to be called a Berkeleyan, yet her bald statement "to perceive a thing is to perceive that it exists"—*percipi* is *esse*—gives no way to distinguish her position from Berkeley's *esse* is *percipi*. Rand apparently was counting on her readers to understand what she meant to say, that is, that *matter* exists, without her having to go to the trouble of proving it.

[42] *Introduction to Objectivist Epistemology*, second edition, 6. Here is what Peikoff wrote about entities: "This term [entity] may be used in several senses. If you speak in the primary sense, `entity' has to be defined ostensively—that is to say, by pointing. . . . 1. An entity means a self-sufficient form of existence—as against a quality, an action, a relationship, etc. . . . An entity is a *thing*. . . . 2. An entity, in the primary sense, is a solid thing with a definite boundary—as against a fluid, such as air. . . . 3. An entity is perceptual in scale, in size. In other words it is a "this" which you can point to and grasp by human perception. . . ." (*The Ayn Rand Lexicon*, 146). It follows, of course, that minds are not entities, nor are any other immaterial things: truth, justice, romantic love, self-interest, *ad infinitum*. In fact, what Peikoff takes to be entities are the furniture of Newtonian physics. Post-Newtonian physics denies that there is anything with a definite boundary; everything is a pulsating field of energy.

[43] *Introduction to Objectivist Epistemology*, 6.

and three implicit concepts[44] are *chronological* stages in the development of human consciousness:

> When a child observes that two objects (which he will later learn to designate as "tables") resemble each other, but are different from four other objects ("chairs"), his mind is focusing on a particular attribute of the objects (their shape), then isolating them according to their differences, and integrating them as units into separate groups according to their similarities.

The process occurs in this chronological order:

(1) observation of two objects, that is, individuals, "entities";
(2) observation of resemblance between the two objects;
(3) observation of differences between the two objects and four other objects;
(4) classification of objects according to resemblances.

The four steps may be shortened to

observation
differentiation
integration.

The first question that must be asked is one that Rand did not even attempt to answer. Like Aristotle, Rand's first "category" (or "axiomatic concept," as she calls it) is "existence." Furthermore, her "primary realities," also like Aristotle, are individuals (or "existents" or "entities," as she calls them). The problems with Rand's epistemology do not begin at the conceptual level, as we have already shown, but at the perceptual and sensational levels, the levels of "entities" and "identities." Her theory is subject to the same difficulties as Aristotle's: What is an entity, what is an individual? Clark explains the difficulty:

---

[44] See section below, "Implicit Concepts."

If the universe is an aggregate of individual things, is Mt. Blanca such an individual thing, or is Mt. Blanca itself a composite of the individual rocks and strata that contribute to its great mass? If Mt. Blanca is the primary reality, a single rock would be but a fraction of an individual; it itself would not be individual and therefore would not be real.[45]

Since Rand uses the examples of tables and chairs for individuals, rather than Aristotle's Mount Olympus (or Clark's Mt. Blanca) the question to be asked is, If a chair is the entity, the individual, the existent, then are its seat, arms, legs, back, and cushions not entities, not individuals, not existent, and therefore not real? In other words, what are individuals, what are the existents that are the basis of Rand's theory of concept formation? On the basis of experience alone, how can one choose the existent to be identified and classified? Are quarks, atoms, and molecules "existents," or entities, or, at the other extreme, is the universe itself the "existent"?

Further, Rand's apparently separable levels of consciousness—sensation, perception, conception—are not so separable and simple as they appear to be. The three levels of consciousness give rise to the three stages through which the *implicit concept* "existent" develops: the implicit concepts entity, identity, unit.[46] "The ability to regard entities as units is man's distinctive method of cognition," Rand wrote.[47] It is "similarity" that binds "units" together into groups: "A unit is an existent regarded as a separate member of a group of two or more similar members." The concept "unit," furthermore, "is not an arbitrary creation of consciousness: It is a

---

[45] Gordon H. Clark, *An Introduction to Christian Philosophy*, 30-31. "The identification of individuals cannot be made on the empirical basis Aristotle adopts." Nor on the empirical basis Rand adopts.

[46] Implicit in Rand's progression—entity, identity, unit—is the idea that entities, individuals, are perceived before identities. This is logically impossible, as we shall see.

[47] *Introduction to Objectivist Epistemology*, 12.

method of identification or classification according to the attributes which a consciousness observes in reality."

In summary, according to Rand, man's consciousness progresses from an undifferentiated chaos, through sensation, to the level of the perception of entities, to the level of the perception of identities, and finally to the uniquely human level of conceptual consciousness. Unfortunately for this schema, Rand failed to explain any of these stages satisfactorily. She claimed that at the conceptual level the "unit" is "not an arbitrary creation of consciousness," but she did not make the same assertion about the "identity." She did not offer a solution to the problem of individuation, which is a problem of first importance to the empiricist. By what data furnished by "undifferentiated chaos" does the mind identify individuals?[48] Rand's position precluded her holding that the mind (or brain) has forms by which the task is accomplished. Man's mind is *tabula rasa*. But as we shall see, Rand asserted that man's mind is both *tabula rasa* and also active according to its own nature. Something similar to Kant's forms of the mind are going to be smuggled through the back door. But we are getting ahead of our story.

There exists an equally serious problem in Rand's account of the formation of concepts from percepts, "units" from "identities." Rand would have us believe that the progression of human consciousness is linear and straightforward, from sensation (a chaos similar to William James' "one great blooming, buzzing confusion"[49]), to the perception of discrete things—"identities"—to the

[48] "No one can perceive literally and indiscriminately every accidental inconsequential detail of every apple he happens to see; everyone perceives and remembers only some aspects, which are not necessarily the essential ones; most people carry in mind a vaguely approximate image of an apple's appearance" (Ayn Rand, *The Objectivist*, April 1971, 3). This statement further complicates Rand's position: How does a perceiver know which details are accidental or inconsequential? If perception and memory are always partial and not necessarily of essentials, if most people's images of something so apparently simple as an apple are only vaguely approximate, how can perception furnish knowledge at all? Worse, some people have no images in their minds at all, vague or clear. What is an empiricist to do with them?

[49] *Principles of Psychology*, I, 488.

formation of concepts and the recognition of existents as "units," that is, as members of groups.

However, to recognize a thing as itself, as an "identity," which means simply to recognize something, one must already be thinking in terms of "units," that is, conceptually. To recognize a table as itself, that is, as a table, one must already have the concept "table" in mind. Not to recognize a table *as a table* is not to recognize it at all. The use of language may not yet be present, but the universal must be present from the beginning of consciousness. Worse still, at least for Rand's theory, to be aware of something at the "lowest," most primitive level requires the use of propositions.

It follows, of course, that concepts or universals do not follow and are not derived from the perception of particulars; they must precede perception. Brand Blanshard, whose book, *The Nature of Thought,* Rand commended highly, wrote: "There is no stage in experience, not even pure sensation, if such a stage exists, in which universals are not present." Furthermore, "What must not be done is to say that we begin with the sensing of bare particulars in which nothing is identical with anything else, and that we somehow find identities as we go on. Identities that are not there cannot be found."[50] I refer the reader to chapter one of *The Nature of Thought* for a much abler and fuller elucidation of the argument than I have given here. It is utterly destructive of Rand's version of empiricism.[51]

Measurement and Science

Rand wrote that the "conceptual level of cognition . . . consists of two interrelated fields: the conceptual and the mathematical. The process of concept-formation is, in large part, a mathematical process. Mathematics is the science of measurement."[52]

We must pause to grasp the import of what Rand wrote here. Mathematics, we are told, is the "science of measurement." Math-

[50] Brand Blanshard, *The Nature of Thought,* I, 63.

[51] Gordon Clark, in turn, destroyed Blanshard's attempt to give a coherent account of perception. See his *Three Types of Religious Philosophy,* 78-80.

[52] *Introduction to Objectivist Epistemology,* 12.

ematics is also the principal basis of concept-formation. This places measurement in a critical position for Rand's theory of knowledge. "Measurement is the identification of a relationship—a quantitative relationship established by means of a standard that serves as a unit."[53] If measurement fails to provide knowledge, Rand's theory is futile. In the statement quoted immediately above, Rand indicates the close connection between measurement and concept-formation by her use of the word "unit." The "unit" is the standard in both measuring and conceiving.

As we examine Rand's theory of cognition and measurement, let us recall her words found in the foreword to *Introduction to Objectivist Epistemology*: "To what precisely do concepts refer in reality? Do they refer to something real, something that exists—or are they merely inventions of man's mind, arbitrary constructs or loose approximations that cannot claim to represent knowledge?"[54] Notice the antithesis between "knowledge" and "inventions," "arbitrary constructs," and "loose approximations." Obviously Rand did not consider inventions, constructs, and approximations knowledge. This understanding is buttressed by Rand's use of the phrases "the most rigorous mathematical precision, the most rigorous compliance with objective rules and facts [that are necessary] if the end product is to be knowledge."[55]

In light of these statements let us proceed to examine her account of measurement, which is the basis of concept-formation. First we encounter the requirements of a standard of measurement, that is, a unit: "that it represent the appropriate attribute [of an existent], that it be easily perceivable by man and that, once chosen, it remain immutable and absolute whenever used."[56] The problems spring like mushrooms from the damp ground: Where on Earth (Rand did not believe in Heaven) are these immutable, absolute,

[53] *Introduction to Objectivist Epistemology*, 13.

[54] *Introduction to Objectivist Epistemology*, 7.

[55] *Introduction to Objectivist Epistemology*, 14.

[56] *Introduction to Objectivist Epistemology*, 13.

and easily perceivable standards without which, she admitted, knowledge is impossible?

Rand's criteria require that her own yardstick as well as the yardstick owned by the Bureau of Standards be immutable and absolute. The problem for which Rand sought to provide a solution is that "The possibility of intelligible speech presupposes the existence of entities that remain unchanged for some finite time; and conversely the theory of universal change makes speech and knowledge impossible."[57] But unlike Christianity, which begins with propositions in the mind of God, Rand's standards and truth cannot originate in the mind of God; they must be found in this world, on this Earth.

By asserting the interdependence and/or similarity of concept-formation and measurement, Rand exposed to full view one of the many fatal errors in empiricism. No absolute and immutable standards of measurement exist in nature; therefore, on Rand's own basis and by Rand's own definition, knowledge is not possible. The platinum bar in the Bureau of Standards is continually changing in length. The weight of a platinum block is continually in flux. Immutability is not a characteristic of physical things. Anyone who has attended to his perceptions or taken Physics 101 should realize that. The scientist in his laboratory (the fictional physicist John Galt, for instance) is Rand's idea of the man in possession of and in pursuit of truth. Let us see how such a scientist behaves in the laboratory:

> To do this, we must more carefully examine the process of experimentation. No matter how intricate an experiment may be, its basic process is the measurement of a line. If a scientist is attempting to determine the boiling point of a fluid, he measures the length of the mercury in a thermometer. If he is interested in the specific gravity of this or that, he measures the distance between a zero mark on a balance and another mark on the scale. Whatever the

[57] Gordon H. Clark, *The Philosophy of Science and Belief in God*, 8.

49

experiment may be, all measurement is measurement of the length of a line.

When this length has been measured once, the scientist in any new and important experiment repeats the experiment and measures the length a second, a third, a fourth time, until he has a long list of readings. These measurements are the experimental factors; these are the observational data; but they are not the sole factors in arriving at [scientific] laws. After the scientist has obtained his list of readings, he notices that they are all different. Water never, well, hardly ever, boils at the same temperature. A cubic centimeter of gold hardly ever weighs the same twice. Thus a list of different readings is an inescapable result of measuring.

With this list of readings the scientist does what seems to be only sound common sense. He adds them and divides by the number of readings; that is, he computes the arithmetic mean. For philosophical purposes this step should be carefully considered. Why is it sound common sense to compute the arithmetic mean? For many people it seems the natural thing to do because they have a notion that we need an average, and the arithmetic mean is the only average they know. But statisticians know two other averages: the mode, or the most frequently occurring number, and the median, or the middle number in the list when arranged in order of magnitude. Why then does the scientist choose the mean rather than one of the other two? This question turns out to be more difficult to answer than at first it might seem; but whatever answer is attempted, clearly nothing in the observational data has dictated its choice. Here is something the scientist himself contributes, no doubt from his theory of mathematics, but certainly neither imposed upon him by, nor discovered by him in, the experimental material.

This is only the beginning of the use of non-empirical factors in the construction of a law of physics. The next step is the scientist's subtraction of each reading from the mean to find the difference. One reading may be .002 above the mean and another .003 below. When these differences are ascertained, the scientist, disregarding the plus or minus signs, adds them and divides by the number of readings, thus computing the arithmetic mean of the differences. This mean he attaches with a plus and minus sign to the original mean (for example, 19.31 ± .0025) and calls it the variable error. Once more the procedure is dictated by something other than the observed data.

After the scientist has done this for a whole series of experiments—for example, the boiling point of a liquid at many pressures, or the force of gravity between the same two bodies at many distances—his next step is a most striking confirmation of the conclusion that a law of physics is a construction and not a discovery of how nature moves. The step from the several means with their variable errors to the equation that will be called the law may be made by plotting these values on a graph. But, of course, instead of indicating a point on the graph, the value of 19.31 ± .0025 indicates a line; the corresponding range of pressure or force indicates another line on the other axis; with the result that the two values enclose a rectangular area on the graph. The scientist marks out a series of such areas, each one corresponding to one of the experiments in the whole set.

Then he passes a curve through these areas, and this curve he calls a law. But here is the trouble. Through one series of rectangles it is possible to pass any number of curves. . . .[58] The empirical data do not necessitate any given curve. In other words, so far as observation is concerned, the scientist could have chosen a law other than the one he actually selected. Indeed, his range of selection was infinite; and out of this infinity he chose, he did not discover, the equation he accepts.

---

[58] It is possible to pass an infinite number of curves through any series of points, as well.

Not only does this consideration show that laws are not discovered in the empirical material, or necessarily deduced from that material, but it also shows that if mathematical equations could describe nature, the chance of choosing the correct description is one over infinity, or zero. Therefore, all the laws of physics are false.[59]

Despite Rand's fondest wishes, objectivity and knowledge do not exist either in measurement or in science; John Galt discovered no truth by the scientific method; he chose equations and called them knowledge. If they worked, that is, if they yielded the results he wished, he accepted them. What Rand regarded as knowledge are, to use her own words, "merely inventions of man's mind, arbitrary constructs and loose approximations that cannot claim to represent knowledge." Moreover, we have been carried to this conclusion precisely because we have exercised "the most rigorous mathematical precision, the most rigorous compliance with objective rules and facts. . . ."[60]

Popper on Science

One of the implications of Clark's logically rigorous analysis of laboratory procedure is this: If there is an infinite number of curves that may be drawn though any series of data-points or data-areas, then one's chances of choosing the correct curve are one in infinity, or zero. That means that all the laws of science are false, and all have the same probability: zero.

So the reader will not imagine that this is a conclusion reached by a Christian philosopher with an axe to grind (as though secular philosophers had no axes to grind), perhaps these words from the atheist philosopher of science Karl Popper and from others,

---

[59] Gordon H. Clark, *The Philosophy of Science and Belief in God*, 58-60.

[60] One might argue, however, that were the scientist to comply rigorously with "objective rules and facts," he would never discover or invent any laws at all, for he would not be allowed to compute averages.

none of whom is a Christian, might be more credible:

> First, although in science we do our best to find the truth, we are conscious of the fact that we can never be sure whether we have got it. . . . [W]e know that our scientific theories must always remain hypotheses. . . . [I]n science there is no "knowledge," in the sense in which Plato and Aristotle understood the word, in the sense which implies finality; in science we never have sufficient reason for the belief that we have attained the truth. What we usually call "scientific knowledge" is, as a rule, not knowledge in this sense, but rather information regarding the various competing hypotheses and the way in which they have stood up to various tests; it is, using the language of Plato and Aristotle, information concerning the latest, and the best tested, scientific "opinion." This view means, furthermore, that we have no proofs in science (excepting, of course, pure mathematics and logic). In the empirical sciences, which alone can furnish us with information about the world we live in, proofs do not occur, if we mean by "proof" an argument which establishes once and for ever the truth of a theory.[61]

> Einstein declared that his theory was false: He said that it would be a better approximation to the truth than Newton's, but he gave reasons why he would not, even if all predictions came out right, regard it as a true theory.[62]

> . . .ever since LaPlace, attempts have been made to attribute to our theories instead of *truth* at least *a high degree of probability*. I regard these attempts as misconceived.
> [I]t can be shown by purely mathematical means that

---

[61] "Two Kinds of Definitions," in *Popper Selections*, 90-91.

[62] "The Problem of Demarcation," in *Popper Selections*, 121.

degree of corroboration can never be equated with mathematical probability. It can even be shown that all theories, including the best, have the same probability, namely zero.[63]

The way in which knowledge progresses, and especially our scientific knowledge, is by unjustified (and unjustifiable) anticipations, by guesses, by tentative solutions to our problems, by conjectures. These conjectures . . . can never be positively justified: They can neither be established as certainly true nor even as "probable". . . . And since we can never know for certain, there can be no authority here nor any claim to authority, nor conceit over our knowledge, nor smugness.[64]

[F]alse theories often serve well enough: Most formulae used in engineering or navigation are known to be false . . . and they are used with confidence by people who know them to be false.[65]

[A]ll scientific statements are hypotheses, or guesses, or conjectures (including Bacon's own) [which] have turned out to be false. . . ."[66]

[O]ur attempts to see and to find the truth are not final, but open to improvement; that our knowledge, our doctrine, is conjectural; that it consists of guesses, of hypotheses, rather than of final and certain truths. . . ."[67]

---

[63] *Conjectures and Refutations*, 192.

[64] *Conjectures and Refutations*, vii.

[65] *Conjectures and Refutations*, 27.

[66] *Conjectures and Refutations*, 138.

[67] *Conjectures and Refutations*, 151.

Russell on Induction

Bertrand Russell, who wrote an essay titled *Why I Am Not a Christian*, was clear-minded enough to understand the logical fallaciousness of induction:

> All inductive arguments in the last resort reduce themselves to the following form: "If this is true, that is true; now that is true: therefore, this is true." This argument is, of course, formally fallacious. Suppose I were to say, "If bread is a stone and stones are nourishing, then this bread will nourish me; now this bread does nourish me; therefore, it is a stone, and stones are nourishing." If I were to advance such an argument, I should certainly be thought foolish, yet it would not be fundamentally different from the argument upon which all scientific laws are based.

That is, all scientific laws are conclusions of logically fallacious arguments.

What Russell was illustrating, of course, is the elementary logical fallacy of asserting the consequent, which is the heart of the scientific method. No competent mechanic would make the same mistake as the scientist in dealing with a car that won't start.

To summarize: There are seven fundamental and insuperable epistemological flaws in science and the scientific method:

1. The unreliability of the senses: Scientists repeat experiments several times and develop special instruments in an effort to overcome this unreliability.
2. The mutability of nature: The things the scientist is attempting to measure are continually changing.
3. The use of arbitrary—here *arbitrary* means not required by the experimental data—methods, choices, and procedures such as averages.
4. The fallacy of induction: Drawing universal conclusions from specific observations.

5. The fallacy of asserting the consequent: If p, then q. Q; therefore, p.
6. The arbitrary choice of an equation from among an infinite
   number of possible equations.
7. The use of assumptions that do not and cannot describe the
   physical world.

The failure of measurement to provide knowledge is part of the
failure of science to provide knowledge, and leads in turn to the
failure of Rand's theory of cognition to provide knowledge, since
both are interrelated. Neither Rand nor any of her disciples attempted to justify logically the scientific method.[68]

Concept Formation

Rand defined a concept as "a mental integration of two or more
units which are isolated according to a specific characteristic(s)
and united by a specific definition."[69] The concept as a *mental* integration is distinguished from the percept, which is "a group of
sensations automatically retained and integrated by the *brain* of a
living organism."[70] Rand wished to differentiate between the integrating functions of the brain, which produces percepts, and the
integrating functions of the mind, which produces concepts. This
distinction implies that percepts are physical things, and concepts
are mental things. What a physical perception would be like is quite
unimaginable.

A concept, Rand wrote, is an integration of "units." What is a
"unit"? It is "an existent regarded as a separate member of a group
of two or more similar members."[71] Using Pascal's advice about
definitions, that is, to substitute the *definiens* for the *definiendum*

[68] See Appendix E, "Science and Truth."

[69] *Introduction to Objectivist Epistemology*, 15.

[70] Emphasis added for clarity, *Introduction to Objectivist Epistemology*, 11.

[71] *Introduction to Objectivist Epistemology*, 12.

whenever it occurs, we find that a concept is a mental integration of two or more existents regarded as separate members of a group, which are isolated according to a specific characteristic(s) and united by a specific definition.[72] "Units," however, we are told, "do not exist *qua* units, what exists are things [i.e. individuals or existents], but units are things viewed by consciousness in certain existing relationships."[73] Thus, the relationships exist; the "things" exist; but the units do not exist. How one can mentally integrate physical things Rand did not explain. A chemist can combine physical things in the laboratory; a philosopher can mentally integrate ideas; but how anyone can mentally integrate physical things is a puzzle. Rand did not solve the puzzle, and she did not appear even to be conscious that there is a puzzle here.

The relationships that Rand said exist are similarity and difference, but similarity and difference are not individuals; they are not existents; they are not things. Rand had already told us that only things—existents, individuals—exist. Rand asserted, contradictorily, that only things exist, and that relationships exist.

These relationships exist, but units *qua* units do not exist, we are told. This is another contradiction. If the relationships exist in the sense that Rand intends to use the word *existence*, they are not solely in the consciousness of the observer: They are external to the observer. That is the only meaning that can be given to the word "exist" in this context, for Rand insists on a distinction between invention (or mental construct) and "perceived in reality." If the *relationships* of similarity and dissimilarity exist in "objective reality," then units *qua* units exist. Similarities (or dissimilarities) that are not there cannot be regarded. And if the similarities and dissimilarities are out there, the groups also are out there. If the groups are out there, the units exist *qua* units, that is, as members of groups. If they did not, no process of concept formation could account for universals. In short, universals that are not out there cannot be validly derived by a *tabula rasa* mind. Why

[72] *Introduction to Objectivist Epistemology*, 15.

[73] *Introduction to Objectivist Epistemology*, 12.

Rand insisted that universals are *not* out there in objective reality while relationships *are* is another puzzle. She rejected Plato's and Aristotle's view that universals exist in reality because (she asserted) only individuals exist. But she asserted that relationships as well as individuals exist in objective reality. If relationships exist, then on what basis did Rand assert that universals do not? Relationships are as non-physical as universals.

There are further difficulties with Rand's definition of a concept as "a mental integration of two or more units which are isolated according to a specific characteristic(s) and united by a specific definition." First, Rand was not clear about the meaning of "integration." She did say, "The uniting involved is not a mere sum, but an integration, i.e., a blending of the units into a single, new mental entity which is used thereafter as a single unit of thought (but which can be broken down into its component units whenever required)."[74] What this metaphor of blending means, we were not told. How one breaks out components that have been "blended" rather than "summed," we were not told. Nor were we told how this blending of physical (that is, brain-constructed) "perceptions" (I assume that Rand did mean units of perception, not sensation) is achieved by the *mind* resulting in a *mental* "unit." Rand simply ignored the crucial and most difficult questions of epistemology, and like Aristotle, provided a figure of speech ("blending") when she should have spoken literally.

Furthermore, Rand's definition of concept as "a mental integration of two or more units which are isolated according to a specific characteristic(s) and united by a specific definition" is circular. Her definition of *concept* and her account of concept formation presuppose both characteristics and definition, *both of which are already conceptual in nature.* Her definition of *concept* fails as a definition altogether, for it presupposes the term to be defined in order to define the term. To have a concept, one must first have a definition.

Concepts, Rand wrote, are formed by "a process of abstraction: i.e., a selective mental focus that takes out or separates a cer-

---

[74] *Introduction to Objectivist Epistemology*, 15.

tain aspect of reality from all others. . . ."[75] This is a very important assertion that I cannot discuss immediately. First, we must discuss language, which is "the exclusive domain and tool of concepts." "Words transform concepts into (mental) entities;[76] definitions provide them with identity."[77] This is a rather extraordinary account of the relationship between language and concepts, and completely at odds with Rand's theory of concept formation, for if words "transform" concepts into mental entities, what are concepts prior to this "transformation"? Are not concepts mental entities already? Rand wrote that:

> When a child observes that two objects (which he will later learn to designate as "tables") resemble each other, but are different from four other objects ("chairs"), his mind is focusing on a particular attribute of the objects (their shape), then isolating them according to their differences, and integrating them as units into separate groups according to their similarities.[78]

Does this statement ("he will later learn to designate as tables") not mean that concepts are formed prior to the use of words? Are the concepts not already mental? On page 16, Rand wrote: "The child does not think in such words (he has, as yet, no knowledge of words), but that is the nature of the process [of concept-formation] which his mind performs wordlessly." If this does not mean that concepts are formed prior to the use of words, then what does it mean? If it does mean this, then how can words transform concepts into mental entities?[79] One begins to suspect that we are on

[75] *Introduction to Objectivist Epistemology*, 15.

[76] An entity, Rand told us earlier, is both physical and perceptible. Here an entity is mental and imperceptible.

[77] *Introduction to Objectivist Epistemology*, 16.

[78] *Introduction to Objectivist Epistemology*, 12.

[79] If language were indeed the exclusive domain and tool of concepts, as Rand asserted, then we have concepts only when we speak.

an epistemological merry-go-round in this account of words and concepts.

Rand proceeded to a discussion of concept formation by abstraction, and we dutifully follow. She selected the concept "length" as her first example:

> If a child considers a match, a pencil and a stick, he observes that length is the attribute they have in common, but their specific lengths differ. The difference is one of measurement. In order to form the concept "length," the child's mind retains the attribute and omits its particular measurements.[80]

I have discussed above some of the problems Rand did not address in her account of measurement. The present problems arise from the process of abstraction.

First, why did Rand assert that length is "the attribute" a match, a pencil, and a stick have in common? Surely there are many empirical attributes which they share: color, extension, width, texture, hardness, and so forth. It is false to say that length is "the attribute" they have in common.

The second problem is the obvious circularity of Rand's definition of "length": "I shall identify ["definitions provide them (concepts) with identity"] as 'length' that attribute of any existent possessing it which can be quantitatively related to a unit of length, without specifying the quantity." The definition of the concept of "length" presupposes the concept of length. Once again Rand offered a circular definition.

Rand wrote that although this definitional process is not explicit in the child's mind (which is a problematic position for a person who believes that man is a being of "volitional consciousness" to take),[81] the process is performed by the child "wordlessly." So, too, all fundamental concepts are formed:

---

[80] *Introduction to Objectivist Epistemology*, 16.

[81] Rand at times spoke in contradiction to her theory of volitional consciousness:

> Man, by his nature, cannot [note well] refrain from generalizing;

He [the child] forms the concept "table" by retaining that characteristic ["a flat, level surface and support(s)"] and omitting all particular measurements, not only the measurements of the shape, but of all the other characteristics of tables. . . .[82]

By observing individuals the child abstracts some particular attribute from them and forms a general idea or concept. Rand seems to have confused her reconstruction of how concepts are formed with the actual psychological development of children: Even Aristotle remarked that the infant calls all men "Daddy." The perception of individuals is a later achievement in knowing, not an earlier.[83]

---

he cannot [note well] live moment by moment without context, without past or future; he cannot [note well] eliminate his integrating capacity, i.e., his conceptual capacity, and confine his consciousness to an animal's perceptual range. . . . The enormously powerful integrating mechanism [note the word *mechanism*] of man's consciousness is there at birth; his only [note well] choice is to drive it *or to be driven by it.* Since an act of volition—a process of thought—is required to use that mechanism for a cognitive purpose, man can evade that effort. But if he evades, chance [note well] takes over: the mechanism [note well] functions on its own, like a machine [note well] without a driver. . . . (*The Romantic Manifesto*, 26-27, emphasis added).

To focus his eyes . . . to perceive the things around him . . . to coordinate his muscles . . . and, ultimately, to grasp the process of concept-formation and learn to speak. . . . These achievements are not conscious and volitional in the adult sense of the terms: an infant is not aware, in advance, of the processes he has to perform in order to acquire these skills, and *the processes are largely automatic* (*The New Left*, 156, emphasis added).

Similar statements could be quoted from other Objectivist works; all such statements conflict with Rand's theory of "volitional consciousness," upon which theory much of her philosophy depends. Rand's aesthetics, however, are based upon her theory of mechanical and automatic consciousness. (For a further discussion of her theory of volitional consciousness, see the next two chapters.)

[82] *Introduction to Objectivist Epistemology*, 16.

[83] "Knowledge is a process from the more abstract to the more concrete, not the reverse, as is commonly supposed" (T. H. Green, *Introduction to Hume*, Sec. 40, as quoted by Brand Blanshard, *The Nature of Thought*, I, 569).

Without a Prayer: Ayn Rand and the Close of Her System

The principal difficulty in Rand's theory of concept formation by abstraction from particulars lies in the fact, which I have already pointed out, that to identify an individual is to identify it as *something* and thus to be already using universals. The universal precedes the particular, not vice versa. Without the universal, one could not identify a particular. In Rand's terms, the "unit" must precede, not follow, the "identity." "To form a concept by abstraction in this way [Rand's way] is to look for the spectacles we are wearing by the aid of the spectacles themselves."[84] Unfortunately, Rand was committed to the view that men wear no spectacles and thus pursued this futile enterprise.

Rand chose "table" as an illustration of concept formation because it was more amenable than other concepts to her theory of abstraction. Her theory, however, must account for all concepts. (It does not account for any, though it is more plausible in some cases than in others.) George Berkeley's famous example of the concept of color must be dealt with in any theory that maintains concepts are formed by abstraction. Thus to form the concept "color," one would have to "select and preserve the common qualities of red, green, blue, burnt sienna, and alizarin crimson. But there are no common qualities. Each color is a distinct 'simple idea.' There is no common quality. The abstract idea of color therefore is an impossibility."[85] Nor is color the only problem. Rand's theory cannot even plausibly explain how concepts of imperceptible things—such as hatred, justice, equality, and mind—are formed.

Rand voiced the opinion that:

> Concepts cannot be formed at random. All concepts are formed by first differentiating two or more existents from other existents. All conceptual differentiations are made in terms of commensurable characteristics (i.e., char-

---

[84] Sigwart, *Logic*, I, 249, as quoted by Brand Blanshard, *The Nature of Thought*, I, 571.

[85] Gordon H. Clark, *The Philosophy of Gordon H. Clark*, 455-456.

acteristics possessing a common unit of measurement). No concept could be formed, for instance, by attempting to distinguish long objects from green objects. Incommensurable characteristics cannot be integrated into one unit.[86]

Why can long objects not be distinguished from green objects? Is not Rand's statement here a simple *fiat* prohibition against something that can very easily be done, is in fact done all the time, and must in fact be done if "long" and "green" are not synonymous? Rand might have objected that the existence of a long, green object could not be integrated into a conceptual scheme in which long objects are distinguished from green objects, but this problem is no different from the existence of primitive living organisms that cannot be classified as either animal or vegetable to the exclusion of the other. The anomaly of the animal-vegetable is no more anomalous than the long-green object.[87]

What Rand seemed to be presupposing, although she did not make the presupposition explicit, is that color and length are or belong to different categories of thought. Rand, however, acknowledged no categories, no forms, of the mind. The mind is *tabula rasa*. Rand did speak of "commensurable characteristics" and remarked that they are essential in the process of concept formation. She christened such characteristics "Conceptual Common Denominators" and defined these CCDs as "Characteristic[s] reducible to ... unit[s] of measurement, by means of which man differentiates two or more existents from other existents possessing [them]."[88]

---

[86] *Introduction to Objectivist Epistemology*, 18.

[87] "In the case of existents whose characteristics are equally balanced between the referents of two different concepts—such as primitive organisms, or the transitional shades of a color continuum—there is no cognitive necessity to classify them under either (or any) concept. The choice is optional . . ." (*Introduction to Objectivist Epistemology*, 73). By this statement, Rand undermined her account of concept formation, for without forms of the mind, which she denied, all cases are "borderline" cases, and the *tabula rasa* brain and mind may combine attributes of entities in any convenient fashion.

[88] *Introduction to Objectivist Epistemology*, 15.

More candidly, these characteristics should be called lowest common denominators, for Rand's view of concepts as abstractions, despite her protests, implies that the more general the concept, the emptier the concept.

Notice that a concept, the means by which a human being grasps reality, can be formed only by abstracting from "two or more existents," a phrase which appears repeatedly in Rand's work. One cannot form a concept from one existent. Rand wrote: "The number 'two' is crucially important epistemologically, because to form concepts you need two or more existents between which you observe similarities."[89] Aristotle correctly concluded from the nature of abstraction that "existents," individuals, the primary realities, were therefore unknowable. Rand agreed with Aristotle that individuals were the primary realities: "The first concepts man forms are concepts of entities—since entities are the only primary existents."[90] Since man grasps reality conceptually, according to Rand, he cannot conceptually grasp individuals, for individuals lie just beyond concepts. A concept is an abstract idea (abstracted from two or more individuals) based on a lowest (conceptual) common denominator. The more general the concept, the lower the denominator, until the most general concept, Rand's "existence," Parmenides' "what is," and Hegel's "being," is reached. That axiomatic concept, being the emptiest concept, is indistinguishable from its opposite, non-existence, non-Being.[91]

Another example of the impossibility of concept formation by a process of abstraction is the concept "figure." Blanshard wrote:

> According to the theory [of concept formation by abstraction] before us, the genus "figure" is reached by omit-

---

[89] *Introduction to Objectivist Epistemology*, 198.

[90] *Introduction to Objectivist Epistemology*, 15.

[91] "Obviously the first category must be the simplest, the emptiest, and the most abstract: pure Being. . . . Pure Being, as mere existence, is not green, or heavy, living or conscious, qualified or quantified, or in any way determined. Pure Being therefore is the equivalent of Nothing" (Gordon H. Clark, *Thales to Dewey*, 461).

ting the differences of the species and retaining only what is common. The species in this case are two, rectilinear figure and curvilinear figure. Hence to reach the genus "figure" we must leave out what makes these different. The "figure" then which we reach as genus will be neither "straight-line figure" nor "curved-line figure" but just "figure." Now no such figure can either exist or be conceived. "Figures composed of lines that are neither straight nor curved" are words without meaning. Figure is figure at all only as it is made of lines; and lines are lines at all only when they have some form. Hence if you take form away, you abolish figure with it.[92]

Rand's theory of abstract universals is incoherent because it cannot solve the problems of abstraction.

Rand stated that the first concepts formed are concepts of entities, since entities are the only primary existents.[93] But in the formation of such concepts, "a child's mind has to focus on a distinguishing characteristic—i.e., on an attribute—in order to isolate one group of entities from all others. He is, therefore, aware of attributes while forming his first concepts, but he is aware of them perceptually, not conceptually."[94]

Once again the suspicion arises that Rand put her cart before her horse. If a child cannot distinguish attributes conceptually, how can he distinguish entities conceptually? To use Rand's own example, a child distinguishes between chairs and tables, that is, between entities, by distinguishing between their shapes, that is, their attributes. If, however, the child has not already conceptually distinguished between c-shape and t-shape, how does he arrive at the distinction between chairs and tables? (Whether the conceptualization of attributes is explicit or not is another question, for neither is the conceptualization of entities according to Rand.)

[92] *The Nature of Thought*, I, 584.

[93] *Introduction to Objectivist Epistemology*, 19.

[94] *Introduction to Objectivist Epistemology*, 15.

In a statement that has implications for her anthropology, Rand wrote: "As far as can be ascertained, the perceptual level of a child's awareness is similar to the awareness of the higher animals: the higher animals are able to perceive entities, motions, attributes, and certain numbers of entities."[95] One peculiarity of this statement is Rand's separate listing of "entities," and "certain numbers of entities." One suspects that Rand was about to smuggle an unwarranted idea into her epistemology by using such a listing, and the suspicion is confirmed in chapter 7, "The Cognitive Role of Concepts." It should be obvious to all that if a being is able to perceive entities, it is also capable of perceiving numbers of entities; the latter phrase is redundant. If consciousness may perceive one entity, why can it not perceive several? Rand's purpose in listing the redundancy is apparently to smuggle conceptualization into animal consciousness as perception. In chapter 7 she wrote of crows which were fooled by the number of hunters entering and leaving the forest. She concluded that: "Apparently, their [the crows'] power of discrimination did not extend beyond three units [*note well*]—and their perceptual-mathematical ability consisted of a sequence such as: one-two-three-many."[96]

Unfortunately for Rand and her crows, we have already been told that "The ability to regard entities as units is man's distinctive method of cognition, which other living species are unable to follow." We have also been informed that: "The process of concept-formation is, in large part, a mathematical process."[97] Now we are

---

[95] *Introduction to Objectivist Epistemology*, 19-20. For the record, let it be noted that Rand also wrote that "no man can fully escape the conceptual level of consciousness . . ." (*For the New Intellectual*, 19); and Nathaniel Branden has written: "There is no way for man to regress to the state of an animal . . ." (*The Objectivist*, May 1966, 3). Therefore, confining the child to the perceptual level, as Rand does here, is not only an impossible situation, but one that contradicts her opinions stated elsewhere, unless Rand believed that a child, or at least some children, are not human beings.

[96] *Introduction to Objectivist Epistemology*, 57, emphasis added.

[97] *Introduction to Objectivist Epistemology*, 12.

told that crows discriminate units and that mathematical ability can be and is perceptual.

To illustrate her point Rand appealed to introspection:

> If we omit all conceptual knowledge, including the ability to count in terms of numbers, and attempt to see how many units (or existents of a given kind) we can discriminate, remember and deal with by purely perceptual means (e.g., visually or audibly, but without counting), we will discover that the range of man's perceptual ability may be greater, but not much greater, than that of the crow: we may grasp and hold five or six units [*sic*] at most.[98]

Here we have crows thinking in *units* and men *perceptually* discriminating units! Rand did not and could not consistently adhere to her own account of concept formation. Indeed, Rand's appeal to introspection is itself problematic, since it is sense perception alone that is the basis of cognition. "Introspection," she wrote, "is a process of cognition directed inward—a process of apprehending one's own psychological actions, . . . such actions as thinking, feeling, reminiscing, etc."[99] How one can do this if the senses are the sole means of gaining knowledge is a puzzle. Rand's empiricism makes knowledge of one's self—since the self is not sense perceptible—impossible. And if that is the case, how does one come by one's knowledge of reason, logic, and cognition itself? Recall that Rand insisted that "man's senses are his *only* direct cognitive contact with reality and, therefore, his *only* source of information. Without sensory evidence, there can be no concepts. . . ."[100]

The question that needs to be raised now is whether the thought experiment Rand proposed in the paragraph quoted above is possible. How can a being who is conceptually conscious by nature divest himself voluntarily of that nature and become an animal?

[98] *Introduction to Objectivist Epistemology*, 62-63.

[99] *Introduction to Objectivist Epistemology*, 29.

[100] *Philosophy: Who Needs It?* 108.

Rand herself said that this cannot be done. On the other hand, Rand might have seen no difficulty in such an achievement, for she maintained that man is a being of "volitional consciousness," an idea which I shall examine in detail later. Perhaps the answer Rand might have given in this specific case—had she bothered to answer any criticism of her theories at all—would have involved reducing the time the "units" are exposed to the observer. This is the normal procedure in such an experiment: Flash a photograph on the screen for a split second and ask the observers how many existents they saw. The point is that such experiments do not (and cannot) measure perceptual as opposed to conceptual ability: Adult human beings cannot observe anything without implicitly (or "subconsciously") counting.[101] The flash experiments and Rand's experiment simply measure how fast persons can count. The concepts are already there. Just as a person can count only so far in a split second, so a crow can count only so far in a much longer time. Just as a person inevitably loses track of his counting after a certain number of units have been counted, so a crow loses track—after only three units have been counted. The fact that Rand says the crows discriminated three *units* obviously implies that crows have limited conceptual ability, not that they have none at all. Such a conclusion, however, contradicts Rand's epistemology. It makes her definition of man as "the" rational animal problematic. It would cause her statement, "We refer to the fact that they [men] are living beings who possess the same characteristic distinguishing them from all other living species: a rational faculty . . ."[102] untrue.

Abstraction

In chapter three of *Introduction to Objectivist Epistemology* Rand ascended higher into clouds of abstraction as she proceeded to ex-

---

[101] "The sensory-perceptual awareness of an adult does not consist of mere sense data (as it did in his infancy), but of automatized integrations that combine sense data with a vast context of conceptual knowledge" (Ayn Rand, *The Objectivist*, April 1971, 2).

[102] *Introduction to Objectivist Epistemology*, 17.

plain how the concept "furniture" is formed by abstraction from the concepts "table," "chair," "bed," "cabinet," etc., "on the principle that a piece of furniture must have some shape [is it only furniture that has shape?], but may have any of the shapes characterizing the various units subsumed under the new concept."[103] What is left after all differentia have been removed is the concept "furniture." We are told that existents qualifying as "furniture" must have some measurements, but all specific measurements are omitted from the concept. Is there any sense in this? Is this not simply a repetition of the definition of the concept "figure" as composed of lines which are neither curved nor straight? Is not "furniture" here defined as objects which have some measurements, but no particular measurements, some shape but no particular shape? But just as a line must be either curved or straight, so must an object, or so must furniture, have some specific measurement(s) and shape. In eliminating the specific quantities or measurements from the concept, Rand has emptied the concept of meaning.

Rand attempted to explain her notion of concepts, but merely dug herself deeper into a hole:

> When concepts are integrated into a wider one, the new concept includes all the characteristics of its constituent units; but their distinguishing characteristics are regarded as omitted measurements, and one of their common characteristics becomes the distinguishing characteristic of the new concept: the one representing their "Conceptual Common Denominator" with the existents from which they are being differentiated.[104]

This explanation is confusing, because Rand seemed to want her concepts both to be abstractions and not to be abstractions. She insisted that "the new concept includes *all* the characteristics of its constituent units," that is, there is no abstraction; but that "their

[103] *Introduction to Objectivist Epistemology*, 22.

[104] *Introduction to Objectivist Epistemology*, 23.

distinguishing characteristics [that is, their differentia], are regarded as omitted measurements . . . ," that is, there is abstraction. Keep in mind that Rand's concepts are *mental* entities; they do not exist outside the mind. One should now see that Rand's two descriptions of a concept are irreconcilable: Either a concept includes all "constituent characteristics" or it does not. Recourse to a phrase such as "regarded as omitted" is impermissible, for such regarding, if a concept contains all the characteristics, must be a cognitive error. Obviously, if characteristics that are included in a concept are regarded as omitted, then the regarding is a serious cognitive error. In my estimation, Rand saw the logical consequences of conceiving of the universal as an abstraction, and wished to maintain that the universal is not an abstraction, yet is "regarded as" an abstraction.[105]

For example, Rand accepted the definition of man as "rational animal." The acceptance of this Aristotelian notion must logically lead one to deny the title *human being* to: (1) an old person who is no longer rational; (2) a fetus (Rand drew the logical conclusion here and advocated abortion-on-demand); (3) a baby; and (4) a person injured in the prime of life who is comatose.[106] None of these creatures is rational. Such conclusions should lead one to re-examine the theory of abstract universals. Rand tried to avoid some of these conclusions by saying:

> Just as the concept "man" does not consist merely of "rational faculty" (if it did, the two would be equivalent and interchangeable which they are not), but includes all the characteristics of "man," with "rational faculty" serving as the distinguishing characteristic. . . .[107]

---

[105] Leonard Peikoff's essay, "The Analytic-Synthetic Dichotomy," includes a notable but unsuccessful effort to explain Rand's theory of the abstract-concrete concept.

[106] Aristotle denied that a sleeping person is an actual man. Man is man only when actually functioning in a distinctly human manner.

[107] *Introduction to Objectivist Epistemology*, 27. Of course, this statement obviously makes Rand's denial of the status of "man" to unborn children problematic.

Now, no one has, I suppose, ever asserted that according to Aristotle or Rand, "man" means only "rational faculty." According to both, "man" means "rational animal." What both Aristotle and Rand said is that the "rational faculty" is the characteristic which distinguishes man from other animals. Therefore, despite Rand's assertion that the definition of man "includes all the characteristics of man," it is obvious that if the rational faculty disappears, "man" disappears, because "rational faculty" is "the" distinguishing characteristic. If the characteristic is no longer present, it cannot distinguish. Rand could have avoided this conclusion only if she had set forth a completely different theory of concept formation, one in which there is not merely one distinguishing characteristic.

Rand widened her argument:

> A widespread error . . . holds that the wider the concept, the less its cognitive content—on the ground that its distinguishing characteristic is more generalized than the distinguishing characteristics of its constituent concepts. The error lies in assuming that a concept consists of nothing but its distinguishing characteristic. But the fact is that in the process of abstracting from abstractions, one cannot know what is a distinguishing characteristic unless one has observed other characteristics of the units involved and of the existents from which they are differentiated.

The simple confusion apparent in this paragraph is the confusion between the concept itself and the process of concept-formation. Quite obviously "abstraction"—if words have their usual meaning —implies a mass from which certain factors are removed (abstracted) and certain factors are not. In this sense, abstraction clearly means—must mean—that there are more characteristics in the entities than in the concept.[108] An implication of the idea of abstraction is that in order to abstract one must be aware of characteristics

[108] "To form a concept, one mentally isolates a group of concretes (of distinct perceptual units) on the basis of observed similarities which distinguish them from all other known concretes (similarity is 'the relationship between the two or more existents which possess the same characteristic(s), but in different measure

that are not abstracted. But it certainly does not follow from this that the concept—the result of the process of abstraction—is as full as the particulars. If this were the case, one could not speak of *abstraction*. Rand's point that in her theory concepts are based upon a wider knowledge of particulars is important. But her insistence that the abstractions are really not abstractions, that is, that concepts are their constituent existents' characteristics without omission is, simply, a contradiction. Rand apparently encountered criticisms of the abstract universal and sought to escape them by asserting that her universal is both abstract and not abstract. She did not escape the criticism; she merely impaled herself on an egregious contradiction.

Ostensive Definition

All concepts (with the exception of concepts referring to sensations, and metaphysical axioms) are definable in terms of other concepts, Rand wrote. As for sensations, one can only define their content "ostensively," that is, by pointing at objects. These "ostensive definitions" are also applicable to axioms: "Since axiomatic concepts are identifications of irreducible primaries, the only way to define one is by means of an ostensive definition—e.g., to define 'existence' one would have to sweep one's arm around and say: 'I mean this.' "[109] The most important elements in Rand's epistemology—the axiomatic concepts and sensations—must be "defined" ostensively.

It is unfortunate for her theory of ostensive definition that Rand had already defined *definition*: "A definition is a statement that identifies the nature of the units subsumed under a concept."[110] Now,

---

or degree'); then, by a process of omitting the particular measurements of these concretes, one integrates them into a single new mental unit: the concept, which subsumes all concretes of this kind (a potentially unlimited number)" (Leonard Peikoff, "The Analytic-Synthetic Dichotomy," 9).

[109] *Introduction to Objectivist Epistemology*, 41. Rand here seems to be saying that her widest abstractions, the axiomatic concepts, are not abstractions at all. One cannot point at a concept.

[110] *Introduction to Objectivist Epistemology*, 40.

a definition is either a statement that identifies the nature of the units subsumed or it is a swinging of the arms; it cannot be both. When Rand declared, "I mean this," she did not tell us what "this" is; the nature of "this" is not identified. "This" might be the act of swinging the arms itself. It might mean whatever one points at, and one cannot point at everything, not even everything perceptible. Worse, a blind person could not see the ostensive "definition." Ostensive "definition," therefore, is a meaningless phrase, and this meaningless contradiction lies at the base of both Rand's epistemology and her metaphysics.[111]

Furthermore, ostensive definition obscures Rand's distinction between the *definition* of a concept and the *meaning* of a concept. The definition of a concept, according to Rand, is a statement presenting the essential characteristic(s) of a group of units. The meaning of a concept is simply the particular referents of the concept, the existents it subsumes.[112] Thus an ostensive definition cannot be a definition at all, but at best a meaning. This is corroborated by the exclamation Rand made while swinging her arms about: "I mean this." One must conclude that concepts of sensations and metaphysical axioms are, by Rand's own terms, *indefinable*. One is reduced to swinging one's arms. This, to say the least, is a curious result for a philosophy that exalts reason and rationality. Had Rand read Augustine's *De Magistro*, available for 1,500 years, she might have learned that ostensive definitions are both useless and impossible. Rand's Objectivism, like the logical positivism of the twentieth century, is based on the logically absurd: ostensive definitions.

---

[111] Leonard Peikoff denies that an ostensive definition is a definition: "This is not a definition [of *entity*], because I'd have to rely ultimately on pointing . . ." (*The Philosophy of Objectivism*, lecture series [1976], lecture three, question period; as quoted in *The Ayn Rand Lexicon*, 146).

[112] "The meaning of a concept consists of the units—the existents—which it integrates, including all the characteristics of these units" (Peikoff, 9). "On the objective, contextual view of essences, a concept does not mean only the essential or defining characteristics of its units. To designate a certain characteristic as 'essential' or 'defining' is to select, from the total content of the concept, the characteristic that best condenses and differentiates that content in a specific cognitive context" (Peikoff, 13).

Open-ended Concepts

Other concepts, the concepts midway between sensations and axioms, are formed contextually, Rand wrote. That is, concepts are and can be formed only on the basis of available evidence, which is always partial; as the evidence grows, the concepts expand or become more refined. Rand insisted that

> If [one's] grasp is non-contradictory, then even if the scope of [one's] knowledge is modest and the content of [one's] concepts is primitive, *it will not contradict the content of the same concepts in the mind of the most advanced scientists.*[113]

This point is crucial to Rand's theory of cognition, for, assuming that all her arguments up to this point had been valid, and this argument was invalid, her entire epistemology would collapse. If concepts are not "open-ended," that is, if later concepts contradict or are inconsistent with earlier concepts, then one cannot claim to have any knowledge. Rand said that definitions and concepts are "contextually absolute" but are not changelessly absolute. This is a rather curious use of the word *absolute*, and one suspects that it has been used for its emotive qualities, not its cognitive.[114]

Rand illustrated her idea of the open-ended concept by imaginatively tracing the development of the concept "man" from that of an infant to that of an adult. According to Rand's imagination, the infant's definition of "man," if articulated, would be: "A thing that moves and makes sounds." The child's definition: "A living thing that walks on two legs and has no fur." The youngster's: "A living thing that speaks and does things no other living beings can do." The adult's: "A rational animal."[115] The latter of these defini-

---

[113] *Introduction to Objectivist Epistemology*, 43.

[114] The phrase "contextually absolute" is a contradiction in terms. One might as well speak of "temporarily eternal," or "relatively absolute." See *Introduction to Objectivist Epistemology*, 47, 85.

[115] *Introduction to Objectivist Epistemology*, 43-44.

tions, Rand wrote, include the earlier, and the last, "rational animal," includes all earlier definitions. But what does it mean to say that the definition "rational animal" "includes" the definition "a thing that moves and makes sounds"? How does one definition "include" another? Do not cars and trucks and cats move and make sounds? Is not a bird a "living thing that walks on two legs and has no fur?" How is the word "include" being used?

Furthermore, one might question how, if concepts are formed and definitions devised contextually, the youngster can define man as doing things "no other living being can do." If the definition had specified "no other living being that I know of," then there would have been no problem—and no knowledge—because the statement would have been tentative and incomplete. The fundamental problem is this, however: If concepts and definitions are formed and devised contextually, how do they develop? Unless one knows *prior* to developing any concept or articulating a defining statement which existents are men, how does one proceed to develop these "open-ended" concepts at all?

One must realize that Rand's illustration of the open-ended concept is an imaginative reconstruction designed to illustrate her theory: It is not a description of the development of the concept "man" in the mind of the child. Rand substituted fiction for history, fiction for truth. But this point is not the most damaging to her theory of open-ended concepts. The fatal flaw is that in her theory, prior concepts, or prior contextual definitions of concepts—such as those of the infant, the child, and the youngster—are verified only by later concepts (or definitions). The implications of this theory should be obvious to all: Any contextual definition cannot be verified or "validated" without using another contextual definition developed later. Therefore, one cannot possibly know that the definition one currently holds is "correct" until it has been replaced by a new definition. Only if the two are logically compatible or consistent can one plausibly assert that the first contextual definition—which is now inadequate and obsolete—had been properly formulated. Rand's theory requires one to be continually "validating" obsolete and inadequate definitions, just as Rand did in her illustration.

However, the difficulties do not end here. Since concepts are open-ended, definitions may be changed *ad infinitum*. Thus one's present definition, which cannot be validated until a later, superior definition has been devised, cannot be used to validate earlier definitions. An open-ended concept is as skeptical an epistemological conclusion as one could imagine, for it rests one's hope for knowledge on an ever-retreating horizon of tentative, elusive, and ever-changing definitions.

Implicit Concepts

Rand's account of knowledge is such a jumble, her ideas so contradictory, that the reader must forgive one more example. In *Introduction of Objectivist Epistemology*, she introduced the idea of "implicit concepts." Now these concepts are not implicit in other concepts, but in things or in percepts, she says:

> Since it [existence] is a concept, man cannot grasp it *explicitly* until he has reached the conceptual stage. But it is *implicit* in every percept (to perceive a thing is to perceive that it exists) and man grasps it implicitly on the perceptual level—i.e., he grasps the constituents of the concept "existent," the data which are later to be integrated. . . . It is this implicit knowledge that permits his consciousness to develop further. (It may be supposed that the concept "existent" is implicit even on the level of sensations. . . . A sensation is a sensation of something, as distinguished from nothing . . .).[116]

What seems to have happened is that Rand recognized that the empiricist account of concept formation is logically impossible (after all, she had apparently read Brand Blanshard's *The Nature of Thought*), but she did not want to admit it. Rand's assertion of the *tabula rasa* mind, and her rejection of innate ideas, so clearly stated

---

[116] *Introduction to Objectivist Epistemology*, 6.

in her works, was contradicted by her assertion of the existence of "implicit concepts" and "implicit knowledge." In her account of axiomatic concepts she wrote:

> Axiomatic concepts identify explicitly what is merely implicit in the consciousness of an infant or of an animal. (Implicit knowledge is passively held material which, to be grasped, requires a special focus and process of consciousness—a process which an infant learns to perform eventually).[117]

This "material," of course, is the concept that is already present at the perceptual, and even the sensational level, if there is such a thing as sensation. Concept formation is not the last step in cognition, as Rand argued, for cognition simply cannot begin without concepts.

What Is Truth?

A discussion of the nature of truth immediately arises from this discussion of changing definitions and concepts. "Truth," Rand wrote, "is the product of the recognition (i.e., identification) of the facts of reality."[118] Now this statement is not very helpful, for we are not told what a fact is, nor what the "product" is.[119] Man's brain organizes sensations into percepts, and his mind organizes percepts into concepts and concepts into propositions. "Every concept stands for a number of propositions."[120] (Did not Rand previously tell us that every concept stands for a number of existents?) We must conclude from these present statements that every proposition is made

---

[117] *Introduction to Objectivist Epistemology*, 57.

[118] *Introduction to Objectivist Epistemology*, 48.

[119] "The English word *fact* has too many connotations to be useful in a carefully formulated theory" (Gordon H. Clark, "Apologetics," in Carl F. H. Henry, editor, *Contemporary Evangelical Thought*, 145).

[120] *Introduction to Objectivist Epistemology*, 46.

of concepts, and every concept is made of propositions. The question of truth or falsehood, or whether the two have any meaning when applied to a concept, is not at all answered by saying that "A definition is the condensation of a vast body of observations—and stands or falls with the truth or falsehood of these observations." How an *observation* can be false is not explained. On the contrary, Rand asserted the infallibility of the senses.

Rand "challenge[d] and reject[ed] the proposition that truth is a matter of propositions."[121] This is an absurd position. Truth is a characteristic of propositions, and of nothing else. How a concept can be true or false she did not explain. "Cat," spoken, heard, or read without context, is not true. It is not false. It is meaningless. If it is an answer to a question, it is an elliptical expression, meaning: "That is a cat," or, "My favorite animal is a cat." But without context, "cat" is as meaningless as "boojum." All by themselves, single concepts and single words are meaningless. They are neither true nor false. Rand made the same mistake that Parmenides, Plato, Aristotle, and Hegel made: thinking that concepts per se are true. If we are to know truth, if we are to discover truth, we must think in terms of propositions, not concepts. Truth—knowledge—comes only in propositions. "Conceptual truth" is a contradiction in terms. Truth is a relationship between a predicate and a subject. If there is no predicate, there is no truth. If there is no subject, there is no truth. Neither an experience, nor an encounter, nor an observation, nor an isolated concept, nor a single word can be true.

Truth, of course, is an insuperable problem for empiricism: Truth cannot be derived from something non-propositional, such as "observations." Unless one starts with propositions, one cannot end with propositions. One cannot logically infer more than one begins with.

Essences

Rand's observations are not observations of essences, for essences

---

[121] *Letters of Ayn Rand*, 527.

are epistemological, not metaphysical as Aristotle and Plato thought. But Rand gave us two differing accounts of essences.

> Objectivism holds that the essence of a concept is that fundamental characteristic(s) of its units on which the greatest number of other characteristics depend, and which distinguishes these units from all other existents within the field of man's knowledge. *Thus the essence of a concept is determined contextually and may be altered with the growth of man's knowledge.*[122]

Now, if the essence of a concept is a characteristic(s) of existents, then essences are, in fact, metaphysical, despite Rand's frequent and insistent declarations that they are not. Essences are not mental at all. Furthermore, may a concept which has changed *essentially* be regarded as the same concept before and after its change? If so, on what basis? But if not, then how can Rand's theory of cognition succeed? If the *essence* of a concept ("a concept is a mental integration") changes as the "context" changes, on what basis is it logically permissible to speak of one and the same concept? Notice that a recourse to "meaning" as opposed to "definition" cannot extricate the Objectivists from the force of this question, for the "context" and the "meaning" are indissolubly linked. If the "context" of a concept changes, this can only mean that some existents or some characteristics of existents that have never before been recognized are now perceived. The meaning of a concept may be thus enlarged or diminished, as the concept's referents (which are its meaning) are increased or decreased in number. Thus the "context" and the "meaning" are equally variable. There is no fixed core in Rand's concepts that one can accurately call knowledge. If the "meaning" of the concept changes, and its definition (essence) changes also, then on what basis may the concept be regarded as unchanged?

Rand repudiated the unchanging metaphysical essences of Plato

---

[122] *Introduction to Objectivist Epistemology*, 52, emphasis added.

and Aristotle; she substituted in their places the changing, contextual, epistemological essences of Objectivism.[123] She declared that essences (concepts, definitions) are mental constructs that change as the context changes, and that there are no extra-mental, unchanging essences. It is worthwhile to recall the function that the notion of unchanging metaphysical essences performed for Plato and Aristotle: Their function was to bridge the gap between consciousness and reality, that is, between one's mind and one's extra-mental environment. Now this function cannot be performed by an essence which is a mental construct. The result is that Rand was left with concepts whose contexts, meanings, essences, and definitions can and do change without limit. One can only conclude, despite her self-serving illustration of the growth of the concept "man," that Rand's open-ended concept is simply a series of puns on the word "man."

Thomas Kuhn, in *The Structure of Scientific Revolutions*, remarked upon "how closely the view of science-as-cumulation is entangled with a dominant epistemology that takes knowledge to be a construction placed directly upon raw sense data by the mind."[124] This, of course, is Rand's position. Rand's imaginative reconstruction of the development of the concept "man" from infancy to adulthood is a yielding to what Kuhn calls "the temptation to write history backward. . . ."[125] Unfortunately for Rand's argument, the question is not whether an intelligent adult may improvise an account of the development of a concept which serves to illustrate that that intelligent adult's theory of cognition and concepts is correct, for it is obvious that this piece of speculative psychological history is easily composed. The question is whether children—any and all children—ever performed the sequential actions that Rand believed necessary. And that question cannot be settled by a liberal use of the imagination. In her example Rand exhibited

---

[123] "Aristotle regarded 'essence' as metaphysical; Objectivism regards it as epistemological" (*Introduction to Objectivist Epistemology*, 52).

[124] *The Structure of Scientific Revolutions*, 95.

[125] *The Structure of Scientific Revolutions*, 137.

a "tendency to make the history of science [cognition] look linear or cumulative. . . ."[126] Such a tendency is, of course, in keeping with her general epistemological theories, and is therefore to be expected, but that does not make such backward histories tenable: It makes them circular.[127]

Axiomatic Concepts

In chapter 6 of *Introduction to Objectivist Epistemology*, Rand formally crossed the line from epistemology to metaphysics with her discussion of axiomatic concepts. The axiomatic concepts bear some similarities to Aristotle's categories:

> An axiomatic concept is the identification of a primary fact of reality, which cannot be analyzed, i.e., reduced to other facts or broken into component parts. It is implicit in

---

[126] *The Structure of Scientific Revolutions*, 138.

[127] In view of Rand's notions of open-ended concept, contextually absolute definitions, and knowledge-as-cumulation, consider the following passages from Lenin:

> Human thought then by its nature is capable of giving, and does give, absolute truth, which is compounded of a sum-total of relative truths. Each step in the development of science adds new grains to the sum of absolute truth, but the limits of the truth of each scientific proposition are relative, now expanding, now shrinking with the growth of knowledge (*Materialism and Empirio-Criticism*, 133-134).
>
> That absolute truth results from the sum-total of relative truths in the course of their development; that relative truths represent relatively faithful reflections of an object existing independently of man; that these reflections become more and more faithful; that every scientific truth, notwithstanding its relative nature, contains an element of absolute truth—all these propositions, which are obvious to anyone who has thought over Engels' *Anti-Duhring*, are for the "modern" theory of knowledge a book with seven seals (319).

For those readers not familiar with the Bible, Lenin is alluding in his last phrase to the fifth chapter of the book of Revelation. It is *not* the book of Revelations.

all facts and in all knowledge. It is the fundamentally given and directly perceived or experienced, which requires no proof or explanation, but on which all proofs and explanations rest.[128]

Rand, like Aristotle and Hegel, insisted on the primacy of concepts: Explicit propositions as such are not primaries; they are made of concepts. The base of man's knowledge—of all other concepts, all axioms, propositions and thought—consists of axiomatic concepts.[129] Earlier, Rand had written: "Every concept stands for a number of propositions . . . on the higher levels of abstraction, a concept stands for chains and paragraphs and pages of explicit propositions. . . ."[130]

The primacy of concepts would certainly appear to be problematic, judging from these two statements. But not only does the concept stand for a number of propositions, it also stands for a number of individuals, and Rand had already told us that concepts are made of percepts, which in turn are made of sensations. Rand wrote: "Axioms are usually considered to be propositions identifying a fundamental, self-evident truth. But explicit propositions as such are not primaries: they are made of concepts. . . ." Rand had told us earlier that concepts are made of percepts, and percepts of sensations. Concepts are not primaries either. Now, however, it seems that not all concepts are made of percepts:

> An axiomatic concept is the identification of a primary
> fact of reality, which cannot be analyzed, i.e., reduced to

---

[128] *Introduction to Objectivist Epistemology*, 55. Aristotle's categories are not, of course, perceived, but they may be intuited. Rand's axiomatic concepts, however, are "directly perceived or experienced," which is a very peculiar statement, since one can neither perceive nor experience a concept, according to Rand. See the next footnote.

[129] "Since concepts are complex products of man's consciousness, any theory or approach which implies that they are irreducible primaries is invalidated by that fact alone" (Peikoff, *Objectivism*, 9).

[130] *Introduction to Objectivist Epistemology*, 48.

other facts or broken into component parts. It is implicit in all facts and in all knowledge. It is the fundamentally given and directly perceived or experienced, which requires no proof or explanation, but on which all proofs and explanation rest. . . . These are irreducible primaries.[131]

This, of course, contradicts her account of concept formation in several ways. First, Rand had already told us that concepts are not irreducible primaries: They are formed from percepts: ". . . all concepts are ultimately reducible to their base in perceptual entities, which are the base (the given) of man's cognitive development."[132] Second, Rand's concepts are epistemological, not metaphysical or perceptual; yet axiomatic concepts are "given" and "directly perceived," that is, they are both metaphysical and perceptible. Third, if these axiomatic concepts are irreducible primaries, they must be first in the order of knowing; that is, the concepts must already be in the infant's mind before he can perceive anything. Indeed, the phrase "axiomatic concept," for anyone who bases cognition on sense experience and rejects forms or categories of the mind, is a contradiction in terms. For an empiricist, a concept cannot be axiomatic, and a starting point cannot be a concept. For Hegel and Plato a conceptual first principle is consistent with the rest of their systems, but it is not consistent with Rand's system.

Rand found three "first and primary axiomatic concepts": existence, identity, and consciousness. She wrote, "Existence, identity and consciousness are concepts in that they require identification in conceptual form."[133] But she had just told us that existence is identified, not in conceptual form, but by swinging one's arms about. Well, let us continue. Rand drew a distinction between the first two axiomatic concepts, existence and identity, which she said are *not* attributes of existents, and consciousness, which *is* an attribute of certain existents.

---

[131] *Introduction to Objectivist Epistemology*, 55.

[132] *Introduction to Objectivist Epistemology*, 15.

[133] *Introduction to Objectivist Epistemology*, 55.

For the sake of argument, my critique of her theory of axiomatic concepts will accede to this distinction Rand drew between existence and identity, and consciousness. The first question which occurs to one to ask is (assuming the existence of certain things), how can one posit consciousness as an axiomatic concept pertaining to "certain living entities"? Is not consciousness, far from being axiomatic, an inference, a conclusion? The consciousness of other living beings besides herself is in no way a logical prerequisite of Rand's consciousness: What she regarded as an axiomatic concept is quite obviously not so. To illustrate what I mean, I shall cite *Atlas Shrugged*: "You cannot prove that you exist or that you're conscious," they [the "neomystics"] chatter, blanking out the fact that proof presupposes existence, consciousness, and a complex chain of knowledge. . . ."[134] Unfortunately, "proof" requires only the consciousness of the prover—not the consciousness of anyone else. Rand's alleged proof in no way presupposed the consciousness of Jesus Christ, or William Shakespeare, or Frank O'Connor—only Ayn Rand. Her assertion that "consciousness" understood in a general sense is an axiomatic concept is obviously untrue, unwarranted, and apparently intended to sweep under the rug the problem of other minds that no empirical philosophy is able to solve. Objectivism must necessarily end in solipsism; Rand could at best establish the existence of only her own consciousness, not the existence of other consciousnesses.

This last sentence forces upon us a recognition of the peculiar way in which Rand opposed (or distinguished between) existence and consciousness. The two, she wrote, are distinct axiomatic concepts, yet one must presume that she in no way meant to imply that "existence" and "consciousness" are separable, but that consciousness *exists*. She did wish to teach, however, that "existence" is the most fundamental, logically and chronologically, of all axiomatic concepts—more fundamental than consciousness. She repeatedly spoke of "existence" as something that precedes consciousness, or is prior to consciousness in the cognitive pro-

---

[134] *Atlas Shrugged*, 1039-1040.

cess:[135] "to perceive a thing is to perceive that it exists." She insisted that her philosophy is based upon the primacy of existence and not, as are some philosophies,[136] upon the primacy of consciousness. Compare this passage from Lenin:

> But the slightest reflection could have shown these people that it is impossible, in the very nature of the case, to give any definition of these two latter concepts [matter and spirit or consciousness] of epistemology save one that indicates which of them is taken as primary. What is meant by giving a "definition?" It means essentially to bring a given concept within a more comprehensive concept. For example, when I give the definition "an ass is an animal," I am bringing the concept "ass" within a more comprehensive concept. The question then is, are there more comprehensive concepts, with which the theory of knowledge could operate, than those of being and thinking, matter and sensation, physical and psychical? No. These are the ultimate concepts, the most comprehensive concepts, which epistemology has in point of fact so far not surpassed (apart from changes in nomenclature, which are always possible). One must be a charlatan or an utter blockhead to demand a "definition" of these two "series" of concepts of ultimate comprehensiveness which would not be a "mere repetition": one or the other must be taken as the primary.[137]

[135] "They [mystics] want to cheat the axiom of existence and consciousness, they want their consciousness to be an instrument not of perceiving but of creating existence, and existence to be not the object but the subject of their consciousness—they want to be that God they created in their image and likeness, who creates a universe out of a void by means of an arbitrary whim" (*Atlas Shrugged*, 1036-1037).

[136] "It must be noted that the Platonist school begins by accepting the primacy of consciousness, by reversing the relationship of consciousness to existence . . ." (*Introduction to Objectivist Epistemology*, 53).

[137] *Materialism and Empirio-Criticism*, 145.

Not only is Rand's position the same as Lenin's, but it indicates that Rand is equivocating on the word *existence*. For example, many would argue that Christianity is based on the primacy of the *existence* of consciousness, the primacy of the *existence* of God. Why then doesn't *that* divine Existent count as the primacy of existence in Rand's philosophy? The only answer seems to be that the Existent God doesn't count, because God, in addition to being existent, is also *conscious*. These considerations force one to conclude that by "existence" Rand, like Lenin, meant *only unconscious* existents, not all existents. Now this conclusion implies that what Rand really meant when she talked of the primacy of existence versus the primacy of consciousness was the primacy of unconscious matter or *Stoff* versus the primacy of conscious mind or ideas. At one point, she referred to man as "the product . . . of nature. . . ."[138] This, given her idea of nature, is materialism.[139] What Rand was saying is that consciousness must be conscious of unconscious matter in order to be conscious. This is, of course, an unwarranted and illogical conclusion.

Rand's "existence," like Parmenides' "what is" and Hegel's "being," is a concept—in fact, the most basic of all her concepts. Keeping that in mind, let us repeat her (circular) definition of a concept: "A concept is a mental integration of two or more units which are isolated according to a specific characteristic(s) and united by a specific definition."[140] Now, how is the concept "existence" formed? Since it allegedly subsumes all that exists, how can one isolate existents and choose a distinguishing characteristic? Concepts, Rand has repeatedly told us, are formed by differentiation and integration. How can one perform such actions and arrive at the concept "existence"? Only if Rand distinguished existence from consciousness could it be done. That would clearly imply that

---

[138] *Capitalism: The Unknown Ideal*, 322.

[139] For a further discussion of "nature" see the next chapter on Objectivist Theology.

[140] *Introduction to Objectivist Epistemology*, 15.

existence is unconsciousness. And that means that Rand is some sort of materialist.

The problem of explaining the formation of this axiomatic concept is not the only problem with "existence." The concept is, by definition, applicable to everything. Everything exists. Trees exist. Rocks exist. Unicorns exist. Minds exist. Dreams exist. Atheists exist. God exists. Hallucinations exist. A term that is predicable of everything, however, means nothing. As Hegel noted, if one thinks of Being, it very soon becomes indistinguishable from non-Being—"existence" is indistinguishable from nothing. Because "existence" is a meaningless term—meaningless precisely because it is a predicate of everything (if everything were white, "white" would have no meaning)—Hegel's, Parmenides', and Rand's first and most basic category is no basis for thought at all.[141] Neither a metaphysics nor an epistemology can be built on the foundation of a meaningless term—and Rand's effort was to ground both disciplines in "existence." Unfortunately her argument is fallacious: Just as the only consciousness presupposed by her thought was her own, and no one else's, so the only existence presupposed by her thought was her own, and nothing else's.[142]

This is not to say that her oft-repeated statement that a consciousness with nothing to be conscious of is a contradiction in terms, for the statement is undeniably correct. What Rand overlooked is

---

[141] "Being and Reality are so universal as to be meaningless. A word that is applicable to everything is applicable to nothing. If trees exist and are real, so do dreams exist and are real. Hallucinations are real hallucinations" (Gordon H. Clark, *The Philosophy of Gordon H. Clark*, 410).

[142] Equivocation on the meaning of "existence" occurs most blatantly in *Atlas Shrugged*. Rand wanted us to understand that "existence" is "objective reality." But watch carefully the philosophical sleight of hand in this argument to demonstrate the "axiom of existence": "When he declares that an axiom is a matter of arbitrary choice and he doesn't choose to accept the axiom that he exists [not that "existence exists," please note], he blanks out the fact that he has accepted it by uttering that sentence, that the only way to reject it is to shut one's mouth, expound no theories and die" (*Atlas Shrugged*, 1040). Rand sounded like Descartes in this passage, but she cannot escape her solipsism.

that consciousnesses are conscious of their contents.[143] Rand never offered any definition of "sensation" or evidence that "sensation" actually occurs. Her equivocation on the word "existence" rests in two assertions: (1) that the contents or objects of consciousness must exist if one is to speak intelligibly about consciousness; and (2) that certain kinds of existents must exist if consciousness is to be conscious, namely, impenetrable, sensible in some sense, hard, inanimate atoms or their twentieth century equivalent. It seems that *mental* existents do not *exist* for Rand. Because Rand did not and could not define "existence" (as pointed out earlier, an "ostensive

[143] "It seems evident, that men are carried, by a natural instinct or prepossession, to repose faith in their senses; and that, without any reasoning, or even almost before the use of reason, we always suppose an external universe, which depends not on our perception, but would exist though we and every sensible creature were absent or annihilated. Even the animal creations are governed by a like opinion, and preserve this belief of external objects, in all their thoughts, designs, and actions. . . .

"But this universal and primary opinion of all men is soon destroyed by the slightest philosophy, which teaches us, that nothing can ever be present to the mind but an image or perception, and that the senses are the only inlets, through which these images are conveyed, without being able to produce any immediate intercourse between the mind and the object.

"The table, which we see, seems to diminish, as we remove farther from it: But the real table, which exists independent of us, suffers no alteration: It was therefore, nothing but its image, which was present to the mind. These are the obvious dictates of reason; and no man, who reflects, ever doubted, that the existences, which we consider, when we say 'this house,' and 'that tree' are nothing but perceptions in the mind. . . .

"By what argument can it be proved, that the perceptions of the mind must be caused by external objects, entirely different from them, though resembling them (if that be possible), and could not arise either from the energy of the mind itself, or from the suggestion of some invisible and unknown spirit, or from some other cause still more unknown to us?

"How shall the question be determined? By experience surely; as all other questions of a like nature. But here experience is, and must be entirely silent. The mind has never anything present to it but the perceptions, and cannot possibly reach any experience of their connection with objects. This supposition of such a connection is, therefore, without any foundation in reasoning" (David Hume, *An Enquiry Concerning Human Understanding*, Chapter XII. London, 1882, II, 124-126).

definition" is a contradiction in terms). Rand was quite able and willing to use whatever meaning of "existence" was required by the context of her argument at the moment. If pressed on the questions, which are the proper epistemological and metaphysical questions, What exists? and How do you know? her equivocations, contradictions, and unwarranted leaps in thought become obvious.

As it is, however, Rand never tired of chanting "existence exists," as if the statement were profound philosophy.[144] Constant repetition of a phrase intended to be understood as a profound philosophical discovery is no substitute for a serious philosophical effort to declare what exists, how we may know that it exists, and what it is. Unfortunately, Rand moved very little beyond chanting her materialist mantra. Any critique, therefore, will have difficulties in criticizing her idea of "objective reality," for the nature of this reality was not clearly discussed by Rand, although she hinted at it. One can say only that the impressions one receives from reading Rand is that "objective reality" or "existence" is "matter" in the ancient Democritean or nineteenth century sense of the term: hard, impenetrable atoms against which a mystic or an altruist is bound to beat his brains out. Yet it is precisely this notion of reality that twentieth-century scientists have found it necessary to abandon, in favor of a quite different view. Materialism, if I understand the developments in modern physics correctly, has been thoroughly repudiated by science, which Rand apparently viewed as the island of rationality in a sea of subjectivism.[145] (Rand had a great animus

---

[144] "If a predicate can be attached to everything without exception, it has no distinct meaning, and this is to say that it has no meaning at all. . . . The predicate *existence* can be attached to everything real or imaginary without exception. Dreams exist, mirages exist, the square root of minus one exists. These statements, however, are meaningless; they tell us nothing about dreams and the square root of minus one. . . . Similarly, the question that needs to be asked about God is not whether he exists, but what he is. Of course God exists. Anything exists, so far as the term has any faint meaning at all" (Gordon H. Clark, *Three Types of Religious Philosophy*, 43-44).

[145] "While scientists were performing astounding feats of disciplined reason, breaking down the barriers of the 'unknowable' in every field of knowledge, charting the course of light rays in space or the course of blood in the capillaries of man's body . . ." (*For the New Intellectual*, 33).

against science since Heisenberg and Einstein, however, precisely because it was not materialist in the nineteenth century sense of the term.) Yet if Rand did not have a nineteenth century conception of matter in mind when she spoke of "objective reality," it is completely unclear what she did have in mind. If she had nothing particular in mind, then she had nothing in mind, and "existence" is shown to be simply a meaningless word whose sole function is to exclude theism without a hearing.

Rand's axiomatic concepts (existence, identity, and consciousness) "identify the precondition of knowledge." They identify the "distinction between existence and consciousness."[146] It is obvious that Rand here implied a view that can accurately be called the primacy of *un*consciousness. She repeatedly emphasized that her philosophy is based on the "primacy of existence" and not on the "primacy of consciousness" as some other philosophies are. This insistence can only be understood if the "primacy of existence" is taken to mean the primacy of *un*consciousness. Matter—whatever matter may be—precedes consciousness, according to Rand, both temporally and logically.[147] Unfortunately the evidence and argument for this are absent. The only consciousness and the only existence necessary for her thinking are her own.[148] The phrase the "primacy of existence" is an ambiguous phrase which obscures the fact that those philosophies (and I am thinking particularly of Christianity) which are based upon what Rand called the "primacy of consciousness" are based, of course, on the primacy of the *existence* of consciousness. She wields the words *existence* and *consciousness* as though they were necessarily mutually exclusive, which they are not.

[146] *Introduction to Objectivist Epistemology*, 57.

[147] I have deferred argument for this statement until the next chapter, where it properly belongs.

[148] "But since no one has seen an external body, no one can compare it with the red he has seen or the hard he has touched. Empiricism therefore furnishes no knowledge of an external world, finds no evidence for its existence, and confines the mind to the mind, i.e., its sensations" (Gordon H. Clark, *Three Types of Religious Philosophy*, 77).

I have already shown that what Rand called axiomatic concepts are not concepts as she defined the term *concept*, nor can she define them. Rand also admitted, "Since axiomatic concepts are not formed by differentiating one group of existents from others, . . . they have no Conceptual Common Denominator with anything else."[149] Now the Conceptual Common Denominator is the essence of the concept; without it there can be no concept in Rand's terms. One begins to wonder why Rand called these words axiomatic concepts at all. They are neither axiomatic nor are they concepts. They have no conceptual common denominators, no essences. She wrote, " 'Existence,' 'identity' and 'consciousness' have no contraries— only a void." But Rand continually used "existence" and "consciousness" as contraries: the primacy of existence *versus* the primacy of consciousness. Consciousness quite obviously has a contrary: unconsciousness, which is apparently the chief characteristic of "existence." Furthermore, existence "is identity," as Rand wrote, and, therefore, all three have contraries; in fact, they are contraries of each other. Consequently her elaborate discussion of the fiction that axiomatic concepts have no contraries is entirely pointless.

One major criticism of axiomatic concepts is applicable to any philosophy which views the most primitive units of knowledge as concepts rather than propositions, whether it be Plato's philosophy, Hegel's, or Rand's. We have already seen the confusion in Rand on the matter, who simultaneously held that concepts are prior or ultimate, and that concepts are simply shorthand notations for systems of propositions. She could not explain whether concepts or propositions were fundamental. Furthermore, it is quite possible to say that concepts are true; it is utterly impossible to derive any intelligible meaning from such a statement. Is "mind" true? Is "existence" true? Truth is not an attribute of concepts, or of feelings, or of percepts. It is an attribute of one thing, and one thing only: propositions. Non-propositional truth—whether it be Aristotelian-Hegelian-Randian categories or axiomatic concepts, or existential encounters, or feelings of dependence—is a meaningless phrase.

[149] *Introduction to Objectivist Epistemology*, 58.

Only propositions can be true or false.[150] It follows that Rand's axiomatic concepts are completely garbled.

Rand wrote: "The units of the concepts 'existence' and 'identity' are every entity, attribute, action, event or phenomenon (including consciousness) that exists, has ever existed or will ever exist."[151] But she had earlier defined a unit as "an existent regarded as a separate member of a group of two or more similar members;"[152] and had said that "existence and identity are not attributes of existents, they are the existents."[153] Exactly how the concepts "similar," (which is indispensable for the formation of a group of units), and its contrary "dissimilar" are applicable to the formation of the group of units designed as "existents"? Existence (Rand told us) is not an attribute, and therefore cannot be a point of similarity among things, nor can it be a point of dissimilarity. Things are not similar because they exist, for the quite simple reason that they cannot be dissimilar to anything because they exist. Rand's account of the formation of the axiomatic concepts existence and identity contradicted her account of concept-formation. This fact makes the basis of her epistemology and metaphysics, the axiomatic concepts, completely incoherent. To illustrate this incoherence again: Rand was quite fond of saying, "existence exists," and yet she also wrote, "It is Aristotle who idéntified the fact that only concretes exist."[154] Which is it? Does "existence" exist or do only concretes exist? Or is existence a concrete? To say "existence" is existents is tantamount to saying that a concept is its referents, thus erasing the

---

[150] "Hegel is not to be rejected because of Herr Krug's pen: even Aristotle admitted that individuals cannot be known. Hegel's fault, or one of them, was to make the concept rather than the proposition the object of knowledge. But a concept is as unknowable as an individual. 'Pen' is neither true or false. Only a proposition can be true. . . . Truth always comes in propositions" (Gordon H. Clark, *The Philosophy of Gordon H. Clark*, 411).

[151] *Introduction to Objectivist Epistemology*, 53.

[152] *Introduction to Objectivist Epistemology*, 6.

[153] *Introduction to Objectivist Epistemology*, 56.

[154] *Introduction to Objectivist Epistemology*, 52.

distinction between the two, overthrowing the representational (algebraic) nature of concepts, abstraction, or any mental process whatever. Rand is egregiously self-contradictory—all in the name of "reason."

Rand wrote: "The units of the concept 'consciousness' are every state or process of awareness that one experiences, has ever experienced or will ever experience (as well as similar units, a similar faculty, which one infers in other living entities)."[155] This quotation bristles with questions that require answers. One question is whether these alleged states or processes of awareness are discrete as Rand obviously thought they are (they are the "units," and the units are the particulars, existents, or concretes subsumed under a concept), or whether consciousness is something entirely different.

Second, the universal "chair," we were told, does not exist outside one's own mind: Rand totally disagreed with Plato and Aristotle on the "external" existence of essences. But Rand believed other consciousnesses do exist extra-mentally, that is, in other bodies, and this is an inference, Rand wrote. Well, is it an inference, or is it axiomatic? If it is an inference, an inference from what? "Consciousness" has been proclaimed as an axiomatic concept—and now we are told that it is by inference in "other living entities." On what grounds is this inference made? What are the steps in the argument? Rand did not tell us any of this. That would mean the axiomatic concept "consciousness" is grounded only in Rand's own states or processes of awareness that she has experienced, is now experiencing, or will ever experience. This, as we noted before, is solipsism.

When one has grasped the incoherence of Rand's notion of axiomatic concepts, and the logical incoherence of her epistemology, it becomes obvious that her assertion that the "statements [of modern philosophers who declare that axioms are a matter of arbitrary choice] imply and depend on 'existence,' 'consciousness,' 'identity,' "[156] is entirely without foundation. Rand attributed to "the

[155] *Introduction to Objectivist Epistemology*, 56.

[156] *Introduction to Objectivist Epistemology*, 58.

enemies of reason" a perspicacity not possessed by reason's alleged defenders, that of seeing that "axiomatic concepts are the guardians of man's mind and the foundations of reason—the keystone, touchstone and hallmark of reason—and if reason is to be destroyed, it is axiomatic concepts that have to be destroyed."[157] Rand was quite right in this: With the collapse of axiomatic concepts, her version of "reason" collapsed.

Open-ended Concepts

Near the end of her monograph, Rand returned to a notion she had discussed before: concepts as open-ended ideas. She again used the example of the development of the child's concept of man, which, she asserted, does not change during the entire process: "What has changed and grown is the knowledge [of man]. The definition of concepts may change with the changes in the designation of essential characteristics, and conceptual reclassifications may occur with the growth of knowledge. . . ."[158] Rand admitted (1) the definition may change; (2) the essential characteristic may change; and (3) the arrangement of concepts may change. But she insisted that the concept "itself" does not change. Is it not obvious that Rand confused the word *man* with the concept man; and the concept man with men?

Second, Rand said that there is no difference between the concept and its referents, that the concept is its referents.[159] How can a concept be its referents, when we have already been informed that the concept is an abstraction and a mental creation that is in no way (as Aristotle and Plato thought) extra-mental? Rand argued that with the growth of knowledge the referents have not changed (but they have), and the concept therefore has not changed. She also seemed to believe that if one realizes aforetime that concepts may change, that is, are open-ended, then concepts really do not change. This is

[157] *Introduction to Objectivist Epistemology*, 60.

[158] *Introduction to Objectivist Epistemology*, 66.

[159] *Introduction to Objectivist Epistemology*, 56.

tantamount to saying that concepts subsume unknown existents and qualities yet to be discovered (how could Rand know this?).[160] If they are truly yet to be discovered, then no evidence exists for them now and the statement is untrue, because it does not have any supporting evidence. Rand's theory seems to be that anticipation of change eliminates change. Such a theory, applied to weather forecasting, would require us to believe that since we anticipate changes in the weather, therefore there is really no change in the weather. That is the meaning of her notion of open-ended concepts.

Near the end of chapter seven Rand introduced her razor: "Concepts are not to be multiplied beyond necessity, . . . nor are they to be integrated in disregard of necessity."[161] One suspects that "necessity," like "reason," is a word of convenience, and that suspicion is confirmed when Rand gave an example of its application: "In case of black swans, it is objectively mandatory to classify them as 'swans,' because virtually all their characteristics are similar to the characteristics of the white swans, and the difference in color is of no cognitive significance."[162] This is offered as an assertion; no reason, no criterion of "cognitive significance" is offered. The second example, a rational spider from Mars, evoked this reply from Rand: "The differences between him and man would be so great that the study of one would scarcely apply to the other and, therefore, the formation of a new concept to designate the Martians would be objectively mandatory."[163] Apparently here there is more cognitive significance, but we are not told how to determine it. Not only would a new concept for the Martians be required, but one could no longer define man as "the rational animal."

---

[160] "The fact that certain characteristics are, at a given time, unknown to man, does not indicate that these characteristics are excluded from the entity—or from the concept. . . . Thus, a concept subsumes and includes all the characteristics of its referents, known and not-yet-known" (Peikoff, "The Analytic-Synthetic Dichotomy," 10).

[161] *Introduction to Objectivist Epistemology*, 65.

[162] *Introduction to Objectivist Epistemology*, 73.

[163] *Introduction to Objectivist Epistemology*, 72.

Volitional Consciousness

One major problem in Rand's epistemology, the notion of "volitional consciousness," requires further comment in this chapter. The reader will find longer discussions of this idea in the next two chapters, but since the Objectivists believe that the theory is established on epistemological grounds, it is necessary to discuss it briefly here. Nathaniel Branden has written:

> I shall confine myself to the analysis of a central and insuperable contradiction in the determinist position—an epistemological contradiction—a contradiction implicit in any variety of determinism, whether the alleged determining forces be physical, psychological, environmental or divine.[164]

The contradiction as Branden (and Rand) saw it is that determinism leaves man no possibility of knowing anything to be true; determinism leads not to truth, but to necessary belief, which, they maintained, are two quite different things:

> That which a man does, declare the advocates of determinism, he had to do—that which he believes, he had to believe—if he focuses his mind, he had to—if he evades the effort of focusing, he had to—if he is guided solely by reason, he had to be—if he is ruled instead by feeling or whim, he had to be—he couldn't help it.
> But if this were true, no knowledge would be possible to man. No theory could claim greater plausibility than any other—including the theory of psychological determinism.

The result of this, according to Branden, is that the determinist, to claim his theory is true, must exclude himself from being determined:

---

[164] *The Objectivist Newsletter*, May 1963, 17.

> Those who expound determinism must either assert that
> they arrived at their theory by mystical revelation, and thus
> exclude themselves from the realm of reason—or they must
> assert that they are an exception to the theory they pro-
> pound, and thus exclude their theory from the realm of
> truth.[165]

Now secular determinists may commit the "fallacy of self-exclusion," as Branden calls it, for they cannot claim that they received their knowledge by divine revelation, since they are committed to an atheistic metaphysics. But Christians, who are not so
committed, can and do claim that revelation is the only basis for
human knowledge. This revelation is not mystical or emotional,
but rational, intelligible, and propositional. Revelation, of course,
excludes Christians from the Objectivist "realm of reason," that is,
reason defined as sense experience, but it does not exclude Christians from the "realm of truth" as the fallacy of self-exclusion does
for secularists.[166] Consistent Christians—Calvinists—easily escape
the dilemma posed by Branden, if one accepts Branden's dilemma
as plausible. His dilemma demonstrates that all secular philosophies (including Objectivism) are internally contradictory, and that
only those who escape from the "realm of [empirical] reason" can
enter the "realm of [propositional] truth."

One of the difficulties of Objectivism is the origin of reason
and "volitional consciousness" from an otherwise absolutely irra-
tionally (non-purposeful, non-thoughtful, unconscious) *determined*

---

[165] *The Objectivist Newsletter*, May 1963, 20.

[166] "Christianity is under no obligation to justify itself as rational in any other
sense [than logical self-consistency], for the history of philosophy has shown
that all the other senses result in skepticism. Therefore to claim that election, or
the atonement, or any other doctrine is 'irrational' is nothing more than to assert
that these doctrines are distasteful to the objector. The accusation is not a substantial intellectual conclusion, but an emotional antipathy. If the Biblical doctrines are self-consistent, they have met the only legitimate test of reason" (Gordon H. Clark, "Special Divine Revelation as Rational," in *God's Hammer: The
Bible and Its Critics*, 79).

universe. That universe, the Objectivists clearly teach, as we shall see in the next chapter, is completely determined. The Objectivists believe, with Friedrich Nietzsche, that reason arose by accident, a pre-determined accident.[167] And yet this belief, according to Branden, undermines all their thought and all their philosophy. In Objectivism, it undercuts the theory of "volitional consciousness," which is the Objectivist version of free will. Branden writes, "Man's freedom to focus or not to focus, to think or not to think, is a unique kind of choice that must be distinguished from any other category of choice."[168] Leonard Peikoff writes: "As far as metaphysical reality is concerned (omitting human actions from consideration, for the moment), there are no 'facts which happen to be but could have been otherwise' as against 'facts which must be.' There are only: facts which are."[169] By these statements, the Objectivists exclude man's "free will" from the causal system in the rest of reality and even from causality in the rest of his own actions. An antinomy splits man down the middle. The mind-body dichotomy returns in Objectivism with a vengeance.[170]

It is necessary, however, to examine more closely Branden's idea of the "insuperable epistemological contradiction" in determinism. One might first say that Branden's contradiction is really a confusion between psychology and logic, between the origination and the verification of ideas; that it is an instance of the genetic fallacy. Branden cannot refute a Christian by saying that because his beliefs are determined by God his beliefs must be untrue. If God predestines a man to go to the city, then the man will not go to the country. If God determines a man to believe the truth, then that man does not believe falsehood.

---

[167] "Reason. How did it come into the world? As is fitting, in an irrational manner, by accident. One will have to guess at it as at a riddle" (Friedrich Nietzsche, *The Dawn*, 123).

[168] *The Objectivist*, February 1966, 6.

[169] "The Analytic-Synthetic Dichotomy," 16.

[170] For further discussion, see the next chapter.

Furthermore, one might point out that not all choices, events, and actions are free, according to the Objectivists. In fact, only one choice, one "event," one "act" is free, that is, undetermined: the choice to think. All other choices are determined by one cause or another. One must conclude from this that all other thoughts are likewise determined; that thought A necessitates thought B. Already the reader will begin to see the difficulties present in Branden's argument. The assertion that all thoughts except one are determined makes Objectivism subject to Branden's own "insuperable contradiction."

There are further considerations. The epistemological argument which Branden makes appears to be merely a variant on the moral argument for free will (or volitional consciousness), namely, that determinism makes knowledge (or virtue or vice) impossible. Neither of these arguments is valid, but here I will confine myself to the epistemological version. Restating that argument, it may be presented as the notion that if a person is compelled (or determined) to think a certain thought, to believe a certain proposition, then he cannot know whether this proposition is true or false. If all a person's thoughts are likewise determined, then he is likewise precluded from knowing anything at all. Determinism and knowledge are mutually exclusive.

Unfortunately this argument disintegrates upon further examination. Consider: If one thinks at all, one must think the law of contradiction. One is *compelled* to think that law. Moreover, if one thinks consistently, all one's thoughts are equally determined, simply because logic, like truth, is thoroughly authoritarian and necessitarian. Now it would be absurd to argue that because everyone is compelled to think the law of contradiction it is, therefore, untrue, or that we cannot know that it is true. So it would be absurd to argue that the most logical minds are devoid of truth because their thoughts (or most of them) follow of necessity from one or a few axioms. To say, therefore, that necessity *per se* excludes truth or knowledge is patently false: The necessity of thinking the law of contradiction is the framework within which any putative system of knowledge must function. If necessity did not exist, if indeter-

minism were the state of affairs, then no knowledge would be possible, for with the termination of necessity comes the end of logic
and truth.

There is a great modern myth that liberty—political, economic,
and intellectual—is incompatible with law. On the contrary, liberty is possible only within the framework of law. We are free to
think only because we *must* think the laws of logic. The "free will"
theory is an instance of this superstition that liberty and law are
antagonistic.

Branden's epistemological argument for free will, like the moral
argument for free will, rests upon a peculiar understanding of knowledge and morality. These ideas, in turn, rest upon a view of man as
possessing a "free will," on man as an autonomous being. In short,
Branden so defines morality and knowledge that free will is an
integral part of their definitions. This procedure makes his arguments
circular, for he assumes that knowledge and morality presuppose
free will. That is why he presents the argument as conclusive.

Unfortunately, the Objectivists have never succeeded in giving
a coherent account of free will (volitional consciousness), a fact
which vitiates the entire argument. In fact, Rand herself made statements that seem to conflict with her idea that conceptual consciousness, human consciousness, must be the result of a deliberate volition. For example, in the essay "Altruism as Appeasement,"[171] Rand
wrote: "Such decisions are seldom, if ever, made consciously. They
are made gradually, by subconscious emotional motivation and
semi-conscious rationalization." Unconscious decision-making
seems to conflict with volitional consciousness. In " 'Extremism,'
or the Art of Smearing"[172] Rand wrote about concept formation:
"And if a man accepts a term with a definition by non-essentials,
his mind will substitute for it the *essential* characteristic of the
objects he is trying to designate. . . . Thus the real meaning of the
term will automatically replace the alleged meaning." But if the
mind does this automatically, can it be said to be volitional, as Rand

[171] *The Objectivist*, January 1966, 2.

[172] *Capitalism: The Unknown Ideal*, 176.

has used the term? Leonard Peikoff, as well as Rand, wrote: "Man's consciousness is not automatic, and not automatically correct."[173] In "The Comprachicos,"[174] Rand wrote: "The subconscious is an integrating mechanism [note well]: when left without conscious control, it goes on integrating on its own—and, like an automatic [note well] blender, his subconscious squeezes its clutter of trash to produce a single basic emotion: fear." These quotations underscore the conflicting statements from Rand about consciousness and concept formation.

In his argument for free will, Branden at best presented the case for saying that man has a will, or at least acts volitionally, and Christianity does not dispute that. His argument is typical of arguments of many if not all indeterminists, who confuse free will and will, the first of which functions in a causal vacuum, and the second within a causal nexus. One difference between a being with a determined will and a robot or a machine, to which the proponents of free will compare determinists, is the fact that a determined person is conscious. The metaphors that equate a determined person to a robot (or puppet) are extremely misleading (unless of course the type of determinism one has in mind is mechanistic like Skinner's, for instance). Mechanical devices have no wills; conscious beings do. "Will" is the term that one gives to consciousness as cause. In this sense, volition and intellection are not separable: "The common opinion that an act of volition is different from an act of intellection is an illusion which results from the restriction of attention to physical acts such as sitting down."[175]

The plausibility of Branden's argument (and the arguments of other indeterminists) stems from the fact that persons are not unconscious and know they are not. But determinism of a non-mechanistic variety, Christian determinism, unlike Skinner's, in no way

---

[173] *The Philosophy of Objectivism*, Lecture 6, as quoted in *The Ayn Rand Lexicon*, 31.

[174] *The New Left*, 218.

[175] Gordon H. Clark, *Religion, Reason and Revelation*, 98-99.

implies that persons are things. Because truth is a system of revealed propositions that can be recognized by its content and its
self-consistency, and because the law of contradiction is an indispensable part of that system, all men are determined to think some
truth(s). It is the theory of free will, not the determinism of the
Bible, that would eliminate knowledge and truth, for such a theory
claims that all knowledge, including the law of contradiction, is
not revealed by God but is discovered by men, who are able to
think falsehood freely.

Causality

The Objectivist theory of causality deserves some comment in this
chapter. The Objectivists hold that "the premise that every action
is only a reaction to an antecedent action, rules out, arbitrarily and
a priori, the existence of self-generated, goal-directed action."[176]
Consequently, they hold that this premise applies to all reality except man. This is the central problem in their theory of free-will.
They also reject the notion that causality is a relationship between
motions, in favor of the view that it is a relationship between things:

> The view of causality as a relationship between mo-
> tions is entirely spurious. It is worth noting that, if one ac-
> cepts this view, there is no way to prove or validate the law
> of causality. If all that is involved is motion succeeding
> motion, there is no way to establish necessary relationships
> between succeeding events: one observes that B follows A,
> but one has no way to establish that B is the effect or con-
> sequence of A. (This, incidentally, is one of the reasons
> why most philosophers, who accept this notion of causal-
> ity, have been unable to answer Hume's argument that one
> cannot prove the law of causality. One can't—unless one
> grasps its relationship to the law of identity. But this en-
> tails rejecting the motion-to-motion view of causality.)

[176] Nathaniel Branden, *The Objectivist*, March 1966, 12.

Furthermore, the motion-to-motion view obscures the explanatory nature of the law of causality. If one wishes to understand why entities act as they do, in a given context, one must seek the answer through an understanding of the properties of the entities involved. And, in fact, any explanation via references to antecedent actions always implies and presupposes this understanding. For example, if one states that the action of a wastebasket catching fire was caused by the action of a lighted match being thrown into it, this constitutes a satisfactory causal explanation only if one understands the nature of paper and of lighted matches; a description of the action sequence, in the absence of such knowledge, would explain nothing.[177]

These paragraphs are a confused defense of causality, for they presuppose that which an empiricist cannot presuppose: that he somehow "knows" the nature (or identity) of a thing apart from observation of it. Observation, of course, does not mean staring at an immutable or unmoving object, but the deliberate manipulation of an object and watching the changes it undergoes or "causes." This is precisely Hume's point, and one which the Objectivist—or any other empiricists—have never been able to refute.

The observation of change (of motion-to-motion causality to use Branden's term) is the only observation that can be made. In the example Branden uses, no empiricist can state truthfully that the lighted match caused the wastebasket to burn. Causation is not *observed* at all. What is observed is a change in the condition of the wastebasket following the placement of a lighted match in it. On empiricist grounds, to say that the latter caused the former is the logical fallacy *post hoc ergo propter hoc*. The Objectivists illegitimately separate knowledge of events (motions) and knowledge of things (identities) and seek to establish causality on the basis of the latter, while conveniently ignoring that knowledge of things (identities), on empirical grounds, must be knowledge of motions.

[177] *The Objectivist*, March 1966, 11-12.

To say that it is the "nature" of a lighted match to ignite a wastebasket is to say no more than, "I (or others) have seen wastebaskets ignite after lighted matches have been dropped into them."

The problems with the Objectivist theory of causality stem from its theory of knowledge, that is, that the mind is *tabula rasa* at birth and that all its knowledge comes by the senses. By accepting this premise, they must also maintain that the laws of thought are derived from experience, unless they wish to deny that the laws are knowledge. But the establishment of the law of identity, for instance, as an ontological law on the grounds of experience, cannot be done. It would involve knowing the objects of experience in some non-sensory manner and comparing this knowledge with one's sensory data.

> Aristotle's claim that the law of contradiction is an ontological law as well as a law of thought involves a *hysteron proteron*. To suppose that logic is adequate to reality requires a knowledge of reality prior to and independent of the law. But the law itself denies that there is any knowledge independent of it. Therefore, concludes Nietzsche, we can never know that the world of things corresponds to our laws of thought.[178]

> Just as the three laws—contradiction, excluded middle, and identity—cannot be established as ontological laws by an appeal to experience, so neither can the knowledge of "identities" be established by experience of events. To claim some sort of superior knowledge of "identities," as the Objectivists do, is to claim a means of knowledge other than the senses. Their view of causality is radically at odds with their epistemology.

The Self

A concluding note on Objectivist epistemology must include a brief

---

[178] Clark, *An Introduction to Christian Philosophy*, 35-36.

discussion of the self, the percipient. In *For the New Intellectual*, Rand wrote:

> When Hume declared that he saw objects moving about, but never saw such a thing as "causality"—it was the voice of Attila that men were hearing. It was Attila's soul that spoke when Hume declared that he experienced a flow of fleeting states inside his skull, such as sensations, feelings or memories, but had never caught the experience of such a thing as consciousness or self.[179]

Are we to conclude, then, that Attila published an essay in *The Objectivist* when we read there:

> Consider the fact that normally man experiences himself as a process—in that consciousness itself is a process, an activity, and the contents of man's mind are a shifting flow of perceptions, thoughts and emotions. His own mind is not an unmoving entity which man can contemplate objectively—i.e., contemplate as a direct object of awareness —as he contemplates objects in the external world.
>
> He has, of course, a sense of himself, of his own identity, but it is experienced more as a feeling than a thought— a feeling which is very diffuse, which is interwoven with all his other feelings, and which is very hard, if not impossible, to isolate and consider by itself. His "self-concept" is not a single concept, but a cluster of images and abstract perspectives on his various (real or imagined) traits and characteristics, the sum total of which can never be held in focal awareness at any one time; that sum is experienced, but is not perceived as such.[180]

It would appear that the philosophy which began with "objective

[179] *For the New Intellectual*, 29.

[180] Nathaniel Branden, *The Objectivist*, December 1967, 3-4.

reality," which insisted on one's own existence as axiomatic, is not even sure what one's self is, or what objective reality is, since one can have no perception of it, but only an "experience."

A Confession of Epistemic Failure

A confirmation of the utter failure of Objectivist epistemology to establish a solid foundation for knowledge came from the Objectivists themselves, though in a political, not an epistemological, context. Specifically, the context is a discussion of the Objectivist position on capital punishment. The writer is Nathaniel Branden:

> If it were possible to be fully and irrevocably certain, beyond any possibility of error, that a man were guilty, then capital punishment for murder would be appropriate and just. But men are not infallible; juries make mistakes; that is the problem. There have been instances recorded where all the available evidence pointed overwhelmingly to a man's guilt, and the man was convicted, and then subsequently discovered to be innocent.[181]

Man, then, can know nothing for certain. Even if all the available evidence points to a particular conclusion, that conclusion may be incorrect. This admission is fatal to Objectivist epistemology. Yet even if Branden had not been kind enough to provide us with it, our analysis would have reached the same conclusion.

Rand's attempt to give a coherent account of concept formation is a determined one, but her failure was foreordained by her acceptance of empiricism, the belief that all knowledge arises from sense experience. Given that premise, any epistemological effort must fail, some more quickly than others. Her inability to provide a coherent epistemological theory automatically destroys the rest of her philosophy: Her metaphysics, her ethics, and her politics have nowhere to stand. This critique of Rand's system could very

---

[181] *The Objectivist Newsletter*, January 1963, 3.

well end here, but for the fact that Rand's adherents will continue to cling to her ethics and politics despite the lack of a coherent epistemological foundation for them. It is necessary to continue destructive criticism of the other branches of her philosophy in order to demonstrate that Objectivist ethical and political theory are as inherently self-contradictory as Objectivist epistemology. Even this demonstration, however, will probably not be sufficient to dislodge the ardent proponents of Objectivism from their failed philosophy; but that fact merely corroborates what this writer wrote earlier: Philosophies are chosen. Except a man's mind be changed by God, it will not be changed. And if a demonstration of the logical incoherence of Objectivism is not sufficient to make Objectivists abandon their system, then they are the very mystics they condemn.

4

IMAGINING GODS
OBJECTIVIST THEOLOGY

Gradually I have come to realize what every great philosophy up to now has been: the personal confession of its
originator, a type of involuntary and unaware memoirs; also,
that the moral (or amoral) intentions of each philosophy
constitute the protoplasm from which each entire plant has
grown. Indeed, one will do well (and wisely), if one wishes
to explain to himself how on earth the more remote metaphysical assertions of a philosopher ever arose, to ask each
time: What sort of morality is this (is he) aiming at?

Friedrich Nietzsche
Beyond Good and Evil

A Childish Atheism

Ayn Rand was an atheist.[1] Formally, to be an atheist is to disbe-
lieve in the existence of a god, and, since our civilization has

---

[1] "A man of reason does not accept ideas on faith. He knows that all of one's
conclusions must be based on and derived from the facts of reality. He is, therefore, an atheist" (Nathaniel Branden, *The Objectivist Newsletter*, April 1963, 15).

"As uncompromising advocates of reason, Objectivists are, of course, atheists. We are intransigent atheists, not militant ones. We are for reason; therefore,

its roots in Christianity, atheism has come to mean disbelief in the existence of the God of the Bible. Rand, however, would have us believe that she disbelieves in all gods—Christian or otherwise—including the anchoritic god of Aristotle. As we have seen in previous chapters, however, philosophy is always the handmaid of theology—faith, if you wish—simply because unproved and indemonstrable axioms must be accepted for any philosophical system to begin. Every philosophy must begin somewhere, if it is to begin at all, and the beginning is just that, a beginning. Nothing precedes the starting point; no proofs, no demonstration; nothing.[2] Reason was not released from its servitude to faith with the advent of the Renaissance and the Reformation; it merely chose new masters to serve when it repudiated Catholicism. Martin Luther and John Calvin chose the Christian axiom of revelation, expressed in the fundamental principle of the Reformation, The Bible alone is the Word of God (*sola Scriptura*); others chose the axiom of sensation (Bacon, Locke, Hume) or the axiom of logic (Spinoza, Descartes, Hegel).

As I have already indicated, Ayn Rand was an atheist in the sense that she did not believe in the God of the Bible: She decided she was an atheist at the age of thirteen, shortly following the athe-

---

as a consequence, we are opposed to any form of mysticism; therefore, we do not grant any validity to the notion of a supernatural being. But atheism is scarcely the center of our philosophical position. To be known as crusaders for atheism would be acutely embarrassing to us; the adversary is too unworthy" (Nathaniel Branden, *The Objectivist Newsletter*, December 1965, 58).

Branden's statement that "atheism is scarcely the center of our philosophical position" conflicts with Rand's assertion of the "primacy of existence." Atheism is indeed the center of Objectivist philosophy because atheism is its metaphysical position. While Rand deliberately remained vague on the nature of reality, she was unmistakably clear that God was not the real. As for crusading for atheism, Rand supported the efforts of Madalyn Murray O'Hair to remove all references to God from public life.

[2] "It is always necessary to begin with some apriori proposition that cannot be deduced from anything more fundamental" (Gordon H. Clark, *The Philosophy of Gordon H. Clark*, 471).

istic Revolution of 1917 in her homeland.[3] Her biographers tell us that at the age of thirteen,

> attempting to formulate her convictions on a number of fundamental issues, she considered the question scrupulously— and concluded that there was no God. She wrote the causes of her conclusion in her diary: first, there are no reasons to believe in God, there is no proof of the belief; and second, that the concept of God is insulting and degrading to man— it implies that the highest possible is not to be reached by man, that he is an inferior being who can only worship an ideal he will never achieve. By her view, there could be no breach between conceiving of the best possible and deciding to attain it. She rejected the concept of God as morally evil.

I have quoted Barbara Branden at length simply because she wrote at length on this point, as the thirteen-year-old Rand herself no doubt thought at length. Close attention to the quoted passage should make clear that although Rand placed the lack of reasons and proof for the existence of God first in her brief list of reasons for not believing in God, this deplorable lack of proof is really subordinate to the second (and primary) reason why Rand decided she was an atheist. The difference in emphasis placed upon the two reasons for Rand's atheism is by itself sufficient indication as to which reason was primary in Rand's mind. Lack of reasons and proof for the existence of God is treated cursorily, almost as if it were obligatory to say something about reason and proof, and not a very pleasant duty at that. On the other hand, the rejection of God on moral grounds[4] occupies most of the attention of the writer—

---

[3] "The second incident occurred when Ayn was not yet fourteen. It consisted of an entry in her diary: 'Today, I decided that I am an atheist'" (Nathaniel and Barbara Branden, *Who Is Ayn Rand?* 129).

[4] Like Kant, whom Rand viewed as her arch-antagonist, Rand's method was quite Kantian: She derived her theology, or more correctly, her atheology, from her ethics. Like Kant, Rand rejected the God of the Bible and chose another god on the basis of her morality. Kant was also an atheist. He asserted that the God of the Bible did not exist. "God" was simply a useful heuristic device.

and the child. Rand was 13 in 1918, and these atheist ideas and arguments were part of the new regime in Russia. They were in the press, in the schools, and in the universities. Perhaps this writer can be forgiven if he suggests that at the age of thirteen Rand was not yet capable of understanding the so-called proofs for the existence of God offered from Aristotle to Anselm, let alone grasping the much more subtle (and Scriptural) position that the God of the Bible is not a matter for demonstration, but the *axiomatic sine qua non* of all logical demonstration and rational thought. Yet, if one is to accept what Mrs. Branden wrote at face value, one must assume that not only had Rand read and studied the various arguments for the existence of God at the age of 13, but also that she had excogitated refutations of them. After all, Mrs. Branden did say 13-year-old Rand "considered the question scrupulously." If this assertion seems a bit too big to swallow, then the importance of the second reason, the alleged immorality of God, increases still more. Perhaps at this point the reader will return to the motto with which this chapter began and wonder whether Nietzsche was always insane.

Rand's belief in the immorality of God is pervasive in her works and philosophy. It is this motive that informs her characterizations of persons who believe in God as mystics, whim-worshipers, and witch doctors;[5] it is this motive that leads her to attack Christian

---

[5] See *For the New Intellectual*. Rand was quite generous in her use of derogatory words and phrases for those with whom she disagreed. However, Rand seemed to be unique in that she called such a procedure a fallacy—the argument from intimidation—and then proceeded to commit the fallacy repeatedly. She described the fallacy as follows:

> The essential characteristic of the Argument from Intimidation is its appeal to moral self-doubt and its reliance on the fear, guilt or ignorance of the victim. It is used in the form of an ultimatum demanding that the victim renounce a given idea without discussion under threat of being considered morally unworthy. The pattern is always: "Only those who are evil (dishonest, heartless, insensitive, ignorant, etc.) can hold such an idea" (*The Virtue of Selfishness*, 139).

Rand frequently used the argument from intimidation, for she sought to make her readers renounce a given idea without discussion, under threat of being considered morally unworthy. Her pattern was always: "Only those who are evil (altruists, mystics, whim-worshipers, witch doctors, Attilas, etc.) can hold such an idea."

doctrine in *Atlas Shrugged* and other works. Her belief that the concept of God is immoral because such a concept would mean that man is not the highest being in the universe is more than slightly reminiscent of Nietzsche's whine (Nietzsche was always whining about something) that there could be no god because he could not endure not being a god.

Excursus on Rand's Attacks on Christian Doctrine

Here are a few examples of Rand's rhetorical and emotional attacks (they rarely rise to the level of reasoned arguments) on Christian doctrines:

> But a "moral commandment" is a contradiction in terms. The moral is the chosen, not the forced; the understood, not the obeyed. The moral is the rational, and the reason accepts no commandments.[6]

Rand presented the reader with false alternatives. The choice is not between the chosen and the forced, nor between the understood and the obeyed. Obviously, to obey a commandment, one must first understand it. Rand's second couplet is absurd because understanding is a prerequisite for obedience. As for the first couplet, one may choose to obey moral commandments, such as the Ten Commandments, or not. What makes them law, what makes them moral *commandments*, is that there are penalties attached for disobeying them. Where there are no penalties, there is no law. Rand's statement would have logically required her to dismiss all laws—civil as well as divine—as "contradictions in terms," because all laws are commands. Her statement—"the reason accepts no commandments"—is logically absurd: It implies that the "reason" accepts no commandments or laws of any kind, including logical laws. The Randian command to focus, for example, is a moral commandment (Rand wrote at length about the penalties involved

---

[6] Galt's rodomontade in *Atlas Shrugged*, 1018.

for disobeying it), and her remark about moral commandments would have logically required her not to accept it.

Here is a second example of Rand's attacks on specific Christian doctrines:

> The name of this monstrous absurdity is Original Sin. A sin without volition is a slap at morality and an insolent contradiction in terms: that which is outside the possibility of choice is outside the province of morality. If man is evil by birth, he has no will, no power to change it; if he has no will, he can do neither good nor evil; a robot is amoral. To hold, as man's sin, a fact not open to his choice is a mockery of morality. To hold man's nature as his sin is a mockery of nature. To punish him for a crime he committed before he was born is a mockery of justice. To hold him guilty in a matter where no innocence exists is a mockery of reason.[7]

These passages disclose little but a complete failure, and perhaps even a complete lack of effort, to understand the Christian doctrines of God, man, and sin.

First, original sin, or more accurately, total depravity, is not "a sin without volition." That indeed would be a logical absurdity. Total depravity is a description of the will, the volition, to use Rand's word. The will, or more accurately, the rational being, must be either good (or neutral), that is, sinless; or evil, that is, sinful; there is no third choice. If to say the will is evil is absurd, then it is equally absurd to say that the will is good. Neither statement is absurd, but one is false.

Second, Rand's assertion—"if man is evil by birth, he has no will" —is logically absurd. If man has no will, if he has no rational faculty, he cannot be evil. The concept of moral "evil," the concept "sinful," requires the concept "will." Rand's subsequent argument based on this absurd statement, therefore, collapses. The last several sentences of the paragraph are not arguments; they are simply rhetoric.

---

[7] Galt's rodomontade in *Atlas Shrugged*, 1025.

Branden, from the point of view of a secular psychologist, wrote:

> It is worth observing, in this connection, that both the religious doctrine of Original Sin and its secular version, the Freudian theory of an id, are disastrous psychologically. Aside from the fact that they are groundless and offensive to reason, they are extremely anti-therapeutic.[8]

Whether an idea is anti-therapeutic from the point of view of secular psychology is, of course, irrelevant to the issue of its truth. Psychology, psychiatry, and psychoanalysis are the best examples of witchdoctory in the twentieth century. How many studies have concluded that persons with "mental problems" solve those problems as well without therapy as they do with therapy?[9]

Branden showed his misunderstanding of the Christian doctrine of sin when he wrote:

> Neither is man born with any sort of Original Sin; if a man feels guilty, it is not because he is guilty by nature; sin is not "original," it is originated. The problem of anxiety is psychological, not metaphysical.[10]

Of course, the doctrine of total depravity does not teach that men feel guilty. It teaches the opposite: They are so depraved, they tend to think they are fine, upstanding, and good. They are confident of their abilities and brimming with self-esteem, never realizing that they are poor, miserable, nasty, and brutish. They imagine that they understand themselves and the world, when they are ignorant of both. The philosophers and philodoxers of the Enlightenment fo-

---

[8] *The Objectivist*, May 1966, 9.

[9] Good critiques of this whole field of pseudo-science are the books of Thomas Szasz (from a secular point of view) and Jay Adams and Martin and Deirdre Bobgan (from a Christian point of view).

[10] *The Objectivist*, November 1966, 12.

cused their energies on denying total depravity, thereby confirming it:

> The concept of original sin is the common opponent against which all the different trends of the philosophy of the Enlightenment join forces. In this struggle Hume is on the side of English deism, and Rousseau of Voltaire; the unity of the goal seems for a time to outweigh all differences as to the means of attaining it.[11]

Rand agreed with Kant's view that ability limits responsibility. Both Rand and Kant rejected the Christian view of men's inability to obey the law of God, and their responsibility to obey. Both Rand and Kant believed that metaphysics—particularly the "free will" of man—was determined by ethical considerations. They both shaped their beliefs about man and the world by what they thought were the requirements of rational ethics. All of this is in contrast to Christianity, which teaches that ethics must be based on, not determinative of, metaphysics.

Just as Rand could not believe in God for moral reasons, neither could Kant.

The Traditional Proofs for God

Much more could be said about the implications of Rand's belief that the idea of God is immoral, and some of those implications will appear as the occasion arises further along in this chapter. We must now turn our attention to the Objectivist arguments countering the traditional Aristotelian-Thomistic "proofs" for the existence of God. The only such argument that they discussed at any length is the argument from causality, which Nathaniel Branden discussed in *The Objectivist Newsletter*.[12] He wrote:

> There are two basic fallacies in this argument. The first

[11] Ernst Cassirer, *The Philosophy of the Enlightenment*, 141.

[12] May 1962, 19.

is the assumption that, if the universe required a causal explanation, the positing of a "God" would provide it. To posit God as the creator of the universe is only to push the problem back one step farther: Who then created God? Was there a still earlier God who created the God in question? We are thus led to an infinite regress—the very dilemma that the positing of a "God" was intended to solve. But if it is argued that no one created God, that God does not require a cause, that God has existed eternally—then on what grounds is it denied that the universe has existed eternally?

In *Atlas Shrugged* Rand wrote: "The only philosophical debt I can acknowledge is to Aristotle."[13] This is a curious statement in many respects. Why was this the only philosophical debt she could acknowledge? Because all the remainder of her ideas were original? Hardly. The educated reader (and, one must assume, Rand herself knew) knows quite well that such is not the case. Was Rand's reluctance to admit any other philosophical debt due to the fact that many of her ideas are the stock-in-trade of a much less reputable group of thinkers than the Aristotelians—the materialists of the eighteenth, nineteenth, and twentieth centuries? As an example of what I mean, consider this passage from Ludwig Feuerbach, one of the most prominent materialists of the early nineteenth century:

Nothing is more absurd than to regard nature as a single effect and to give it a single cause in an extra-natural being who is the effect of no other being. If I cannot refrain from spinning out fantasies, from looking further and further afield, if I am unable to stop with nature and content my intellectual need for causes with the universal action and interaction of nature, what is to prevent me from going beyond God? What is to prevent me from looking for a ground and cause of God as well? Do we not in God find the same situation as in the concatenation of natural causes and ef-

---

[13] "About the Author."

fects, the very situation that I wished to remedy by positing the existence of God?[14]

Surely the refutation of the first cause argument offered by the Objectivists is not original—thus it is a philosophical debt. But this refutation was not authored by Aristotle, it was offered by the materialists. Aristotle, in fact, is the *source* of the traditional proofs for God. One may find his arguments in the *Physics*. Rand's affinity to the materialists and her rejection of the thoroughly Aristotelian arguments for the existence of God will become quite clear as this chapter progresses. It is this debt that must be grasped if one is to understand Objectivism.

Consider this passage from Friedrich Engels, friend and financier of Karl Marx, co-author of *The Communist Manifesto*: "But nowadays, in our evolutionary conception of the universe, there is absolutely no room for either a Creator or a Ruler; and to talk of a Supreme Being shut out from the whole existing world, implies a contradiction in terms. . . ."[15] Engels sounded very much like Branden: "To demand a cause for all of existence is to demand a contradiction; if the cause exists, it is part of existence; if it does not exist, it cannot be a cause."[16] Actually, of course, it was Branden who was echoing Engels. And Branden was equivocating on the word "existence." He is smuggling into Objectivism, without argument, the notion that "existence" means "matter." Branden sought to instill the notion that "Existence" and "God" are mutually exclusive concepts when he wrote, "Existence—not 'God'—is the First Cause." Unfortunately, Branden has so misrepresented the Thomist argument that his attempted refutation refuted an argument never made by Thomas, that God is somehow non-existent. Because God exists, according to Thomas, he "causes" other existents to exist. To say, as Branden does, that therefore "Existence,

---

[14] *Lectures on the Essence of Religion,* 101.

[15] *Socialism: Utopian and Scientific,* 14.

[16] *The Objectivist Newsletter,* May 1962, 19.

not 'God' is the First Cause" is tantamount to saying that existence (since all causes exist) is the cause of every thing and action, which is an uninformative and meaningless statement. This writer believes the Aristotelian-Thomistic arguments for the existence of God are invalid, but he also believes they ought to be refuted, not by misrepresentation or legerdemain, but by logic. If Rand and Branden were correct about "existence," then all statements such as "A causes B" are incorrect, for, since A exists, it is actually "existence" which causes B. Such an argument is devoid of meaning and sense.

One should note that the Objectivist denial of the only true God does not eliminate the attributes of God; at least some of God's attributes are simply reassigned to some other being, in this case, the universe, nature, or objective reality, meaning, of course, the physical universe. The physical universe is the cause of itself. The universe is eternal. Matter is *causa sui*.[17]

Another example of this Objectivist redistribution of divine attributes to the physical universe is Rand's transmogrification of the Christian doctrine that God is love into the doctrine of the "benevolent universe." This is an excellent example of the pathetic fallacy. Only a person can be "bene-volent" or "male-volent," for "volent" means will. When Rand called the universe benevolent, rather than malevolent, she was not making an intelligible statement, unless she was implying that the universe is both living and conscious, or is the product of some being who is living and conscious. If she was not speaking literally, but using a figure of speech, she was committing the pathetic fallacy, personifying nature.

Leonard Peikoff, writing in 1976, may have had this objection in mind (I first published it in 1974 in *Answer to Ayn Rand*) when he wrote: "The 'benevolent universe' does not mean that the universe feels kindly to man, or that it is out to help him achieve his goals. No, the universe is neutral; it simply is; it is indifferent to you. [So *benevolent* really means *neutral, indifferent.*] But real-

---

[17] "We may regard the material and cosmic world as the supreme being, as the cause of all causes, as the creator of heaven and earth" (Lenin, quoting Dietzgen with approval, *Materialism and Empirio-Criticism*, 251).

ity is 'benevolent' [of course, we put words between inverted commas when we do not really mean what they seem to say] in the sense that if you do adapt to it—i.e., if you do think, value, and act rationally, then you can (and barring accidents you will) achieve your values. . . . Pain, suffering, failure do not have metaphysical significance—they do not reveal the nature of reality. . . ."[18]

Of course, Peikoff's last sentence is an example of what Rand called "blanking out" or "faking reality." Pain, suffering, and failure are as real and as objective as pleasure, enjoyment, and success. By what queer argument are these things denied metaphysical significance? Both Rand and Peikoff preferred to fake reality.[19]

Other attributes of God (see below) are similarly transferred to the physical universe—yet we are asked to believe that the Objectivists do not believe in any gods.

Objectivism's First God

If existence is a god of Objectivism, what is the nature of this god? As I argued in the previous chapter, the answer appears to be: Objective reality is material. Existence is matter—indestructible matter. This metaphysical belief is the indispensable basis, not only of Objectivist theology, but of Objectivist ethics as well, as we shall see in the next chapter. Rand wrote:

> There is only one fundamental alternative in the universe: existence or nonexistence—and it pertains to a single

---

[18] *The Philosophy of Objectivism*, 1976, Lecture 8, as quoted in *The Ayn Rand Lexicon*, 51.

[19] When it was convenient to do so, Rand took a decidedly different view: "Without machines and technology, the task of mere survival is a terrible, mind-and-body-wrecking ordeal. In 'nature,' the struggle for food, clothing and shelter consumes all of a man's energy and spirit; it is a losing struggle—the winner is any flood, earthquake or swarm of locusts. (Consider the 500,000 bodies left in the wake of a single flood in Pakistan; they had been men who lived without technology.) . . . [L]ife in nature, without technology, is wholesale death" (*The New Left*, 149, 142).

> class of entities: to living organisms. The existence of in-
> animate [Rand should have said *inorganic*, and her mis-
> statement appears to be deliberate] matter is unconditional,
> the existence of life is not: it depends on a specific course
> of action. Matter is indestructible, it changes its forms, but
> it cannot cease to exist.[20]

Matter, objective reality, is everlasting, indestructible. Another attribute of God has been transferred to nature. As we have already seen, there is no argument demonstrating that we should accept this doctrine of indestructible matter as objective reality; indestructible matter was postulated by Rand for the purpose of lending plausibility to her ethical system. But this dogmatic assertion of indestructible matter did establish Rand's membership in the materialist school.

Rand formulated this metaphysical postulate in the simple proposition, "existence exists." Existence, she wrote, is an axiomatic concept that all thought presupposes; "existence exists" is a way of translating this axiomatic concept into the form of an axiom. It is this axiom that forms the basis of Rand's philosophical system.[21] Rand was clear on the nature of existence. She was vigorous in her attack against those philosophers whom she regarded as adherents of the "primacy of consciousness"—Descartes, Kant, and Hegel; and insistent upon her adherence to the "primacy of existence."[22] Since she chose to oppose the terms "consciousness" and "existence," we are compelled to conclude that she believed in the primacy of *un*consciousness, of inorganic, indestructible matter and energy. Existence is unconsciousness. This inference is required

---

[20] *The Virtue of Selfishness*, 15. See *Atlas Shrugged*, "This Is John Galt Speaking."

[21] "We, the men of the mind, are now on strike against you in the name of a single axiom, which is the root of our moral code, just as the root of yours is the wish to escape it: the axiom that existence exists" (*Atlas Shrugged*, 1015).

[22] Lenin is quite as insistent as Rand on this point in his *Materialism and Empirio-Criticism*.

by her distinction between the primacy of existence and the primacy of consciousness.[23] "Existence," then, is everlasting (indestructible), immutable,[24] omnipresent[25] matter.[26] Existence is unconsciousness.

> The earlier, naturalistic revolution against God replaced
> the name "God" by the name "Nature." Almost everything
> else was left unchanged. Theology, the science of God, was
> replaced by the science of Nature; God's laws by the laws
> of Nature; God's will and power by the will and power of

[23] "If nothing exists, there can be no consciousness: a consciousness with nothing to be conscious of is a contradiction in terms. A consciousness conscious of nothing but itself is a contradiction in terms: before it could identify itself as consciousness, it had to be conscious of something. If that which you claim to perceive does not exist, what you possess is not consciousness" (*Atlas Shrugged*, 1015).

[24] "This means that although reality is immutable and, in any given context, only one answer is true . . ." (Ayn Rand, *The Objectivist Newsletter*, February 1965, 7). In this sentence Rand transfers another attribute of God, immutability, to nature. One wonders where Rand observed this immutable reality. Sensible reality is always changing.

[25] "Existence exists; you cannot go outside it, you cannot get under it, on top of it or behind it. Existence exists—and only existence exists; there is nowhere else to go" (Nathaniel Branden, *The Objectivist Newsletter*, May 1962, 19).

[26] Some readers may still question whether Rand actually believed in matter as the nature of existence. Perhaps another quotation from *Atlas Shrugged* will clarify her position:

> All thinking is a process of identification and integration. Man
> perceives a blob of color; by integrating the evidence of his sight and
> his touch, he learns to identify it as a solid object; he learns to identify
> the object as a table; he learns that the table is made of wood; he learns
> that the wood consists of cells, that the cells consist of molecules, that
> the molecules consist of atoms (1016).

In addition, Nathaniel Branden wrote: "It is necessary to mention that many of Professor Blanshard's own philosophical premises are deeply at variance with those of Objectivism. He is a representative of the Absolute Idealist school of thought . . ." (*The Objectivist Newsletter*, February 1963, 8).

Nature (the natural forces); and later God's design and God's judgment by Natural Selection. Theological determinism was replaced by naturalistic determinism; that is, God's omnipotence and omniscience were replaced by the omnipotence of Nature and the omniscience of science.[27]

In the previous chapter on Objectivist epistemology we examined and found wanting the category of Being; we concluded that it was indistinguishable from Nothing, and that Hegel's fancied movement from Being to Nothing was only the movement from one word to another. We shall not repeat that analysis here; we shall be satisfied with the conclusion that existence for Rand is material. Now that is passable nineteenth-century physics, but physics in the twentieth century long ago discarded any belief in matter. Nathaniel Branden at one point seemed to realize that twentieth century physicists have eliminated the last vestige of matter from the universe, for he wrote: "Long after the time when the mechanical 'model' was recognized by physicists as inapplicable to many aspects of the physical world, i.e., inapplicable even to many inanimate, deterministic systems within the universe: . . ."[28] Yet earlier in the same essay he apparently contradicted this statement by saying: "The actions of a stone, for example, are only reactions to other objects or forces; a stone, which moves by a mechanistic type of causation. . . ."

Both Rand and Branden attacked twentieth-century physics because it wasn't materialistic enough for their taste. But late in life Rand herself expressed some skeptical views:

How can we make conclusions about the ultimate constituents of the universe? For instance, we couldn't say: everything is material, if by "material" we mean that of

[27] Karl Popper, *Conjectures and Refutations*, 346.

[28] *The Objectivist*, March 1966, 11. The sentence continues: "a disastrous legacy remained: the insidiously persistent notion that every action, including every action of man, is only a reaction to some antecedent action or motion or force."

which the physical objects on the perceptual level are made.
... If this is what we mean by "material," then we do not
have the knowledge to say that ultimately everything is
subatomic particles which in certain aggregates are matter.
... The only thing of which we can be sure, philosophically, is that the ultimate stuff, if it's ever found, will have
identity.... What if they [the ultimate stuff] are solid flows
of energy, but each is indivisible, and it moves. ... We
can't claim [that they will have extension ... or shape].[29]

One might conclude from these statements that Rand and
Branden were uncertain as to the status of matter and mechanism.
One might even argue that Rand here admits epistemological defeat: "If it's ever found." But whether they are uncertain or dogmatic, the Objectivist distinction between the non-human universe
and man, especially in the field of meta-ethical theory, depends
upon the existence of both indestructible matter and fragile consciousness. It is Rand's theory of ethics that required her to adopt a
materialist position in metaphysics.

Objectivism's Second God

The existence of indestructible matter is only part of Objectivist
theology. The other part is consciousness, a specific kind of consciousness, conceptual consciousness, man's consciousness. The
fact that Rand regarded man as a god (or men as gods) is hardly to
be denied; the evidence for such as assertion abounds in her works.[30]

Let us begin with *Atlas Shrugged*, where allusions to and overtones of Christianity are ever-present. For example, one of the
principal doctrines of the Christian faith is the sovereign election

[29] Rand, *Introduction to Objectivist Epistemology,* 290-291.

[30] "This philosophy [Feuerbach's] has for its principle ... a real being, the true
ens realissimum—man; ... It generates thought from the opposite of thought,
from matter, from existence, from the senses ..." (Feuerbach, *Essence of Christianity*, xxxv).

of God; that is, God chooses some people to be saved and predestines others to be damned.[31] In *Atlas Shrugged* it is John Galt who performs this function of choosing people to be saved, that is, to go to Galt's Gulch. Galt himself comes as a thief in the night to take the suffering saints to be with him in Galt's Gulch—the suffering saints are even castigated by the worldlings as "Puritans." The overtones of Christianity are so obvious as to eliminate any doubt that Rand knew what she was doing. When Henry Rearden, one of the suffering Puritans, sees Ragnar Danneskjold for the first time, Danneskjold looks like "an avenging angel."[32] He informs Rearden that there is a "large bank account waiting for him" in Atlantis, that is, Galt's Gulch; and refers to the *Parousia*—the presence, or the *coming*—of John Galt as the "day of deliverance."[33]

It was Augustine who wrote that the elect person—the chosen person—is not at peace until he knows God, and that the need for God will result in an endless restlessness until the elect one sees God face to face. But it is Dagny Taggart who thinks:

> You—she thought—whoever you are, whom I have always loved and never found, you whom I expected to see at the ends of the rails beyond the horizon, you whose presence I had always felt in the streets of the city and whose world I had wanted to build, it is my love for you that had kept me moving, my love and my hope to reach you and

[31] The doctrine of predestination, despite the denials of most churches and millions of professed Christians, is explicitly and implicitly taught in hundreds of passages, such as Exodus 33:19, Psalm 33:12, Matthew 11:27, John 10:24-29, John 17, Romans 8:28-30, and Romans 9:10-24. The fact that most churches deny this clear teaching of Scripture, a teaching far more pervasive than the doctrine of the Trinity (which is also Biblical), indicates how far they are from being Christian churches.

[32] *Atlas Shrugged*, 574.

[33] *Atlas Shrugged*, 581. One will of course recognize the doctrine of Christianity that the saved will receive rewards in Heaven, and at his return, Christ will deliver the saints from the tribulations of the world. *Parousia* is the Greek word used in the New Testament to refer to the second coming of Christ.

my wish to be worthy of you on the day when I would stand before you face to face. . . .[34]

Later in the novel Dagny realizes who it was that she was so longing to see: John Galt, Rand's surrogate for the Messiah, Jesus Christ.[35] When Dagny was admitted to Atlantis and saw all those men who had been disappearing from the Earth,[36] her experience is described by Rand as an entrance into Heaven:

> "This?" She laughed suddenly, looking at the faces of the men against the golden sunburst of rays filling the great windows. "This looks like. . . . You know, I never hoped to see any of you again, I wondered at times how much I'd give for just one more glimpse or one more word—and now—now this is like that dream[37] you imagine in childhood, when you think that some day, in heaven, you will see those great departed whom you had not seen on earth. . . ."[38]

One of those great departed, Ken Danagger, a persecuted "Puritan," replied:

---

[34] *Atlas Shrugged*, 634. The phrase is apparently taken from Scripture: "For now we see through a glass, darkly; but then face to face: now I know in part; but then shall I know even as also I am known" (1 Corinthians 13:12).

[35] "John, that night, it was you that I was thinking of . . . only I didn't know it . . ." (958). The fictional Dagny found her fictional messiah; Rand, the Russian Jew, never found hers; she fabricated him.

[36] "Then shall two be in the field; the one shall be taken, and the other left. Two women shall be grinding at the mill; the one shall be taken, and the other left. Watch therefore: for you know not what hour your Lord comes" (Matthew 25:40-42).

[37] "Religion is the dream of the human mind" (Feuerbach, *Essence of Christianity*, xxxix). "Men create gods—and demons—in their own likeness; mystic fantasies, as a rule, are invented to explain some phenomenon for which men find no explanation" (Ayn Rand, *The Objectivist*, July 1971, 7).

[38] *Atlas Shrugged*, 735.

"That's not all," said Danagger. "There's something you'd want to hear from them. I didn't know it, either, until I saw him for the first time"—he pointed to Galt— "and he said it to me, and then I knew what it was that I had missed all my life. Miss Taggart, you'd want them to look at you and to say, 'Well done.' "[39]

The reward of Dagny in Atlantis is to see John Galt smile;[40] need it be said that a smile can be considered a reward only by the devout believer who has loved his Lord full and well? And Dagny, we are told, thought of John Galt the way a Christian must think of Jesus Christ: "Once they have seen him—thought Dagny—can they wish to look at anybody else?"[41]

In the fictional character of John Galt, Rand fabricated her own messiah, and the resemblances between Galt and the Messiah Jesus of Nazareth are remarkable in some respects. For example, *Atlas Shrugged* opens with a curse: "Who is John Galt?" The name "John Galt" had become a form of profanity, just like the name "Jesus Christ." Further, Galt is mentioned early in the book—he appears only in disguise and only briefly, almost as a spectator, just as Christ briefly appears in the Old Testament. Then in the last third of *Atlas Shrugged*, Galt appears in two chapters—his first coming, as it were—then disappears until the climax, the second coming, when he returns to Earth to set up his kingdom (and to sacrifice his life for his chosen one Dagny, if need be). Rand's messiah does not live on Earth in *Atlas Shrugged*; he is off-stage throughout most of the book, yet he is very much in control of the situation, too. The parallels between Rand's novels and the Bible's history and theology are more than coincidental. Rand, having rejected the Messiah, had to create her own fictional god-man, John Galt, whose

[39] *Atlas Shrugged*, 735-736. "His Lord said unto him, 'Well done, you good and faithful servant; you have been faithful over a few things, I will make you ruler over many things: enter into the joy of your Lord" (Matthew 25:21, 23).

[40] "Her reward was to see Galt smile . . ." (*Atlas Shrugged*, 803).

[41] *Atlas Shrugged*, 1123.

words later assumed the character of quasi-scripture in her non-fiction works.

I have not cited these allusions to Christianity simply to show that Rand read the Bible, but also to show that her many allusions are not accidental,[42] but conscious. Rand was quite consciously smuggling some Christian ideas into her theology;[43] she was deliberately investing the creature with the attributes of the Creator. By her disguised and undisguised allusions to Christianity she gave us to understand that the reader should not overlook the fact that Objectivism has a very definite theology, despite the claim of atheism.

Rand wrote that "the sense of life dramatized in *The Fountainhead* [is] man worship."[44] Yet neither *Atlas Shrugged* nor *The Fountainhead* provided the best demonstration that for Rand, "theology

---

[42] "A few years ago, Ayn Rand gave a series of private lectures on the art of fiction-writing. During a discussion period, she happened to remark that there was not a single word in her novels whose purpose she could not explain" (Nathaniel Branden, *Who Is Ayn Rand?* 110-111).

[43] Rand launched a vigorous attack on Christian theology in *Atlas Shrugged*; she attacked the "mystics of the spirit" for presenting as knowledge negative definitions: "God is a non-man, heaven is non-earth, soul is non-body, virtue is non-profit, A is non-A, perception is non-sensory, knowledge is non-reason. Their definitions are not acts of defining, but of wiping out" (1035). One might compare this passage to Feuerbach: "Religion is the disuniting of man from himself; he sets God before him as the antithesis of himself. God is not what man is—man is not what God is. God is the infinite, man the finite being; God is perfect, man imperfect; God eternal, man temporal; God almighty, man weak; God holy, man sinful. God and man are extremes: God is the absolutely positive, the sum of all realities; man the absolutely negative, comprehending all negations" (*Essence of Christianity*, 33).

Ronald Merrill, an Objectivist, in his book *The Ideas of Ayn Rand*, thought Rand was using Jewish symbolism (61). But Merrill garbled the account of Sodom and Gomorrah and missed the pervasive Christian symbolism completely. That illustrates how defective an education at one of America's first-class universities (MIT) may be.

[44] *The Objectivist*, March 1968, 5. Rand seeks to account for "religious emotions" by seeking their true object(s) in the visible world:

> Religion's monopoly in the field of ethics has made it extremely difficult to communicate the emotional meaning and connotations of a

is anthropology."[45] Her theological work *par excellence* is *Anthem*,[46] one of her earliest and shortest novels.

Anthem

Anthem describes the emergence of the individual from a totalitarian society in the future. Its theme is the transition from the Sovereign State to the Sovereign Individual. This theme has, of course, significant implications for Rand's political theory, as we shall see. In its first ten chapters the book briefly describes the life and physical escape of Equality 7-2521 and Liberty 5-3000, two subjects of the Sovereign State. Rand hesitated to make the Sovereign Individual emerge alone: He is quickly followed by another, who becomes his wife. But Rand clearly wrote that the Sovereign Individual could have achieved his escape and lived a human life alone:

---

rational view of life. Just as religion has pre-empted the field of ethics, turning morality against man, so it has usurped the highest moral concepts of our language, placing them outside this earth and beyond man's reach. 'Exaltation' is usually taken to mean an emotional state evoked by contemplating the supernatural. 'Worship' means the emotional experience of loyalty and dedication to something higher than man. 'Reverence' means the emotion of a sacred respect, to be experienced on one's knees. 'Sacred' means superior to and not-to-be-touched by any concerns of man or this earth. Etc. . . .

"It is this highest level of man's emotions that has to be released from the murk of mysticism and redirected at its proper object: man" (4-5).

Compare Rand's statement to Feuerbach's: "The purely, truly human emotions are religious; but for that reason the religious emotions are purely human. . ." (*Essence of Christianity*, 282).

[45] Feuerbach, *Essence of Christianity*, xxxvii.

[46] According to the *Oxford English Dictionary*, an anthem is "1. a composition, in prose or verse, sung antiphonally, or by two voices or choirs, respectively; 2. a composition in unmeasured prose (usually from the Scriptures or Liturgy) set to music; 3. loosely in poetry; a song, as of praise or gladness. Also used in the English 'National' or 'Royal' anthem,' which is technically a hymn."

Then a blow of pain struck us [Equality 7-2521], our
first and our only. We thought of the Golden One [Liberty
5-3000]. We thought of the Golden One whom we shall
never see again. Then the pain passed. It is best. We are
one of the Damned. It is best if the Golden One forget our
name and the body which bore that name.[47]

We are thus given to understand that the autonomy of the Sovereign Individual remains unbreached by the emergence of two Sovereign Individuals.

Chapter eleven begins the intellectual emergence: Equality 7-2521 discovers the word "I." Escape has already occurred—physically; now begins the process of intellectual liberation. The chapter begins: "I am, I think, I will."

If Rand wished us to understand that these three states or actions are logically and/or temporally in order, then she contradicted herself. Despite her emphasis elsewhere on the absolute priority of "existence," she wrote in *The Virtue of Selfishness:* "He [man] can abandon his means of survival, his mind, he can turn himself into a subhuman creature and he can turn his life into a brief span of agony. . . . Man has to be man by choice. . . ."[48] "As man is a being of self-made wealth, so he is a being of self-made soul."[49] As thoroughly as any existentialist,[50] Rand believed that man makes himself, that, for man at least, existence precedes essence. Rand's position is that man's fundamental decision, "to think or not to think," determines the answer to the question, "to be or not to be?"

---

[47] *Anthem*, 86.

[48] *Anthem*, 24-25. This passage in turn contradicts other passages in which Rand denies this to be possible. We quoted one or two of these in an earlier chapter.

[49] *Anthem*, 27. "Are you a thinking being before you think? In creating the first thought you create yourself, the thinking one . . ." (Max Stirner, *The Ego and His Own*, 31).

[50] Rand "could have" and apparently did consider calling her philosophy *Existentialism* at one point, according to Leonard Peikoff. See also Sciabarra, *Ayn Rand*, 402.

The implications of this position are far-reaching for all branches of her philosophy.

Making the incorrect choice at this level has metaphysical implications. This notion led Rand into insoluble antinomies. If "man has to be man by choice," who is it that makes the choice? Rand repeatedly committed the fallacy of the stolen concept, a fallacy which she detected exclusively in others.[51] The notion that man makes himself, that "man is a being of self made soul," is a logical contradiction. Rand's series in *Anthem*, "I am. I think. I will," should have been reversed in order to be consistent with her theory of volitional consciousness: "I will. I think. I am." Such a reversal, which would be consistent with her position in *The Virtue of Selfishness*, would accentuate the primacy of the will in this aspect of her theory. It is by an act of will that a "subhuman being" chooses to become a man. The being lifts itself by its bootstraps. The being is its own creator.[52] Rand's idea of volitional consciousness is one of the most blatant examples of the fallacy of the stolen concept that this writer has encountered.

Anthem does not end, however, with the affirmation of the deity of man: Man is owner of all creation: "My hands . . . My spirit . . . My sky . . . My forest . . . This earth of mine. . . ."[53] The new individual god-man, who has replaced the old collective god, is here asserting his ownership of all. Both gods are all-inclusive; both gods are unlimited; both gods are the *summum bonum*: "This, my body and spirit, this is the end of the quest. I wished to know the meaning of things. I am the meaning. I wished to find a warrant

---

[51] This fallacy will be discussed more fully in the chapter on Objectivist ethics.

[52] "Man is the sole animal capable of working his way out of the merely animal state—his normal state is one appropriate to his consciousness, one that has to be created by himself" (Friedrich Engels, *Dialectics of Nature*, in *Marx and Engels on Religion*, 192). It is quite interesting that Rand, despite her atheism, seemed reluctant to refer to man as an animal. Apparently she had serious doubts about the theory of evolution, perhaps realizing what havoc it would wreak on her concept of man.

[53] *Anthem*, 108.

for being. I need no warrant for being, and no word of sanction upon my being. I am the warrant and the sanction."[54]

The godhood of the Sovereign Individual is absolute:

> It is my eyes which see, and the sight of my eyes grants beauty to the earth. It is my ears which hear, and the hearing of my ears gives its song to the world. It is my mind which thinks, and the judgment of my mind is the only searchlight that can find the truth. It is my will which chooses, and the choice of my will is the only edict I must respect.[55]

Here, stripped of the camouflage of pedantic philosophy, is the spirit that informs Objectivism. Here first appears the insoluble antinomy in Objectivist theology: consciousness *versus* existence. Something similar to Kantianism appears: But for me, there would be no beauty, no song, no truth, no morals. I am the creator of beauty, sound, truth, and morality. Very little is left of "objective reality," for if the beauty is due to me, why not the form? If the song is my creation, why not the singer? If the truth . . . the implications for Rand are philosophically disastrous. If the morality decreed by my Sovereign Will is true morality, then I am beyond good and evil. Rand seemed to draw the same conclusion herself: "Everything that we discuss, *everything*, is done from the human

[54] Pages 108-109. "Man, especially the religious man, is to himself the measure of all things, of all reality" (Feuerbach, *Essence of Christianity*, 22). In her *Introduction to Objectivist Epistemology*, Rand wrote: "It is here that Protagoras' old dictum may be given a new meaning, the opposite of the one he intended: 'Man is the measure of all things.' Man is the measure, epistemologically—not metaphysically. In regard to human knowledge, man has to be the measure, since he has to bring all things into the realm of the humanly knowable" (13-14).

[55] *Anthem*, 109. "The distinguished type of human being feels himself as value-determining; he does not need to be ratified; he judges that 'which is harmful to me is harmful as such'; he knows that he is the something which gives honor to objects; he creates values. This type honors everything he knows about himself; his morality is self-glorification" (Friedrich Nietzsche, *Beyond Good and Evil*, IX, 260).

viewpoint and has to be, because there is no such thing as "reality in itself."[56]

Rand recognized and made explicit this primacy of the will: "Many words have been granted me, and some are wise, and some are false, but only three are holy: 'I will it!'"[57] This is the motive and the goal of Rand's atheism: Man, specifically Rand, and by implication each individual man, is a god. Man's will is holy; his decrees are definitive; his acts are creative. Man is the way, the truth, and the life: "Whatever road I take, the guiding star is within me; the guiding star and the loadstone [*sic*] which point the way. They point in but one direction. They point to me."

Rand adopted one of Kant's ethical ideas as her own: Man is an end in himself. "And my happiness needs no higher aim to vindicate it. My happiness is not the means to any end. It is the end. It is its own goal. It is its own purpose. Neither am I the means to any end others may wish to accomplish. I am not a tool for their use."[58]

Furthermore, man is his own miracle: "I am a man. This miracle of me is mine to own and keep, and mine to guard, and mine to use, and mine to kneel before!"[59] With the banishment of God from the universe, man becomes a miracle and a god. It would seem that arguments against miracles are useful only for showing the impossibility of miracles not performed by man. Rand's worship of man[60] was conscious; her language imitated that of the Bible: "I guard my treasures: my thought, my will, my freedom. And the greatest

---

[56] *Introduction to Objectivist Epistemology*, 193-194.

[57] *Anthem*, 109.

[58] *Anthem*, 109-110. "But neither politics nor ethics nor philosophy are ends in themselves, neither in life nor in literature. Only Man is an end in himself" (Ayn Rand, *The Romantic Manifesto*, 129).

[59] *Anthem*, 110.

[60] "The motive and purpose of my writing can best be summed up by saying that if a dedication page were to precede the total of my work, it would read: To the glory of man" (*The Romantic Manifesto*, 137).

of these is freedom."[61] Freedom is sovereignty, the absence of a superior, the non-existence of the Creator. Rand rightly said, "the greatest of these is freedom," for by this declaration of independence she sought to establish her own will as autonomous. This was her faith; this was her theology: "And now I see the face of god, and I raise this god over the earth, this god whom men have sought since men came into being, this god who will grant them joy and peace and pride. This god, this one word: 'I.' "[62] The deification of man is complete and explicit.[63]

In the twelfth chapter of *Anthem*, this god becomes the savior

---

[61] *Anthem*, 110. Nor is this the only imitation of the Bible. The allusions are almost too numerous to mention: "Your will be done" (105), an echo of the Lord's Prayer; the end of chapter 11, which is quoted in the text, is an allusion to the first chapter of John's Gospel. The religious words and phrases in *Anthem* are even more conspicuous than the imitations of Biblical phrases. I refer the reader to pages 11, 53, 55, 63, 85, 90, 93-97, 104-123. Unfortunately, many of her readers, having been educated in government operated or funded schools, are unfamiliar with the Bible and are unaware of what Rand was doing.

[62] *Anthem*, 112-113. "The criticism of religion ends with the teaching that man is the highest essence for man . . ." (Karl Marx, *Contribution to the Critique of Hegel's Philosophy of Right*, in *Marx and Engels on Religion*, 50).

[63] Both Feuerbach and Kant reached similar conclusions about the divinity of man: "Man has his highest being, his God, in himself; not in himself as an individual, but in his essential nature, his species" (*Nature of Christianity*, 281). "Man is certainly unholy enough, but humanity in his person must be holy to him. Everything in creation which he wishes and over which he has power can be used merely as a means; only man, and with him, every rational creature, is an end in itself. He is the subject of the moral law which is holy, because of the autonomy of his freedom" (Immanuel Kant, *Critique of Practical Reason*, 90). Kant in his *Religion Within the Limits of Pure Reason* wrote: "Much as my words may startle you, you must not condemn me for saying: every man creates his god. From the moral point of view . . . you even have to create your God, in order to worship in him your creator. For in whatever way . . . the Deity should be made known to you, and even . . . if he should reveal himself to you: it is you . . . who must judge whether you are permitted to believe in him, and to worship him." Kant prefaced this passage by saying that "our own reason is capable of revealing it [the moral law] to us" and "we ourselves judge revelation by the moral law" (Chapter 4, Part 4, paragraph 1, footnote).

of all mankind: "It was when I read the first of the books I found in my house that I saw the word 'I.' And when I understood this word, the book fell from my hands, and I wept, I who had never known tears. I wept in deliverance and in pity for all mankind."[64]

The savior, the Sovereign Individual, then calls his wife, and in an imitation of Genesis gives names to himself and to her. The names are quite significant: Prometheus and Gaea: Prometheus, because "he took the light of the gods and he brought it to men, and he taught men to be gods. And he suffered for his deed as all bearers of light must suffer."[65] Gaea, because she was "a goddess . . . who was the mother of the earth and of all the gods. . . ."[66]

The similarity between Rand and Karl Marx at this point is startling. Rand quite obviously believes man to be a "product of . . . nature."[67] Marx wrote: "Man is directly a natural being."[68] Furthermore Marx, like Rand, believed man to be his own creator: "the whole of what is called world history is nothing but the creation of man by human labor, . . . he, therefore, has the evident and irrefutable proof of his self-creation, of his own origins."[69]

In a passage which Rand herself might have appended to *Anthem*, Marx wrote:

> A being does not regard himself as independent unless he is his own master, and he is only his own master when he owes his existence to himself. A man who lives by the favor of another considers himself a dependent being. But I live completely by another person's favor when I owe to him not only the continuance of my life but also its cre-

---

[64] *Anthem*, 114.

[65] *Anthem*, 115.

[66] Gaea (or Gaia), of course, is what the environmental pantheists call their god.

[67] *Capitalism: The Unknown Ideal*, 322.

[68] *Early Writings*, ed. Bottomore, 206.

[69] *Early Writings*, 166.

ation—when he is its source. My life has necessarily such a cause outside itself if it is not my own creation.[70]

This is the motive of all humanism: the desire to be free of God.

Marx goes on to say, however, that "the idea of creation is thus one which it is difficult to eliminate from popular consciousness. This consciousness is unable to conceive that nature and man exist on their own account, because such an existence contradicts all the tangible facts of practical life." Marx wanted to deny such "tangible facts" and replace them with his doctrine of the self-creation of man. It is because of this motive that he, like Rand, idolized Prometheus:

> Philosophy makes no secret of it. Prometheus' admission: ["In sooth all gods I hate"] is its own admission, its own motto against all gods, heavenly and earthly, who do not acknowledge the consciousness of man as the supreme divinity. There must be no god on a level with it.[71]

Marx, like Rand, did not report the reply to Prometheus' expression of hatred for the gods: "It appears you have been stricken with no small madness." As Voegelin remarked: "Anyone who does not know *Prometheus Bound* must conclude that the quoted 'confession' sums up the meaning of the tragedy, not that Aeschylus wished to represent hatred of the gods as madness."[72]

By choosing the name Prometheus for her hero in *Anthem*, Rand unmistakably declared her position, and has inadvertently implied that the hero is mad in his self-deification: "Not until the gnostic revolt of the Roman era do Prometheus, Cain, Eve, and the serpent become symbols of man's deliverance from the power of the tyrannical god of this world."[73]

---

[70] *Early Writings*, 165.

[71] Karl Marx, Foreword to his doctoral dissertation: *The Difference between the Nature Philosophy of Democritus and the Nature Philosophy of Epicurus*, in *Marx and Engels on Religion*, 14-15. (Marx quotes the original Greek.)

[72] Eric Voegelin, *Science, Politics, and Gnosticism*, 36-37.

[73] *Science, Politics, and Gnosticism*, 37.

Without a Prayer: Ayn Rand and the Close of Her System

In *Atlas Shrugged*, Rand's god John Galt says:

> What is the nature of the guilt that your teachers call his Original Sin? What are the evils man acquired when he fell from a state they consider perfection? Their myth declares that he ate the fruit of the tree of knowledge; he acquired a mind and became a rational being. It was the knowledge of good and evil—he became a moral being. He was sentenced to earn his bread by his labor—he became a productive being. He was sentenced to experience desire—he acquired the capacity for sexual enjoyment. The evils for which they damn him are reason, morality, creativeness, joy—all the cardinal values of his existence.[74]

The Fall was really an ascent; Adam and Eve were courageous pioneers; and the serpent was the means of their, and our, liberation.

Rand's Prometheus names his wife Gaea, "who was the mother of the earth and of gods." This is done, for she is to be "the mother of a new kind of gods."[75] The implications of this are not difficult to see. Prometheus hates all the gods, and Gaea is the mother of gods. Inadvertently Rand revealed the inevitable consequence of her humanism: the murder of man. By her symbols, she unwittingly instructed us that the new world that Prometheus has begun is as totalitarian as the world from which he "escaped." Rand's heroes are supermen, *ubermenschen*, and their sovereignty results not in a free society but in a totalitarian society.

> Man cannot transform himself into a superman; the attempt to create a superman is an attempt to murder man. Historically, the murder of God is not followed by the superman, but by the murder of man: the deicide of the gnostic

---

[74] *Atlas Shrugged*, 1025-1026. "Why were the men of Babel punished? Because they attempted to build a tower to the sky" (Rand, *The Objectivist*, July 1971, 8).

[75] *Anthem*, 115-116.

theoreticians is followed by the homicide of the revolutionary practitioners.[76]

Let me present my argument that humanism is inherently murderous more fully.

The War of the Gods

One insoluble contradiction in Rand's theology lies in its gods: man and objective reality, or Man and Nature. We have already seen how objective reality is to be understood as matter—indestructible, determined matter. The Communists were quite as eager as Rand to defend objective reality. Lenin, for instance, wrote:

> Once you deny objective reality, given us in sensation, you have already lost every one of your weapons against fideism, for you have slipped into agnosticism or subjectivism—and that is all fideism wants. If the perceptual world is objective reality, then the door is closed to every other "reality" or quasi-reality. . . .[77]

Engels wrote:

> The material [*stofflich*], sensuously perceptible world to which we ourselves belong is the only reality; and . . . our consciousness and thinking, however suprasensuous they may seem, are the products of a material, bodily organ, the brain. Matter is not a product of mind, but mind itself is merely the highest product of matter.[78]

---

[76] *Science, Politics, and Gnosticism*, 64.

[77] *Materialism and Empirio-Criticism*, 37.

[78] *Marx and Engels on Religion*, 230-231.

Again, Lenin:

> We ask, is man given objective reality when he sees
> something red or feels something hard, etc., or not? . . . If
> you hold that it is not given, you . . . inevitably sink to sub-
> jectivism and agnosticism. . . . If you hold that it is given, a
> philosophical concept is needed for this objective reality,
> and this concept has been worked out long, long ago. This
> concept is matter. Matter is a philosophical category desig-
> nating the objective reality which is given to man by his
> sensations, and which is copied, photographed and reflected
> by our sensations, while existing independently of them.[79]

Rand was equally clear about the nature of "objective reality." It
remains to be seen, however, exactly what she thought man is.

At one point Rand defines *man* as "an indivisible entity, an
integrated unit of two attributes: of matter and consciousness. . . ."[80]
Rand was adamantly opposed to what she called the "soul-body
dichotomy": "They [the 'mystics'] have taught man that he is a
hopeless misfit made of two elements [a 'corpse' and a 'ghost'],
both symbols of death."[81] Yet Objectivism insists that man is fundamentally different from the rest of nature. Although man is a
product of nature,[82] "Nature has not 'programmed' him to think
automatically."[83] Man has one (but only one) free choice: "In the
choice to focus or not to focus, to think or not to think, to activate
the conceptual level of his consciousness or to suspend it—and in
this choice alone—is man psychologically free."[84]

This doctrine of limited free will is of fundamental importance

---

[79] *Materialism and Empirio-Criticism*, 128.

[80] *Atlas Shrugged*, 1019.

[81] *Atlas Shrugged*, 1026.

[82] *Capitalism: The Unknown Ideal*, 322.

[83] Nathaniel Branden, *The Objectivist*, February 1966, 7.

[84] Nathaniel Branden, *The Objectivist*, January 1966, 12.

in the Objectivist system, and it will be discussed at greater length in the chapter on Objectivist ethics. It is important in Objectivist theology, for it establishes an insoluble antinomy at the very foundation of the system, an antinomy as irreconcilable as Kant's antinomy between the *homo noumenon* and *homo phenomenon*. If you will recall, Kant separated the noumenal world and the phenomenal world. The latter is the world of appearance, mechanism, and determinism. The former, in the case of man, is the world of freedom. The world of nature, including man's body (*phenomenon*) is deterministic, but the world of the inner man, consciousness (*noumenon*), is the world of freedom: "Freedom, however, among all the ideas of speculative reason, is the only one whose possibility we know a priori. We do not understand it, but we know it as the condition of the moral law which we do know."[85]

The Objectivists also use Kant's argument, as we have seen in their attacks on the doctrine of sin. In chapter three a critique of the other Objectivist argument for free will—the argument from knowledge—was presented. Let it suffice here to say that Rand believed that man is qualitatively different from the remainder of nature. While the universe is *causa sui*, so is man:

> The primary choice to focus, to set one's mind to the purpose of cognitive integration, is a first cause in man's consciousness. On the psychological level, this choice is causally irreducible; it is the highest regulator in the mental system; it is subject to man's direct, volitional control.[86]

Both man and nature are first causes or prime movers; that is, both beings have attributes usually assigned to God.[87] Because of

---

[85] Immanuel Kant, *Critique of Practical Reason*, 4.

[86] Nathaniel Branden, *The Objectivist*, February 1966, 7. "In this issue, man is a prime mover" (March 1966, 13).

[87] " 'Free will'—in the widest sense of the term—is the doctrine which holds that man is capable of performing actions that are not determined by forces outside his control; that man has the power of making choices which are, causally, primaries—i.e., not necessitated by antecedent factors" (Nathaniel Branden, *The*

this, a tension arises between the gods, a tension that is aptly caught by one of Rand's favorite (though never acknowledged) quotations from Francis Bacon: "Nature, to be commanded, must be obeyed." The contradiction in Rand's doctrine of man, between his constituent matter and his sovereign reason,[88] cannot be resolved by recognizing man's consciousness as the image of God; Objectivism holds that man, including man's capacity to reason, is a product of inanimate nature. Nature has determined that man shall not be determined. This position is logically impossible.[89] Mind, consciousness, in both Marx and Rand, is an epiphenomenon of matter, yet mind has the capacity to master matter.

The derivation of mind from matter, of reason from unreason, of consciousness from unconsciousness, of freedom from mechanism, is an enormous and insoluble problem for Objectivism, as it is for other varieties of naturalism. It must be underscored that man, for the Objectivists, even though he differs essentially from the rest of reality, is still regarded as an integral part and product of nature. The Objectivist position on the relationship between mind and pre-existing matter is indistinguishable from the general materialist position of the nineteenth century. Feuerbach wrote:

> My doctrine or view can therefore be summed up in two words: nature and man. The being which in my thinking man presupposes, the being which is the cause or ground of man, to which he owes his origin and existence, is not God—a mystical, indeterminate, ambiguous word—but nature, a clear sensuous, unambiguous word and thing. And the being in whom nature becomes personal, conscious, and rational is man. To my mind, unconscious nature is the eternal, uncreated being, the first being—first, that is, in time

---

Objectivist Newsletter, January 1964, 3). "A man's choice to focus is a primary, a first cause in consciousness" (April 1964, 15).

[88] "Fight for the essence of that which is man: for his sovereign rational mind" (*Atlas Shrugged*, 1069).

[89] See Gordon H. Clark's *Behaviorism and Christianity*.

but not in rank, physically but not morally; man with his consciousness is for me second in time, but in rank the first.[90]

Both Engels and Lenin, like Rand, rejected the "vulgar material-ist" idea that the brain secretes thought as the liver secretes bile: "One day we shall certainly 'reduce' thought experimentally to molecular and chemical motions in the brain, but does that exhaust the essence of thought?"[91] Only the non-dialectical vulgar materi-alists "assumed that thought is secreted by the brain as bile is se-creted by the liver," wrote Lenin in *Materialism and Empirio-Criti-cism*.

Rand's distinction between the looters and the producers—a distinction which forms a major theme of *Atlas Shrugged*—between the men who seek power over other men and the men who seek not to rule others, but to conquer nature, breaks down precisely be-cause in Rand's philosophy *man is wholly a part of nature*. He is a natural product of nature, not the special creation of a supernatural Creator. The distinction Rand made between the peaceful bene-factors of mankind who have sought only to conquer nature and the violent malefactors of mankind who have only lusted for power over their fellow human beings is obscured by the fundamental premise of Objectivist theology that man is wholly a natural being. Because Rand repudiated the idea of the special creation of man by a rational, omnipotent God, she committed herself to the destruc-tion of man. Because she is a naturalist, the conquest of nature is, finally, the conquest of man.

I am only making clear what man's conquest of nature really means and especially that final stage in the conquest, which, perhaps, is not far off. The final stage is come when man by eugenics, by pre-natal conditioning, and by an edu-cation and propaganda based on a perfect applied psychol-ogy, has obtained full control over himself. Human nature

[90] *Lectures on the Essence of Religion*, 21.

[91] Engels, *Dialectics of Nature*, in Wette, *Dialectical Materialism*, 493-494.

will be the last part of nature to surrender to man. The battle will then be won.[92]

What Rand (and others) have disguised in the phrase "man's conquest of nature," is the fact that "What we call man's power is, in reality, a power possessed by some men which they may, or may not, allow other men to profit by."[93] What we call man's power over nature turns out to be a "power exercised by some men over other men with nature as its instrument."[94]

When Ayn Rand made man his own creator, giving him the power to choose to be a man or not, she also made man his own destroyer. Her total and complete repudiation of Christianity as lies hatched by the minds of men[95] has put her in the position of repudiating man. Such a conclusion was to be expected: When she repudiated the God of the Bible, she also began the inexorable sequence of thought that must conclude in the elimination of the image of God: man.[96]

Man's conquest of nature, if the dreams of some scientific planners are realized, means the rule of a few hundreds of men over billions upon billions of men. There

---

[92] C. S. Lewis, *The Abolition of Man*, 72.

[93] *The Abolition of Man*, 68.

[94] *The Abolition of Man*, 69. "It is, of course, a commonplace to complain that men have hitherto used badly, and against their fellows, the powers that science has given them. But that is not the point I am trying to make. I am not speaking of the particular corruptions and abuses which an increase of moral virtue would cure: I am considering what the thing called 'man's power over nature' must always and essentially be."

[95] "Religious abstractions are the product of man's mind, not of supernatural revelation" (*The Objectivist*, March 1968, 4).

[96] "The source of all contrasts between paganism and Christianity is the difference in their concepts of God. In any system the ultimate principle determines the form of the whole and shows its implications in the details of ethics, physics, and epistemology" (Gordon H. Clark, *Thales to Dewey*, 183).

neither is nor can be any simple increase of power on man's side. Each new power won by man is a power over man as well. Each advance leaves him weaker as well as stronger. In every victory, besides being the general who triumphs, he is also the prisoner who follows the triumphal car.[97]

Rand's theology, of course, did not consist merely of two gods, man and nature, but of billions of gods. Each sovereign individual is his own god, his own "I." This is part of the appeal of her books. This polytheism also leads to all sorts of conflicts among the gods, and we shall get a glimpse of those conflicts in the next chapter.

---

[97] *The Abolition of Man*, 71.

5

IMAGINING VALUES
OBJECTIVIST ETHICS

In every system of morality, which I have hitherto met with, I have always remark'd, that the author proceeds for some time in the ordinary way of reasoning, and establishes the being of a God, or makes observations concerning human affairs; when of a sudden I am surpriz'd to find, that instead of the usual copulations of propositions, *is,* and *is not*, I meet with no proposition that is not connected with an *ought*, or an *ought not*. This change is imperceptible; but is, however, of the last consequence. For as this *ought*, or *ought not*, expresses some new relation or affirmation, 'tis necessary that it shou'd be observ'd and explain'd; and at the same time that a reason should be given, for what seems altogether inconceivable, how this new relation can be a deduction from others; which are entirely different from it. But as authors do not commonly use this precaution, I shall presume to recommend it to the readers; and am persuaded, that this small attention wou'd subvert all the vulgar systems of morality, and let us see, that the distinction of vice and virtue is not founded merely on the relations of objects; nor is perceiv'd by reason.

David Hume
Treatise of Human Nature

Imagining Values

> So convenient a thing it is to be a reasonable creature,
> since it enables one to find or make a reason for everything
> one has a mind to do.
>
> Benjamin Franklin
> *Autobiography*

Ayn Rand believed that she answered some important questions in ethics; it is our duty to examine her answers for their logical consistency, for therein lies the possibility of their truthfulness. Her ethical system rests upon her claim to have derived the *ought* from the *is*, which David Hume denied to be possible. The central argument for and statement of her ethics appears in the essay "The Objectivist Ethics," chapter 1 of *The Virtue of Selfishness*. It is with this essay that we shall largely concern ourselves.

Definitions

Rand began by defining "morality, or ethics" as "a code of values to guide man's choices and actions—the choices and actions that determine the purpose and the course of his life."[1] This is an ambiguous statement, and the first question that must be asked is whether the latter phrase is more restrictive than the former, that is, does man need a "code of values" to guide *all* his "choices and actions" or *only* "the choices and actions that determine the purpose and the course of his life"? Or are the two phrases synonymous? If not, how does one distinguish between the two classes of actions? In short, did Rand believe in good, bad, and indifferent actions, or only good and bad actions? Unfortunately, she never told us.[2]

---

[1] *The Virtue of Selfishness*, 13.

[2] "Secondly, while she provides us with a theory of 'value' . . . she does not go on to define any sort of practical criteria for choosing between values. At basis, she leaves a large number of significant questions unanswered: Are some types of wealth . . . preferable to others? Do material values differ in kind or only in degree? . . . Is quantitative profit the sole criterion for choosing between alternative courses of action? . . ." (William F. O'Neill, *With Charity Toward None*, 177). O'Neill's point, of course, is that Rand did not furnish us with a useful ethical system at all.

Rand insisted that the first question one must ask in any discussion of ethics is not *which* moral system should man accept, but rather, Does man need a moral code at all, and, if so, why?[3] It is upon this question that we must concentrate, she says, if we wish to construct a valid meta-ethical theory. It is ironic, given the direction in which Rand developed her ethical theory, that the fundamental question in her meta-ethical inquiry is based on need: Does man *need* a moral code? As we shall see, need, or at least perceived need, plays an indispensable role in Rand's ethics. There is, of course, no ethical value or import in "need," until an argument can demonstrate that value. Here at the beginning of her ethics, here in her meta-ethical theory, Rand simply assumes that because one needs something, one ought to have it. Specifically, because men need a code of value, they ought to have one. Hume would chortle at this shift from one relation to another. Rand apparently never realized that her entire ethical theory rests on the morally loaded term *need*.

After raising her initial question, however, Rand lapsed into a digression that we must reluctantly pass over at this point.[4] She came finally to an important issue, a definition of *value*. " 'Value' is that which one acts to gain and/or keep."[5] It follows, of course, that anything can be a value: snorting cocaine, frequenting prostitutes, stealing money, achieving health, engaging in altruistic actions, and so on. Value, moreover, "is not a primary; it presupposes an answer to the question: of value to whom and for what? It presupposes an entity capable of acting to achieve a goal in the face of an alternative. Where no alternative exists, no goals and no values are possible."

The first inkling of waiting disaster should be the assertion that value presupposes the answer to the question, of value to whom and for what? Value, then, presupposes value.

---

[3] See the opening pages of *The Virtue of Selfishness*.

[4] *The Virtue of Selfishness*, 14-15.

[5] *The Virtue of Selfishness*, 15.

Rand proceeded to quote from Galt, that is, herself,[6] about "indestructible matter," which is opposed to "living organisms," which, far from being indestructible, are very fragile. In that distinction, said Rand, lies the clue to a rational ethical system: "It is only a living organism that faces a constant alternative: the issue of life or death. . . . It is only the concept of 'life' that makes the concept of 'value' possible."[7]

The Alternative

The alternatives living organisms face are existence or nonexistence, life or death, survival or decease. One must not lose sight of the fact that it is biological survival that forms the basis of Rand's ethics. Physical survival. It is the concept of biological life—not man's life, nor man *qua* man—that makes the concept value intelligible. On Rand's own terms, it is *physical survival* which forms the indispensable basis for a code of morality: "What standard determines what is proper in this context? The standard is the organism's life, or: that which is required for the organism's survival."[8] To be certain she was not misunderstood, Rand repeated her statement: "An organism's life is its standard of value: that which furthers its life is the good, that which threatens it is the evil."[9]

[6] "Perhaps Miss Rand's favorite type of verification is self-quotation. She never tires of quoting her own eloquent words, frequently expressed by various characters in her novels, in order to establish a point. *Atlas Shrugged* frequently assumes the proportions of sacred writ in her subsequent writings" (*With Charity Toward None*, 22).

[7] *The Virtue of Selfishness*, 15-16. "The existence of inanimate [Rand should have said inorganic] matter is unconditional, the existence of life is not; it depends on a specific course of action. Matter is indestructible, it changes its forms, but it cannot cease to exist" (*Atlas Shrugged*, 1012).

[8] *The Virtue of Selfishness*, 16.

[9] *The Virtue of Selfishness*, 7. "The falseness of a given judgment does not constitute an objection against it, so far as we are concerned. . . . The real question is how far a judgment furthers and maintains life. . . . We are, in fact, fundamentally inclined to maintain that the falsest judgments . . . are the most indispensable to us . . ." (Friedrich Nietzsche, *Beyond Good and Evil*, I, 4). Nietzsche

Rand immediately began to muddy the waters to hide her next move. The muddying is accomplished in part by the use of the vague and indefinite verb "furthers." Does "furthers" mean extend temporally, or to increase the "quality of life"? Of course, if physical survival is the standard, it must mean extend temporally, for there is no basis on which to judge between different qualities of life. There is only quantity—length—of life. Rand stressed the point: "the fact that living entities exist and function necessitates the existence of values and of an ultimate value, which for any given living entity is its own life."[10] Here is pure subjectivism, renamed Objectivism.

"The fact that a living entity *is*, determines what it ought to do. So much for the issue of the relation between 'is' and 'ought'."[11] Unfortunately, "so much" is not quite enough. The fact that a living entity *exists* does not "determine" whether it *ought* to continue in existence. Perhaps it ought to die. From an ethical position quite different from Rand, we can logically assert that many living entities should die: the Ebola virus, the polio virus, child-rapists, kidnappers, mass murderers, and rabid dogs—to name just a few. But in Rand's ethical theory, the "ultimate value" for each of these living entities is "its own life." Her ethics would seem to permit, if not require, murderers to fight against their just punishment. In doing so, they would be acting morally, furthering their own lives.

Rand argued that the great alternative is between life and death, existence and non-existence, physical survival or physical demise. The fact that a living being lives might allow it to choose between alternatives, but it does not decide the choice. Why one should choose to live is the unanswered and, on Rand's ethical theory, the unanswerable question. That Rand's ethics is not a deduction from her axioms about reality may be seen in this statement from *Atlas*

---

recognized the distinction between truth and survival value, between truth and utility. Rand did not and could not, for it would have been fatal to her epistemology as well as her ethics.

[10] *The Virtue of Selfishness,* 17.

[11] *The Virtue of Selfishness*, 17.

Shrugged: "My morality, the morality of reason, is contained in a single axiom: existence exists—and in a single choice: to live. The rest proceeds from these."[12] On what basis Rand makes this most fundamental and important *choice* is not explained and cannot be explained. It is a completely a-moral choice. First need, and now an unjustified and unjustifiable choice, are the basis—the *sine qua non*—on which all other choices are made, on which all other choices depend; but Rand did not give and could not give a reason for acknowledging need or making the choice. She gave us no basis on which to decide the question, To be or not to be?

In ethics, as in every other branch of philosophy, Rand taught a logical contradiction: that biological life is beyond values and the basis for values, and that biological life is the ultimate value. If she had denied that life is the ultimate value, the end in itself, her ethical system would have collapsed for lack of a *summum bonum*. On the other hand, if Rand had denied that life is beyond (the presupposition of) value, her hierarchy of concepts would have collapsed. The confusion, of course, was already contained in her initial and absurd assertion that value presupposes value.

In "The Objectivist Ethics" Rand argued that an indestructible robot could have not values:

> . . . try to imagine an immortal, indestructible robot, an entity which moves and acts, but which cannot be affected by anything, which cannot be changed in any respect, which cannot be damaged, injured, or destroyed. Such an entity would not be able to have any values: it would have nothing to gain or to lose. . . . It could have no interests and no goals.[13]

This analogy, like all analogies, fails, but this particular illustration seems to have been deliberately loaded. If it was meant to illustrate Rand's contention that life, and life alone, is the basis for

---

[12] *Atlas Shrugged*, 1018.

[13] *The Virtue of Selfishness*, 16.

values, then Rand should not have added such touches as that it cannot be affected by anything, cannot be changed in any respect, cannot be damaged or injured. Rand's point, we must keep in mind, is that the great alternative, existence or non-existence, is the *only* alternative that makes values possible or necessary. But that is clearly not true, even within the context of her own argument. Even an immortal robot would face many alternatives that could affect it without killing it. That means, of course, that life—survival—is neither the sole nor the sufficient explanation for ethics. Rand loaded the illustration by denying that the robot can be affected in any way whatever. Had she constructed the illustration correctly, the robot would have been indestructible, but not impassible. There are many alternatives short of life and death that even an inde-structible robot would face. It is false to say that physical survival or death is the only alternative that makes values possible. Life, that is, biological life, may be a prerequisite for valuing and seek-ing goals, but it does not follow therefrom that life must be the ultimate value, or the basis of all values. Mastering arithmetic may be the prerequisite for mastering calculus, but it does not follow that arithmetic is the ultimate value or the end in itself of the math-ematician. Indeed, biological life is merely an instrumental value, so that one may pursue other, more important goals.[14]

Suicide

The question of suicide is not simply one ethical question among many ethical questions. It is logically the most fundamental ques-tion in ethical theory, and every ethical decision implicitly includes a decision to commit or not to commit suicide. The alternative of life and death is not one that is faced once and for all; it is faced every moment of every day; it is part of every choice one makes. Therefore, to place this decision outside one's ethical system is to

---

[14] See the instructive essay by J. Charles King, "Life and the Theory of Value: The Randian Argument Reconsidered," in *The Philosophic Thought of Ayn Rand*, Rasmussen and Den Uyl, editors, 102-121.

place all decisions outside one's ethical system. Until the problem of suicide is solved, no other ethical problem can be.

The fundamental issue of suicide is entirely unresolved by Rand's attempt to construct a rational, that is, secular, ethics. Why one should choose to live is the question forced outside of her ethical system; all the "why's" can be asked only of secondary, subordinate, dependent choices and values. To say that life is the highest (or ultimate) value because the concept value presupposes the concept life is a logical *non sequitur*. To say that one should choose to live because life is the standard of value is to speak nonsense. To say that one must make this most fundamental choice—the choice on which all other choices admittedly depend—without any ethical guidance is to confess the failure of one's attempt to construct a rational ethics. It was apparently easy for Rand to recommend one goal before another, given that the basic choice to live or not to live had already been made. But, as Rand said, that choice is the most fundamental of all, and she furnished no basis on which it may rationally be made. We must conclude that her efforts to derive normative commands from descriptive propositions failed.[15]

Let us return for a moment to a statement Rand made about value: Value "is not a primary; it presupposes an answer to the question: of value to whom and for what?"[16] Now, we can understand Rand's assertion that values are values to a living organism (each individual organism has its own values) for the purpose of furthering its own life. On this schema, the organism's life is not itself a moral value. Rand wished to hold that the greatest good of a living being is its biological survival, and that this highest value is neither good nor evil, but beyond good and evil: "that which furthers its [the organism's] life is the good, that which threatens it is the evil."[17] The initial plausibility of Rand's construction lies in the fact that she has read the "one fundamental alternative in the

---

[15] "The disparity between normative principles and descriptive statements is one of the basic objections to naturalism" (Gordon H. Clark, *William James and John Dewey*, 87).

[16] *The Virtue of Selfishness*, 15.

[17] *The Virtue of Selfishness*, 17.

universe"[18] completely out of her ethical system. Her program is "rational" only if one always evades the "one fundamental alternative." If one has previously chosen to survive, then it becomes plausible to assert that one should choose those means that seem to conduce to one's biological survival. But the questions—Why ought I choose to live, why should I choose survival, why ought I not choose to destroy my life—are not answered and cannot be answered by Objectivist ethics.

Readers of *Atlas Shrugged* will recall that John Galt[19] threatened to commit suicide, should the collectivists capture and torture Dagny Taggart. He explained that it would not be an act of self-sacrifice: "I do not care to live on their terms, I do not care to obey them and I do not care to see you enduring a drawn-out murder. There will be no values for me to seek after that—and I do not care to exist without values. I don't have to tell you that we owe no morality to those who hold us under a gun."[20]

This statement, of course, is empty rhetoric, not substantial argument. Rand had already said that only living beings have values and that they have values because they are living. Here, in a gush of emotion and rhetoric, however, Galt-Rand tells us that Galt's life "after that," that is, after Dagny's death, would be without values for John Galt. On Rand's theory *Dagny* would have no more values because she would be dead, but *Galt*, being a living organism, would and must have values. Rand relied on her considerable literary power and rhetoric to score points with her readers to which she had no logical or philosophical right.

Compare Rand's argument to this argument from Feuerbach:

> But what is this supreme being in man, on whom all other supreme beings, all gods outside him depend? It is

---

[18] *The Virtue of Selfishness*, 15.

[19] It is an odd fact that Rand's attorney was named John Gall. See *Letters of Ayn Rand*.

[20] *Atlas Shrugged*, 1091. In her other novels, the good guys do commit suicide: Andrei in *We, the Living* and Gail Wynand in *The Fountainhead*. Dominque Francon mutilates and almost kills herself in *The Fountainhead*.

the aggregate of all his human drives, needs, predispositions, it is his existence, his life, which encompasses all the rest. Man makes a god or divine being of what his life depends on only because to him his life is a divine being, a divine possession or thing. Men have been known to say that "life is not the highest good"; but only where life is taken in a secondary sense, where man is in a state of unhappiness, of conflict, and his life is not normal. Then, to be sure, he rejects and despises life, but only because his life lacks qualities or advantages that are essential to normal life; only because it has *ceased to be life*. When, for example, a man is deprived of freedom, when he is a slave to arbitrary power, he can and should despise life, but only because it is then a deficient, meaningless life, lacking in the most essential condition and attribute of human life, which is freedom of movement and freedom to exercise his own will. This is also the cause of suicide. A man who kills himself does not take his life, it has already been taken from him. That is why he kills himself; he destroys only a semblance of himself; what he casts away is a mere shell whose kernel, whether by his fault or not, has long since been eaten away. But a healthy normal life—if life is taken to mean the aggregate of the properties pertaining to man—is and should be man's highest good, his supreme being.[21]

Compare this passage from Feuerbach with Rand's words:

Then she [Cheryl Taggart] ran, ran by the sudden propulsion of a burst of power, the power of a creature running for its life, she ran straight down the street, that ended at the river—and in a single streak of speed, with no break, no moment of doubt, with full consciousness of acting in self-preservation, she kept running till the parapet barred her way and, not stopping, went over into space.[22]

---

[21] *Lectures on the Essence of Religion*, 52.

[22] *Atlas Shrugged*, 908.

In these passages lies the explanation of Rand's appeal: Her rhetoric, her ability to tell a story, even her eloquence, are the reasons she has attracted so much attention and will continue to attract attention. It is not her argumentation, which is hopelessly illogical, but the emotional appeal of her stories that keeps Rand's works in print.

Why, to ask the proper question, would not John Galt's or Cheryl Taggart's suicides "be an act of self sacrifice"? Are we to understand that suicide "furthers" their biological survival, as Rand's theory requires? Did Rand forget that whatever does not further survival is evil? Apparently she did, for Rand explicitly wrote that Taggart was "acting in self-preservation" by killing herself. Rand obviously smuggled something other than biological survival into her argument, something to which she had no philosophical claim. If suicide is now good, if the death of the organism is now a moral value, indeed the highest and final value, then all Rand's arguments stating the opposite must be abandoned.

It must be emphasized that this contradiction exists because John Galt is the paragon of egoism, of "rational self-interest," of the virtue of selfishness, and the originator of the Objectivist oath.[23] The contradiction arises because life is the ultimate value, and Galt had previously chosen life. Now, however, he chooses death. Rand, of course, denied, despite the appearances, that there is any real contradiction involved in her perfect egoist committing suicide. In one sense, she might have been right, but it is a sense that she does not explain, indeed could not explain, without subverting her whole argument.

As I have pointed out, in the Objectivist ethics the "one fundamental alternative"—the continued existence or non-existence of living organisms, life or death—is not an ethical choice at all: It is meta-ethical. Rand's ethics is based on the assumption that the prob-

---

[23] "I swear by my life and my love of it, that I will never live for the sake of another man, nor ask another man to live for mine" (*Atlas Shrugged*, 732). Galt swore by his life, because there was nothing greater for him. In Rand's ethical theory, each organism's life is its ultimate value.

lem of suicide has been solved. To put it another way, the "one fundamental choice" between life and death in Rand's philosophy may be made either way, with equal rationality (or irrationality), for Rand offered no ethical guidance or argument on how to make that fundamental choice. When, therefore, Rand made Galt choose suicide, and made Taggart, Wynand, and Andrei commit suicide, there is no contradiction at all between what Rand wrote and what she made her characters do. But Rand can escape the charge of contradiction only by admitting that she has no ethical system at all, and her characters are free to do whatever they please, including killing themselves. Her ethical philosophy is completely compatible with a pro-death, pro-suicide, point of view. What her philosophy cannot logically justify is a pro-life ethic. Rand failed to give a reason why one should choose to live.

I must point out the irony of the situation. Rand claimed to offer an ethics for "living on Earth," a "rational ethics," but her ideal man chose to commit suicide. Rand wrote much about the value of life, but death became her perfect man's highest value. While this outcome is ironic, it must be expected, for Rand did not and could not solve the problem of suicide. Furthermore, like the fundamental choice to think, to focus, the fundamental choice to die is always with us. That choice is not made once, but continually, hourly, as long as one lives. Rand could not offer any *reason* why one should not choose death, and her hero did in fact choose death, when it was convenient for him to do so.

Two of Rand's academic defenders, Douglas J. Den Uyl and Douglas B. Rasmussen, have argued:

> Given that life is a necessary condition for valuation, there is no other way we can value something without also (implicitly at least) valuing that which makes valuation possible. Paradoxically perhaps, we could value not living any longer, but in making such a value [judgment] we must nevertheless value life.[24]

[24] "Nozick on the Randian Argument," *The Personalist*, April 1978, 191.

To the extent that this argument has any merit, it proves the truism that the person who has decided to commit suicide must be alive to do so. It does not demonstrate that the suicide must hold, as Rand argued, life as the ultimate value, or his own life as an end in itself. Living, if it has any value to a person intent on committing suicide at all, has merely an instrumental value: It is needed to achieve death. The argument that the idea of value logically presupposes the idea of life, even if valid, does not imply that one ought to value life. Rand, Rasmussen, and Den Uyl all confuse logical priority with moral obligation.

Pleasure and Pain

The next topic to be discussed is the central role of pleasure and pain in Rand's ethics. Rand inextricably linked good and evil with pleasure and pain:

> The physical sensation of pleasure is a signal indicating that the organism is pursuing the right course of action. The physical sensation of pain is a warning signal of danger, indicating that the organism is pursuing the wrong course of action. . . .[25]

The first thing to be noticed is that Rand emphatically wrote and repeated, "physical sensation."

The second thing to be noticed is that Rand asserted that "Just as sensations are the first step of the development of a human consciousness in the realm of cognition, so they are its first step in the realm of evaluation."[26]

At this point, our earlier analysis of Rand's epistemology must be recalled. If the senses do not provide true information about

---

[25] *The Virtue of Selfishness*, 17-18. If this be so, then using crack and heroin for recreational purposes, and eating arsenic, for it is sweet, are manifestly right.

[26] *The Virtue of Selfishness*, 17. As we have already seen, however, Rand asserted that sensations per se are neither experienced nor remembered.

reality, if they fail in the realm of cognition, why should we suppose they provide truth in the realm of evaluation? If they are unreliable in epistemology, why should we rely on them in ethics?

In the foreword to *Introduction to Objectivist Epistemology* Rand asseverated that "the arguments of those who attack the senses [i.e., the accuracy or reliability of man's senses] are merely variants of the fallacy of the 'stolen concept.' "[27] The argument for such an assertion is absent. We are to take it "for granted."[28] Now we must determine whether Rand believed that the senses as the means of evaluation are as infallible as the senses as the means of cognition. She obviously does so believe, simply because the ethical situation is analogous to the epistemological situation. Since there is no other source of knowledge in her system, sense experience must be the infallible source; since there is no other source of morality in her system, sense experience (pleasure and pain) must be the infallible source. Indeed, there is a great deal of persuasiveness in the argument that, from an Objectivist viewpoint, the two roles of the senses cannot be separated, for morality is within the province of reason, that is, sensation.

If, then, pleasure and pain are trustworthy guides to morality, we have here a formulation for ethical hedonism.[29] Infallible guides to right and wrong courses of action are not to be disobeyed, particularly when such infallible guides are the unique and exclusive source of moral knowledge. Whatever would overrule these sen-

---

[27] *The Virtue of Selfishness*, 9.

[28] For a person who professes not to accept anything on faith, this is a rather peculiar position, just as the title of the book (*Introduction*) is a rather peculiar title. The book is really an excerpt from the middle of an undeveloped epistemological theory, which in turn rests on an enormous *petitio principii*, namely, that sense experience is accurate and reliable, an assumption that sense experience itself refutes.

[29] "Ethical hedonism is the doctrine that pleasure is the standard of moral value, the criterion to be used in determining good and evil, virtue and vice—that the right action in any situation is the action which produces the most pleasure (and/or the least pain)" (Leonard Peikoff, *The Objectivist Newsletter*, February 1962, 7).

sible, infallible guides—pleasure and pain—must be suspect, for on what other basis are contrary judgments to be made? Identification of the good with pleasure and the evil with pain is hedonism. Rand wrote: "Sensations are an automatic response, an automatic form of knowledge, which a consciousness can neither seek nor evade. An organism that possesses only the faculty of sensation is guided by the pleasure-pain mechanism of its body, that is: by an automatic knowledge and an automatic code of values."[30]

With this material in mind, let us turn to a brief essay by Leonard Peikoff detailing the reasons why Objectivism rejects hedonism. Peikoff wrote, "[T]he feeling of pleasure, however, like any emotional response, is not a psychological primary; it is a consequence, an effect, of one's previously formed value-judgments."[31]

Here the conflict is joined: Are pleasures primary (as Rand said they are), "an automatic form of knowledge and an automatic code of values," or are they derivative, "a consequence, an effect" as Peikoff said they are? Or shall the response of the Objectivists be that they are speaking of different "pleasures," that is, equivocating on the word *pleasure*? Or shall they respond that they are referring to the pleasures of irrational animals and the pleasures of rational animals? If the last be their response, then they are obliged to show how the addition of a human consciousness changes the basis of human and animal consciousness, sensations.

In any case, the Objectivists are forced to accept one of the following alternatives: (1) Rand's and Peikoff's statements are contradictory; (2) Peikoff equivocated in using the word *pleasure* in two ways: as a "sensation" and as a "feeling"; or, as an animal sensation and as a rational animal sensation. If Peikoff now wishes to expound on a distinction between a "sensation" and a "feeling" and thereby seek to overcome his at least verbal contradiction of

[30] *The Virtue of Selfishness*, 18-19. I must point out that "automatic knowledge" is the "contradiction" that Objectivists reject in their epistemological argument for "volitional consciousness." Since morality is a code of values, according to Rand, organisms that possess only the faculty of sensation have an automatic morality.

[31] *The Objectivist Newsletter*, February 1962, 7.

Rand, he must simultaneously admit that he has thereby demonstrated that Objectivism does not reject the most thorough-going hedonism of all, that of the Cyrenaics. Peikoff thus either contradicted Rand (and since Rand was the editor of *The Objectivist Newsletter,* Peikoff's argument falls within the canon of Objectivism, and Rand thereby contradicted herself) or he failed to show why Objectivism rejects hedonism. His argument relied upon a pun on the word *pleasure.*

Plants, Animals, and Men

At this point Rand began to expand her argument, differentiating plants, animals, and man, rather than dealing with "living organisms." Plants are simply unconscious, though they are living. In her brief discussion of plants, confusion abounds. Plants

> can survive by means of their automatic physical functions.
> . . . A plant has no choice of action. . . . Nourishment, water, sunlight are the values its nature has set it to seek. . . .
> But whatever the conditions, there is no alternative in a
> plant's function: it acts automatically to further its life. . . .[32]

Unfortunately, we have already been told that value "presupposes an entity capable of acting to achieve a goal in the face of an alternative. When no alternative exists, no goals and no values are possible."[33] Now we are told that values are possible, even though the plant has no alternative. The argument is confused. Do plants have an alternative(s) and thereby have values? Or do they act "automatically" with no alternative(s) and thus have no values? Do they

---

[32] *The Virtue of Selfishness*, 18.

[33] *The Virtue of Selfishness*, 15. Leonard Peikoff later distinguished between a "choice" and an "alternative" and held that while plants have no choice, they do have alternatives. This distinction is quite legitimate, but it simply, by contrast, demonstrates the confusion of Rand's thought.

have alternatives but no choices? Perhaps there is no contradiction lurking in the confusion, but there certainly is no clarity.

Worse, it is biological life—not sentient or intellectual life—that is the basis and standard for ethics, according to Rand. Plants have biological life. Why, then, does she exclude them from having a code of morality?

Epistemology and Ethics

The argument proceeds, not upon ethical grounds, but upon epistemological. Up to this point I have said little about the enormous epistemological assumptions of Rand's ethical theory, but Rand found it necessary to make her epistemology, such as it is, explicit in her discussion of ethics. I shall have to digress as she digressed. Please bear with us.

Rand wrote: "The higher organisms [meaning animals and man] possess the faculty of retaining sensations, which is the faculty of perception."[34] We have already been told, however, that sensation "lasts for the duration of the immediate moment, as long as the stimulus lasts and no longer."[35] How are sensations, which last "no longer" than the stimulus, "retained"? Unfortunately, Rand did not enlighten us on this point. Rand reverted again to asseveration: A "perception is a group of sensations automatically retained and integrated by the brain of a living organism, which gives it the ability to be aware, not of single stimuli, but of entities, of things."[36]

Did Rand wish to assert that not only sensations furnish automatic and infallible knowledge, but also that perceptions do? Apparently she did, for she wrote that an animal is guided "by an integrated awareness of the perceptual reality confronting it."[37]

[34] *The Virtue of Selfishness*, 19.

[35] *The Virtue of Selfishness*, 18.

[36] *The Virtue of Selfishness*, 19.

[37] *The Virtue of Selfishness*, 19. Is "retaining" the same as "remembering"? In *Introduction to Objectivist Epistemology*, Rand said that sensations cannot be remembered.

"[I]ts senses provide it with an automatic code of values, an automatic knowledge of what is good for it or evil. . . ."[38] Animals, apparently, are in the same situation as plants, so far as automatic, unavoidable knowledge, values, and actions go, and the same confusion clouds both discussions. Since their actions and knowledge are unavoidable and automatic, may they be said to have values? But the author of the confusion can no longer dispel it, and I can only point it out.

After this introduction, Rand dropped the bombshell: "Man has no automatic code of survival. . . . His senses do not tell him automatically what is good for him or evil. . . ."[39] The question to be asked is, How did Rand know this? We had previously been informed that the senses provide an "automatic knowledge and an automatic code of values."[40] How do man's senses (or sensations) differ in principle from those of other animals? Why do "infallible guides" in lesser animals suddenly become fallible in the greater animal, man? Do the senses fail as tools of cognition in man, just as they do as tools of evaluation? If not, why not? Can the two, in fact, be separated into discrete functions?

Rand's assertion is immediately followed by this bit of nonsense: "[M]an is the only living entity born without any guarantee of remaining conscious at all."[41] Many living entities are born that

---

[38] The alert reader will recall that the major Objectivist argument supporting "volitional consciousness" is that "automatic knowledge" is alleged to be a contradiction in terms, for knowledge requires a means of validation, which determinism allegedly precludes.

[39] Compare this passage: "Just as the pleasure-pain mechanism of man's body works as a barometer of health or injury, so the pleasure-pain mechanism of his consciousness works on the same principle, acting as a barometer of what is for him or against him . . ." (Nathaniel Branden, *The Virtue of Selfishness*, 61). Unexplained by Branden is the distinction between the pleasures of the body and the pleasures of consciousness. Are not all pleasures of consciousness? Does not the concept of pleasure presuppose the concept consciousness? (Notice, once again, the repeated reference to *mechanism* with regard to both body and consciousness.)

[40] *The Virtue of Selfishness*, 18-19.

[41] *The Virtue of Selfishness*, 19.

never have consciousness, and those that do have consciousness do not have any guarantees of remaining conscious. That is immortality by definition. Apparently we are to conclude that animals are immortal, that is, they have a guarantee of remaining conscious, while man is mortal. Any other meaning would turn on a dangerous equivocation in the word "conscious." From this ambiguity Rand derived what she regarded as a cardinal point in her philosophy: "Man's particular distinction from all other living species is the fact that his consciousness is volitional."[42]

Volitional Consciousness

Earlier we discussed the "fallacy of the stolen concept," by which Rand dismissed attacks on empiricism. That fallacy, as explained by Nathaniel Branden in *The Objectivist Newsletter* and summarized by Rand, is "the act of using a concept while ignoring, contradicting or denying the validity of the concepts on which it logically and genetically depends."[43] I suggest that there could not be a better example of such a fallacy than the statement "man is a being of volitional consciousness," for the simple reason that the concept volition *presupposes* the concept consciousness. Rand and Branden blatantly—brazenly—committed the fallacy of the stolen concept. It is upon this fallacy that Rand based her ethical system. A perceptive reader of *The Objectivist Newsletter* pointed out the problem in the following words: "With regard to the principle that man is a being of volitional consciousness, does not a man have to be thinking already in order to 'choose' to think?"[44]

Nathaniel Branden was assigned the task of answering the question. Branden wrote: "A man's choice to focus is a primary, a first

---

[42] *The Virtue of Selfishness,* 19-20.

[43] *Introduction to Objectivist Epistemology,* 9. We have already discussed this notion in chapters three and four as it impinges on both epistemology and theology. I must point out here that Branden's word "genetically" seems to introduce the genetic fallacy: He should have said only "logically."

[44] *The Objectivist Newsletter,* April 1964, 15.

cause in consciousness."[45] But how can Branden's statement be true? How can a choice be a *first* cause in consciousness? Does *man* choose? If, as Rand wrote in *The Virtue of Selfishness*, "Man has to be man by choice," how can a man choose to be man as a *first* cause? The statement, "man has to be man by choice," is logically absurd, because man must exist before man can choose. As Branden wrote, "The perceptual level, which man shares with animals, is automatic." How can this *automatic* perceptual consciousness choose? Yet Branden, contradicting himself and Rand, wrote:

> [T]here are degrees of consciousness; the alternative is not simply absolute unconsciousness or optimal consciousness. The choice to focus (or to think) does not consist of moving from a state of literal unconsciousness to a state of consciousness. This clearly would be impossible. . . . To focus is to move from a lower level of consciousness to a higher level. . . .[46]

Now, since there are only two levels of consciousness, according to both Rand and Branden, namely animal (perceptual, "automatic") consciousness, and rational animal (conceptual, "volitional") consciousness, we must assume that Branden meant that one moves from animal consciousness to rational animal consciousness by an act of choice. Unfortunately, we have already been instructed that animal consciousness is "automatic," that is, it is incapable of making such choices. How this lower level of consciousness can "choose" to become human is an insoluble problem in Objectivism. It is an insoluble problem within Existentialism as well. Both Rand and the Existentialists taught that for man, existence precedes essence.

Should Branden or Rand have tried to retort that they mean levels of consciousness within a spectrum called "human," they

---

[45] Once one has denied God, his attributes do not disappear; they reappear elsewhere; in this case, as a characteristic of man.

[46] *The Objectivist Newsletter,* April 1964, 15.

have simply begged the question: They have assumed the existence of man *qua* man in order to "prove" that man exists by choice. The Objectivist theory of volitional consciousness—like the Objectivist theory of the *tabula rasa* mind—is logically absurd. The proper and honest answer to the reader's question would have been a candid admission of the internal contradiction in the notion of "volitional consciousness." Unfortunately, that was not the answer given.

Branden ended his argument in this manner: "[W]hen a man is awake and his brain and nervous system are structurally normal, he is conscious—if only passively. This basic level of consciousness is given to him by nature, as it were." Compare Rand's first sentence in *Introduction to Objectivist Epistemology*: "Consciousness, as a state of awareness, is not a passive state, but an active process that consists of two essentials: differentiation and integration."[47] Reconciliation of the two statements is a proper task for only the most befuddled Russian thinker.[48]

Rand continued the argument (which long ago became absurd) by writing: "Man's actions and survival require the guidance of *conceptual* values derived from *conceptual* knowledge. But *conceptual* knowledge cannot be acquired automatically."[49] Again, as before, the requisite argument is missing. We have instead unsupported assertion with which one must agree on pain of being called a mystic or an altruist.

Rand proceeded to define a concept as "a mental integration of two or more perceptual concretes, which are isolated by a process of abstraction and united by means of a specific definition." A little

---

[47] *Introduction to Objectivist Epistemology*, 11.

[48] One further note: Having banned God as first cause, Branden labeled animal consciousness as the "first cause of consciousness." No doubt had Mr. Branden pursued the matter he would soon have arrived at the lowest common denominator and assigned that the office of "first cause." As the apostle Paul explained two thousand years ago, men who will not worship God end up worshiping some aspect of creation.

[49] *The Virtue of Selfishness*, 20. Compare *The New Left*, 156.

later she wrote: "The process of concept-formation does not consist merely of grasping a few simple abstractions, such as 'chair,' 'table,' 'hot,' 'cold,' and of learning to speak." These things are, however, conceptual in nature, as Rand admitted: "Every word of man's language, with the exception of proper names, denotes a concept. . . ." Why then is she insistent upon driving a wedge between such obvious examples of concept formation and what she calls "conceptualizing"? For one reason only: to lend plausibility to her earlier assertion that man's consciousness is volitional. Yet the procedure she describes and then denies to be conceptualizing simply emphasizes the equivocation present in her statement that man is a being of volitional consciousness.

"Reason," we learn, "is the faculty that identifies and integrates the material provided by man's senses. It is a faculty that man has to exercise by choice." Here again is the fallacy of the stolen concept. We are asked to believe that unreasoning men, brutes, make a choice to reason. What is the meaning of the word "choice" in the context of unreasoning men? Do such beings have any more choice than plants or animals?

Free Will and Determinism

In previous chapters we examined the notion of "volitional consciousness" in its epistemological and theological aspects. We must now turn our attention to the Objectivist version of free will.

In *Atlas Shrugged* Rand wrote:

> That which you call your soul or spirit is your consciousness, and that which you call "free will" is your mind's freedom to think or not, the only will you have, your only freedom, the choice that controls all the choices you make and determines your life and your character.[50]

We have already seen the incredible muddle the notion of volitional consciousness creates in epistemology and theology, that is,

[50] *Atlas Shrugged*, 1017.

that one must already be a man before one can "choose" to be a man. It is this absurdity that vitiates any plausibility Rand's doctrine of free will might have, for Rand asserts simultaneously that a man is a man and yet must choose to be a man, and that it is upon this choice made by a man who is not yet a man that all morality hangs.

But the muddle is just beginning. In the quotation above, one choice, the impossible choice, "*controls* all the choices you make, and *determines* your life and your character."

Yet the Objectivists also believe that if man's choices were determined, he would not be responsible for his actions.[51] In their view, freedom—free will—and responsibility are inseparably connected; responsibility, and with it the possibility of and the need for a system of morality, is possible only for a being who is not determined by external factors, but has an autonomous will.

> "Free will"—in the widest sense of the term—is the doctrine which holds that man is capable of performing actions that are not determined by forces outside his control; that man has the power of making choices, which are, causally, primaries—i.e., not necessitated by antecedent factors.[52]

Yet the Objectivists also asserted that choices and actions made by man are *not* free, but are determined. Nathaniel Branden expressed the Objectivist position quite clearly:

> When a man chooses to pursue a given course of action, the cause of his action is the mental operations that

---

[51] "A man's behavior, i.e., his actions, proceed from his values and premises, which in turn proceed, in the context of knowledge available to him, from his thinking or non-thinking. His actions may be said to be free in that they are under the control of a faculty which is free, i.e., which functions volitionally. That is the reason why a man is held responsible for his actions" (Nathaniel Branden, *The Objectivist*, February 1966, 9-10.

[52] Nathaniel Branden, *The Objectivist Newsletter*, January 1964, 3.

precede his choice; these mental operations express and are the result of his values, premises, knowledge and thinking—whether he is fully aware of it or not. Sometimes, through incompetence at introspection, a man is ignorant of the causes of his actions; sometimes ... the preceding mental operations are so rapid that he is unconscious of them. But the choice to perform an action is not and cannot be an irreducible, causal primary.

The Objectivists asserted, then, that man both has free will and does not have free will. He has free will in one choice only—the choice to think—and he does not have free will in any other choice.

The primary choice to think[53]—i.e., to focus one's mind, to set it to the purpose of active integration—must be distinguished from any other category of choice. It must be distinguished from the decision to think about a particular subject, which depends on one's values, interests, knowledge and context; and it must be distinguished from the decision to perform a particular physical action, which again depends on one's values, interests, knowledge and context. These decisions involve causal antecedents of a kind which the choice to focus does not.[54]

Unfortunately, the argument establishing the logical distinction between the choice to focus and all other choices seems to be missing. The Objectivist theory of free will rests upon pure asseveration. Are we to understand that this choice, which is not made once, but hourly, repeatedly, is not influenced or determined by "one's values, interests, knowledge, and context"? On what grounds are we to accept Branden and Rand's assertion that this one choice is made in a causal vacuum? The Objectivists presented an argument detailing the alleged "contradiction of determinism," but as

[53] As you recall, in *Atlas Shrugged* the primary choice is to live or die.

[54] Nathaniel Branden, *The Objectivist Newsletter*, April 1964, 15.

we have seen, the argument does not hold water: It is invalid if one is referring to that form of divine determinism, predestination, as taught in the Bible. The Objectivists should have presented a theory of free will supported by arguments, by evidence—and this they have not done. Yet it is upon this unsupported and contradictory theory that the Objectivist ethics rests—surely a poor foundation for an ethical system that was supposed to revolutionize philosophical thought. Worse, it is upon this impossible choice made in a causal vacuum that the nobility of man allegedly rests: "[M]an, who has no automatic values, has no automatic sense of self-esteem and must earn it by shaping his soul in the image of his moral ideal, in the image of Man, the rational being he is born able to create, but must create by choice."[55]

The attentive reader will not have overlooked the similarity between Rand's and Kant's doctrines of the autonomy of the will. A long quotation from Kant will reinforce the belief that far from being antipodes in philosophy, Rand and Kant occupy common ground at times:

> Nature has willed[56] that man should produce entirely by his own initiative everything which goes beyond the mechanical ordering of his animal existence, and that he should not partake of any other happiness or perfection than that which he has procured for himself without instinct and by his own reason. For nature does nothing unnecessarily and is not extravagant in the means employed to reach its ends. Nature gave man reason, and freedom of will based upon his endowments. For it showed that man was not meant to be guided by instinct[57] or equipped and instructed by innate knowledge; on the contrary, he was meant to produce everything out of himself. Everything had to be en-

---

[55] Ayn Rand, *Atlas Shrugged*, 1020-1021.

[56] Kant, like Rand, also committed the pathetic fallacy.

[57] "An 'instinct' is an unerring and automatic form of knowledge" (Galt's rodomontade, 1013).

tirely of his own making—the discovery of a suitable diet, of clothing, of external security and defence. . . . It seems as if nature had intended that man, once he had finally worked his way up from the uttermost barbarism to the highest degree of skill, to inner perfection in his manner of thought and thence (as far as is possible on Earth) to happiness, should be able to take for himself the entire credit for doing so and have only himself to thank for it. It seems that nature has worked more with a view to man's rational self-esteem than to his mere well-being.[58]

The Objectivists are caught in the contradiction of maintaining that man is determined to be undetermined, forced to be free, and a product of nature which is not a secondary but a primary cause. Placing man inextricably within a web of mechanistic causation— just as Kant did—they roundly assert that he is really free. Believing man to be capable of knowing the truth, they maintain that he is a highly organized collocation of atoms, that his consciousness is a recent epiphenomenon of unconscious matter, that he is not a rational creature of the logical God, but the accidental product of the mindless universe. Holding these positions, they encounter a contradiction that Kant also encountered—and tried to escape by creating the noumenal and the phenomenal worlds.

> The union of causality as freedom with causality as the mechanism of nature, the first being given through the moral law and the latter through natural law, and both as related to the same subject, man, is impossible unless man is conceived by pure consciousness as a being in itself in relation to the former, but by empirical reason as appearance in relation to the later. Otherwise the self-contradiction of reason is unavoidable.[59]

[58] Kant, *Political Writings*, 43.

[59] Immanuel Kant, *Critique of Practical Reason*, 6n3.

The insistence of the Objectivists that the choice to focus one's mind is unique, always possible to man, and never determined or influenced by external factors as other choices are, is a reversion to the noumenal world of Kant, the world that is uninfluenced by the events of the phenomenal world. It is only by the invention of two such entirely disparate categories of choice that the Objectivists could hope to forestall further collapse of their edifice—and yet such an invention carries them back into the arms of Immanuel Kant, whom they profess to abhor. The noumenal choice—to think —is to be distinguished from phenomenal choices—to think about something, to perform an action. Yet what is the meaning of the choice "to think" apart from "to think about something"? One cannot choose to think about nothing. Yet that is what the noumenal choice to think implies.[60]

To muddle the notions of volitional consciousness and free will further, the Objectivists do not always seem to imply that the primary choice is a primary at all:

> In some cases, the motive of non-thinking is anti-effort, i.e., a disinclination to exert the energy and accept the responsibility that thinking requires. In other cases, the motive is some wish, desire or feeling which one wants to

---

[60] "Such, then, is the distinctive nature of the Objectivist theory of free will: it locates man's volition, not in the sphere of action or desire [the phenomenal world], but in the sphere of cognition [the noumenal world]—in the choice to activate his mind or to suspend it" (Nathaniel Branden, *The Objectivist Newsletter*, January 1964, 3).

Although the Objectivists maintained that the choice to "focus" is the only and primary choice, which is not subject to past experiences, values, desires as other choices are, they also maintained, "The more consistently and conscientiously a man maintains a policy of being in full mental focus, of thinking, of judging the facts of reality that confront him, of knowing what he is doing and why, the easier and more 'natural' the process becomes (Nathaniel Branden, *The Objectivist*, February 1966, 8). "Conversely, the more a man maintains a policy of focusing as little as possible, and of evading any facts he finds painful to consider, the more he sabotages himself psychologically—and the more difficult the task of thinking becomes for him" (9).

indulge and which one's reason cannot sanction. . . . In other cases, the motive is escape from fear. . . . These motives are not causal imperatives; they are feelings which a man may choose to treat as decisive.[61]

A question we have asked before again arises: If a person can make free choices in this matter, if he can choose to regard or disregard these motives, then on what grounds did the Objectivists deny that a person can disregard motives in other situations? No grounds, of course, were stated. The argument ultimately comes down to this: Ayn Rand said so. Asseveration supplanted argument, rhetoric supplanted logic—and acceptance of Objectivism requires one to swallow contradictions.

The Objectivists presented the contradictions themselves: "In a given moment, a man may be so overcome by a violent [*violent*? perhaps *strong*?] emotion—particularly fear—that he may find it difficult or impossible to think clearly."[62] If this be so, then the choice to think is not a primary, and a man may not disregard his motives. Yet on the same page Branden reasserted the contradictory Objectivist position that man does indeed have a choice to think.[63] He wavered between asserting free will and admitting determinism:

A man's social environment can provide incentives to think or it can make the task harder. . . . But the social en-

---

[61] Nathaniel Branden, *The Objectivist*, February 1966, 7. Is the choice to treat these feelings as decisive determined?

[62] *The Objectivist*, February 1966, 9.

[63] "An incentive is not a necessitating cause. The fact that a man has good reasons to want to think about some issue, does not guarantee that he will do so; it does not compel him to think." On page 10 Branden wrote: "As to man's desires and emotions, a man cannot will them in or out of existence directly; but he is not compelled to act on them if and when he considers them inappropriate." Here it is the phenomenal choices which are free—an inversion of the central Objectivist contention that in fact a man's desires and emotions and related factors *do* determine all man's actions except one.

vironment cannot determine a man's thinking or non-thinking. It cannot force him to exert the effort and accept the
responsibility of cognition and it cannot force him to
evade; . . . In this issue, man is inviolably a self regulator.[64]

It is conceivable, of course, that a young child could be
subjected, from the first months and years of his life, to
such extraordinarily vicious irrationality . . . that it would
be impossible for him to develop normally, impossible to
establish any firm base of knowledge on which to build.[65]

Here, of course, in this impossibility, free will has disappeared.

Man Qua Man

An important reason for Rand's equivocation on the word "consciousness" came to light later in her essay when she tried to substitute the survival of "man *qua* man" for man *qua* living being.
She said and repeated: "Consciousness—for those living organisms
which possess it—is the basic means of survival."[66] For man, "the
basic means of survival is reason."[67] How she substituted the survival of "man *qua* man" for mere physical survival is a lesson in
clever and invalid argumentation. After much rhetoric, Rand wrote:
"The standard of value of the Objectivist ethics—the standard by
which one judges what is good or evil—is man's life, or: that which
is required for man's survival *qua* man."[68] In making such a statement Rand begged all ethical questions. By what steps did the
argument move from physical survival as the ethical standard to

[64] *The Objectivist*, February 1966, 10.

[65] *The Objectivist,* February 1966, 11.

[66] *The Virtue of Selfishness*, 18, 21. "Man's mind is his basic tool of survival"
(*Atlas Shrugged*, 1012).

[67] *The Virtue of Selfishness*, 21. "The fact that reason is your means of survival
. . ." (*Atlas Shrugged*, 1012).

[68] *The Virtue of Selfishness*, 23.

"man *qua* man," that is, to a standard already bristling with value judgments? Rand provided no steps. It was one small step for Rand, but one giant leap for logic.[69]

Making this substitution permitted Rand to attack as "evil" an action that leads to physical survival, because it does not lead to the quality of life she implicitly and without argument selected as proper for man.[70] Rand smuggled ethics into her system by the backdoor: She switched the fundamental ethical standard from survival to the highest quality of life. Perhaps it is best to emphasize here that the *physical* survival of man is in fact the survival of man *qua* man. After all, man does not become a plant or an animal simply because he wants to survive at any price. Rand, however, denied that physical survival and the survival of man *qua* man are equivalent. Therefore, what Rand meant by the phrase "man *qua* man" is already ethically loaded.

Rand's surreptitious introduction of a moral standard without any argument illuminates the importance of what might be called the doctrine of forfeiture in her ethics and politics: The doctrine consists of the notion that men who act in a certain way or ways forfeit their humanity.[71] John Locke relied upon this doctrine in his

---

[69] Rand's notion that man's "nature" determines what he ought to do was standard fare for eighteenth century atheists. Holbach, for example, wrote: "The morality suitable to man should be founded on the nature of man" (*Systeme Social*, I, 58). Going back even further, the Stoic philosopher and tyrant, Marcus Aurelius, wrote: "nothing is evil which is according to Nature" *(Meditations*, II, 17).

[70] "The man who, in any and all circumstances, would place his physical self-preservation above any other value, is not a lover of life, but an abject traitor to life—to the human mode of life—who sees no difference between the life proper to a rational being and the life of a mindless vegetable. His treason is not that he values his life too much, but that he values it too little" (Nathaniel Branden, *The Objectivist Newsletter*, April 1964, 15-16).

[71] "No, you do not have to live as a man; it is an act of moral choice. But you cannot live as anything else [note well]—and the alternative is that state of living death [note the rhetorical use of a contradiction] which you now see within you and around you, that state of a thing unfit for existence, no longer human [note well] and less than animal [note well], a thing that knows nothing but pain and drags itself through its span of years in the agony of unthinking self-destruction" (*Atlas Shrugged*, 1015).

Treatise of Civil Government in the seventeenth century. (I shall have occasion to return to the doctrine in the chapter on Rand's politics.) The doctrine assumes that men are volitional humans, that man makes himself. Rand wrote: "Nothing is given to man on earth except a potential and the material on which to actualize it. The potential is a superlative machine:[72] his consciousness; but it is a machine without a spark plug, a machine of which his [whose?] own will[!] has to be the spark plug, the self-starter and the driver. ... Man has to be man—by choice. ..."[73]

To return to the argument proper: Rand was unwilling to admit that men remain men as long as they live, and unwilling to admit that men may survive by immoral means, because such statements would undermine her ethical philosophy. Despite her efforts to camouflage her smuggling of unwarranted value judgments into her ethics, the phrase "the life proper to man" indicates that such smuggling has taken place. "Man *qua* man" is a *petitio principii*: It assumes that the problem of ethics has been solved. Rand makes a leap from physical survival and ethical hedonism as the basis for ethics at the beginning of her argument, to something called "man *qua* man," details to be furnished later. Rand wrote: ". . . man has to choose his course, his goals, his values in the context and terms of a lifetime."[74] To ask the proper question: Why? All Rand had warrant for saying (if we disregard her logical blunders thus far) is that man must choose to survive, and one does not survive lifetime by lifetime, but moment by moment. The concept "lifetime" is another meaningless notion in this context: One does not know, nor can one know, how long a lifetime is. It may be one minute or it may be threescore and ten years. What Rand arbitrarily demanded is that one make choices on the basis of an unknown, and an unknowable, factor. On the other hand, sensations, as she said, are immediately known, because they are moment-by-moment sense

---

[72] It is remarkable—and entirely consistent with her materialism—how Rand continually referred to man's mind as a "mechanism" and a "machine."

[73] *The Virtue of Selfishness*, 22-23.

[74] *The Virtue of Selfishness*, 24.

experience. By what valid argument has the basis of action been shifted from infallible sensation to an indefinite factor called a "lifetime"? The argument I am making, please note, is not that men must not plan ahead: They ought to, and Objectivists, like all atheists, should plan ahead much further than they do. That is not the issue. The issue is, How does Rand support her contention that men must plan for a lifetime? As a Christian, I can give reasons and argumentation for my belief in planning in terms of a lifetime; I do not leap as Rand does from physical survival to "the life proper to man," from short-term survival to lifetime-planning. The desirability of the conclusion is no substitute for argument, and those who allow themselves to be deceived by arguments because they like the conclusions are poor philosophers.

Rand made her substitution of the new standard, and her contradiction, explicit: "It does not mean a momentary or a merely physical survival." "The Objectivist ethics holds man's life as the standard of value—and his own life as the ethical purpose of every individual man."[75] If one has not yet grasped the magnitude of the philosophical smuggling which has occurred here, let me repeat Rand's initial proposition: "An organism's life is its standard of value: that which furthers its life is the good, that which threatens it is the evil."[76] The contradiction between the two propositions is glaring. For the organism's life, that is, physical survival, Rand substituted "man's life." She hastened to define "standard" as the ethical norm, "an abstract principle that serves as a measurement or gauge to guide a man's choices in the achievement of a concrete, specific purpose."[77] What she failed to establish by valid argumentation, namely, a basis for an ethical system, she attempted to establish by rhetoric. The rhetoric flows uninterruptedly until the end of the essay ten pages later. It is through this extensive use of rhetoric, asseveration, and ipsedixitisms that Rand sought to es-

[75] *The Virtue of Selfishness*, 25.

[76] *The Virtue of Selfishness*, 17.

[77] *The Virtue of Selfishness*, 25.

tablish her ideas in the minds of her readers, and she succeeded to a remarkable degree. I have attempted to deal with what little serious argument she used; I shall not attempt to match her remarkable powers of asseveration.

Excursus on Good and Evil

Rand's view of man as morally neutral at birth, is, of course, not a new idea, and it has a history. Perhaps the most famous advocate of the idea in the history of Christian theology was Pelagius, a fourth century theologian, whose theories were demolished by Augustine. Augustine's arguments work equally well against Rand. Perhaps her central argument is that from causality.

If man is morally neutral at birth, if he makes himself by his actions, if he is a being of self-made soul, how does this morally neutral being commit evil acts? Evil acts can easily be explained on the basis of Biblical theology, which teaches that men do evil things because they are first sinners. Their ideas and actions, their fruit, reveal what sort of men they are. But the fruit do not make the tree. The tree makes the fruit. It seems that Rand, like Pelagius, got cause and effect reversed. Apples do not make a tree an apple tree. Rather, an apple tree, because it is not neutral, bears apples. Actions do not make men evil; evil actions reveal the nature of men. Things act, as Rand was fond of saying, according to their own nature. But Rand would have us believe that men at birth have no moral nature, that their moral nature—their soul—is something that they create through their action. In this aspect of her thinking, she was as irrational as any Existentialist. Just as a *tabula rasa* consciousness is a contradiction in terms, so is a *tabula rasa* moral nature. A being of self-made soul is a contradiction, because nothing can cause itself.

There is, however, a further problem with Rand's view of good and evil. At times she wished to say that only actions are evil or good; at other times, many other times, she said that thoughts are evil or good. She wished, for example, to deny that one could have evil thoughts, because she wished to oppose censorship. But she regarded Kant, for example, as the most evil man who ever lived. Now, what did Kant do except think and express his thoughts? Did he murder Jews? Did he exterminate the Kulaks? Yet Kant is more evil, according to Rand, than Stalin or Hitler, because he furnished the ideas that made them possible. Now I happen to agree with Rand that thoughts, just as much as actions, can be good or evil, and that some evil thoughts are worse than some evil actions. Moreover, all evil actions originate in evil thoughts. I believe these things, however, on the basis of what the Bible says; Rand cannot appeal to the Bible. The problem for Rand is her ethical system, which permits only actions—actions that threaten one's survival—to be evil.

Conclusion

In conclusion, Rand sought to derive an ethical system from a metaphysical axiom and a meta-ethical choice.[78] This primary choice—the choice to live—is made amorally: It is not part of her ethical system, but prior to it. Rand failed to solve the problem of suicide, and all her ethical philosophy is an evasion of this fundamental question. She castigated those who disagreed with her—as though this choice were part of a rational ethical system, and she relied on rhetoric to score her points. She attacked those who do not accept her ethics of rational self-interest as holding a "Morality of Death. Death is the standard of your values, as death is your chosen goal. . . ."[79] This condemnation is pronounced by John Galt in a tone of moral self-righteousness, when, in fact, Rand had and could have no logical objection to those who do "choose death," because that choice is outside of her ethical system. In fact, death was *Galt's* chosen goal at one point. Given her premises, Rand could not logically say that such a choice and such a standard are wrong, because they are meta-ethical. Rand therefore has no logical basis from which to criticize "mystic" or "altruist" ethics.

---

[78] "My morality, the morality of reason, is contained in a single axiom: existence exists—and in a single choice: to live. The rest proceeds from these" (*Atlas Shrugged*, 1018).

[79] *Atlas Shrugged*, 1025.

Rand's ethical philosophy led to some odd conclusions. For example, even though she stressed the importance of right thinking, she wrote: "There are no evil thoughts except the refusal to think."[80] Only actions—and not all actions at that—could be evil. So the thought of murder, theft, idolatry, altruism, and lust could not be evil. Moreover, her ethics are not applicable to emergencies. One could morally kill those in the lifeboat if their continued existence was a threat to one's own life.[81] Rand justified murder.

Furthermore, as we have seen, even given the choice to live, Rand's morality of "rational self-interest" is a *non sequitur*, for "to live" as opposed to "to die" can only mean physical survival. It most certainly does not mean something called the life of "man *qua* man," for this is precisely the question Rand ought to be answering: What is the life proper to man? For her to assume that ``man's life" is the standard in ethics is a *petitio principii*. Unfortunately, few readers of Rand's works have become aware of the philosophical smuggling in which Rand engaged, especially her attempt to construct an ethics and politics. One might well keep in mind Gordon Clark's warning on humanist ethical theory:

> Even if the humanist professes to discover in experience certain moral ideals and spiritual values that are at least superficially similar to those of the Bible, it can well be supposed that he actually learned them from his Christian heritage and not from an independent study of nature and man. The kindly atmosphere of humanitarianism is notably absent from societies to which the Christian message has not been taken.[82]

In view of such a warning, it is curious to note that Rand bestowed her greatest praise for Christianity on its ethics: "His [Kant's] ver-

---

[80] Quoted in *The Ideas of Ayn Rand*, 117.

[81] See "The Ethics of Emergencies" in *The Virtue of Selfishness*.

[82] Gordon H. Clark, "Special Divine Revelation as Rational," in *God's Hammer: The Bible and Its Critics*, 65.

sion of morality makes the Christian one sound like a healthy, cheerful, benevolent code of selfishness. Christianity merely told man to love his neighbor as himself; that's not exactly rational—but at least it does not forbid man to love himself."[83]

Indeed, her list of virtues contains some that bear a superficial resemblance to Christianity, and since her ethics of rational self-interest[84] has no rational justification, one must conclude that she smuggled a good deal into Objectivism from Christianity. Unfortunately she failed to smuggle all of Christianity into Objectivism, and thus undermined whatever might be of value in her system. Unlike Nietzsche, Rand failed to realize that:

> When one gives up the Christian faith, one pulls the right to Christian morality out from under one's feet. This morality is by no means self-evident: this point has to be exhibited again and again, despite the English flatheads. Christianity is a system, a whole view of things thought out together. By breaking one main concept out of it, the faith in God, one breaks the whole: nothing necessary remains in one's hands.[85]

---

[83] Ayn Rand, "Faith and Force," 7. Rand saved most of her vitriol for Kant: "The monster is Immanuel Kant." "Kant is the most evil man in mankind's history" (*The Objectivist*, September 1971, 3-4). In a 1946 letter to a fan Rand wrote of Jesus: "There is a great, basic contradiction in the teachings of Jesus. Jesus was one of the first great teachers to proclaim the basic principle of individualism . . . the basic principle of Jesus—the preeminence of one's own soul . . ." (*Letters of Ayn Rand*, 287-288).

[84] This ethic leads Rand to a peculiar horror of "sacrifice," which she illustrated by saying: "If you exchange a penny for a dollar, it is not a sacrifice; if you exchange a dollar for a penny, it is" (*Atlas Shrugged*, 1028). Unfortunately, this definition is at odds with the meaning of *sacrifice*, and when Rand encountered a writer who spoke of sacrifice, she invariably imputed her definition to him, and sought thereby to demonstrate how despicable anyone who speaks of sacrifice is. Rand should have gone to more baseball games.

[85] *Twilight of the Idols*, 515-516.

6

IMAGINING JUSTICE, PEACE, AND FREEDOM
OBJECTIVIST POLITICS

> Aristotle and Rousseau, not to mention Spengler, have
> come to a common conclusion in politics: totalitarianism.
> Since these men had such different backgrounds, this agree-
> ment seems to be more than a coincidence. It must be the
> result of a common presupposition held, perhaps uncon-
> sciously, by them all. This underlying presupposition seems
> to be a non-theistic world view.
>
> Gordon H. Clark
> *A Christian View of Men and Things*

Objectivism's political theory rests on its ethics:

> Since every political system rests on some theory of
> ethics, I suggest to those readers who are actually inter-
> ested in understanding the nature of capitalism, that they
> read first *The Virtue of Selfishness*, . . . which is a neces-
> sary foundation for this present book.[1]

If the Objectivist ethics is internally contradictory, as I have

---

[1] Ayn Rand, *Capitalism: The Unknown Ideal*, ix. "Politics is based on three
other philosophical disciplines: metaphysics, epistemology, and ethics . . . " (vii).

180

demonstrated in the previous chapter, then the foundation upon which the Objectivist theory of politics must be built is missing.

Objectivists "advocate capitalism because it is the only system geared to the life of a rational being"[2] However, Rand did not establish the "life of a rational being" as an ethical norm in *The Virtue of Selfishness*. Therefore, the Objectivist position in politics rests upon an unproved ethical theory. This alone would be enough to discredit their politics, but internal criticism of Objectivist political thought becomes necessary for a complete critique of the philosophy, and to demonstrate once again that all secular philosophy, because it is non-Christian, is internally contradictory. In addition, secular political philosophy is either anarchist or totalitarian, if indeed an intelligible distinction can be made between the two.[3] As we shall see, Rand's political philosophy is anarchist first, and ultimately totalitarian in its consequences.

The Incoherence of Natural Rights

The transition pieces between Rand's ethics and her politics are two essays printed in both *The Virtue of Selfishness* and *Capitalism: The Unknown Ideal*, entitled "Man's Right's" and "The Nature of Government." Rand opened "Man's Rights" by writing:

> If one wishes to advocate a free society . . . one must

[2] *Capitalism: The Unknown Ideal,* vii.

[3] This may strike the reader as a peculiar statement; I only point out here that the growth of government in the United States has been paralleled by a growth of both individual and governmental lawlessness. Big government is itself lawless, and becomes more so as it enacts more statutes, prints more regulations, and issues more decrees. Those statutes, decrees, rules, and regulations are the opposite of the rule of law, which requires that law be understandable, applicable to all equally, prospective rather than retrospective, permanent, and constitutional. A totalitarian society and an anarchic society are both *law-less* societies. Neither is governed by the rule of law. It follows from this that it is not anarchy and totalitarianism that are opposites, but lawless anarchy-totalitarianism and the rule of law.

realize that its indispensable foundation is the principle of individual rights.[4]

"Rights" are a moral concept—the concept that provides a logical transition from the principles guiding an individual's actions to the principles guiding his relationship with others ... the link between the moral code of a man and the legal code of a society, between ethics and politics. Individual rights are the means of subordinating society to moral law.

I have quoted Rand at length precisely because the concept of natural rights is central to her political philosophy; if her concept of natural rights stands (ignoring for the moment the absence of an ethical base on which to stand), then her politics stands; if it falls, then her politics falls, too.

Before proceeding with her argument, Rand launched an attack on the "variants of the altruist-collectivist doctrine which subordinated the individual to some higher authority. ... Under all such systems, morality was a code applicable to the individual but not to society. Society was placed outside the moral law. ..." Rand regarded Christianity as a variant of the "altruist-collectivist doctrine," and thus implied that Christian moral law—the Ten Commandments—does not apply to society.

Leaving aside this false categorization of Christianity, it simply is not true that Christianity places society outside moral law. Many Christian philosophers and theologians have written about the Ten Commandments, asserting that the commandments apply to all men both as individuals and as institutions, corporations, and rulers. Governments, that is governors, as well as private individuals, can lie, covet, steal, murder, blaspheme, profane the Sabbath, and become idolatrous, and they have done so with great frequency throughout history. Governments, as institutions, cannot commit adultery or dishonor their parents, but governors have and con-

---

[4] *Capitalism: The Unknown Ideal*, 320.

tinue to do so. All governors will be held accountable by God for their violations of his commandments and will be punished for those violations.

Rand ignored the obvious differences between Christianity and other religions and philosophies in her efforts to establish her philosophy as unique. In fact, had she been better acquainted with English and American history, she would have known that subjecting governors and governments to moral law was accomplished by Christians applying Christian ideas to politics. It was Christian moral law to which the governments were subjected.[5] Because of her humanist bias, Rand ignores the overwhelming testimony of history.

Rand returned to her argument by defining a right as "a moral principle defining and sanctioning a man's freedom of action in a social context."[6] Rights, Rand gave us to understand, are not a gift of society or of God, but are innate or inherent: "The source of man's rights is not divine law or congressional law, but the law of identity. A is A—and Man is Man."[7]

Then the equivocations began to appear. Notice how slippery the word "right" becomes in these two sentences: "If man is to live on earth, it is right for him to use his mind, it is right to act on his

---

[5] The literature corroborating this point is immense. One might survey the following books as an introduction to the subject: *Political Sermons of the American Founding Era*, edited by Ellis Sandoz; *Faith and Freedom* by Benjamin Hart; *Puritan Political Ideas*, edited by Edmund S. Morgan; *Law and Revolution* by Harold Berman; *The Emergence of Liberty in the Modern World*, by Douglas Kelley; *The Origins of Modern Freedom in the West*, edited by R. W. Davis; *Constitutionalism and Resistance in the Sixteenth Century*, edited by Julius H. Franklin; and *War Against the Idols* by Carlos M. N. Eire. Time permitting, one might read the relevant works of John Calvin, Martin Luther, James Madison, and Patrick Henry, as well as some 19th century historians, such as Leopold von Ranke.

[6] *Capitalism: The Unknown Ideal*, 32. She also defined a right as "the sanction of independent action. A right is that which can be exercised without anyone's permission" ("Textbook of Americanism," 5).

[7] *Capitalism: The Unknown Ideal*, 322.

own free judgment, it is right to work for his values and to keep the product of his work. If life on earth is his purpose, he has a right to live as a rational being. . . ."[8]

The first three times Rand used the word *right*, she used it as an adjective modifying an action; the fourth time she used it as a noun, denoting an attribute of a person. The connection between the two concepts is not mentioned, but the reader is expected to believe there is one, apparently for no better reason than that the two words are spelled and pronounced alike.

Objectivist politics depends on this equivocation: "To violate man's rights means to compel him to act against his own judgment, or to expropriate his values." How are these rights, one must ask, related to the alleged fact that "it is right for him to use his mind"? (Rand's ethics failed to establish that it is right to use one's mind.) Let us assume, *arguendo*, that Rand had demonstrated that it is right for a person to use his mind. How does it follow that it is wrong for another person to force him to use it in a specified way? Even if it could be shown on Objectivist foundations that such an action would be morally wrong, how does this violate a right? Does not a man, according to Rand, have the right *not* to use his mind? If a person has the right *not* to use his mind, where did this right come from? Did Rand insist that it is right not to use one's mind? (To be consistent, she should have.) Just as Rand made an unexplained leap in her ethics between survival and the "life proper to man," so she made another leap in her meta-politics between "right actions" and "rights."[9]

Rand asserted: "Basically, there is only one way to do it [vio-

---

[8] *Capitalism: The Unknown Ideal*, 323.

[9] In *Atlas Shrugged* Rand passed off the same equivocation as profound argument: "The source of man's rights is not divine law or congressional law, but the law of identity. A is A—Man is Man. Rights are conditions of existence required by man's nature for his proper survival. If man is to live on earth, it is right for him to use his mind, it is right to act on his own free judgment, it is right to work for his values and to keep the product of his work. If life on earth is his purpose, he has a right to live as a rational being . . ." (1061).

late a person's "rights"]: by the use of physical force."[10] By her use of the word "basically" she protected herself against a rigid dogmatism on the point.[11] However, her formulation immediately raises a question: Why cannot a man violate his own rights? If it is right for him to work for his values and to keep the product of his work, is it not wrong and therefore a violation of his rights if he refuses to work or works and gives away his income? If it is right for him to act on his own free judgment, is he not violating his own rights by allowing his judgment to become un-free through the use of drugs or alcohol or submission to an organization like the Roman Catholic church, which requires implicit obedience? If it is right for him to use his mind, is it not wrong and therefore a violation of his rights for him to live on a "subhuman" level? If it is right for him to live, and rights are inalienable, is it not a violation of his rights to commit suicide?

If the reader is inclined to object that these questions are nonsense questions, I can only reply that, if they are, it is only because the concept "right" as developed by Rand is incoherent.

If the proper function of government is "to secure these rights," does it not follow that it is the proper function of government to see that every man uses his mind, his judgment, forces him to work and to keep the product of his work, that is, to do those things that Objectivism says are right? If one finds these consequences distasteful, one should re-read Rand's argument and find where the train of thought has derailed. Petulance is not an argument. If the source of man's rights is himself, and those rights are based on right actions, then man also becomes a source of violations of his

---

[10] *Capitalism: The Unknown Ideal*, 323. "This recognition of individual rights entails the banishment of physical force from human relationships: basically, rights can be violated only by force. In a capitalist society, no man or group may initiate the use of physical force against others."

[11] However, in her "Textbook of Americanism" Rand wrote: "A right cannot be violated except by physical force. . . . Whenever a man is made to act without his own free, personal, individual, voluntary consent—his right has been violated" (6).

own rights. Rights can then be violated by a Robinson Crusoe—his own—simply because he may act against his own best interests.

The Initiation of Force

"Rights" as developed by Rand is an equivocal concept. Yet she proceeded to argue as though she had provided a logical justification for rights in order to conclude that the government "may use force only in retaliation and only against those who initiate its use."[12] Rand informed us: "Basically, there is only one way [to violate rights]: by the use of physical force." She also told us that government may in fact use physical force, as long as it is in "retaliation" and not "initiation." As with her other central ideas, Rand offered no valid argument—indeed little argument at all—to justify this moral distinction between initiated force and retaliatory force. If Rand had been guided by logic, she would have been forced to conclude that retaliatory force is a violation of right.[13] That is the requirement of logic, but not the conclusion of Rand. She preferred to differentiate, for some unspoken reason, between initiated and retaliatory force.

Now such a moral distinction may strike the reader as plausible, and that is what Rand was counting on: It relieved her of showing, on the basis of her own theory, how retaliatory force does not violate rights while initiated force does. She followed this assertion by several paragraphs of rhetoric, apparently hoping that no reader would be perceptive enough to raise the important ques-

---

[12] *Capitalism: The Unknown Ideal*, 323. "Now it is important to remember that all actions defined as criminal in a free society are actions involving force—and only such actions are answered by force" ("Textbook of Americanism," 7).

[13] "Since Man has inalienable individual rights, this means that the same rights are held, individually, by every man, by all men, at all times" ("Textbook of Americanism," 6). This is the only logically consistent logical formulation of the notion of inalienable rights. It quite obviously follows from this and from Rand's statement about force being used to violate rights that the use of force against any man, whether initiated force or retaliatory force, is a violation of that man's rights, which he possesses "at all times."

tion. The essay concludes without any argument offered for her moral distinction between initiated and retaliatory force. Rand appealed to the distinction between murder and self-defense as a distinction her readers already accepted to illustrate her distinction between initiated and retaliatory force. Unfortunately she appealed to a distinction she was required to establish; that is, she begged the question. If all men have the same rights at all times, as Rand said, then how are murder and self-defense to be morally distinguished? Her view of inalienable natural rights permits no moral distinction between murder and self-defense. "Since Man has inalienable individual rights, this means that the same rights are held, individually, by every man, by all men, at all times." If that is true, there can be no moral distinction between initiated and retaliatory force.

In her essay, "The Nature of Government," Rand dropped the cautious "basically" and asserted: "Man's rights can be violated only by the use of physical force."[14] Notice the "only": This statement logically implies that blackmail, fraud, perjury, pollution, breach of contract, embezzlement, misprision of a felony, misrepresentation, conspiracy, child neglect, adultery, libel, slander, and other actions correctly recognized as crimes, but which do not involve the use of physical force, are not violations of man's rights.[15]

Furthermore, Rand asserted that rights can be violated *only* by means of physical force—initiated physical force. But her next step in the argument was that all initiated physical force is therefore a

[14] *Capitalism: The Unknown Ideal*, 330. This, of course, is a repetition of her position in "Textbook of Americanism."

[15] It is doubtful that government can exist without initiating some force. In addition to laws against all the crimes listed in the text, in punishment of which the government initiates force, there are procedural powers as well: subpoena, arrest, and detention pending trial. Neither a free society nor a government could survive without these powers of using force. Even Rand admitted that one of the primary functions of government is to settle disputes among its citizens, but she never showed how such disputes could be resolved without the powers of subpoena, laws against perjury, arrest, and injunction, all of which are initiations of force.

violation of right. Unfortunately for her political theory, this is an elementary logical blunder, the fallacy of the converse. The proposition that all violation of rights is by initiated physical force does not imply that all initiated physical force is a violation of rights, any more than the statement that all dogs are canines implies that all canines are dogs (or that all Chinese are humans implies all humans are Chinese). Her argument and her political theory—as well as the political theories of secular libertarians who have followed Rand on this point—depend on this elementary logical blunder. All *p* is *q* does not logically imply all *q* is *p*. Rand asserted that it does.

Rand then attempted to justify her earlier distinction between initiated and retaliatory force:

> The necessary consequence of man's right to life is his right to self-defense. In a civilized society, force may be used only in retaliation and only against those who initiate its use. All the reasons [Rand had stated no reasons; she was counting on her readers to supply them from their own resources] which make the initiation of physical force an evil, make the retaliatory use of physical force a moral imperative.[16]

If, as Rand maintained, force may be properly used only in retaliation and only against those who initiate its use, all court proceedings and wars involve some immorality. A free society could not morally defend itself against either criminals or international aggression. It is one of the characteristics of litigation and war that some innocent people are subjected to the use of force.

Retaliation and Self-Defense

In the quotation above, Rand erroneously equated retaliation with self-defense. This identification does not meet the objection that she failed to explain the moral distinction between initiated and

---

[16] *Capitalism: The Unknown Ideal*, 330.

retaliatory force on the basis of her new theory, and it opens up further objections.

Is not self-defense a violation of rights? If rights are innate and inalienable, how can a criminal lose his rights? If rights come from his identity as a man, is not a criminal still a man, and therefore a possessor of rights? If rights are inalienable by nature, by the law of identity, how can they be alienated? And if a criminal cannot alienate his rights, how can it be maintained that the use of force against him is not a violation of his rights? Rand maintained: "When we say that we hold individual rights to be inalienable, we must mean just that. Inalienable means that which we may not take away, suspend, infringe, restrict or violate—not ever, not at any time, not for any purpose whatsoever."[17] That statement precludes punishment, and therefore, precludes justice.

I will grant, merely for the sake of argument, that a criminal who initiates force violates the inalienable rights of his victim. Does it not follow that the prospective victim also violates the inalienable rights of the criminal by using force against him? If it is right for a man to use his mind, is it not a violation of his rights to force him to stop using it? If it is right for a man to act on his free judgment, is it not a violation of his rights to force his judgment?

In *Atlas Shrugged*, Rand presented one argument in an attempt to show that the use of retaliatory force is proper, and the use of initiated force improper:

> It is only as retaliation that force may be used and only against the man who starts its use. No, I do not share his evil or sink to his concept of morality. I merely grant him his choice, destruction, the only destruction he had the right to choose: his own. He uses force to seize a value; I use it only to destroy destruction. A holdup man seeks to gain wealth by killing me; I do not grow richer by killing a holdup man. I seek no values by means of evil, nor do I surrender my values to evil.[18]

[17] "Textbook of Americanism," 12.

[18] *Atlas Shrugged*, 1024.

This is an interesting argument. If one ignores the rhetoric (for example: "destroy destruction"), it would appear that the moral distinction between the holdup man and his victim is that the victim *does not* profit from his use of force, while the holdup man *does*. The holdup man "seeks values," he seeks to "gain wealth," while the victim does not seek values, nor seek to "grow richer." And it is upon this difference that Rand based her moral distinction between initiated and retaliatory force. Now this is obviously a rather peculiar argument for a person who believed gain to be the only proper motive for all action, for Rand argued that it is the criminal who is seeking values and gain. That is what makes his actions wrong. By contrast, the intended victim, acting in self-defense, seeks no values or gain. That is what makes his action right. Were Rand consistent with her basic ethical theory, the holdup man who seeks to gain wealth would be the more moral of the two, not the man who seeks no gain.

Rand, of course, also ignored the question of whether a man has a right to commit suicide; she simply assumed, without evidence or argument, that he does, and that this right is actually what is being exercised when a holdup man is killed. This is obviously a rhetorical obliteration of the difference between suicide and self-defense.

Excursus on the Initiation of Force in the Welfare State

Rand, of course, was vehemently opposed to the taxation and redistribution of wealth by government. But her argument in favor of taking government grants and scholarships contradicted that position. She wrote:

> The recipient of a public scholarship is morally justified *only so long as he regards it as restitution and opposes all forms of welfare statism.* Those who advocate public scholarships, have no right to them; those who oppose them, have. . . . The victims do not have to add self-inflicted martyrdom to the injury done to them by others; they do not

have to let the looters profit doubly by letting them distribute the money exclusively to the parasites who clamored for it. Whenever the welfare-state laws offer them some small restitution, *the victims should take it. . . .*

The same moral principles and considerations apply to the issue of accepting social security, unemployment insurance or other payments of that kind. It is obvious, in such cases, that a man receives his own money which was taken from him by force. . . .[19]

Not only does this argument—offered as advice to students, social security recipients, unemployment recipients, and anyone else receiving money from the government—contradict her libertarian strictures against legalized theft, it is patently invalid. It is not obvious, nor is it true (to challenge her last statement) that a person who accepts a government grant, whether it be a scholarship or social security, is merely getting his own money back. In fact, "his money," paid in taxes, has already been spent. It is already gone. The government spends money faster than it collects taxes. Therefore, a person cannot get his own money back. Any money he receives is stolen from someone else. He cannot get even without injuring others.

Furthermore, these welfare state programs are not offered as a means of restitution, as Rand said, but as a means of redistribution. Regarding them as restitution, as Rand advocated, is an excellent example of faking reality, to which Rand claimed to be opposed. It seems, however, that Rand believed one may and should fake reality, if such faking results in getting a check from the government.

Worse, notice that Rand wrote that those who are opposed to these programs have a right to them. What kind of right is this? A right to a welfare program only if you oppose welfare programs? Could Ellsworth Toohey himself have thought of, let alone advocated, anything so irrational?

Rand, beginning as an advocate of limited government, private

---

[19] *The Objectivist*, June 1966, 11.

property, and justice, ended by advising her readers to grab whatever they can get from the government, so long as they also oppose "welfare statism." Whatever monies they receive are merely restitution for the harm done to them and to their ancestors. Many, perhaps all, thieves convince themselves that what they are stealing is really theirs by right. The rich really owe the money to the poor, having first stolen it from them, right? The employers really owe the money to the underpaid workers, *n'est pas*? The bourgeoisie, through its exploitation of the working class, deserves to be expropriated, *nicht*? Don't many, perhaps most, thieves think they are only taking what they deserve? Rand's advocacy of legalized thievery is no different in principle from the rationalizations that common thieves and revolutionary Communists have fabricated to justify the evil they are doing. Rand's argument illustrates how easily "rational ethics" can be turned whichever way one wishes.

The Crime of Punishment

If men have natural inalienable rights, then all punishment is immoral. It is immoral because punishment is a violation of inalienable rights. Execution is a violation of the inalienable right to life. Imprisonment is a violation of the inalienable right to liberty. Fines are violations of the inalienable right to property. It is no accident that the erosion of justice and the collapse of the criminal justice system in the United States have been fueled by demands for the recognition of rights. What has occurred over the last 40 years is the outworking in practice of what the notion of inalienable rights implies in theory. The theory of natural rights logically requires that there be no punishment, for punishment is itself a crime, a violation of those rights. If rights are indeed inalienable, then nothing a person can do can make him lose those rights. There is a fundamental logical incompatibility between justice and inalienable rights, and for the past 40 years, justice has been vitiated by the doctrine of inalienable rights.

Further objections to Rand's equation of self-defense and retaliation are simply that punishment is not self-defense, yet it is retaliatory; neither are governmental acts self-defense, unless Rand wished to say (and I believe it is implicit in her version and in every version of the social compact theory),[20] *l'état, c'est moi.*

Rand ignored the differences between self-defense, retaliation, and punishment, treated them all as identical, and proceeded to argue that retaliatory force must be organized, "objective," and monopolistic. Let's examine the last putative characteristic of government first. Rand believed that "government holds a monopoly on the legal use of physical force."[21] Such a bald assertion is simply and obviously untrue. Parents legally use physical force regularly; moreover, unless they live in some socialist hive, they initiate it regularly in the discipline of their children. Secondly, in the United States, at least in theory (and in practice at one time) no single government—local, state, or national—has a legal monopoly on the use of force. The genius of federalism (a system of government that Rand seemed not to understand) is to deny explicitly that any one government should have a legal monopoly on the use of force. The entire theory of both the division and separation of powers is a denial that there is any government or any part of government that has such a monopoly.

The Consent of the Governed

The two other characteristics of a free society according to Rand are that the use of retaliatory force is organized, that is, in a government, and "objective," that is, under law. Furthermore, "The source of the government's authority is the consent of the governed." This means that the government as such has no rights except the rights delegated to it by the citizens for a specific purpose.[22]

[20] Rand rather obviously believed in some version of the social compact theory: "Men delegate to the government the power to use force in retaliation—and only in retaliation" ("Textbook of Americanism," 7).

[21] *Capitalism: The Unknown Ideal,* 331.

[22] *Capitalism: The Unknown Ideal,* 332. "The phrase, the consent of the governed, makes a good slogan; but, if it means that no government rules by right unless it has been established by a unanimous vote—and Locke as well as

Without a Prayer: Ayn Rand and the Close of Her System

We are given to understand, then, that government and its just powers are entirely derivative: The consent of the governed creates and informs the institution of government. This is obviously good Lockean or Jeffersonian theory, but it is not necessarily true. Locke and Jefferson had one or two false ideas. All governments in one sense—a somewhat trivial sense—rest on consent. The Austrian economist Mises expressed this by saying that in the long run, there is no such thing as an unpopular government. But this meaning of consent is obviously not that intended by Jefferson or Rand; for them, consent is the secular substitute for divine ordination: It is not a passive acceptance, but a creative moral action. Nor is popular consent merely the means of instituting a government, as it was, for example, in ancient Israel, when the people consented to the constitution God had written for them. Popular consent, in Rand's theory, is the source of moral authority for government. It is to this notion of consent that we must direct our attention.

The Depravity of Men

Our first question must be, If government is merely the right of self-defense externalized and objectified, how can men delegate their inalienable rights to government? Natural rights are by definition inalienable; and if English words mean anything, inalienable rights cannot be alienated. Second, if government is merely the right of self-defense externalized, are men under any moral obligation to delegate their rights to the state? How did this moral obligation arise? Unlike Plato and Aristotle, who taught that the state is prior to individual,[23] Rand taught that the individual is prior

---

Rousseau required a unanimous vote—the consequence is that no actual government is justified. No government rules, nor has any been initiated by unanimous consent" (Gordon H. Clark, *An Introduction to Christian Philosophy,* 109-110). Sir Robert Filmer was probably the most brilliant critic of the social compact theory. For a study of his thought, see the author's unpublished Ph.D. dissertation, *The Political Thought of Sir Robert Filmer* (The Johns Hopkins University, 1973).

[23] "Now, if Plato's theory is a form of communism, perhaps Aristotle could be called fascist. The important point is that they are both totalitarian" (Gordon H. Clark, *A Christian View of Men and Things,* 109).

to the state. The priority may not be temporal, but it is logical and moral. Why, then, should individuals surrender their rights to an external agency? The answer Rand gave appeared to be: because men are evil: "Such, in essence, is the proper purpose of a government, to make social existence possible to men, by protecting the benefits and combating the evils which men can cause to one another."[24]

Lest my argument be misunderstood, the question is not whether some (or all) men commit specific evil actions, for Rand was quite willing to admit that some men do and thereby deserve to be called evil men. The question is whether all men are ethically evil by nature, whether there is a one hundred percent chance of a man thinking and doing evil. It is this idea of sin that Rand castigated as a "monstrous absurdity."[25] For Rand, as for the Enlightenment thinkers, nature was normative: "To hold man's nature as his sin is a mockery of nature." We must conclude, then, that Rand believed man to be naturally good. Now these two beliefs, namely that government is necessary and that man is good, are in conflict. The conflict erupts into view in Rand's essay, "Conservatism: an Obituary." Rand attacks the view that government is necessary because man is depraved:

This argument runs as follows: since men are weak,

---

[24] *Capitalism: The Unknown Ideal*, 334. "The use of physical force—even its retaliatory use—cannot be left at the discretion of individual citizens. Peaceful coexistence is impossible if a man has to live under the constant threat of force to be unleashed against him by any of his neighbors at any moment. Whether his neighbors' intentions are good or bad, whether their judgment is rational or irrational, whether they are motivated by a sense of justice or by ignorance or by prejudice or by malice—the use of force against one man cannot be left to the arbitrary decision of another" (*The Virtue of Selfishness*, 108-109).

[25] *Atlas Shrugged*, 1025. As we have seen, Rand believed in "free will," that is, she believed that man was born with a good nature. In good Pelagian fashion she attacked those who might seek a compromise between Scripture and Pelagius: "Do not hide behind the cowardly evasion that man is born with free will, but with a 'tendency' to evil. A free will saddled with a tendency is like a game with loaded dice. . . . If the tendency is of his choice, he cannot possess it at birth; if it is not of his choice, his will is not free."

fallible, non-omniscient and innately depraved, no man may be entrusted with the responsibility of being a dictator and of ruling everybody else; therefore, a free society is the proper way of life for imperfect creatures. Please grasp fully the implications of this argument: since men are depraved, they are not good enough for a dictatorship; freedom is all that they deserve; if they were perfect, they would be worthy of a totalitarian state.[26]

Rand's argument is plausible only because Rand juxtaposed two implicitly contradictory concepts: perfect man and totalitarian state. This is an example of the fallacy of the stolen concept: The concept "totalitarian state" presupposes the concept "evil men." There can be no totalitarian state in a world of perfect men. Her rhetoric is persuasive but fallacious.

As noted, it is not a question of whether men will perform evil acts that is at issue: Rand said that they will. The problem is more profound:

The possibility of human immorality is not the only objection to anarchy: even a society whose every member were fully rational and faultlessly moral could not function in a state of anarchy; it is the need of objective laws and of an arbiter for honest disagreements among men that necessitates the establishment of a government.[27]

Let us examine this assertion carefully. The first point to be noted is that Rand put great emphasis on "need," as though need justifies doing whatever is allegedly needed. This is obviously at odds with her many denunciations of the concept of need as having any value in ethical theory. "Need" is also the morally loaded word that allows her to slip unnoticed from the realm of the "is" to the realm of the "ought," from the indicative to the imperative. But the

[26] *Capitalism: The Unknown Ideal*, 198-199.

[27] *Capitalism: The Unknown Ideal*, 334.

alleged fact that men "need" (in some sense) government does not and cannot logically entail the conclusion that government is, on the basis of that "need," logically justified. "Need" is the vague, ambiguous, and morally loaded term that Rand used to play her philosophic tricks in both ethics and politics. In ethics, it is man's alleged "need" of a moral code that Rand used to try to justify her moral theory; in politics it is man's alleged "need" of a government that Rand used to try to justify her theory of government. In neither case is her argument logical.

The next question which arises is, How can "fully rational and faultlessly moral" men disagree? The question arises because (1) a fully rational man will draw the proper conclusions from the knowledge available to him; and (2) these conclusions will necessarily be consistent with those of any other fully rational man who happens to possess more (or less) or the same information.

Rand wrote:

> If his [fully rational man's] grasp is non-contradictory, then even if the scope of his knowledge is modest and the content of his concepts is primitive, it will not contradict the content of the same concepts in the mind of the most advanced scientists.[28]

"Honest disagreements" and "fully rational men" are mutually exclusive concepts. Rand's argument contains another illustration of the fallacy of the stolen concept: The concept "honest disagreement" presupposes men who are not fully rational. The concept "dishonest disagreement" presupposes men who are not faultlessly moral.

For the sake of argument alone, however, I will accept Rand's assertion that fully rational men are able to have honest disagreements. Unfortunately, it still does not follow that government is necessary. One must keep in mind Rand's definition of government: an agency with a monopoly on the legal use of physical force

---

[28] *Introduction to Objectivist Epistemology*, 42.

in a geographical area.[29] Keeping that definition in mind, why do "fully rational and faultlessly moral" men need a *monopolistic agency of physical force?* Are we to assume that perfect men are not able to settle any honest disagreements without the use of force, or the threat of force? Apparently we are, for if they could, there would be no need of government.

Rand thus implicitly admitted that man is innately depraved: Even "perfect" men would need to use force to settle their differences. But she is caught in a contradiction. The contradiction has its basis in the fact that her philosophy posited the priority of man and the derivative nature of government. Starting with such an assumption, she must logically conclude that anarchy is the only proper and moral social arrangement. Unlike Aristotle, whom she so much admired, she did not believe in the priority of the state; consequently she is not the explicit totalitarian Aristotle was. She is an implicit anarchist instead.

Objectivism leads logically to anarchy, because no sovereign individual—and we are all sovereign, aren't we?— may be forced to delegate his rights to government. The sovereign individual[30] has every right to refuse to pay taxes, ignore subpoenas, ignore courts of law, resist arrest, and take all measures necessary to the preservation of his rights, including one supposes, since government is entirely derivative, issuing subpoenas, forming his own army, and establishing his own courts and judicial procedures, and punishing people.

Rand, however, vociferously maintained that she did not advocate an anarchic society:

> I disapprove of, disagree with and have no connection with, the latest aberration of some conservatives, the so-called "hippies of the right," who attempt to snare the

---

[29] "A government is an institution that holds the exclusive power to enforce certain rules of social conduct in a given geographical area" (*The Virtue of Selfishness*, 107).

[30] The sovereign individual is, as we have seen, the hero of *Anthem*.

younger or more careless ones of my readers by claiming simultaneously to be followers of my philosophy and advocates of anarchism. Anyone offering such a combination confesses his inability to understand either. Anarchism is the most irrational, anti-intellectual notion ever spun by the concrete-bound, context-dropping, whim-worshiping fringe of the collectivist movement, where it properly belongs.[31]

What was obviously missing in her attack on anarchism was any intellectual argument concerning the distinction(s) between her version of a free society and anarchy. Rather than explanation, Rand supplied only denunciation.

As we have already shown, such a distinction between a free Objectivist society and anarchy would be difficult for her to maintain. Take, for example, her description of Atlantis (Galt's Gulch), the society which the most rational and most moral men on Earth create as a refuge from the "moral cannibalism" of the rest of the world:

> We have no laws in this valley, no rules, no formal organization of any kind.[32]

> We have no rules of any kind.[33]

> We are not a state here, not a society of any kind— we're just a voluntary association of men held together by nothing but every man's self-interest. I own the valley and I sell the land to the others, when they want it. Judge

---

[31] *The Objectivist*, September 1971, 2. Karl Marx scorned the anarchist Bakunin as "a man devoid of theoretical knowledge" and "a nonentity as a theoretician," whose "programme was a superficially scraped together hash of Right and Left" and "rubbish" (Marx to Botte, 23 November 1871, in *Selected Correspondence*, 316-317).

[32] *Atlas Shrugged*, 714. The speaker is John Galt.

[33] *Atlas Shrugged*, 747.

Narragansett is to act as our arbiter, in case of disagreements. He hasn't had to be called upon, as yet.[34]

If these words are not descriptions of anarchy, a description of anarchy does not exist. It is most interesting to note that in the last quotation Rand contrasted her ideal association with a state or a society by saying that the perfect association is "voluntary" and "held together by nothing but every man's self-interest." This clearly implies that in Rand's mind the state *qua* state, society *qua* society, is to some extent an involuntary association held together by something other than every man's self-interest. The unmistakable implication of these statements is that states, societies, and governments are incompatible with her idea of a free society—that, in fact, her idea of the perfect association is anarchy.

Taxation and Government Finance

This implication is corroborated by her description of the proper powers of government. She insisted that a proper government may use force only in retaliation.[35] This is because the citizens have delegated their rights to use force in retaliation to the government.[36] Consequently, since taxation is an initiation of force, it cannot be used by the government of a free society.[37] Of course, as I have

[34] *Atlas Shrugged*, 747-748. The speaker is Midas Mulligan.

[35] ". . . the Objectivist principle that the government of a free society may not initiate the use of physical force and may use force only in retaliation against those who initiate its use" (*The Virtue of Selfishness*, 116).

[36] "The source of the government's authority is 'the consent of the governed.' This means that the government is not the ruler, but the servant or agent of the citizens; it means that the government as such has no rights except the rights delegated to it by the citizens for a specific purpose" (*The Virtue of Selfishness*, 110). Rand confused force used in retaliation with force used in self-defense, that is, she confused punishment and prevention of crime. She spoke alternately of delegating the right to use force in retaliation and the right to use force in self-defense to the government. See *The Virtue of Selfishness*, 110.

[37] "In a fully free society, taxation—or, to be exact, payment for governmental services—would be voluntary" (*The Virtue of Selfishness*, 116).

pointed out above, if the government is not to initiate force, several other powers besides that of taxation must be eliminated, too. Taxation, however, was the only issue that Rand dealt with at any length. As alternative methods of "payment for governmental services," Rand first suggested a government lottery.[38] Then she suggested an alternative method of financing:

> One of the most vitally needed services, which only a government can render, is the protection of contractual agreements among citizens. Suppose that the government were to protect—i.e., to recognize as legally valid and enforceable—only those contracts which had been insured by the payment, to the government, of a premium in the amount of a legally fixed percentage of the sums involved in the contractual transaction. Such an insurance would not be compulsory; there would be no legal penalty imposed on those who did not choose to take it. . . . The only consequence would be that such [uninsured] agreements or contracts would not be legally enforceable; if they were broken, the injured party would not be able to seek redress in a court of law.[39]

What Rand apparently failed to realize is that in seeking to restrict government to the use of force only in retaliation, she was

---

[38] *The Virtue of Selfishness*, 116. Interestingly, Rand in *For the New Intellectual* regarded gambling as a pleasure of the lowest type of human being: Attila. "His [Attila's] pleasures are closer to the level of sensations than of perception: food, drink, palatial shelter, rich clothing, indiscriminate sex, contests of physical prowess, gambling—all those activities which do not demand or involve the use of the conceptual level of consciousness" (16). If gambling is to be used in Rand's fully free society as a method of governmental financing, the society must be populated by Attilas.

[39] *The Virtue of Selfishness*, 116-117. Rand concluded: "This particular 'plan' is mentioned here only as an illustration of a possible method of approach to the problem—not as a definitive answer nor as a program to advocate at present. The legal and technical difficulties involved are enormous . . ." (117).

eliminating government from her society. She no longer spoke of the authority of government; she spoke only of "government services."[40] It is no wonder that the theory of competing governments[41] emerged from Objectivist circles—Rand herself chose to speak of government as a provider of services to the market.[42]

Furthermore, it is unlikely that, as Rand maintained, the only consequence would be that contracts not insured by the government would not be legally enforceable. What would prevent such parties from insuring their contracts with competing insurance agencies? Once Rand's voluntary government has entered the market selling its "governmental services," it cannot prevent similar agencies from entering the market, that is, it cannot maintain its monopoly on the use of force in a geographical area, except by initiating the use of force or the threat of force against those competing agencies. The result?

> Instead of a single, monopolistic government, . . . there [would] be a number of different governments in the same geographical area, competing for the allegiance of individual citizens, with every citizen free to "shop" and to patronize whatever government he chooses.[43]

Rand's theory of a monopolistic government voluntarily fi-

---

[40] "The premise to check (and to challenge) in this context is the primordial notion that any governmental services (even the legitimate ones) should be given to the citizens gratuitously" (*The Virtue of Selfishness*, 119).

[41] "A recent variant of anarchistic theory, which is befuddling some of the younger advocates of freedom, is a weird absurdity called 'competing governments.' Accepting the basic premise of the modern statists—who see no difference between the functions of government and the functions of industry, between force and production . . ." (*The Virtue of Selfishness*, 112).

[42] It is quite true that Rand wished to distinguish between the "services" provided by a government and those provided by an industry—but so do the anarchists. Neither Rand nor the anarchists believed that the governmental services should be paid for or provided for in any way different from the services provided by business.

[43] *The Virtue of Selfishness*, 112-113.

nanced by a contract insurance program rests on the fallacy of the stolen concept: A monopoly can be maintained only by the use or threat of force, that is, by the initiation of force.[44] Therefore, a government that does not initiate force is a contradiction in terms—in Rand's own terms, simply because governments are monopolies. Her argument presented consistently would lead to anarchy.

Totalitarianism and the Doctrine of Forfeiture

Anarchy is where the doctrine of the inalienable rights of man must logically lead.[45] Rand drew back from this conclusion only by contradicting herself. She could not logically advocate a free society simply because she rejected the Christian axiom of revelation.[46] It is only on the basis of Scripture that one may advocate a free society without self-contradiction, because one does not have to choose between the priority of the collective (totalitarianism) or the priority of the individual (anarchy). All secular political philosophy has been based on one or the other of these premises, and the mad veerings of history are testimony to the inherently unstable nature of institutions established on these principles. Christianity—the propositions written in the Bible—and Christianity alone, furnishes the only logical foundation for a free and stable society. Neither the individual nor the collective is sovereign: God and God alone possesses the attribute of sovereignty. God is prior: Both man and

[44] See Branden's article "Common Fallacies About Capitalism" in *Capitalism: The Unknown Ideal*, 72-77.

[45] "Thus, in one or the other of its two forms—avowed materialism or deism—it became the creed of the whole cultured youth of France; so much so that, when the Great Revolution broke out, the doctrine hatched by English Royalists gave a theoretical flag to French Republicans and Terrorists, and furnished the text for the Declaration of the Rights of Man" (Friedrich Engels, *Socialism: Utopian and Scientific*, 20).

[46] "Christian presuppositions justify civil governments of limited rights, whereas humanistic principles imply either anarchy or totalitarianism" (Gordon H. Clark, *A Christian View of Men and Things*, 143). For a discussion of the axiom of revelation, see Clark, *An Introduction to Christian Philosophy*.

government are derivative. Man is a creature of God; government is an ordinance of God. It is limited by his law, not by any inherently contradictory notion of human rights. The notion of innate and inalienable human rights does not appear in the Bible. Rather than rights, it is God's law that limits government; nature is not normative, the Word of God is. Christ's command to render unto Caesar the things that are Caesar's and to God the things that are God's should be regarded as the Magna Carta of liberty, for it clearly denied, in opposition to all secular philosophy, that Caesar (nor any other creature) is God, and Caesar's powers are limited, in fact, limited by God. Jesus Christ, not the fascist Aristotle, was America's first "Founding Father."[47]

The doctrine of inalienable human rights has never received a logical philosophical foundation, and Ayn Rand's punning attempt to establish it was as inadequate, if not more so, than other attempts which have been made by other philosophers. Because it lacks a logical foundation, the notion of inalienable rights leads to insoluble antinomies, one of the most obvious being the doctrine of forfeiture.

Rand believed that man makes himself; that man must be man by choice. This is a metaphysical statement: By an act of his will a being can chose to become human. By an act of his will a man can choose to become subhuman. Accepting Aristotle's definition of man as the rational animal, Rand believed, quite literally, that man is an animal that can choose to be, or not to be, human. A man who initiates force, who seeks to live not by producing but by looting, has publicly declared his decision to be subhuman and thereby becomes subhuman. It is by this means that Rand sought to achieve a reconciliation between the logically contradictory ideas of inalienable rights and self-defense, and the logically incompatible ideas of inalienable rights and punishment. On the basis of inalienable rights, self-defense and punishment of criminals would be forbidden, for if rights are by nature *inalienable*, nothing a person can do can alienate his rights, and therefore any force used against him is

---

[47] "What this country needs is a philosophical revolution—a rebellion against the Kantian tradition—in the name of the first of our Founding Fathers: Aristotle" (Ayn Rand, *The New Left*, 98).

a violation of his rights. If man possesses rights by virtue of the fact that he is a man, that is, he possesses rights by nature, then he possesses those rights at all times and in all circumstances. Rand "solved" the problem, however, just as John Locke did: She eliminated inalienable rights by eliminating human nature. Both Rand and Locke posit a metaphysical consequence of an act of the will. Locke in his *Second Treatise of Government* wrote:

> Every Man in the State of Nature, has a Power to kill a Murderer . . . to secure Men from the attempts of a Criminal, who having renounced Reason, . . . hath by the unjust Violence and Slaughter he hath committed upon one, declared War against all Mankind, and therefore may be destroyed as a Lyon or a Tiger, one of those wild Savage Beasts. . . .[48]

Locke and Rand both believed that an aggressor may be destroyed because an aggressor quite literally is not human: Since "reason" is the defining characteristic of man, a being who is not acting with "reason" is not human. The rights of man may be inalienable, according to Rand, but the mannishness of man is not. By choosing not to think, by renouncing reason, by initiating force, a person forfeits his status as a human being. A man cannot lose his rights, but he can forfeit his humanity.

Eating Babies for Breakfast

Once one has accepted the Aristotelian definition of man as a rational animal, as Rand did, and also the notion of man as a being of volitional consciousness, the doctrine of forfeiture follows. The implication of the doctrine of forfeiture is that some beings who look like men, who are descended from men, are not men, for man's differentia is metaphysical.[49] Abortion, for example, becomes moral,

[48] John Locke, *Two Treatises of Government*, Laslett, ed., 314-315.

[49] For Aristotle, women were misbegotten males. He thought that the deliberative faculty is not present at all in the slave, it is inoperative in the female, and in the child undeveloped.

for the abortionist is not initiating force against a human being. Since a human being is by definition a being who has chosen to think conceptually, an unborn child is not a human being. Rand wrote: "An embryo *has no rights*. Rights do not pertain to a *potential*, only to an actual being."[50] She obviously used some sort of Aristotelian theory of potentiality and actuality in her defense of abortion. But neither Aristotle nor Rand told us what the terms mean. Aristotle furnished illustrations, but no non-circular definition, and Rand did not even try to explain.

But more to the present point, Rand presented no argument for her assertion that rights do not "pertain" to "potentials." She simply made the statement. This ipsedixitism leads her into some difficulties. For example, "A child cannot acquire rights until it is born." That would imply that children, that is, all of us, at some point in time *acquire* our rights. That seems to imply that since our rights are acquired, we do not possess our rights by nature, unless, of course, we also acquire a nature. Rights may be inalienable, but natures are not. Rand's view seems to imply that the process by which one acquires rights is locomotion, specifically, moving from the womb to the crib. One acquires inalienable rights by changing location.

In the same passage Rand announced that abortion "is a moral right—which should be left to the sole discretion of the woman involved. . . ." Nowhere, to my knowledge, did Rand make similar statements about other medical procedures being moral rights. For some reason, she seemed to have a great deal of emotion invested in the question of abortion. Furthermore, she asserted that abortion is to be left to the *sole discretion of the woman:* That clearly implies that her husband has no moral rights in the matter—and therefore should have no legal rights; that her parents, if she is a minor, have no moral rights; and, obviously, the government, which is charged with the purpose of defending individual rights, has no role either. While Rand usually denounced whims and wishes elsewhere, on the question of abortion, "nothing other than her wish

[50] *The Objectivist*, October 1968, 6.

. . . is to be considered." In abortion, the woman's wish reigns supreme.

Finally, Rand asked, "Who can conceivably [I surmise she intended no pun] have the right to dictate to her what disposition she is to make of the functions of her own body?"—but that is a different, and an irrelevant, question. It is irrelevant, unless we are to understand that the unborn child's body is actually the woman's body—in which case the woman has two brains, heads, and hearts; four eyes, ears, arms, and legs; and may be both male and female—or unless we are to understand that the child is a "function" of the woman's body, analogous to elimination, respiration, or reproduction. But even the most obtuse abortionist—and Rand is not obtuse—would not confuse feces with the bodily function of elimination, nor carbon dioxide with the bodily function of respiration, nor babies with the bodily function of reproduction.

In other places Rand referred to the idea that an embryo has a right to life as "vicious nonsense" and "unspeakable": "a piece of protoplasm has no rights"—and note the next phrase—"and no life in the human sense of the term."[51] Elsewhere she wrote: "a proper, philosophically valid definition of man as 'a rational animal,' would not permit anyone to ascribe the status of 'person' to a few human cells."[52] In *Philosophy: Who Needs It?* Rand, who wrote of a "piece of protoplasm" and a "few human cells," wrote: "Observe that . . . the egalitarians' view of man is literally the view of a children's fairy tale—the notion that man, before birth, is some sort of indeterminate thing, an entity without identity, something like a shapeless chunk of human clay. . . ."[53] Apparently her view of abortion is a children's fairy tale.

Rand did not draw back from some of the logical consequences of her view of man. She vigorously supported the elimination of laws regulating or outlawing abortion, a position quite consistent

[51] *The Ayn Rand Lexicon*, 2, 3.

[52] *The Objectivist Forum*, June 1981, 3.

[53] *Philosophy: Who Needs It?* 133.

with her doctrine of man.[54] But there are further implications of the view. Not only are unborn children not human, born children are not human either. Aristotle in his *Politics* wrote that

> There should certainly be a law to prevent the rearing of deformed children. . . . The proper thing to do is to limit the size of each family, and if the children then conceived in excess of the limit so fixed, to have miscarriage induced before sense and life have begun in the embryo.[55]

Aristotle apparently did not realize that a human being lives from conception—and thus he had an excuse which Rand did not have.

When Harry Binswanger was editing *The Ayn Rand Lexicon*,[56] he reports, "Miss Rand became increasingly enthusiastic about the project. One value of the book had special meaning to her: it eliminates any shred of excuse . . . for the continual gross misrepresentation of her philosophy at the hands of hostile commentators. As

[54] The October 1968 essay continues: "The living take precedence over the not-yet-living (or the unborn). . . . The Catholic Church is responsible for this country's disgracefully barbarian anti-abortion laws, which should be repealed and abolished" (Ayn Rand, *The Objectivist*, October 1968, 6). Rand apparently did not understand much American history; otherwise, she would not have made such a foolish statement about the Roman Catholic church.

[55] *Politics*, 1335b. Far from being the first of the founding fathers of America, Aristotle is one of the founding fathers of totalitarianism. Communist China has put his prescriptions for population control into effect. Rand wrote: "There are few political actions today that we can support without supporting a number of dangerous contradictions at the same time. The abortion-law reform is one such action; it is clear-cut, unequivocal and crucially important. It is not a partisan issue in the narrow sense of practical politics. It is a fundamental moral issue of enlightened respect for individual rights versus savagely primitive superstition" (Ayn Rand, *The Objectivist*, February 1969, 4). Notice how easily Rand's concern for human rights leads to her justification of killing. Rand's vehemence on this issue leads one to suspect that she may have had a bad conscience.

[56] The *Lexicon* has some curious lacunas. For example, there are four pages on "love"; none on "fact." There are four pages on "romanticism," only two-thirds of a page on "science," and seven *lines* on "induction and deduction." There are no entries at all for "industry," "industrial revolution," or "objective reality."

she quipped to me, 'People will be able to look up BREAKFAST and see that I did not advocate eating babies for breakfast.' "[57] Considering her views on abortion, one wonders why Miss Rand objected to eating babies for breakfast. Simply discarding their bodies seems a waste of good, tender, and possibly quite tasty, meat.[58] If they are indeed not human beings, as Rand so vociferously insisted, why not offer the meat for sale, or at least sell their bodies for medical parts? What possible moral objection, consistent with her views on abortion and the rights of the mother, could Miss Rand have had to such things? None, of course.

Life Unworthy of Living

Since infants as well as unborn children are not human by Rand's definition (they, too, are only potentially human, not actually human), there can logically be no immorality in infanticide. To my knowledge Rand did not publicly endorse infanticide, but infanticide is a logical consequence of her Aristotelian views, and Aristotle explicitly advocated it. If Rand did not, she was inconsistent with her own definitions.

For the same reason, Rand's philosophy leads logically to the approbation of other types of murder. Because men make themselves, some men are better made than others, who are rather shoddy merchandise. Some are not men at all. Logically then, Objectivists must approve the liquidation of imbeciles, morons, idiots, the retarded, the mediocre who don't think, the men who "do not choose to think, but survive by imitating and repeating, like trained animals, the routine of sounds and motions they learned from others, never making an effort to understand their own work . . . mental parasites . . . ,"[59] until the small group known as Objectivists is all

[57] *The Ayn Rand Lexicon*, ix.

[58] See "The Ethics of Abortion," in *The Trinity Review*, March/April 1982.

[59] *The Virtue of Selfishness*, 23. Merrill and Sciabarra point out two revealing passages from the first and second editions of *We, The Living*. The passages report a conversation between the semi-autobiographical Kira and Andrei. The Communist. Andrei assumes that Kira likes the Communists' ideals but hates

that is left alive. By that time, however, Rand's following will have increased greatly, as people seek to prove their humanity to an Objectivist government. Where Christians would fit in among these subhuman animals is debatable. Their continued existence under an Objectivist government has already been the subject of debate in Objectivist circles, for two reasons: (1) Christians are obviously mystics, that is, people who choose not to think—and are therefore subhuman; and (2) Christianity is a type of extortion and fraud. As such it ought to be outlawed in a free atheist society. One's hopes are not encouraged by Peikoff's ascribing to Christianity partial responsibility for Nazism:

> On the road leading from the ancient world to the eth-
> ics of Nazism, the first major landmark is the development

---

their methods. In the first edition Kira replies: "I loathe your ideals. I admire your methods. If one believes one's right, one shouldn't wait to convince millions of fools, one might just as well force them. Except that I don't know, however, whether I'd include blood in my methods." In the second edition, published in 1959, Kira says simply, "I loathe your ideals."

In the first edition, Rand had Andrei say, ". . . we can't sacrifice millions for the sake of the few." To which Kira replied: "You can! You must. When those few are the best. Deny the best its right to the top—and you have no best left. What are your masses but mud to be ground underfoot, fuel to be burned for those who deserve it? What is the people but millions of puny, shriveled, helpless souls that have no thoughts of their own, no dreams of their own, no will of their own, who eat and sleep and chew helplessly the words others put into their mildewed brains? And for those you would sacrifice the few who know life, who are life? I loathe your ideals because I know no worse injustice than justice for all. Because men are not born equal and I don't see why one should want to make them equal. And because I loathe most of them."

In the second edition Kira says: "Can you sacrifice the few? When those few are the best? Deny the best its right to the top–and you have no best left. What are your masses but millions of dull, shriveled, stagnant souls that have no thoughts of their own, no dreams of their own, no will of their own, who eat and sleep and chew helplessly the words others put into their brains? And for those you would sacrifice the few who know life, who are life? I loathe your ideals because I know no worse injustice than the giving of the undeserved. Because men are not equal in ability and one can't treat them as if they were. And because I loathe most of them."

of Christianity. But Christianity is merely the necessary condition of all that followed; by itself, it could not—and did not—lead to Nazism. Kant could. His ethics is the second, and towering, landmark on that road.[60]

Peikoff, a secular Jew, does not think it important or necessary to demonstrate his accusation against Christianity. Nor does he find Aristotle and his totalitarianism a factor in the rise of the pagan Nazi movement. Peikoff is so obtuse he cannot see the logical implications of his own political philosophy. Peikoff's intellectual history is about as accurate as Mary Ann Sures' political and cultural history. In 1969 she published "Metaphysics in Marble" in *The Objectivist*. Sures wrote:

> Ancient Greece tore away the heavy shroud of mysticism woven for centuries in murky temples, and achieved, in three centuries, what Egypt had not dreamed of in thirty: a civilization that was essentially pro-man and pro-life. The achievements of the Greeks rested on their confidence in the power of man's mind–the power of reason. . . . The Greeks built temples for their gods, but they conceived of their gods as perfect human beings. . . .[61]

Hardly. Sures'—and Rand's—romantic notions of ancient Greece bear little resemblance to what we know of that civilization. The Greek and Roman gods and goddesses were men and women larger than life. They fought, schemed, lied, got drunk, raped, committed incest, gambled, stole, murdered, and so on— hardly perfect human beings. As far as being pro-man and pro-life, the Greek city-states were founded on slavery, practiced infanticide and euthanasia, encouraged suicide, and were continually at war. Murray tells us:

> For most of the time which Plato describes [mislead-

---

[60] *The Objectivist*, September 1971, 4-5.

[61] *The Objectivist*, February 1969, 12.

ingly, in his dialogues], Athens was fighting a long and
bloody war in which at least half the population died, many
of them from a particularly horrifying plague which scarred
even those who survived it, and which was partly the consequence of the unsanitary conditions in which vast numbers of citizens were camped . . . on every available space
of open or sacred land within the city walls.[62]

Greece and Rome were built on slave labor; their philosophers defended slavery (Aristotle, for example, believed that reason—the
deliberative faculty—was not present in slaves, was inoperative in
females, and was undeveloped in children); recommended abortion and infanticide—to be enforced by the rulers, if needed to control population growth; and favored and practiced euthanasia. Far
from being "pro-man" and "pro-life," the Greek city-states were
totalitarian church-states.[63]

Animal Rights

One further consideration on the matter of rights is necessary. Permit me to put before you again Rand's attempted derivation of the
concept of rights:

> Rights are conditions of existence required by man's
> nature for his proper survival. If man is to live on earth, it
> is right for him to use his mind, it is right to act on his own
> free judgment, it is right to work for his values and to keep
> the product of his work. If life on earth is his purpose, he
> has a right to live. . . .[64]

Now this series of puns—or in more formal terms, this equivo-

---

[62] Oswyn Murray, "Life and Society in Classical Greece," *The Oxford History of the Classical World*, 1986, 205.

[63] See Appendix G: "Christ and Civilization."

[64] *Capitalism: The Unknown Ideal*, 323.

cation—is supposed to be an argument establishing man's rights as an intelligible concept; I have already commented on this point. What I have not yet pointed out is that the same argument may be applied to non-human animals. Their purpose is obviously "to live on earth"; to do so they must use whatever rudimentary minds they have; they, too, must act on their own judgments, which they may believe to be as free as we believe our judgments to be; they, too, must work for their values and retain the product of their work. Since life on Earth is their purpose, they, too, have a right to live. The advocates of the rights of only rational animals may reject this argument for the rights of all animals, including men, yet they will lack logic in their rejection, for Rand's derivation of rights applies equally to all animals, rational or otherwise. And at least one prominent person in the Objectivist movement is also a leader in the animal rights movement.

Indeed, it might even be argued that Rand's rights argument establishes rights for plants, which, as Rand herself wrote, have values, live on Earth, work for their values, and keep them. Unfortunately, plants do not have minds or make judgments (although some recent authors might dispute this), but this does not impair the validity of the argument: Plants live; their existence is not unconditional like stones; they have values; they have an automatic morality; and therefore they have a right to live. . . .

Rand herself pointed out, "On the physical level, the functions of all living organisms, from the simplest to the most complex—from the nutritive function in the single cell of an amoeba to the blood circulation in the body of a man—are actions generated by the organism itself and directed to a single goal: the maintenance of the organism's life."[65] Cells, bacteria, viruses, and human embryos, because they are living entities, have goals and values. They live on Earth, work for their values, and keep them. They may not have minds, but their existence is not unconditional, like that of stones. They have values and an automatic code of morality. What furthers their lives is good; what thwarts their lives is evil. It is

[65] *The Virtue of Selfishness*, 16.

therefore immoral for anyone to violate their rights, to seek to kill them. Objectivist political philosophy logically implies two doctrines: a pantheistic "reverence for life" and a totalitarian survival of the most human.

I must conclude, then, that Rand failed to present either a coherent ethical theory or a logically consistent political theory. Her political philosophy, like all secular political philosophies, leads logically to anarchy and/or totalitarianism. It cannot furnish the basis for a free society, despite the brilliant rhetoric that seeks to persuade in lieu of logic. Its acceptance by a large segment of the American citizenry will hasten the future of the "boot stamping on the human face forever."[66]

Furthermore, Rand's express advocacy of a free society ought to be disregarded, for a reason that one of her own disciples stated: "a philosopher's [political] views, to the extent that they contradict the essentials of his system, have comparatively little historical significance."[67]

---

[66] George Orwell, *1984.*

[67] Leonard Peikoff, *The Objectivist*, April 1969, 1. Peikoff wrote, defending Aristotle: ". . . the primary significance of Aristotle, or of any philosopher, does not lie in his politics. It lies in the fundamentals of his system: his metaphysics and epistemology" (*The Ominous Parallels*, 21).

7

AYN RAND AND THE CLOSE OF HER SYSTEM

Mistakes of this size are never made innocently.

Ayn Rand
Atlas Shrugged

One of the ways in which the damned will be con-
founded is that they will see themselves condemned by their
own reason, by which they claim to condemn the Christian
religion.

Pascal
Pensées

In *Who Is Ayn Rand?* Nathaniel Branden boasted: "No one has
dared publicly to name the essential ideas of *Atlas Shrugged*
and to attempt to refute them."[1] That boast, still carried on copies
of *Who Is Ayn Rand?* published in 1996, has not been true since
1974, when this author named the essential ideas of *Atlas Shrugged*
and refuted them. In both that book and this one, the clarification

[1] *Who Is Ayn Rand?* 51.

and refutation of Rand's ideas have proceeded simultaneously; in large part, their clarification is their refutation. Once the ideas are examined, stripped of Rand's literary prose, it becomes clear that they are blatantly self-contradictory.

Rand summarized her philosophy while standing on one foot;[2] we might do the same, summarizing the logical conclusions of her premises:

> Metaphysics: Indestructible Matter
> Epistemology: Skepticism
> Ethics: Hedonism
> Politics: Anarcho-totalitarianism.

Her metaphysics, despite some more skeptical statements near the end of her life, consists of a belief in the primacy of indestructible matter. Her epistemology, sensation plus abstraction, leads only to skepticism, not to knowledge. Our dissection of her epistemology reveals the many ambiguities and difficulties in Rand's theory and concludes with Branden's admission that even though all the evidence might point to a specific conclusion, the conclusion might be wrong. This, of course, is skepticism. Rand's ethics, being founded on an amoral, unjustified choice, and guided by sensation, results in hedonism. Then her entire ethical edifice collapses because she built it on an imaginary bridge across Hume's gap between the "is" and the "ought," a bridge called "need." Her politics, deriving from her theory of the sovereign individual, leads to anarchism and totalitarianism.

Rand frequently complained about the plight of American philosophy. It is indeed indicative of the bankruptcy of contemporary American philosophy that Rand's sophomoric arguments and ideas must be seriously considered. Rand was primarily a novelist; without the novels, few would pay any attention to her philosophy; indeed, many people ignore the philosophy while enjoying the novels. But Objectivism is another illustration of the cyclical nature of

---

[2] *The Objectivist Newsletter*, August 1962, 35.

secular philosophy: It turns from great theoretical systems purport-
edly giving a comprehensive view of reality to critiques of those
systems, which critiques then result in skepticism. When the depths
of skepticism are reached, some new philosopher erects another
edifice of human thought, only to have that edifice eroded by the
logical criticisms of other scholars, resulting in a new skepticism.
So the cycle turns, from Parmenides to the Sophists, from the Sophists to Plato; from Plato to the sophists, from the sophists to Augustine; from Augustine to the sophists, from the sophists to
Descartes; from Descartes to the sophists, from the sophists to
Hegel; from Hegel to the sophists. The history of secular philosophy is the history of failure, but secular philosophers will not give
up their futile attempts to build a tower unto Heaven.

The Perennial Failure of Secular Philosophy

A student of philosophy might ask why all secular philosophies
have failed to withstand logical scrutiny, why the cycle of epistemological optimism and pessimism has existed for well over two
thousand years. To answer the question one ought to examine the
premises of the various philosophies, and there one finds a common element: the rejection of propositional revelation. All secular
philosophies—indeed, most religious philosophies—reject Biblical revelation. Objectivism is no exception. Yet the repeated philosophical failures have not resulted in a repudiation of this axiom,
only in more determined efforts to attain knowledge by some means
other than revelation. Lessing's famous alternative between accepting truth from the hand of God as a gift, and eternally searching
for, but never finding truth, is the alternative faced by all thinkers.
All non-Christian thinkers have chosen an endless, irrational, and
futile quest, just as Lessing did. The choice as outlined by Lessing
is a choice that must be made by all men. Shall I accept revelation
or not? Is the Bible the Word of God or not? Non-Christian philosophers (and some philosophers who profess to be Christian) have
chosen the futile search. Many believe that the search is not futile
at all, but will one day succeed. It will not. Objectivism will be

eclipsed by a new surge of skepticism, and rightly so, for it has furnished no good reasons for believing in the ability of the human mind to create a system of knowledge.

The natural antipathy of the human mind to accepting an epistemological gift from God—revealed propositional truth—is obvious and ever present. It is the explanation for the cycle of secular philosophy. Faced with the alternative of accepting knowledge as a gift of God and finding knowledge on his own, the rebellious human being will always refuse the gift of knowledge and seek to erect his own philosophical system, his own Tower of Babel. This book has been written with the purpose of speeding the collapse of this newest form of secular philosophical optimism, so that men may be forced to admit that the choice is nihilism or Christianity; skepticism or revelation. The choice is not, as Rand has said, between Communism and Objectivism,[3] for those two philosophies are actually quite similar: Both are materialistic, both are empiricist, and both are anarchistic. Rand escaped physically from the Communists in the mid-1920's, but she has never escaped intellectually from the Communists. Rather than being diametrically opposed, Objectivism and Communism share common premises, and attack a common foe, Christianity.

Marx wrote:

The materialist doctrines of original goodness, equal intellectual endowments of men, and the all-importance of experience, custom, education, and environmental conditions are necessarily connected to communism and socialism. *If man derives all his knowledge and his perception, etc., from the world of the senses and from experience, in the world of the senses,* it is our business to so order the empirical world that man shall have truly human experiences in it, shall experience himself to be a human being. *If self-interest rightly understood is the basic principle of morality,* it behooves us to make sure that the private inter-

---

[3] "Faith and Force," 14.

est of the individual shall coincide with the general human interest.[4]

While Objectivism and Communism share fundamental ideas, the antithesis between those two philosophies and Christianity is unmistakable: God or Matter? Propositional revelation or sensation? God's law or man's wishes? Limited government or totalitarian anarchy? Only one system of thought challenges Communism in all its ramifications, and that system is not Objectivism. That system is Christianity.

The Promise of Christianity

This book is a defense of Christianity against one secular philosophy. The author hopes the reader will not stop with these pages, but will proceed to check his premises and the premises of other thinkers. To aid the inquiring reader, this writer has edited and published dozens of books on philosophy and Christianity—books discussing science, historiography, language, logic, psychology, ethics, epistemology, education, and ancient, medieval, and contemporary philosophies. The conclusion of those discussions is that the axiom of revelation—the proposition "The Bible alone is the Word of God"—contains the only solution to man's epistemological problem, for it provides truth—metaphysical, epistemological, theological, ethical, and political truth—that cannot be deduced from any non-Christian axiom. Propositional revelation avoids the insuperable difficulties encountered in any form of empiricism. Revelation is not a shortcut to knowledge, as though there were other, longer routes; the history of philosophy shows that propositional revelation is the only way to knowledge. All other routes are dead ends.

Biblical revelation does not mean, of course, mystical experience: Revelation is intelligible, communicable, and propositional information. By revelation we have been given not only a coherent epistemology, but a coherent theology, ethics, and politics.

[4] Karl Marx and Friedrich Engels, *The German Ideology*, emphasis added.

There are, of course, many who will persist in their refusal to accept knowledge as a gift from God and continue to attempt to find knowledge by their own efforts. The history of philosophy is the history of that intellectual rebellion. These persons will argue against Christianity on many grounds. I cannot anticipate and reply to all those arguments here. But if the reader is serious about learning what those replies are, he may consult the list of books at the end of this book for his answers.

One ubiquitous objection to Christianity is that this is a modern, scientific age in which it is impossible to believe myths such as are recounted in the Bible. Every scientific advance, from the discovery of germs to the successful placing of a man on the Moon, further destroys the credibility of the Bible and enhances the reputation of science. "In our age," wrote Barbara Branden, "in the presence of the triumphs of science, no thinking man will listen to the voices from the Dark Ages speaking of Original Sin and the futility of human endeavor; no thinking man will reject reason and the achievement of man's mind."[5]

Unfortunately, this argument is a logical fallacy: Branden assumed that science must be true because it succeeds so well. But truth, unfortunately for the Objectivists, the scientists, and the pragmatists, is not necessarily that which works. The backdoor acceptance of pragmatism forms a strong undercurrent in all of Rand's works. Perhaps it can best be seen in *Atlas Shrugged*, which emphasizes not only that only the truth will work, but that what does work is the truth. Engels, in his introduction to *Socialism: Utopian and Scientific*, gave the reason why empiricists embrace pragmatism:

> From the moment we turn to our own use these objects [sense objects], according to the qualities we perceive in them, we put to an infallible test the correctness or otherwise of our sense-perceptions. If these perceptions have been wrong, then our estimate of the use to which an object

---

[5] *The Objectivist Newsletter*, March 1962, 11.

can be turned must also be wrong, and our attempt must fail. But if we succeed in accomplishing our aim, if we find that the object does agree with our idea of it, and does answer the purpose we intended it for, then that is positive proof that our perceptions of it and its qualities, so far, agree with reality outside ourselves.[6]

Engels' argument is, of course, the elementary logical fallacy of asserting the consequent.

The "triumphs of science" are technological triumphs, not epistemological triumphs, and they can constitute no logical objection to belief in the truth of the Bible. There is no clash between "truths discovered by science" and revealed truth, because science discovers no truths.[7] More fundamentally, sense experience provides no truths.[8]

There are, of course, many other standard objections to Christianity, some more important than others. Some will object that I have not proved that God exists, and I will be among the first to admit that I have not. Nor is it logical to ask me to do so: God is contained in the axiom of revelation, and one does not prove axioms, one chooses them.

This fact brings us to an objection that is a favorite with many: If axioms are matters of choice, then all philosophies are arbitrarily

[6] *Marx and Engels on Religion*, 296.

[7] "At this point we must pause to clarify the logic both of this particular situation and of experimental verification in general. A simple argument of verification proceeds as follows: the given hypothesis implies certain definite results; the experiment actually gives these results; therefore the hypothesis is verified and can be called a law. Obviously, this argument is the fallacy of asserting the consequent; and since all verification must commit this fallacy, it follows that no law or hypothesis can ever be logically demonstrated" (Gordon H. Clark, *The Philosophy of Science and Belief in God*, 71).

[8] "Of all empiricists Hume most clearly shows not only that experience cannot prove the existence of God, but also and perhaps reluctantly, that nothing whatever can be learned from experience" (Gordon H. Clark, *Three Types of Religious Philosophy*, 76).

chosen. Since there can be no demonstration of axioms, one philosophy is as good as another, and philosophy becomes futile. This objection overlooks the fact that while axioms cannot be proved, they can be disproved. If an axiom implies a contradiction, it must be rejected. That is the way to judge an axiom: by its logical implications. If they are contradictory, the axiom must be rejected.

> Choice [of axioms], however, is unavoidable because first principles cannot be demonstrated, and though some choices are arbitrary, the philosophical choice has regard to the widest possible consistency. Choice therefore is as legitimate as it is inevitable.[9]

It is not enough to dismiss Christianity as irrational, mystical, or foolish because it is based on faith, for such words have no meaning until they are defined, and an act of definition presupposes a body of propositions in which the definition appears, i.e., a philosophy. Such perfunctory dismissals are merely expressions of the speaker's emotional and irrational aversion to Christianity, not an intellectual critique of it.

Solving the Epistemological Problem

We have seen the insuperable difficulties faced by an Objectivist theory of epistemology: the problems of abstraction, of moving from sensation to perception, and from perception to conception. Throughout this process we are given to understand that the given to the mind is a representation of the real world, not the real world itself. The perceptions and conceptions are mental representations of the real existents. As we saw in the chapter on epistemology, this view of cognition leads to further difficulties:

> Every thinker must decide for himself whether the X that is immediately in the mind is the real object or a repre-

[9] Gordon H. Clark, *A Christian View of Men and Things*, 33-34.

sentation of it. Those who base knowledge on sensation have only two alternatives: They may, like Aristotle, assert that a sensory image is the result of and represents an external object. But in this case . . . there is no way to check the representation. Not only is it impossible to know whether or not an image is a faithful image; it is empirically impossible to know whether it represents anything at all. The second alternative is to deny the external object. Then we have images or sensations that represent nothing. They and they alone are the objects of knowledge. But in this case you cannot have my image any more than you can have my headache. . . .

What is worse (or is it better?) there is no one to communicate with. Not only is it impossible to know another's thought, it is impossible to know that there is another. Each of us, or rather I alone, know only my ideas, and what I call you is only one of my headaches. In technical language, empiricism results in solipsism.[10]

Christian philosophy—Scripturalism—avoids all these difficulties because its theory of cognition, revelation, does not rely on sensation, abstraction, and representationalism. Christian philosophy is epistemological realism; that is, the X present to the mind does not represent something else,[11] but is itself the object of knowledge. In distinction to some philosophies that hold a superficially

[10] Gordon H. Clark, *Three Types of Religious Philosophy*, 121.

[11] "Sensory experiences, such as the sensation of red, or loud, or sweet, are mental events and take place only in the mind. People often suppose that these qualities are copies of, or resemble, things external to the mind. However, it is difficult, or rather impossible, to imagine how a sensory quality can resemble anything other than a sensory quality. How can a color resemble something invisible? How can the sensation hard resemble anything intangible? Note that the alleged external objects are not perceptions. Therefore they are non-perceptible. Only perceptions are perceptible. No one has ever seen a material body. Colors are only mental events" (Gordon H. Clark, *Three Types of Religious Philosophy*, 76).

similar position, Christian philosophy asserts that propositions, not concepts, are the objects of knowledge, for only propositions can be true or false. Equally important, for this forms the uniqueness of Christian epistemology, these propositions are propositions in the mind of God. Christian epistemology avoids not only the problems of empiricism, it avoids the problems of idealism Plato enumerated in the *Parmenides*, particularly the problem of how the human mind and the objects of knowledge (the Ideas) are brought into conjunction. Since persons and truth are propositions in the mind of God, there is no gap between the phenomenal world and the noumenal world which must be bridged. We ourselves are in the mind of God. "In him we live and move and have our being."[12] Thus the myriad problems faced by Aristotle (or Rand) on the one hand and Plato on the other are seen to be philosophogenic: they are caused by the philosophers themselves. The problems do not inhere in the state of affairs: they are created by the false premises of the philosophers.

As for theology, it should be manifest that the state of affairs to which Objectivist theology leads cannot arise when God is the object of devotion, and not nature or man. The deification of nature, which has become pronounced since Darwin published his theological work *On the Origin of Species*, has led to Nazism, Communism, and the popular pantheism of the day, environmentalism. It is only when both man and nature are seen as creatures, and therefore as undeserving of the primacy that must lead to the destruction of both man and nature, that the consequences of idolatry can be avoided.

The precepts of God as presented in the Scriptures are not subject to the criticisms I have made of Objectivist politics. Authority is not derived from man, but from God, and he has ordained government for one specific purpose: the defense of the good and the punishment of evildoers.The anarchistic and totalitarian consequences flowing from the primacy of the state or of the individual are entirely avoided by positing sovereignty in God alone, neither in the state nor in the individual.

[12] Acts 17:28.

In ethics proper, the hedonism to which any theory of plea-sure-as-the-good leads is avoided by Christianity, which teaches that no knowledge, including knowledge of good and evil, can be gained by sense experience. Rather, the moral law has been spelled out in the Scripture. Unlike the generalities which form Rand's ethics,[13] Christian ethics has content that is not ambiguous. The Bible gives both general principles and detailed practical moral guidance; Ayn Rand gave us neither. She did not and could not tell us whether monogamy, polygamy, or adultery is good or bad; whether het-erosexuality or homosexuality is good or bad; whether marriage or divorce is good; whether and under what circumstances killing is permissible; whether children should be spanked; whether there is a just war; whether capital punishment is legitimate; and so on. None of Rand's general principles is supported by logic, and even if they were, one could not derive the sort of detailed guidance necessary for daily living from her general principles. Her ethics fails on both counts: It provides no principles, and it provides no details.

Conclusion

I began this chapter with two mottos, one from Rand, the other from Pascal. They are complementary, but one might wonder what

---

[13] The ambiguities of Rand's ethics allowed her to come down on both sides of an issue. For example, she said a number of times, "where a gun begins, moral-ity ends," meaning, apparently, that all actions taken under duress are amoral. She further stated that it is even improper to tender advice to someone "under the gun": "Morally, no one can give advice in any issue where choice and deci-sions are not voluntary: 'morality ends where a gun begins.' As to practical al-ternatives available, the best thing to do is to consult a good lawyer" *(Capital-ism: The Unknown Ideal*, 235).

Yet after all this she holds that disobedience to a law, except for the purpose of testing its constitutionality, is wrong: "Civil disobedience may be justifiable, in some cases, when and if an individual disobeys a law in order to bring an issue to court, as a test case. But there is no justification, in a civilized society, for the kind of mass civil disobedience that involves the violation of the rights of others—regardless of whether the demonstrators' goal is good or evil" (*Capi-talism: The Unknown Ideal*, 256).

I had in mind by placing them at the beginning. An exposition of their full meaning would require another volume, so I will suggest only one thing: Rand recognized the law of contradiction as governing all thought, and yet she chose—worse, she created—a philosophy full of contradictions. She stands condemned by her own standard.

> If we think at all, we think the laws of logic. Truth is inherent or innate in the mind. But God is truth. Therefore it is impossible to annihilate God in thought. He exists so truly that he cannot even be conceived not to exist.[14]

It is Rand's choice that makes her guilty, her choice of a contradictory philosophy, her choice of a secular philosophy, her choice of Objectivism.

[14] Gordon H. Clark, *Three Types of Religious Philosophy*, 39.

APPENDIXES

A

THE OMINOUS PARALLELS

In 1982 Leonard Peikoff published *The Ominous Parallels: The End of Freedom in America*, which Rand described in her Introduction as "the first book by an Objectivist philosopher other than myself" (vii). Her reaction to the book was a paraphrase of *Atlas Shrugged*: "It's so wonderful to see a great, new, crucial achievement which is not mine."

The book, which is a useful contribution to political philosophy only in the number of quotations from other sources that it furnishes the reader, is a poorly written, sophomoric attempt at intellectual history. Nevertheless, some of the quotations Peikoff provides are quite fascinating. For example, this one from Herman Goering: "Just as the Roman Catholic considers the Pope infallible in all matters concerning religion and morals, so do we National Socialists believe with the same inner conviction that for us the Leader is in all political and other matters concerning the national and social interests of the people simply infallible." Or this from the Nazi Minister of Church Affairs: "Adolf Hitler is the true Holy Ghost!" And from Hitler himself: "People have set us down as enemies of the intelligence. We are. But in a much deeper sense than these conceited dolts of bourgeois scientists ever dream of."

Peikoff, in fact, furnishes us with more than one quotation that might have been spoken by Ayn Rand or Karl Marx. For example, the instrumental use of reason for physical survival: "Men misuse their intelligence. It is not the seat of a special dignity of mankind, but merely an instrument in the struggle for life." Or, in Randian phraseology, man's mind is his only means of survival. And just as Rand argued that truth was "contextual," so the Nazis argued that it is relative to the situation.

One of Peikoff's most annoying errors is his habit of imputing his own definitions (or rather, Rand's definitions) to terms used by others, rather than trying to understand how they define their own terms. So if someone uses the term *faith*, he redefines it his way. If the term is *sacrifice*, it must have the meaning that Rand gave it. Such a procedure is, of course, the opposite of scholarship; it is a deliberate refusal to try to understand what an author is saying. Rand made a virtue of such deliberate misunderstanding: "I am incapable of switching definitions of my concepts to fit each separate occasion and of letting them mean one thing when I use them, but another when Bertrand Russell uses them, and a third when you [John Hospers] use them."[1] One would hate to attend a baseball game with either of those two.

In attempting to trace the intellectual origins of Nazism, Peikoff somehow misses the greatest superstition of the twentieth century, evolution (there is no entry for evolution, Charles Darwin, or Ernst Haeckel in the index), which has fueled all forms of totalitarianism in the twentieth century. Instead, Peikoff has to go back 400 years to Martin Luther's anti-Jewish statements to "explain" Hitler. Once again, scholarship suffers at the hands of an ill-educated man. Hitler, and many of his accomplices, of course, were members of the Roman Catholic Church.

That absolute monarchy, ruled by an arrogant man who claims to be a miracle-worker and God's representative on Earth, because it is quasi-Aristotelian, is the ecclesiastical organization that many Objectivists and libertarians seem to respect the most. For example, Murray Rothbard, a Jewish atheist, hated Calvinism passionately, and favored Catholicism. The anarchist Rothbard favored the to-

---

[1] *Letters of Ayn Rand,* 536.

talitarian Roman church. There is an underlying consistency in this apparent conundrum: It is a willingness to believe anything but the truth. Like Peikoff, Rothbard was a prodigious researcher (when I worked for Congressman Ron Paul in the late 1970s and early 1980s, I advised the Congressman to hire Rothbard to draft an historical chapter for the Congressman's book *The Case for Gold*), but he did not have an accurate understanding of the ideas and institutions he was writing about.

Finding the totalitarianism of Plato a source of Nazism, Peikoff ignores the totalitarianism of Aristotle. But Peikoff has some kind words even for Plato, because he was a pagan, which saved him from being totally evil. Kant, however, is another matter; lacking Plato's philosophically redeeming paganism, Kant is pure evil. Hegel, whom Peikoff describes as "Kant's chief heir," is the cause of much damage. This is neither serious history nor serious philosophy. Behind Kant, Peikoff asserts, is "the ethics of Christianity, which Kant carried to its climax." "Christianity prepared the ground. It paved the way for modern totalitarianism." Peikoff continues the Pharisees' war against the Messiah. Peikoff's virulent hatred of the good for being good comes across most clearly in his diatribe against Calvinism, which was "the worst of the ideas of the old world" (105).

Contrary to Rand, who carried on her own war against Messiah, *The Ominous Parallels* is neither a great nor a crucial book. It is, rather, a work of desipience.

B

OBJECTIVISM:
THE PHILOSOPHY OF AYN RAND

Peikoff himself has an ambivalent attitude toward this book, so one can hardly expect a critic to be more favorably inclined. He begins by raising canonical problems, even suggesting that "some of Ayn Rand's most important ideas are expressed only briefly or not at all in her books."[2] Now that is an extraordinary statement. It seems to mean that over a writing career that spanned five decades, Rand was either a poor writer who could not express her most important ideas in print, or that she did not wish to put her most important ideas into print and had an esoteric doctrine as well as an exoteric doctrine.

Peikoff claims that his book is based on the ideas that somehow never found their way into Rand's books, on his audiotaped course on Objectivism, which Rand described in 1976 as "the only authorized presentation of the entire theoretical structure of Objectivism, i.e., the only one that I know of my own knowledge to be fully accurate." Despite this statement, Peikoff writes: "nor can this book be properly described as 'official Objectivist doctrine.' " " 'Objectivism,' " Peikoff writes, "is the name of Ayn Rand's philosophy as presented in the material she herself wrote or endorsed."[3]

[2] *Objectivism*, xiv.

[3] *Objectivism*, xv.

And since Rand neither wrote nor endorsed this book, it is not Objectivism, despite its title. On the other hand, "The present book is the first comprehensive statement of her philosophy."[4] Peikoff finishes (but does end the confusion) this confused account by calling the book "the definitive statement of Ayn Rand's philosophy— as interpreted by her best student and chosen heir."

The confusion, rather than dissipating, deepens. On page 1, Peikoff quotes Rand: "You have no choice about the necessity to integrate your observations, your experiences, your knowledge into abstract ideas, i.e., into principles." Query: Whatever happened to volitional consciousness?

Existence

One page 4, discussing the axiomatic concept existence, Peikoff tells us, "This axiom does not tell us anything about the nature of existents; it merely underscores the fact that they exist." This is both meaningless and disingenuous. If the concept does not tell us anything about the nature of existents, then it is meaningless. If it underscores that they exist, then it is trivial. Let me repeat: Everything exists. So far as a term has any faint meaning at all, it exists. Unicorns exist. Dreams exist. Hallucinations exist. Illusions exist. God exists. Klingons exist. The square root of minus one exists. If Peikoff now wants to back away from the materialism so clearly taught in Rand's books, then the axiom of existence is meaningless. Peikoff obviously wants to do so, for he writes that "The concept [of existence] does not specify that a physical world exists."[5] Now that statement may come as a shock to many, for Rand had drilled into her readers the concept of "Objective Reality," that is, the physical world of indestructible matter. If that is not what Objectivists mean by the concept and the phrase, then it is difficult to distinguish their view from the views of idealists and Christians. If "objectively real" does not mean physical, I definitely believe in the objective reality of the God of the Bible.

[4] *Objectivism*, xiii.

[5] *Objectivism*, 5.

Peikoff also tells us that "The concept of 'existence' is the widest of all concepts. It subsumes everything—every entity, action, attribute, relationship (including every state of consciousness)—everything which is, was, or will be." And that is precisely why the concept of existence is meaningless. Any concept that applies to everything without exception has no meaning. If everything were black, "black" would have no meaning. The law of contradiction requires a term, if it is to have meaning, to mean not-something. But "existence" applies to everything without exception. It is, therefore, absolutely meaningless.

Worse still, Peikoff, quoting Rand, tells us that an axiomatic concept is "a primary fact [what a "fact" is neither Rand nor Peikoff is saying] of reality that cannot be analyzed. . . . It is the fundamentally given and directly perceived or experienced, which requires no proof or explanation, but on which all proofs and explanations rest." Furthermore, "Axiomatic concepts are not subject to the process of definition. Their referents can be specified only ostensively, by pointing to instances." "One knows that the axioms are true not by inference of any kind, but by sense perception."[6]

I have examined the many errors in these statements in the discussion of *Introduction to Objectivist Epistemology*. I shall merely summarize them here.

First, ostensive definition is a contradiction in terms.
Second, at the very root of Rand's philosophy is something, we know not what, called "existence," that is both unanalyzable and unexplainable. (No mystic could ask for more.)
Third, this "concept" is "given" by sense experience. But Rand has told us that only percepts, not concepts, are given in sense experience.
Fourth, those who have no or defective sense experience obviously cannot get to the axioms.
Fifth, knowledge of the truth of the axioms rests on sense experience, not on inference of any kind. But if sense experi-

---

[6] *Objectivism*, 7, 8.

ence either logically or chronologically precedes knowledge of the axioms, then the axioms are not axioms at all, but derivatives. Objectivism's axioms are not first principles (and "axiom" means "first principle") but second, third, or seventeenth principles.

Validation

Peikoff, realizing that Objectivism's major ideas cannot be logically proven, invents a new concept to conceal the difficulty: validation. On page 8 he writes:

> The above is the validation of the Objectivist axioms. "Validation" I take to be a broader term than "proof," one that subsumes any process of establishing an idea's relationship to reality, whether deductive reasoning, inductive reasoning, or perceptual self-evidence. In this sense, one can and must validate every item of knowledge, including axioms. The validation of axioms, however, is the simplest of all: sense perception.

What the rules of validation are, Peikoff does not say. He does not even attempt to justify inductive reasoning. Yet validation is the undescribed (and perhaps indescribable) procedure that the Objectivists have substituted for deductive proof. Peikoff has confirmed one of my primary criticisms of Objectivism: Far from being too logical, as some of its critics have maintained, Objectivism is not nearly logical enough. It wants a "broad" process by which to justify its claims. It does not wish to be restricted to deductive reasoning. It wants to be irrational and illogical.

Ethics

Bringing clearly into view the implications of Objectivist epistemology for natural law, Peikoff distinguishes between the "metaphysical" and the "man-made" in terms of law: "The law of gravity

is metaphysically given; the laws against murder are man-made."
Now Peikoff, apparently operating in the world of eighteenth-century science, seems to believe in Newtonian natural laws. But moral law, he writes, is man-made. It is not metaphysical; it is not natural. That would remove Objectivist ethics and politics from the so-called natural law or natural rights position, for there are no ethics or laws in nature, just as there are no universals in nature. Natural rights ideas are derived from what Peikoff calls the "intrinsicist" school, the school of thought to which Plato, Aristotle, and Hegel belonged. This has profound implications for all of Objectivism, for it places Objectivism closer to Protagoras than to Aristotle. Man really is the measure of all things, both for Peikoff and for Protagoras.

Materialism

Peikoff's command of philosophy is as weak in this book as his command of history is in *The Ominous Parallels*. He distorts the views of the materialists on page 33. He writes: "Materialists—men such as Democritus, Hobbes, Marx, Skinner—champion nature but deny the reality or efficacy of consciousness. Consciousness, in this view, is either a myth or a useless byproduct of the brain or other motions." Now Skinner may have thought consciousness is a myth (John Dewey, whom Peikoff does not mention, explicitly said it is),[7] but Marx did not. Peikoff presents this caricature of the materialists (not all materialists are behaviorists like Dewey and Skinner) in an attempt to distinguish Objectivism from materialism. Now Objectivism may not be behaviorism, but it is materialism. As I have shown by dozens of quotations in the body of this book, Marxism and Objectivism are quite similar. So when Rand denounces the mystics of muscle, her rhetoric is hollow.
    Peikoff explains the atheism of Objectivism on pages 32 and 33:

[Objectivism] does not accept God or any variant of the

---

[7] See Gordon Clark, *William James and John Dewey*. The Trinity Foundation, 1995.

supernatural. We are *a-theist,* as well as a-devilist, a-demonist, a-gremlinist. We reject every "spiritual" dimension, force, Form, Idea, entity, power, or whatnot alleged to transcend existence. We reject idealism. To put the point positively: we accept reality, and that's all.

Now this bit of disingenuousness passes for brilliant philosophy in Objectivist circles. If one listens carefully, one can see that Objectivism rejects all forms of idealism: Platonic (Idea), Aristotelian (Form), and Christian (theist). But none of these three philosophies advocated anything that transcended existence, as Peikoff alleges. All asserted that the Ideas, or Forms, or God, *exist.* "Existence," quite obviously, means "sensible," or "physical," or "material" to the Objectivists. Despite Peikoff's claim that Objectivists are not materialists, they are. They think that even Aristotle was too much of a "supernaturalist." That places them among the Democriteans.

Consciousness

Explaining his view of consciousness, Peikoff declares:

> Consciousness is an attribute of perceived entities here on earth. It is a faculty possessed under definite conditions by a certain group of living organisms. It is directly observable (by introspection). It has a specific nature, including specific physical organs, and acts accordingly, i.e., lawfully. It has a life-sustaining function. . . . There is nothing unnatural or supernatural. There is no . . . hint of immortality. . . . The soul is a biological datum open to observation, conceptualization, and scientific study.[8]

Of course, it is not consciousness *per se* that is directly observable on this scheme, but only one's own consciousness. The consciousnesses of others, if there be such, are inferences. This con-

[8] *Objectivism*, 33-34.

sciousness, Peikoff writes, "has a specific nature." That is what Kant said, of course. It is not what Aristotle said. Kant and Aristotle agreed that if the mind has a nature of its own, it cannot grasp reality. In the interest of defending knowledge of reality, Aristotle denied that the mind is actually anything before it thinks; Kant asserted that the mind has forms and can never know things in themselves. How Kantian Peikoff is quickly becomes obvious.

The concept of consciousness, Peikoff writes, "can be specified only ostensively." Now, of course, one cannot specify any concept ostensively, since only existents, not concepts, exist, according to the Objectivists. One cannot point to a concept. Their main complaint against Plato and Aristotle is that those two giants made concepts exist outside the mind. They were "intrinsicists." But to say that consciousness can be specified "only ostensively" is to talk utter nonsense. One cannot point either to consciousness or to specific consciousness. Consciousness is not an object of perception.

Sense Perception

Sense perception itself, Peikoff writes, "is an axiom." The senses provide "data," which are "the primaries of cognition, the unchallengeable, the *self-evident*." All concepts must be traced back to sense data. The senses are inerrant, or "valid." Their validity, infallibility, or inerrancy is "an axiom."[9] They are "unchallengeable." The account that Peikoff gives of sense perception is materialist to the core.

> Sensory experience is a form of awareness produced by physical entities (the external stimuli) acting on physical instrumentalities (the sense organs), which respond automatically, as a link in a causally determined chain. Obeying inexorable natural laws, the organs transmit a message

---

[9] *Objectivism*, 39.

to the nervous system and the brain. Such organs have no power of choice, no power to invent, distort, or deceive.[10]

Now, all of this is pure asseveration. No argument or evidence whatsoever is offered. We have, therefore, no reason to believe it. But the statement itself is implausible. We all have experience (and empiricists certainly cannot object to an appeal to experience, can they?) with various electronic gadgets that obey "inexorable natural laws," yet which do indeed invent, distort, and deceive. This writer has experienced various distortions listening to a radio or speaking on the telephone. Sometimes the distortions are so bad that one cannot tell what the message is. Obeying inexorable natural laws, those devices are transmitting messages inaccurately. Or, for an example of systematic deception, not occasional distortion, consider the television. There is no moving image on the cathode ray tube. There appears to be a moving image, but there are simply chemicals affixed to the inside of the tube that glow different colors when irradiated. Nothing moves on the tube. In a movie theater, there appear to be moving images on the screen. The figure that appears to move from left to right is an illusion. So much for the reliability and accuracy of mechanical devices in transmitting messages. Despite the silliness of his statement, Peikoff unabashedly asserts that "*All* sense perceptions are necessarily valid."[11] Whatever "valid" means, it cannot mean "accurate."

In a quasi-Kantian admission, except that Peikoff makes the sense organs as well as the mind form our sensations, Peikoff writes:

> Our sensations are caused in part by objects in reality. They are also—an equally important point—caused in part by our organs of perception, which are responsible for the fact that we perceive objects in the form of sensations of color, sound, smell, and so forth. A being with radically different senses would presumably perceive reality in correspondingly different forms.

[10] *Objectivism*, 40.

[11] *Objectivism*, 41.

So Peikoff's analogy with the mechanical transmission of messages, misleading as it is anyway, is also quite wrong. According to Peikoff, our sense organs cause our sensations. Notice the sensations they cause: "color, sound, smell, and so forth." Now any reader of Rand's books would have learned that these very things that Peikoff ascribes to the sense organs are actually parts of "objective reality." Now, Peikoff tells us, they are actually "forms" (the word is Peikoff's) created by our sense organs, and the world really is not colored, or noisy, or aromatic. In fact, if we had different sense organs, "reality" would be quite different for us. Each consciousness necessarily and inescapably lives within its own "reality." All the "evidence of the senses" is really caused by our sense organs, which react in certain ways to stimuli. Reality, for example, is not colored. We have color hallucinations. We see it as colored, but reality in itself is uncolored.

How does Peikoff tackle color blindness? Incredibly he writes:

> Such a difference [in perception] does not pertain to cognitive content and does not indicate any disagreement among the parties. The senses of a man with normal vision, to take the standard example, do not contradict those of a color-blind man. When the former says about some object, "It is red," he must in reason mean by the statement: "It is an entity in reality of a specific nature such that, when it acts on my senses, I perceive it in the form of red color." That is true; that is what it is. Similarly, if the color-blind man says "It is gray," he has to mean: "It is an entity in reality of a specific nature such that, when it acts on my senses, I perceive it in the form of gray color." That also is true; that is what it is. Neither statement conflicts with the other. Both men are perceiving that which is and are doing so in a specific form.[12]

Now this explanation is brazenly false. Neither man means nor intends to say what Peikoff imputes to him. Each means to say:

[12] *Objectivism*, 42.

That apple is red, or, that apple is gray. Their statements contradict each other. That is why one is called blind. Second, if this difference in perception does not pertain to "cognitive content," to what does it pertain? What cognitive content is there in vision except color? All we see and all we can see are colors. If objective reality is not colored, as Peikoff says, then we are not seeing objective reality. Third, and once again, it has become clear that for the Objectivists, as well as for Protagoras, man, the individual, is the measure of all things. Objectivism is really subjectivism.

In anti-Kantian fashion, Peikoff writes:

> Since the objects we perceive have a nature independent of us [how does Peikoff know there are such objects?], it must be possible to distinguish between form and object; between the aspects of the perceived world that derive from our form of perception (such as colors, sounds, smells) and the aspects that belong to metaphysical reality itself, apart from us.

The difficulty is, of course, that Peikoff simply asserts this; he does not argue it. Kant was too smart to make such an unwarranted statement. If we always perceive forms, then it is impossible to distinguish between forms and objects. Peikoff sort of senses the futility of philosophy when he passes the buck to physics: "The task of identifying the nature of physical objects as they are [*Ding an sich* was the way Kant put it] apart from man's form of perception does not belong to philosophy, but to physics. ... Whatever such attributes turn out to be, however, they have no *philosophic* significance, neither in regard to metaphysics nor to epistemology."[13]

Trying to eat his forms and have them too, Peikoff writes: "Nor do Objectivists speak of 'things in themselves,' which Kantians contrast to 'things in relation to consciousness.' The very terminology insinuates the notion that consciousness, by the mere fact of existing, is an agent of distortion." Peikoff brazenly denies what

[13] *Objectivism*, 44.

he is obviously doing. Is there any difference between Kant's phrase "things in themselves" and Peikoff's phrase "physical objects as they are"? Of course, if our senses cause us to see and hear as colored and noisy things that in themselves ["physical objects as they are" is the phrase Peikoff uses] are not colored, then consciousness is in fact an agent of distortion. Kant, it would appear, has more respect for objective reality than Peikoff does. Peikoff, superstitiously, thinks that by avoiding Kant's terminology, he has avoided the epistemological problem.

Peikoff tells us in one breath, that "Man perceives reality directly, not some kind of effects different from it. He perceives reality *by means of* its effects on his organs of perception." Now if perception is direct, then it cannot be by means of something else. And we have already been told that the effects on our organs really are different from reality (gray and red). Peikoff seems to want to contend that because the resulting solution is blue when one mixes two chemicals in the laboratory, that one or both of the chemicals was blue to begin with. The compound is different from its ingredients.

In presenting his account of consciousness, Peikoff asserts that "The first [chronological] stage of consciousness is that of sensation," but epistemologically, "the perceptual stage comes first." What he apparently means by this is: "The integration of sensations into percepts . . . is performed by the brain automatically. Philosophy, therefore, has no advice to offer in this regard."[14] Once again, philosophy defers to science, and the foundations of Objectivist epistemology will, we are told, be provided later, by the scientists, not by Leonard Peikoff. All we need to know now is that such processes are done "automatically." Such a position is not philosophy; it is the abdication of philosophy.

Concept Formation

Peikoff, echoing Rand, sees some similarities between mathematics and concept formation. Without the concept of unit, man could not reach the conceptual stage of knowledge, nor could he count,

---

[14] *Objectivism*, 54.

measure, and identify quantitative relationships. "It suggests that concept-formation is in some way a mathematical process."[15] On the contrary, it suggests that mathematics is a conceptual process. Rand and Peikoff got things backwards, and touted their confusion as a revolutionary discovery in epistemology.

As I have written in the body of the book, Rand's use of "implicit concepts" is a dishonest device for trying to avoid one fatal embarrassment every form of empiricism faces: how to account for universals. Rand makes them "implicit" right at the beginning. And then, *abracadabra*, she pulls them from her epistemologer's hat at the end of the process of concept formation. "Implicit" must mean logically implicit. So there is no development of the concept from perceptions and sensations. The development is actually in the other direction, from concept, to percept, to sensation.

On page 79 Peikoff asserts, "Only concretes exist. If a concept is to exist, therefore, it must exist in some way as a concrete. That is the function of language." And this, of course, is the language of nominalism.

Does not a concept exist before a word is assigned to it? To what is a word assigned, if the concept does not already exist? And if the concept already exists, then Peikoff's ipsedixitism, only concretes exist, is false. Do "implicit concepts" exist?

Peikoff attempts to illustrate concept formation by using the concept "length." Quoting Rand, "I shall identify as 'length' that attribute of any existent possessing it which can be quantitatively related to a unit of length, without specifying the quantity." Apparently the obvious circularity of such a "definition" escaped both Rand and Peikoff.

After telling us that "Words are essential to the process of conceptualization and thus to all thought,"[16] Peikoff also tells us that "This is the process—performed by the mind wordlessly—which enables the child . . . to integrate. . . ."[17] What is the Objec-

[15] *Objectivism*, 76-77.

[16] *Objectivism*, 79.

[17] *Objectivism*, 83.

243

tivist position? Words are essential to all thought, but the mind can think wordlessly. Go figure.

Rand's account of concept formation not only rests on "implicit concepts," but on implicit propositions. One appears on page 83: "the relevant measurements must exist in some quantity, but may exist in any quantity." Another appears on pages 84 and 85:

> His [a child's] mind . . . is governed by a wordless policy applicable to all future knowledge. This policy, which represents the essence of the conceptual process, amounts to the following: "I know certain attributes of tables. Whatever other attributes I discover, the same process will apply: I will retain the attribute and omit its measurements.

Rand and Peikoff, who asserted that man's mind at birth is *tabula rasa*, found it impossible to account for knowledge except on the basis of implicit concepts and propositions, which they call "policies."

Contradiction follows contradiction. After having it drummed into our thick skulls that man is a being of volitional consciousness, that our knowledge is neither innate nor automatic, Peikoff tells us:

> The process of measurement-omission [which is the process of concept formation] is performed for us by the nature of our mental faculty, whether anyone identifies it or not. To form a concept, one does not have to know that a form of measurement is involved; one does not have to measure existents or even know how to measure them. On the conscious level, one need merely observe similarities.[18]

In short, not only are the actual measurements omitted during concept formation, but the process of measurement is completely irrelevant: One does not have to know measurement is involved; one

[18] *Objectivism*, 95.

does not have to measure; one does not even have to know how to measure: One need merely observe similarities. Our "mental faculty" performs the function of concept formation automatically. It is "performed for us." Clearly this is not an account of concept formation at all. And just as clearly, measuring and measurement-omission have nothing whatever to do with concept formation.

Furthermore, Rand's view of concept formation as a process of measurement omission cannot account for all concepts, nor even plausibly for very many. For example, how is the concept "color," or the concept "justice" formed by measurement omission? How is the concept "one" formed by measurement omission? Or the concept "concept"? If the theory has any plausibility whatsoever (and in philosophy, we are interested in truth, not plausibility), then it is plausible only with regard to concepts of extended objects. It is not even remotely plausible with concepts whose referents are non-extended or spiritual.

The contradictions continue. After telling us that all concept formation is a process of measuring, with the specific values omitted (neither Rand nor Peikoff stated it quite like this, for they do not write this clearly on the subject), Peikoff tells us that

> Measurement as a conscious process presupposes a substantial conceptual development. It presupposes that one has already conceptualized separate attributes, knows how to count, and has defined suitable units and a method of relating objects to them in numerical terms.[19]

Now if that is true, then concept formation cannot involve a process of measurement, for measurement presupposes concepts. Furthermore, it is not just "measurement as a conscious process" that presupposes concepts; whether the process is conscious or "unconscious," the logical status is the same: Measurement cannot be the basis for concept formation, because measurement presupposes concepts. Rand's theory that concept formation is a process of

---

[19] *Objectivism*, 86.

measurement is backward; it gets the mathematical cart before the conceptual horse. Mathematics presupposes concepts that are not learned from experience. Unless epistemology begins where the Gospel of John begins—with the *Logos*, the divine logic, the divine wisdom, the divine ideas, that light every man—it can offer no coherent account of human knowledge.

While maintaining that measurement presupposes substantial conceptual development, Peikoff asserts that "measurement also plays a special role in the first step of concept formation: the differentiation of a group from other things."[20] Which comes first, measurement or concepts? The incoherence of the Objectivist theory is painfully obvious.

So when Peikoff asseverates that "The measurement involved in forming concepts, however, which may be described as 'implicit' measurement, does not require such knowledge," he is simply trying to prop up an epistemological theory that has no foundation, and his assertion is contradicted by the logic of the situation. Peikoff seems to think (and this is what the word "implicit" is used to imply) that the mind requires certain concepts to function, but that those concepts are not really there in the mind. He seems to think that they are logically implicit, but psychologically absent. "Implicit concepts and policies" seem analogous to "innate ideas." What the differences between the two are we are not told.

If the idea, if the concept, if the policy, is implicit, then it is present already in the mind at birth, and the appearance of knowledge at a chronologically later time is simply the blooming of what is already implicitly in the mind. The mind does not obtain these ideas and concepts and policies elsewhere; they are already (implicitly) there. Therefore, the Objectivist account of concept formation is completely false.

Algebra

Rand and Peikoff see an analogy between concepts and algebraic symbols.

[20] *Objectivism*, 87.

The basic principle of concept-formation (which states that the omitted measurements must exist in some quantity, but may exist in any quantity) is the equivalent of the basic principle of algebra, which states that algebraic symbols must be given some numerical value, but may be given any value.

Now that seems to translate into this analogy:

    omitted measurements : actual measurements
    :: algebraic symbols : actual values

But Rand (and Peikoff) continue:

The relationship of concepts to their constituent particulars is the same as the relationship of algebraic symbols to numbers.

Now that seems to translate into this analogy:

concepts : constituents :: algebraic symbols : numbers.

Obviously, the two proportions are not the same, yet Rand (and Peikoff) seems oblivious to that fact. The confusion, unfortunately, deepens.

In the equation $2a = a + a$, any number may be substituted for the symbol "a" without affecting the truth of the equation. . . . In the same manner, by the same psycho-epistemological method, a concept is used as an algebraic symbol that stands for any arithmetical sequences of units it subsumes. Let those who attempt to invalidate concepts by declaring that they cannot find "manness" in men, try to invalidate algebra by declaring that they cannot find "a-ness" in 5 or 5,000,000.

Now presumably Rand and Peikoff do not mean to argue that concepts, like algebraic symbols, are completely arbitrary. Yet that is what their argument implies. If they were speaking about words, that is, the verbal symbols for concepts, then such an implication would be quite correct: It does not matter whether one calls a dog *dog*, *Hund*, or *chien*. Any word is as good as another, for the word is simply a verbal symbol for an intellectual object. But Peikoff's argument does not concern words; it concerns concepts, and concepts are not arbitrary. Rand and Peikoff seem to have confused words and concepts. In doing so, they have destroyed their theory of concepts. Rand should have chosen an equation like this: $2a + 1 = 3$. Had she done so, she would have realized that a cannot mean any number, but only very definite numbers.

More Conceptual Confusion

On page 91, Peikoff writes: "There are no such things as 'organisms' to be seen—there are only men, dogs, roses." Actually, Peikoff has forgotten that one cannot see any concepts, either organisms or dogs. One can see only "existents." Men, dogs, and roses are units.

Since all concept formation according to Rand and Peikoff consist of two processes, differentiation and integration, one must ask: From what other mental activities is thinking differentiated? From what other entities is existence differentiated? It seems that the axiomatic concepts are exceptions to the rule. When Peikoff writes that "The final step in concept formation is definition. This step is essential to every concept except axiomatic concepts and concepts denoting sensations," we see clearly that the so-called axiomatic concepts are not concepts at all. They are not formed by differentiation and integration and they cannot be defined. While mystics wax lyrical about the ineffableness of their experience, Objectivists wax pedestrian about the ineffableness of their most fundamental "concepts." Both groups talk nonsense.

Here is some more Peikoffian nonsense: "Content [of thought] is a measurable attribute [of thought], because it is ultimately some aspect of the external world. As such, it is measurable by methods applicable to physical existents." The content of a thought—say, the thought of justice—is measurable by methods applicable to physical existents. Therefore, justice is measurable in inches, or angstroms, or light years, right? Justice is 5 feet tall, even though my thought of justice is only 5 millimeters tall. This inane statement is about as reductionistic as one finds in philosophy, yet the Objectivists insist they are neither reductionists nor materialists.

Definitions

Peikoff appeals frequently to ostensive definition, which, of course, is not definition at all, but silence and pointing with the finger. The axiomatic concepts are "defined" ostensively. He even speaks of contextual definitions and implicit definitions. He asserts that "Definitions (like all truths) are thus 'empirical' statements. They derive from certain kinds of observations. . . ."[21] So it would seem that only statements that can be "derived" in some way from observations are true. The logical positivist test of truth is also the Objectivist test of truth. But how does one "derive" anything propositional, such as a definition, from non-propositional experience? What is this process of derivation? Rand and Peikoff apparently believe that geometry is about visible points, lines, planes, and figures. Give them an "F" and put them back into tenth grade. They deserve to flunk for teaching that all concepts, all knowledge, and all propositions, if they are "valid," can be reduced to observational data.[22]

"Proof" in Objectivism, is not valid deductive reasoning, but "a form of reduction. . . . Proof is thus a form of retracing the hierarchical steps of the learning process," all the way down to sense data.[23]

A definition—say of a geometric plane—"is the condensation of a vast body of observations—and it stands or falls with the truth or falsehood of those observations."[24] Now many definitions do

[21] *Objectivism*, 99.

[22] *Objectivism*, 137.

[23] *Objectivism*, 138.

[24] *Objectivism*, 101.

not depend on observation at all. Worse, Rand and Peikoff have already told us that there are no false observations. Observation is always correct. So it would seem that definitions are always correct.

But Peikoff backs away from his own method of "reduction": "Let me caution you to apply the method in essential terms only. Trying to work backward through every intermediate cognition involved would be excruciating and pointless."[25]

Proof of Objectivist ideas, in short, is excruciating and pointless. To be even more blunt, proof is impossible, and that is why Peikoff abandons the method almost as soon as he mentions it.

Concepts, unlike definitions, never change: "a concept, once formed, does not change."[26] Knowledge grows, definitions change, but "the concept, the mental integration, remains the same." These statements, on which Rand rests her claim that Objectivist epistemology furnishes knowledge, simply confuse a concept with its constituents. Peikoff and Rand, as I point out in the text, continually confuse a concept with its constituents. A concept, Peikoff, writes, means its existents and all their attributes. A concept is both an integration[27] and not an integration.[28]

"A consciousness without concepts could not discover even the most elementary fact about man. . . ."[29] But all our consciousnesses, according to the Objectivist theory, are at one time without concepts. All our minds are blank at birth.

Truth, according to Peikoff, is correspondence to fact.[30] But what can "correspondence" mean when we have already been told that perceptual existents are colorless, soundless, tasteless, and odorless? What empirical proposition is there that corresponds to

[25] *Objectivism*, 139.

[26] *Objectivism*, 104.

[27] *Objectivism*, 106.

[28] *Objectivism*, 102-103.

[29] *Objectivism*, 106.

[30] *Objectivism*, 146.

"fact"? "I see a green plant" is patently false, for plants are not green and they cannot be seen. And the "truth" that plants are not green does not correspond to any fact that we are aware of by observation.

Oddly enough, Peikoff seems to say that "valid" ideas may be false. He writes:

> . . . one cannot demand omniscience. One cannot ask: "How do I know that a given idea, even if it has been proved on the basis of all knowledge men have gained so far, will not be overthrown one day by new information as yet undiscovered?"

Peikoff says this question cannot be asked. Why not? It goes to the heart of the epistemological problem. If what I "know" today may in fact turn out to be wrong tomorrow, then my "knowledge" is, at best, opinion. At any given time, it is tentative. It is not "knowledge" in the sense that Plato, Aristotle, and the Bible use the term; it has no finality. It is conjecture. It is not knowledge. By making all "knowledge" contextual, Peikoff has eliminated knowledge from Objectivist epistemology.

Furthermore, this question is not a demand for omniscience. It is a demand for an explanation of how we can know one—just one— proposition to be true. Rand and Peikoff failed to provide that explanation.

Man and Ethics

According to Peikoff, "units" do not exist in reality, because concepts are mental, not real. Only entities exist in reality. Yet on page 186 he says that man (not men) is an entity. Now he seems to think he can deal with man as an entity, but according to Objectivist ontology, only individual things (men, presumably) exist in reality, not man. Perhaps this is just a slip of the pen, but I think not.

Thinking requires the use of universals. Yet universals, according to the Objectivists, are not real. They do not inhere in reality.

251

Neither Plato nor Aristotle's versions of realism are acceptable to the Objectivists. That implies that what Peikoff is describing when he discusses "man," or "dog," or any other concept is a mental construct that is not real. He is not describing actually existing things.

Nevertheless, Peikoff discusses "man" as if it were an entity. "Man," we are told, is "self-created, self-directed, and self-responsible."[31] This entity needs ethics for his survival (yet on page 219, Peikoff attacks this idea). I have discussed the Objectivist ethics at length in the body of this book.

Peikoff brings up the subject of lying and tells us that lying is permissible, even virtuous. This, of course, is because rules for conduct, like rules for thinking, are not absolute, but contextual and conditional. Lying to a criminal is "not wrong." In fact, "the victim has not only the right but also the obligation to lie and do it proudly."[32] Proud lying does, however, contradict Rand's strictures about "faking reality." Peikoff simply denies that is true: "The man who tells a lie in this context is not endorsing any antireality principle. On the contrary, he is now the representative of the good and the true." Lying is virtuous when it is done to "dictators, criminals, and snoopers."[33]

Peikoff expands this discussion to an all-out attack on moral rules:

> In discussing integrity, I said that to be good is to be good "all of the time." I can be more precise now. To be good is to obey moral principles faithfully, without a moment's exception, within the relevant context—which one must, therefore, know and keep in mind. Virtue does not consist in obeying concrete-bound rules ("Do not lie, do not kill, do not accept help from others, make money, honor your parents, etc."). No such rules can be defended or consistently practiced.

[31] *Objectivism*, 202.

[32] *Objectivism*, 275.

[33] *Objectivism*, 276.

Several aspects of this paragraph require comment. First, Peikoff asserts that to be good is to be good all the time. In that, he agrees with Christianity, which teaches that no ordinary man is or can be good, precisely because innocence requires perfection. But notice how Peikoff now wants to weasel out of that requirement. Virtue is contextual, that is, situational. In this way, the Objectivist ethics is really little different from that of Joseph Fletcher, whose books also launched an attack on ethical rules, an attack, one must say, much more ably conducted than Peikoff's.

Objectivism advocates a situational (contextual) ethics. Worse, what Peikoff refers to as concrete-bound rules are not concrete-bound at all, they are abstract and universal. It is Peikoff's contextual ethics that is concrete-bound, and as each concrete situation changes, so do the rules. Furthermore, abstract rules can be applied to every situation, if one gets them from the Bible, rather than from ethics textbooks: You shall not murder; you shall not steal; you shall not covet; you shall not commit adultery; you shall not bear false witness; you shall not lie; you shall not worship or serve any other gods; you shall love God with all your soul, mind, and strength, and so on. Peikoff's attack on moral rules is the result of his desire to say that Ayn Rand was good even in committing adultery. But he cannot have it both ways. If, as Peikoff says, integrity requires innocence, then anything less is not virtue, but evil. That requires one to say that Ayn Rand was evil, and we are back to the Christian doctrine of total depravity. It is to avoid that inexorable conclusion that Peikoff makes ethics situational.

Peikoff argues that "Since the moral is the volitional, there is no rule to the effect that all men are good, evil, or mixed."[34] But he had earlier ruled out the possibility of "mixed" men when he wrote: "To be evil 'only sometimes' *is* to be evil. To be good is to be good *all* of the time. . . ."[35] Therefore, all men are either good or evil; the proportion of their "good" deeds to their "evil" deeds is irrelevant; one evil deed is enough to make them evil. Therefore, we must conclude, all men are evil.

[34] *Objectivism*, 281.

[35] *Objectivism*, 266.

Peikoff finally recognizes, as this writer pointed out in 1974, that the fundamental choice, the choice to live, in Objectivism "is not a moral choice; it precedes morality. . . ."[36] That means the most important choice is outside morality. It means that one cannot be faulted for choosing death. Suicide, Peikoff writes in good paradoxical fashion, may be a reaffirmation of life.[37] The Objectivist ethics has some plausibility only because it does not deal with the most fundamental ethical choice: to be or not to be. It assumes that problem is solved, just as its epistemology assumes the problems of sense perception and universals have been solved.

Needs and Economics

Peikoff writes very little about economics, and we ought to be glad for that, for what he does write indicates he does not understand the subject at all: "Economics is not a [part of philosophy]; its concern is not universal principles of human action, but a specialized subject matter."[38] Incredibly, Peikoff chose the phrase used by Mises to show that economics, if it is anything at all, *is* universal principles of human action.

One final comment about needs. In reading Rand and Peikoff one notices their utter contempt for the word "need" as a justification for anything. One also notices his earlier statements that human perception is "direct perception of physical objects and their properties." Now perception is "conditioned." It is "processed." He quotes from *Introduction to Objectivist Epistemology*: " 'All knowledge *is* processed knowledge—whether on the sensory, perceptual, or conceptual level. . . . [T]he satisfaction of every need of a living organism requires an act of *processing* by that organism, be it the need of air, food or of knowledge.' "[55] In Peikoff's book, the contradictions continue and expand.

---

[36] *Objectivism*, 244-245.

[37] *Objectivism*, 248.

[38] *Objectivism*, 379.

C

THE EVIDENCE OF THE SENSES

Writing a brief analysis of David Kelley's book is difficult, not because he is a poor writer (he is actually very good), but because Rand's quasi-Aristotelian epistemology is transformed by Kelley into a quasi-Kantianism. What is worse, Kelley apparently performs this trick by extrapolating from statements made by Rand herself, not in her books, but in speeches and seminars delivered in the closing decade of her life, and from statements made by Leonard Peikoff.

Kelley's book is an attempt to fill a large lacuna in Rand's own writings: Kelley strives to provide an argument for the "validity" of the senses. Kelley, as is typical of epistemologists today, including Rand, scorns those who are seeking "infallible" knowledge. Kelley, for example, writes contemptuously of those who pursue what he calls the "Cartesian quest for an infallible type of knowledge" (168). Now my *Merriam-Webster's* defines *infallible* as "incapable of error; sure, certain." *Fallible*, on the other hand, is "liable to be erroneous." So it would seem that those who attack infallibility in knowledge and favor fallibility in knowledge, are trying to make room for error in knowledge. But if *knowledge* is used by these people as it is used in standard English, as apprehension of truth, then there can be no error in knowledge, because there can be no error in truth. Truth and error are opposites. Truth, by definition, neither contains error, nor is uncertain, nor is liable to error.

Knowledge, by definition, is apprehension of what is true. One cannot be said to *know* what is false. One can have false information, but one cannot have false knowledge. "False knowledge" is a contradiction in terms. What is true cannot be in error. What is known cannot be false. Therefore, knowledge is infallible. If it contains error, if it is liable to error, it is not knowledge, but merely opinion, information, or speculation. If what Kelley and other empiricists are apprehending is not truth, their information is not knowledge. The epistemological problem is to provide a true theory of how one knows. That is the problem that those who rail against "infallible knowledge" are trying to avoid solving. Their reasons for doing so will become apparent.

Now, of course, *knowledge* and *know* can be used more loosely as well: "He knows how to ride a bicycle," for example. Or, he knows that "Columbus sailed the ocean blue." But in philosophy, we must use words precisely, as Rand herself said, and *knowledge* means nothing less than and nothing other than apprehension of the truth. Epistemology—from the Greek *episteme* and *logos*—is the branch of philosophy that deals with theories of knowing, theories of knowledge, theories of truth. It is not concerned with opining or speculating, except as they are distinguished from knowing. All those modern epistemologists who despise infallibility despise knowledge. The measure of their scorn is the measure of their realization (and their fear) that *their* epistemological theories can provide *no knowledge whatever* in the strict and indispensable meaning of the term, so they are trying to substitute for knowledge a vaguer, broader, and less rigorous epistemological standard that perhaps their theories *can* meet. They are not writing epistemology; they are writing doxalogy—from the Greek *doxa*, opinion. Karl Popper, for example, admitted that science discovers no knowledge in the strict meaning of the term:

> First, although in science we do our best to find the truth, we are conscious of the fact that we can never be sure whether we have got it. . . . [W]e know that our scientific theories always remain hypotheses. . . . [I]n science

there is no 'knowledge' in the sense in which Plato and Aristotle used the word, in the sense which implies finality; in science, we never have sufficient reason for the belief that we have attained the truth. . . .

Popper's position, if it is generalized from the philosophy of science and is understood as an epistemological theory, reduces to a thoroughgoing skepticism, and thereby refutes itself. Any theory of "fallible knowledge" does the same.

Despite their war against "infallible knowledge," the Randian empiricists believe, inconsistently, that the senses and the evidence of the senses are indeed infallible. Our sense organs, being mechanisms in a physical and material world, have no ability to misrepresent the facts of reality. They are as completely reliable as even a Descartes could wish. Kelley, for example, writes: "There is—there could be no such thing—as a non-veridical percept."[1] So perception is infallible. These empiricists want to assert infallible knowledge when it comes to perception (there infallibility is inescapable) and deny it when it comes to thought (there infallibility is impossible). Their denial of infallibility is a transparent attempt to hide their failure to provide a coherent account of how we know. Their assertion of infallibility is a transparent attempt to maintain we know in one way only, through the senses, without having to prove it.

Kelley begins his book by asserting his basic materialism: "We live our lives bathed in streams of physical energy: sound waves, electromagnetic fields, mechanical forces of every kind."[2] Of course, the world Kelley takes so much for granted is not a perceptually obvious world at all. The Nobel Prize winning physicist Percy Bridgman, for example, argued that there were no such things as electromagnetic fields, and no evidence to support their postulated existence. Sound waves and mechanical forces are inferences, not perceptions (assuming, for the sake of argument, that perceptions

[1] *The Evidence of the Senses: A Realist Theory of Perception,* 93.

[2] *The Evidence of the Senses,* 1.

257

themselves are not inferences). None of these things—sound waves, electromagnetic fields, mechanical forces—is sensed or perceived. As Kelley puts it: "In perception we never perceive the means by which we are aware of objects."[3]

Kelley's next words are important, for they indicate that we miss most of the world: "Much of this energy passes us by, leaving behind no discernible trace." That means, if one may use an analogy, that we are like concert-goers who can hear only a few pitches and tones. We hear, or think we hear, "Happy Birthday" being played by the orchestra, but the orchestra is actually playing Beethoven's Ninth Symphony. Most of the notes pass us by, leaving no discernible trace. And we, an audience of sophisticated empirical philosophers, think we know what the orchestra is playing.[4] Kelley has not made it through his first paragraph without making statements subversive of, and fatal to, any claim that sense perception furnishes knowledge.

He continues: "But some of it [energy], at every moment, sets off reactions in the cells we call sense receptors, and these in turn set off electrical impulses that reverberate through the physical structure we call the nervous system. Like radios, we are tuned to a portion of the energy that eddies around us." Notice that this mystical, ineffable energy[5] sets off reactions in sense receptor cells "at every moment." When we are sleeping, we are sensing. Sensing, then, seems to be a purely mechanical process, not dependent on an active consciousness.

[3] *The Evidence of the Senses*, 36n38.

[4] Being atheists, we have all rejected the Concert Program, the written, propositional revelation from the Composer. We are independent beings, standing on our own two feet, and we are quite capable of figuring out the program without the aid of some mystical Composer, whom no one has ever seen at a concert anyway. All we have seen is the ushers handing out his Program. (This problem with the limitations of perception, even if all perceptions were accurate, is also a problem with history. Without a written revelation, history is a tale told by an idiot, full of sound and fury, signifying nothing. It is utterly arrogant of us to think we can know anything without propositional revelation.)

[5] John Locke defined *matter* as "something, I know not what."

Kelley continues his materialistic account of knowing: "Unlike any electronic device, the nervous system gives rise to conscious experience of the world around it. The resonance of my brain to the flow of energy makes it happen. . . . We call this process perception." So one's vibrating brain "gives rise to" consciousness. Well, maybe the Beach Boys were right, and Kelley is indeed picking up good vibrations.

After furnishing this inane account of perception, Kelley discloses the conclusion of his theory: "I argue that in perception we are directly aware of physical objects and their properties, and that perceptual judgments about those objects and properties can be based directly on perception, without the need for any inference."[6] Now what is remarkable about this statement is that it is so thoroughly and repeatedly contradicted by the arguments that Kelley is about to present.

Kelley makes it clear that he "reject[s] the classical representationalist view that we directly perceive not physical objects themselves but certain mental entities (images, ideas, sense-data) which represent them."[7] That means, of course, that Kelley has parted company with the greatest empiricists, Aristotle, Thomas Aquinas, John Locke, and David Hume, and with Rand herself, for they all were representationalists. Since he rejects the "classical representationalist view," we must conclude from this statement and from his earlier statements that Kelley asserts that we directly perceive "physical objects and their properties" themselves. That is what he means by the term *realism*. Realism is opposed to representationalism.

Furthermore, Kelley "argue[s] . . . that the integrative processes which produce a percept are automatic and fully compatible with the directness of perceptual awareness" and "hold[s] that perceptual discrimination is preconceptual." So even though there are "complex neural processes that lie behind even the simplest percept," we "directly" perceive the physical object. What "direct" might mean in such a statement is obscure. The relevant meanings

[6] *The Evidence of the Senses*, 2.

[7] *The Evidence of the Senses*, 3.

in *Merriam Webster's* are: "stemming immediately from a source
. . . marked by absence of an intervening agency, instrumentality,
or influence. . . ." *Direct,* however, cannot mean immediate, since
there are complex processes involved, so it must be something else,
perhaps "uninterrupted." I take "direct" to be a synonym for "automatic," which means "largely or wholly involuntary." Perception,
thus, is a function of a preconceptual automaton. That account certainly fits Kelley's materialistic view of the world.

Kelley asserts that "[P]erception is a pre-conceptual mode of
direct awareness of physical objects." Perception is a "mode of
awareness," but it uses no concepts. "[P]erception provides adequate
evidence or justification for our beliefs about such [physical] objects, but that the evidence is non-propositional. That is, I reject
the common assumption that a belief can be justified only by another belief, judgment, or other propositional state. . . ."

Here Kelley has exposed another problem of empiricism: If it
is true that propositions can be justified only by other propositions,
as logic requires, then empiricism must be false. He correctly recognizes that empiricism requires that propositions be justified by
"non-propositional evidence," whatever that phrase might mean.
Of course, what Kelley is implicitly rejecting is the laws of logic.
It is those laws that require a valid inference to be derived from
propositions. Kelley does not seem to understand (or he denies)
that all truth is propositional; that the phrase "non-propositional
truth" is meaningless verbiage; and that the laws of logic apply
only to propositions. There is no other way of drawing a valid inference than by means of the laws of logic. In Kelley, as in Aristotle
and Rand, empiricism is in conflict with the laws of logic. Kelley
rejects the "common assumption," that is, the fundamental requirement of logic, not because of some powerful argument, but simply
because he realizes that empiricism cannot hope to survive if it is
true that only propositions can justify propositions. In rejecting the
"common assumption," Kelley is rejecting logic.

Kelley distinguishes his realism from representationalism, idealism, and phenomenalism.[8] He clarifies his view that perception

[8] *The Evidence of the Senses,* 7.

is "direct awareness of objects in the physical world, objects which exist and are what they are independently of our awareness of them. . . . It is a more structured and integrated form of awareness than sensation is, but perception is itself the basis for further integration at the conceptual level."[9] As we shall see shortly, Kelley's account of perception is hopelessly at odds with this statement.

Kelley brings up a common argument for the reliability of the senses on page 15 in his discussion of Descartes:

> The first such grounds [for doubting the truth of his ideas] he [Descartes] finds—sensory illusions and dreams—are actual occurrences, and in these cases we know that reality is not what it seems. For that reason, however, these occurrences could not raise the general question whether reality exists beyond our ideas; to identify any experience as an illusion, one must have enough knowledge of the objective facts to know that he is misperceiving them.

Now perhaps Kelley has not understood the skeptical argument. One need not have any "knowledge of the objective facts to know that he is misperceiving them." One need only be aware that one has perceptions that conflict with one another: The eye sees the railroad tracks converging; the hand feels them running parallel. One need not know which one, if either, perception is correct; one need know only that the tracks cannot be both converging and parallel, which is a rule of logic, not perception. But one neither can nor is required to tell which conflicting perception, if either, is correct, in order to conclude that the senses are unreliable. Therefore, one is left without any knowledge gained from perception.

Worse, at least for Kelley, he is shortly going to tell the reader that "reality is not what it seems." In fact, it is never what it seems, according to Kelley.

Like the empiricists who are representationalists, Kelley asserts the correspondence theory of truth: "[R]epresentationalists side

---

[9] *The Evidence of the Senses*, 8.

with realists in maintaining the correspondence theory of truth and the independent existence of the ultimate (though not immediate) objects of knowledge."[10] The correspondence theory of truth, however, rests on a representation, which must correspond to reality, if one's perception is true. But Kelley has asserted that perception of physical objects and their properties is "direct." How one can be a realist and adhere to the correspondence theory of truth is a mystery. Furthermore, Kelley's distinction between ultimate and immediate objects of knowledge indicates that perception is not direct, that the objects perceived are not the objects of "objective reality," and that Hume's two tables continue to plague empiricists.

Consciousness, Kelley asserts, "is radically noncreative, radically dependent on existence [unconsciousness] for its contents." Furthermore, "consciousness is not an entity but a functional capacity of the brain."[11] Having made these statements, Kelley repeats: "The object of awareness *is* the object as it actually exists."[12]

But on page 37 Kelley embarks on his neo-Kantian quest for knowledge. He attacks the idea—the Aristotelian idea, let it be said—that consciousness is "diaphanous." Aristotle held that a mind is actually nothing until it thinks. Aristotle recognized that if mind contributed anything of its own to perception, then one could not know the objective facts.

> Therefore, since everything is a possible object of thought, the mind, in order, as Anaxagoras says, to dominate, that is, to know, must be pure from all admixture; for the co-presence of what is alien to its nature is a hindrance and a block: it follows that it too, like the sensitive part [senses], can have no nature of its own, other than that of having a certain capacity. Thus that in the soul which is

---

[10] *The Evidence of the Senses*, 28.

[11] *The Evidence of the Senses*, 29.

[12] *The Evidence of the Senses*, 31.

called mind (by mind I mean that whereby the soul thinks and judges) is, before it thinks, not actually any real thing.[13]

Nothing could be more diaphanous than nothing.

It was Kant who insisted, in opposition to Aristotle, that the mind has a form, a nature of its own, that it was actually something, not actually nothing. It was Kant's view that knowledge is a combination of sensation and the forms of the mind that Rand was concerned to refute. But it is Kelley's view that knowledge is a combination of "objective facts" and consciousness. The view that he attacks, which he alternately calls the "traditional" view and the "diaphanous model," is that of Aristotle, and of the original Rand. Kelley describes this view as one in which awareness "is a direct confrontation between mind and object, that the mind in cognition becomes identical with the object . . . taking on its form without its matter."[14] That is virtually a quotation from Aristotle. (Rand, of course, did not believe in forms.) Aristotle insisted that "Actual knowledge is identical with its object."[15] Kelley insists, despite all the nice words about "directly perceiving physical objects and their properties," that actual knowledge is never identical with its object. In fact, in Kelley's epistemology, just as in Kant's, we cannot know the things in themselves. Kelley himself quotes John Hermann Randall, whose book on Aristotle Rand endorsed in the May 1963 issue of *The Objectivist Newsletter*: " 'If *nous were* something—if it had a definite and determinate structure of its own—then men could not transparently 'see' and know what is, without distortion. They could not really 'know' things as they are, but only things mixed with the structure of *nous*. Such a *nous* would have turned Kantian: it would have become 'constitutive' and 'creative' (*Aristotle* [New York, 1960], 91)."

For the same reason, Aristotle insisted that not only the mind, the *nous*, is transparent, or "diaphanous," but so are the senses. If

---

[13] *Of the Soul (De Anima)*, III, 4.

[14] *The Evidence of the Senses*, 38.

[15] *Of the Soul*, III, 5.

they were not, then what one perceives is not objective reality. It is this Aristotelian view that both Peikoff and Kelley reject.

Kelley praises Kant: "Kant recognized that awareness is always and necessarily conditioned by the means which produce it. A faculty of cognition must have an identity which affects the content of the conscious experiences it gives rise to. . . . Kant rejects the diaphanous model."[16] So, of course, does Kelley.

Now the problem for Kelley is that this conflicts with his earlier statements that human perception is "direct perception of physical objects and their properties." Now perception is "conditioned." It is "processed." He quotes from *Introduction to Objectivist Epistemology*: " 'All knowledge *is* processed knowledge—whether on the sensory, perceptual, or conceptual level. . . . [T]he satisfaction of every need of a living organism requires an act of *processing* by that organism, be it the need of air, food or of knowledge.' "[17]

It seems obvious, then, continuing with this analogy between digestion and cognition, that the nutrients the body receives from the food it ingests, chemically and mechanically broken down by the body's own processes and combined into new material (or even manufactured by the body itself, for example, vitamin D)—that these nutrients have little resemblance to the food the body eats, or to the physical cattle, clams, or corn that exist in objective reality.

Kelley asserts: "Consciousness is not metaphysically active. It no more creates its own contents than does the stomach."[18] This statement betrays an ignorance of the processes of digestion as well as of cognition. The stomach does manufacture some of its own contents. Kelley should decide whether or not he believes in the diaphanous model of digestion and cognition and then stick to it. Instead he veers from one opinion to the other.

At this point in his argument, Kelley sounds a new note: appearances: "In perception, the way objects appear to us is partly

[16] *The Evidence of the Senses*, 39.

[17] *The Evidence of the Senses*, 40.

[18] *The Evidence of the Senses*, 41.

determined by our perceptual apparatus; . . . the objects themselves we are aware of by means of their appearances." Has he already forgotten that we "directly" perceive "physical objects and their properties"? And if these appearances are determined by our perceptual apparatus, then we are not perceiving those objects as they are. He continues: "certain aspects of the content we immediately perceive are the product of an interaction between external objects and our senses."[19] Now, far from perceiving physical objects and their properties directly, we perceive "contents" and "products."

Kelley senses that his argument is in great danger here, and he insists that the contents of our consciousnesses, since our minds are not "metaphysically active," are all derived from "reality." The question to ask is, So what? Are not the colors and shapes reflected in a fun house mirror all derived from "reality"? Are we therefore to conclude that the mirror is an accurate reflection of reality? In belaboring this argument Kelley misses the point entirely: It is not enough that the contents of our consciousnesses be derived from "reality," but our consciousnesses must not distort or change that data. That he does not, and cannot, show. As a matter of fact, however, it is not true that our consciousness are "metaphysically inactive." We have many ideas that are not derived from or dependent on physical objects, including the laws of logic themselves. Furthermore, even if our minds are "metaphysically active," are they not part of reality, and thus their products are products of reality?

Kelley moves further away from Aristotle and direct perception of physical objects and their properties: "[C]ertain qualitative aspects of what we perceive must be assigned to the sensory systems, not to the objects in themselves."[20] But if that is so, then direct perception has disappeared. We are left only with the fleeting contents of our consciousnesses.

In his second chapter Kelley focuses on sensation and perception. He opens the chapter by describing the room in which he is sitting. He lists many things that he calls "facts": green leaves,

[19] *The Evidence of the Senses*, 42.

[20] *The Evidence of the Senses*, 43.

blue-gray cigarette smoke, and numerous other perceptions. These, he says, "were given. I had only to look, or listen, or smell, and they were there."[21] But many if not all these facts, as he calls them, are products of our awareness, products of our sensory apparatus and our minds, not properties of objects in reality. This raises the question: What is a fact? In Kelley's usage it may be either something existing in reality, or something "contributed" by the sensory apparatus. He seems to make no distinction. He says further that these facts are "given." But what can "given" mean when our own sensory apparatus is contributing facts that are not found in reality?

After this initial muddle at the beginning of chapter two, Kelley proceeds with an impossible account of sensation and perception. I have thoroughly discussed that account in the chapters on epistemology in the body of this book. I shall not repeat my arguments here as to why non-conceptual sensation and perception are impossible.

On page 55 he tackles anew the problem of perspective: "Do things really look this way? Yes and no. The railroad tracks stretching into the distance look parallel . . . ; but they also look convergent." Now if this statement were true, by itself it would be grounds for not trusting the senses: They yield contradictions. But the statement is not true: The tracks do not look parallel; at least they do not look parallel to me. Kelley simply asserts that they do. Perhaps to him they do. He writes: "A person far away looks normal, of human size, but he also looks tiny." Well, my sensory apparatus seems to give me quite different perceptions than Kelley's apparatus gives him. Apparently our physiologies are different. Since "perception . . . is a unitary product of *physiological* causes," and my physiology is as good as Kelley's physiology, then my perceptions are as good as his, and therefore my facts are as good as his facts. Kelley's empiricism is relativism. We have arrived back at the position Protagoras took 2,500 years ago.

In chapter three Kelley turns his attention to sensory qualities. He distinguishes between an object and its appearances. "The moon

---

[21] *The Evidence of the Senses*, 45.

looks larger near the horizon than overhead, food tastes different if one is sick, a healthy face turns ghostly pale under a street lamp."[22] All of this, of course, contradicts his initial position that we directly perceive "physical objects and their properties." Furthermore, he says, "such relativity exists in regard to every [note well] perceptible attribute of things, in every [note well] modality of sense. That fact poses a central problem for the philosophy of perception." Indeed it does. There is no modality and no perception that is not relative and changing.

He writes: "The way an object appears is a joint product of the object itself and of the means by which we perceive it."[23] To explain what he intends to say, Kelley introduces the concept of, believe it or not, form. Shades of Kant. But Kelley's forms are different from Kant's forms. "A form of perception is obviously not subjective in the ordinary, commonsense meaning of the term—it is not something we make up arbitrarily...."[24] Nor, of course, were Kant's forms. They were not subjective at all in this sense. "It [a form] is an inexorable causal product of the interaction among the objects perceived, the physical organs of perception, and the external conditions in which they operate." Here Kelley introduces a third element for the first time: He started by asserting that we perceive "physical objects and their properties" directly. Then he distinguished between objects and how they appear to us. Then he asserted that those appearances are the product of the physical objects and our sensory apparatus. Now a new element, "the external conditions in which they operate" has been added to the mix in order to explain the relativity of all our perceptions. With each new ingredient, the direct perception of physical objects and their properties recedes further into the distance, and with it goes any plausible claim to obtain knowledge through the senses, or any plausible claim to realism. It is not the real object we perceive, but the complex product of the object, our mechanical senses, and circumstances.

[22] *The Evidence of the Senses*, 81.

[23] *The Evidence of the Senses*, 84.

[24] *The Evidence of the Senses*, 88.

Colors, for example, which Kelley at one point called "facts," turn out not to be facts at all. Rather, colors are "dependent on the visual systems of perceivers and do not exist in objects apart from them. . . . There is nothing [note well] in the objects themselves, or in the light they reflect, that would account for this [perception of color]. If so, there is no reason for attributing colors to objects apart from our visual systems."[25]

Just to reassure the reader that we have presented Kelley's "realistic" view correctly, here is another quotation:

> We know that color cannot be located in external objects as an intrinsic property, since it depends on a relationship. . . . But the facts do not justify locating color anywhere else. When an object looks red, the red is not in the light, the eye, or the nervous system. And we certainly have no basis for saying it exists in the mind of the perceiver. The facts show only that it results from the interaction of two physical systems, the external environment of objects and light, and the physiology of a perceiver. Indeed, as the product of an interaction, color cannot be located anywhere, as an intrinsic property of some participant in that interaction—any more than the weight of an object or the violence of an automobile collision can be so located.[26]

All this quite clearly says or implies that color is not a property of the world around us. But what can Kelley mean by denying that color is in the mind as well? If color is not in his mind, how does Kelley know he sees red? If color is not in his mind, Kelley cannot be aware of it.

Kelley's subjectivism, which he calls realism, appears quite clearly a few pages later:

> The way a thing looks *is* its effect on a perceiver with a specific nature. A thing acts differently on sense organs of

[25] *The Evidence of the Senses*, 98.

[26] *The Evidence of the Senses*, 99-100.

different types, and looks different as a result. There is no right way for it to look in abstraction from a specific type of sense organ. . . . We can now see that the color *qualia* themselves are also forms. . . . Nevertheless, it is a fact and it requires us to identify the *qualia* as forms, since they are aspects of the way objects appear to us which are determined by our means of perceiving them.[27]

Strangely, Kelley insists that "Color is not in the mind in any sense. From the standpoint of the subject [the perceiver], color is not in or a feature of his perceptual awareness. The physical facts show that color is a relational property. . . ." What can the words "color is not in . . . his perceptual awareness" mean? What do the words "in any sense" mean? Does Kelley mean, simple-mindedly, that our minds, our awarenesses, our consciousnesses, our souls, are not colored? Whoever said they were? I know of no empiricist foolish enough to make such an absurd statement. And no idealist would even think of it. Worse, the words "in any sense" imply that no one is aware of color. That is a very strange position for any empiricist to take.

Color, of course, is merely an illustration and example of a general position that Kelley is disclosing one step at a time. No sensory *qualia* is in the objects perceived. All perceptions, not merely perceptions of color, are products of physical objects, the external conditions, and our sensory apparatus.

. . . the feeling of warmth or coolness is the form in which we detect the kinetic energy of the molecules in substances touching the skin;[28] that sensations of sound are the form in which we perceive certain events in the environment; and that flavors and odors are the form. . . .[29]

---

[27] *The Evidence of the Senses*, 110.

[28] This makes no sense. Assuming the theory of heat Kelley is proposing, the same "kinetic energy" feels cool to some, warm to others, and both cool and warm to the same person at the same time. Hues, sounds, tastes, smells, and so on are equally subjective.

[29] *The Evidence of the Senses*, 111.

Kelley's account of perception takes a more complicated turn when he tries to defend the concept "red."

> ... the concept of red picks out a class of objects which in fact possess certain reflectance properties in common, as well as the relational property of being perceived in a certain form by ordinary perceivers in ordinary conditions.

Granting, for the sake of argument, that the concept of "reflectance property" has some meaning that is neither empty nor tautological, Kelley's position disintegrates because he introduces, as he must, the concepts of "ordinary perceivers" and "ordinary conditions." Which are those perceivers and conditions? The answer is obvious, is it not? They are the perceivers and conditions that support Kelley's theory. Anything else is extraordinary.

Kelley shields his theory from refutation by accumulating scientific evidence, and in so doing, he presents a view of the perceptual world that is quite different from the standard Lockean account. Indeed, it reads more like Bishop Berkeley.

> ... the concept of perceptual form is capable of assimilating any sort of perceptual relativity that science provides evidence of [Kelley obviously assumes that science is a cognitive enterprise], and that the concept [of form] allows us to classify the different levels of relativity. ... Nor would the analysis be refuted should future scientific discoveries provide evidence that at a still deeper level, even the primary qualities [size, shape, motion, rest, number, position], even the entire spacial world, is relative to our senses. We can imagine, for example, that properties of extension and location in space are not causal primaries, that they depend on some underlying energy phenomenon, and that they exist only as products of an interaction between external instances of that phenomenon and the instances we call our senses. We would then have to say that shape, size, and position are forms in which we perceive those underlying properties of energy.

Though he has long since abandoned direct perception of physical objects and their properties, Kelley insists that our experiences of colors are not illusory, and in this world, shapes, locations, and extension would not be illusory either. Because perception is a physical process, it is an infallible, a veridical, process. That characteristic, of course, applies to all perceivers and conditions, not just ordinary ones. Kelley has constructed a physical theory of perception in which there can be neither truth nor error; what he calls perceptions are physical events. Truth, however, is a quality only of propositions; it is not a characteristic of chemical or electrical reactions. In his theory of perception there is no truth in any sense; there are only complex reactions to complex circumstances. One reaction is as good as another.

Kelley's explanation of his theory of "realism" seems to me to be a process of digging a deeper and deeper hole. Take these sentences:

> That my awareness occurs now, at a given moment, does not mean that its object, qua object of awareness, must also exist now. This is not true of memory or historical knowledge generally;[30] and the time lag in perception shows that it is not true of perception either. The objects of perceptual awareness, I have argued, are real—they exist. But there is no reason to assume a priori that they must exist at the moment of the awareness of them, or that at that moment they must be exactly as they are perceived to be.[31]

Perception, then, is not necessarily, in fact it cannot be, perception of present objects; it is always perception of objects that may no longer exist. In fact, building on what Kelley said earlier, none of our perceptions—shape, color, sound, odor, number, location, mo-

---

[30] Of course, both the things remembered and history are indeed present to the remembering mind now; the past no longer exists outside the mind. Kelley should read R. G. Collingwood, and especially Gordon H. Clark's *Historiography*.

[31] *The Evidence of the Senses*, 132.

tion, taste—might resemble the existent world at all, which could be an undulating flow of mystical energy. Worse, at any given moment, our awareness of this world, a world that our sensory apparatus has made for us, must be out of date. By the time we "perceive" anything, the conditions that gave rise to that perception will have changed. I detect less and less difference between Kelley's "realism" and say, Hinduism.

Kelley's argument takes a thoroughly irrational turn at this point. Because this is the way perception is, he writes, that makes perception "valid."

> Perceptual awareness is a natural phenomenon, occurring as the result of definite causes. By the nature of those causes, we could not possibly be aware of the object as it is after it has set in motion the causal sequence that produces our awareness of it. By what right then, do we assume that for perception to be valid, its object must be given in some other way?

This is a thoroughly perverse argument. If the word "valid" has any meaning in this context,[32] it must mean that we accurately perceive the world that exists. Since Kelley has repeatedly admitted that we cannot do so, he now asserts that "valid" means the way our sensory apparatus works. He has demonstrated that our perceptions cannot be valid, that is, accurate, but rather than admit it, he attempts to change the meaning of the word *valid.*

When tackling the problem of hallucinations, Kelley rejects the reports of those who have experienced them: "Although it is beyond doubt that some vivid imagery occurs, we cannot take the report of subjects as evidence about the degree of similarity between hallucinations and perception."[33] Kelley, the empiricist, rejects the empirical evidence out of hand. Why? Because it would subvert his theory.

---

[32] Validity is, of course, a quality only of inferences, just as truth is a quality only of propositions. But Kelley insists that perceptions are not inferences.

[33] *The Evidence of the Senses,* 135.

He continues his discussion of hallucinations:

> Thus the best explanation of what happens in halluci-
> nation would be that the capacity for recalling and rear-
> ranging perceptual experiences is set in operation by causes
> that prevent one from experiencing them as recalled or made
> up. But this is a distortion, an aberration. It does not mean
> that one is actually in the same state as when he perceives;
> it only means he cannot tell that he is not.

The odd thing about Kelley's arguments is that they so obviously
destroy his own case for empiricism, yet he is completely blind to
the skeptical implications of his own arguments. If, as Kelley says,
a person cannot tell whether he is perceiving or hallucinating, then
he can place no confidence in his awareness at all.

Kelley furnishes us with one lethal quotation after another. He
imagines an experiment in which a subject is connected to a device
that changes his perceptions. If the subject's motor neurons were
wired to the device so that they could alter the device, "the subject
could explore his world [notice the subjectivism]. ... Of course
his experience would not be similar to the objects he perceives [be-
cause his experience is altered by the device], but then normal experience is not similar to its objects either. *Perceptual awareness
cannot be compared to its objects at all on the ground of similarity
or dissimilarity.*"[34] Could there be a more thoroughgoing skepticism than this? Could constant hallucinations be worse? Could there
be a more thoroughgoing agnosticism? It is amazing that a work
such as Kelley's is so widely accepted by those who purport to be
defending the accuracy of the senses.

In chapter 5, "The Nature of Perception," Kelley provides an
account of perception that makes it logically prior to sensation,
and achieved only by paying attention. In short, Kelley's account,
far from being empiricist, is almost Augustinian. Now if he could
only see that perception logically presupposes concepts (one must

---

[34] *The Evidence of the Senses*, 141.

know apple before one can identify an apple, as Luttwidge Dodgson so cleverly pointed out), and that concepts logically presuppose propositions (one of which is, A is not not-A), we might be making some headway. But such an account is the reverse of the empiricist account of sensation and perception. It is, in fact, the Christian account.

In his account of "Perceptual Judgments" (chapter 7), Kelley distinguishes between judgments such as "this is a desk, that it is brown," and "far more sophisticated judgments," which, nevertheless, "are often made in a way that is experienced psychologically as direct."

> These latter judgments obviously rest on a body of experience which includes much more than the particular experiences that occasion them. In this respect they differ in degree from the judgments concerning the desk. But I would deny that there is a difference in kind. . . . As I will argue later, any judgment "goes beyond" what is given, by assimilating to abstract types and attributes. . . . In this respect there is no difference in kind between the simpler and the more sophisticated judgments mentioned above.[35]

If every judgment, including every perceptual judgment, goes beyond what is given, then every judgment is an invalid inference. If that "going beyond" is an "assimilating to abstract types and attributes," then every judgment, including every perceptual judgment, requires the uses of concepts, or, as Kelley calls them, abstractions.

Kelley provides several examples of what "going beyond" means. For instance, "I have argued that to perceive a thing as a whole, one does not have to perceive the whole of it—front, back, and inside." But is Kelley not equivocating on the word "perceive" in such a statement? In the first instance, "perceive" actually means something like "understand" or "judge"; in the second instance, "perceive" means literal perception.

---

[35] *The Evidence of the Senses*, 209-210.

He continues:

> Nor does one have to perceive the whole of a thing to be justified in forming a [perceptual] judgment about it. I can identify the creature across the room as a cat, even though its body is hidden by a chair. The subject of my [perceptual] judgment is of course the whole animal, not merely that portion of it reflecting light to my eyes—if the judgment were about the latter "entity," it would be false.

This argument requires several comments. First, Kelley has either abandoned perception as the basis of perceptual judgment, or, if the reader prefer, he has admitted that all perceptual judgments are based on inadequate perceptions, for nothing is ever perceived "as a whole." Therefore, no perception can ever justify a perceptual judgment. Second, Kelley admits that all perceptual judgments are false, because no one ever perceives an entity. Since the cat's head is not an entity (I can only assume that that is what the quotation marks around "entity" mean in Kelley's sentence), then no perception is ever perception of an entity, for the simple reason that nothing is ever perceived entire. Presumably a cat is something more than a patch of color [Kelley makes his situation even more problematic by denying that cats are colored], but that is all Kelley ever sees.

He continues: "But neither am I discriminating just that portion [what appears to be the head of a cat]. The visible border between the cat and chair is experienced as an edge of the chair, not of the cat; I experience the cat as extending beyond that accidental limit to my vision. . . ." The last clause is simply false: Kelley is not experiencing the cat. He is inferring the cat.

Kelley, like Rand and Branden, unwittingly admits epistemological defeat on page 196:

> Any simpleminded realist theory which treats our knowledge as a mirror of reality [that is, as accurate] is easily shown to be false; conceptual thought is no more

diaphanous [transparent] than perception is. We must take account of the specific and fallible means by which cognition occurs, thus allowing for the relativity of the *form* in which we know objects and for the possibility of error.

In the end, all we can have are perceptual forms, which can and do vary from person to person and from time to time in the same person, all of which forms are relative, and none of which accurately reflects—mirrors—reality. In Kelley's theory, cognitive error is not merely possible, it is unavoidable.

D
GOD AND LOGIC

In thinking about God, Calvinists almost immediately repeat the Shorter Catechism and say, "God is a spirit, infinite, eternal, and unchangeable." Perhaps we do not pause to clarify our ideas of spirit, but hurry on to the attributes of "wisdom, holiness, justice, goodness, and truth." But pause: Spirit, Wisdom, Truth. Psalm 31:5 addresses God as "O Lord God of *truth.*" John 17:3 says, "This is life eternal, that they might know thee, the only *true* God. . . ." I John 5:6 says, "the Spirit is *truth.*" Such verses as these indicate that God is a rational, thinking being whose thought exhibits the structure of Aristotelian logic.

If anyone objects to Aristotelian logic in this connection—and presumably he does not want to replace it with the Boolean-Russellian symbolic logic—let him ask and answer whether it is true for God that if all dogs have teeth, some dogs—spaniels—have teeth? Do those who contrast this "merely human logic" with a divine logic mean that for God all dogs may have teeth while spaniels do not? Similarly, with "merely human" arithmetic: Two plus two is four for man, but is it eleven for God? Ever since Bernard distrusted Abelard, it has been a mark of piety in some quarters to disparage "mere human reason"; and at the present time existentialistic, neo-orthodox authors object to "straight-line" inference and insist that faith must "curb" logic. Thus they not only

277

refuse to make logic an axiom, but reserve the right to repudiate it. In opposition to the latter view, the following argument will continue to insist on the necessity of logic; and with respect to the contention that Scripture cannot be axiomatic because logic must be, it will be necessary to spell out in greater detail the meaning of Scriptural revelation.

Now, since in this context verbal revelation is a revelation from God, the discussion will begin with the relation between God and logic. Afterward will come the relation between logic and the Scripture. And finally the discussion will turn to logic in man.

Logic and God

It will be best to begin by calling attention to some of the characteristics the Scriptures attribute to God. Nothing startling is involved in remarking that God is omniscient. This is a commonplace of Christian theology. But, further, God is eternally omniscient. He has not learned his knowledge. And since God exists of himself, independent of everything else, indeed the Creator of everything else, he must himself be the source of his own knowledge. This important point has had a history.

At the beginning of the Christian era, Philo, the Jewish scholar of Alexandria, made an adjustment in Platonic philosophy to bring it into accord with the theology of the Old Testament. Plato had based his system on three original, independent principles: the World of Ideas, the Demiurge, and chaotic space. Although the three were equally eternal and independent of each other, the Demiurge fashioned chaotic space into this visible world by using the Ideas as his model. Hence in Plato the World of Ideas is not only independent of but even in a sense superior to the maker of Heaven and Earth. He is morally obligated, and in fact willingly submits, to the Ideas of justice, man, equality, and number.

Philo, however, says, "God has been ranked according to the one and the unit; or rather even the unit has been ranked according to the one God, for all number, like time, is younger than the cosmos, while God is older than the cosmos and its creator."

This means that God is the source and determiner of all truth. Christians generally, even uneducated Christians, understand that water, milk, alcohol, and gasoline freeze at different temperatures because God created them that way. God could have made an intoxicating fluid freeze at zero Fahrenheit and he could have made the cow's product freeze at forty. But he decided otherwise. Therefore, behind the act of creation there is an eternal decree. It was God's eternal purpose to have such liquids, and therefore we can say that the particularities of nature were determined before there was any nature.

Similarly in all other varieties of truth, God must be accounted sovereign. It is his decree that makes one proposition true and another false. Whether the proposition be physical, psychological, moral, or theological, it is God who made it that way. A proposition is true because God thinks it so.

Perhaps for a certain formal completeness, a sample of Scriptural documentation might be appropriate. Psalm 147:5 says, "God is our Lord, and of great power; his understanding is infinite." If we cannot strictly conclude from this verse that God's power is the origin of his understanding, at least there is no doubt that omniscience is asserted. 1 Samuel 2:3 says "the Lord is a God of knowledge." Ephesians 1:8 speaks of God's wisdom and prudence. In Romans 16:27 we have the phrase, "God only wise," and in 1 Timothy 1:17 the similar phrase, "the only wise God."

Further references and an excellent exposition of them may be found in Stephen Charnock, *The Existence and Attributes of God*, chapters VIII and IX. From this distinguished author a few lines must be included here.

> God knows himself because his knowledge with his will is the cause of all other things; . . . he is the first truth, and therefore is the first object of his understanding. . . . As he is all knowledge, so he hath in himself the most excellent object of knowledge. . . . No object is so intelligible to God as God is to himself . . . for his understanding is his essence, himself. God knows his own decree and will, and

therefore must know all things. . . . God must know what he hath decreed to come to pass. . . . God must know because he willed them . . . he therefore knows them because he knows what he willed. The knowledge of God cannot arise from the things themselves, for then the knowledge of God would have a cause without him. . . . As God sees things possible in the glass of his own power, so he sees things future in the glass of his own will.

A great deal of Charnock's material has as its purpose the listing of the objects of God's knowledge. Here, however, the quotations were made to point out that God's knowledge depends on his will and on nothing external to him. Thus we may repeat with Philo that God is not to be ranked under the idea of unity, or of goodness, or of truth; but rather unity, goodness, and truth are to be ranked under the decree of God.

Logic Is God

It is to be hoped that these remarks on the relation between God and truth will be seen as pertinent to the discussion of logic. In any case, the subject of logic can be more clearly introduced by one more Scriptural reference. The well-known prologue to John's Gospel may be paraphrased, "In the beginning was Logic, and Logic was with God, and Logic was God. . . . In Logic was life and the life was the light of men."

This paraphrase—in fact, this translation—may not only sound strange to devout ears, it may even sound obnoxious and offensive. But the shock only measures the devout person's distance from the language and thought of the Greek New Testament. Why it is offensive to call Christ Logic, when it does not offend to call him a word, is hard to explain. But such is often the case. Even Augustine, because he insisted that God is truth, has been subjected to the anti-intellectualistic accusation of "reducing" God to a proposition. At any rate, the strong intellectualism of the word *Logos* is seen in its several possible translations: to wit, computation, (financial) accounts, esteem, proportion and (mathematical) ratio, explanation, theory or argument, principle or law, reason, formula, debate, narrative, speech, deliberation, discussion, oracle, sentence, and wisdom.

Any translation of John 1:1 that obscures this emphasis on mind or reason is a bad translation. And if anyone complains that the idea of *ratio* or debate obscures the personality of the second person of the Trinity, he should alter his concept of personality. In the beginning, then, was Logic.

That Logic is the light of men is a proposition that could well introduce the section after next on the relation of logic to man. But the thought that Logic is God will bring us to the conclusion of the present section. Not only do the followers of Bernard entertain suspicions about logic, but even more systematic theologians are wary of any proposal that would make an abstract principle superior to God. The present argument, in consonance with both Philo and Charnock, does not do so. The law of contradiction is not to be taken as an axiom prior to or independent of God. The law is God thinking.

For this reason also the law of contradiction is not subsequent to God. If one should say that logic is dependent on God's thinking, it is dependent only in the sense that it is the characteristic of God's thinking. It is not subsequent temporally, for God is eternal and there was never a time when God existed without thinking logically. One must not suppose that God's will existed as an inert substance before he willed to think.

As there is no temporal priority, so also there is no logical or analytical priority. Not only was Logic the beginning, but Logic was God. If this unusual translation of John's Prologue still disturbs someone, he might yet allow that God is his thinking. God is not a passive or potential substratum; he is actuality or activity. This is the philosophical terminology to express the Biblical idea that God is a living God. Hence logic is to be considered as the activity of God's willing.

Although Aristotle's theology is no better (and perhaps worse) than his epistemology, he used a phrase to describe God, which, with a slight change, may prove helpful. He defined God as "thought-thinking-thought." Aristotle developed the meaning of this phrase so as to deny divine omniscience. But if we are clear that the thought which thought thinks includes thought about a world to be created—in Aristotle God has no knowledge of things inferior to him—the Aristotelian definition of God as "thought-thinking-thought" may help us to understand that logic, the law of contradiction, is neither prior to nor subsequent to God's activity.

This conclusion may disturb some analytical thinkers. They may wish to separate logic and God. Doing so, they would complain that the present construction merges two axioms into one. And if two, one of them must be prior; in which case we would have to accept God without logic, or logic without God; and the other one afterward. But this is not the presupposition here proposed. God and logic are one and the same first principle, for John wrote that Logic was God.

At the moment this much must suffice to indicate the relation of God to logic. We now pass to what at the beginning seemed to be the more pertinent question of logic and Scripture.

Logic and Scripture

There is a minor misunderstanding that can easily be disposed of before discussing the relation of logic to the Scriptures. Someone with a lively historical sense might wonder why Scripture and revelation are equated, when God's direct speech to Moses, Samuel, and the prophets is even more clearly revelation.

This observation became possible simply because of previous brevity. Of course God's speech to Moses was revelation, in fact, revelation par excellence, if you wish. But we are not Moses. Therefore, if the problem is to explain how we know in this age, one cannot use the personal experience of Moses. Today we have the Scripture. As the Westminster Confession says, "It pleased the Lord ... to reveal himself ... and afterwards ... to commit the same wholly unto writing, which maketh the holy scripture to be most necessary, those former ways of God's revealing his will unto his people being now ceased." What God said to Moses is written in the Bible; the words are identical; the revelation is the same.

In this may be anticipated the relation of logic to the Scripture. First of all, Scripture, the written words of the Bible, is the mind of God. What is said in Scripture is God's thought.

In contemporary religious polemics, the Biblical view of the Bible, the historic position of the Reformation, or what is the same thing—the doctrine of plenary and verbal inspiration—is castigated as bibliolatry. The liberals accuse the Lutherans and Calvinists of worshipping a book instead of worshipping God. Apparently they think that we genuflect to the Bible on the pulpit, and they deride us for kissing the ring of a paper pope.

This caricature stems from their materialistic turn of mind—a materialism that may not be apparent in other discussions—but which comes to the surface when they direct their fire against fundamentalism. They think of the Bible as a material book with paper contents and a leather binding. That the contents are the thoughts of God, expressed in God's own words, is a position to which they are so invincibly antagonistic that they cannot even admit it to be the position of a fundamentalist.

Nevertheless we maintain that the Bible expresses the mind of God. Conceptually it is the mind of God, or, more accurately, a part of God's mind. For this reason the Apostle Paul, referring to the revelation given him, and in fact given to the Corinthians through him, is able to say, "We have the mind of Christ." Also in Philippians 2:5 he exhorts them, "Let this mind be in you which was also in Christ Jesus." To the same purpose is his modest claim in I Corinthians 7:40, "I think also that I have the Spirit of God."

The Bible, then, is the mind or thought of God. It is not a physical fetish, like a crucifix. And I doubt that there has ever been even one hillbilly fundamentalist ignorant enough to pray to a black book with red edges. Similarly, the charge that the Bible is a paper pope misses the mark for the same reason. The Bible consists of thoughts, not paper; and the thoughts are the thoughts of the omniscient, infallible God, not those of Innocent III.

On this basis—that is, on the basis that Scripture is the mind of

God—the relation to logic can easily be made clear. As might be expected, if God has spoken, he has spoken logically. The Scripture therefore should and does exhibit logical organization.

For example, Romans 4:2 is an enthymematic hypothetical destructive syllogism. Romans 5:13 is a hypothetical constructive syllogism. I Corinthians 15:15-18 is a sorites. Obviously, examples of standard logical forms such as these could be listed at great length.

There is, of course, much in Scripture that is not syllogistic. The historical sections are largely narrative; yet every declarative sentence is a logical unit. These sentences are truths; as such they are objects of knowledge. Each of them has, or perhaps we should say, each of them is a predicate attached to a subject. Only so can they convey meaning.

Even in the single words themselves, as is most clearly seen in the cases of nouns and verbs, logic is embedded. If Scripture says, David was King of Israel, it does not mean that David was president of Babylon; and surely it does not mean that Churchill was prime minister of China. That is to say, the words *David, King,* and *Israel* have definite meanings.

The old libel that Scripture is a wax nose and that interpretation is infinitely elastic is clearly wrong. If there were no limits to interpretation, we might interpret the libel itself as an acceptance of verbal and plenary inspiration. But since the libel cannot be so interpreted, neither can the Virgin Birth be interpreted as a myth nor the Resurrection as a symbol of spring. No doubt there are some things hard to be understood which the unlearned wrest to their own destruction, but the difficulties are no greater than those found in Aristotle or Plotinus, and against these philosophers no such libel is ever directed. Furthermore, only some things are hard. For the rest, Protestants have insisted on the perspicuity of Scripture.

Nor need we waste time repeating Aristotle's explanation of ambiguous words. The fact that a word must mean one thing and not its contradictory is the evidence of the law of contradiction in all rational language.

This exhibition of the logic embedded in Scripture explains why Scripture rather than the law of contradiction is selected as the axiom. Should we assume merely the law of contradiction, we would be no better off than Kant was. His notion that knowledge requires *a priori* categories deserves great respect. Once for all, in a positive way—the complement of Hume's negative and unintentional way—Kant demonstrated the necessity of axioms, presuppositions, or *a priori* equipment. But this *sine qua non* is not sufficient to produce knowledge. Therefore the law of contradiction as such and by itself is not made the axiom of this argument.

For a similar reason, God as distinct from Scripture is not made the axiom of this argument. Undoubtedly this twist will seem strange to many theologians. It will seem particularly strange after the previous emphasis on the mind of God as the origin of all truth. Must not God be the axiom? For example, the first article of the Augsburg Confession gives the doctrine of God, and the doctrine of the Scripture hardly appears anywhere in the whole document. In the French Confession of 1559, the first article is on God; the Scripture is discussed in the next five. The Belgic Confession has the same order. The Scotch Confession of 1560 begins with God and gets to the Scripture only in article nineteen. The Thirty-Nine Articles begin with the Trinity, and Scripture comes in articles six and following. If God is sovereign, it seems very reasonable to put him first in the system.

But several other creeds, and especially the Westminster Confession, state the doctrine of Scripture at the very start. The explanation is quite simple: our knowledge of God comes from the Bible. We may assert that every proposition is true because God thinks it so, and we may follow Charnock in all his great detail, but the whole is based on Scripture. Suppose this were not so. Then "God" as an axiom, apart from Scripture, is just a name. We must specify which God. The best known system in which "God" was made the axiom is Spinoza's. For him all theorems are deduced from *Deus sive Natura*. But it is the *Natura* that identifies Spinoza's God. Different gods might be made axioms other systems. Hence the important thing is not to presuppose God, but to define the mind of the God presupposed. Therefore the Scripture is offered here as the axiom. This gives definiteness and content, without which axioms are useless.

Thus it is that God, Scripture, and logic are tied together. The Pietists should not complain that emphasis on logic is a deification of an abstraction, or of human reason divorced from God. Emphasis on logic is strictly in accord with John's Prologue and is nothing other than a recognition of the nature of God.

Does it not seem peculiar, in this connection, that a theologian can be so greatly attached to the doctrine of the Atonement, or a Pietist to the idea of sanctification, which nonetheless is explained only in some parts of Scripture, and yet be hostile to or suspicious of rationality and logic which every verse of Scripture exhibits?

Logic in Man

With this understanding of God's mind, the next step is the creation of man in God's image. The nonrational animals were not created in his image; but God breathed his Spirit into the earthly form, and Adam became a type of soul superior to the animals.

To be precise, one should not speak of the image of God in man. Man is not something in which somewhere God's image can be found along with other things. Man is the image. This, of course, does not refer to man's body. The body is an instrument or tool man uses. He himself is God's breath, the spirit God breathed into the clay, the mind, the thinking ego. Therefore, man is rational in the likeness of God's rationality. His mind is structured as Aristotelian logic described it. That is why we believe that spaniels have teeth.

In addition to the well-known verses in chapter one, Genesis 5:1 and 9:6 both repeat the idea. 1 Corinthians 11:7 says, "man . . . is the image and glory of God." See also, Colossians 3:10 and James 3:9. Other verses, not so explicit, nonetheless add to our information. Compare Hebrews 1:3, Hebrews 2:6-8, and Psalm 8. But the conclusive consideration is that throughout the Bible as a whole the rational God gives man an intelligible message.

It is strange that anyone who thinks he is a Christian should deprecate logic. Such a person does not of course intend to deprecate the mind of God; but he thinks that logic in man is sinful, even more sinful than other parts of man's fallen nature. This, however, makes no sense. The law of contradiction cannot be sinful. Quite the contrary, it is our violations of the law of contradiction that are sinful. Yet the strictures which some devotional writers place on "merely human" logic are amazing. Can such pious stupidity really mean that a syllogism which is valid for us is invalid for God? If two plus two is four in our arithmetic, does God have a different arithmetic in which two and two makes three or perhaps five?

The fact that the Son of God is God's reason—for Christ is the wisdom of God as well as the power of God—plus the fact that the image in man is so-called "human reason," suffices to show that this so-called "human reason" is not so much human as divine.

Of course, the Scripture says that God's thoughts are not our thoughts and his ways are not our ways. But is it good exegesis to say that this means his logic, his arithmetic, his truth are not ours? If this were so, what would the consequences be? It would mean not only that our additions and subtractions are all wrong, but also that all our thoughts—in history as well as in arithmetic—are all wrong. If for example, we think that David was King of Israel, and God's thoughts are not ours, then it follows that God does not think David was King of Israel. David in God's mind was perchance prime minister of Babylon.

To avoid this irrationalism, which of course is a denial of the divine image, we must insist that truth is the same for God and man. Naturally, we may not know the truth about some matters. But if we know anything at all, what we must know must be identical with what God knows. God knows all truth, and unless we know something God knows, our ideas are untrue. It is absolutely essential therefore to insist that there is an area of coincidence between God's mind and our mind.

Logic and Language

This point brings us to the central issue of language. Language did not develop from, nor was its purpose restricted to, the physical needs of earthly life. God gave Adam a mind to understand the divine law, and he gave him language to enable him to speak to God. From the beginning, language was intended for worship. In the *Te Deum,* by means of language, and in spite of the fact that it is sung to music, we pay "metaphysical compliments" to God. The debate about the adequacy of language to express the truth of God is a false issue. Words are mere symbols or signs. Any sign would be adequate. The real issue is: Does a man have the idea to symbolize? If he can think of God, then he can use the sound *God, Deus, Theos, or Elohim.* The word makes no difference, and the sign is *ipso facto* literal and adequate.

The Christian view is that God created Adam as a rational mind. The structure of Adam's mind was the same as God's. God thinks that asserting the consequent is a fallacy; and Adam's mind was formed on the principles of identity and contradiction. This Christian view of God, man, and language does not fit into any empirical philosophy. It is rather a type of *a priori* rationalism. Man's mind is not initially a blank. It is structured. In fact, an unstructured blank is no mind at all. Nor could any such sheet of white paper extract any universal law of logic from finite experience. No universal and necessary proposition can be deduced from sensory observation. Universality and necessity can only be *a priori.*

This is not to say that all truth can be deduced from logic alone. The seventeenth-century rationalists gave themselves an impossible task. Even if the ontological argument be valid, it is impossible to deduce *Cur Deus Homo,* the Trinity, or the final resurrection. The axioms to which the *a priori* forms of logic must be applied are the propositions God revealed to Adam and the later prophets.

Conclusion

Logic is irreplaceable. It is not an arbitrary tautology, a useful framework among others. Various systems of cataloging books in libraries are possible, and several are equally convenient. They are all arbitrary. History can be designated by 800 as easily as by 400. But there is no substitute for the law of contradiction. If dog is the equivalent of not-dog, and if 2 = 3 = 4, not only do zoology and mathematics disappear, Victor Hugo and Johann Wolfgang Goethe also disappear. These two men are particularly appropriate examples, for they are both, especially Goethe, romanticists. Even so, without logic, Goethe could not have attacked the logic of John's Gospel (I, 1224-1237).

> Geschrieben steht: "Im anfang war das Wort!" Hier stock ich schon! Wer hilft mir weiter fort?

> Mir hilft der Geist! Auf einmal seh' ich Rath und schreib' getrost: "Im Anfang war die That!"

But Goethe can express his rejection of the divine Logos of John 1:1, and express his acceptance of romantic experience, only by using the logic he despises.

To repeat, even if it seems wearisome: Logic is fixed, universal, necessary, and irreplaceable. Irrationality contradicts the Biblical teaching from beginning to end. The God of Abraham, Isaac, and Jacob is not insane. God is a rational being, the architecture of whose mind is logic.

Gordon H. Clark
1966

E
SCIENCE AND TRUTH

Centuries ago it may have been possible to ignore science—in fact centuries ago there was little science to ignore—but today its successes are so phenomenal that it is usually accorded the last word in all disputes. The younger generation can hardly realize that so simple a thing as the incandescent electric bulb came only yesterday. Today science receives its praise and respect by reason of the atomic bomb, bacteriological warfare, and the possibility of interplanetary travel. None of this may be desirable, but truth is not a matter of desire; and the methods that have produced these wonderful products of civilization are capable of answering every question.

T. H. Huxley asserted that the foundation of morality is to renounce lying and give up pretending to believe unintelligible propositions for which there is no evidence and which go beyond the possibilities of knowledge. In a similar vein W. K. Clifford said, "It is wrong always, everywhere, and for anyone to believe anything upon insufficient evidence." The import and context of these statements is a general repudiation of theism in favor of a scientific method that obtains indisputable truth.

Science and Christianity

To show the bearing of science on theism, some quotations from distinguished contemporary scientists should be made. Without doubt Professor A. J. Carlson is a distinguished scientist, as is attested by his writings and by his presidence over the American Association for the Advancement of Science. Religious ideas and their relation to science have attracted his attention, and his conclusions are found in the twice-published article, "Science and the Supernatural." One must note what he says on the nature of science as well as what he says on its relation to religion. He writes, "Probably the most common meaning of science is a body of established, verifiable, and organized data secured by controlled observation, experience, or experiment. ... The element in science of even greater importance than the verifying of facts, the approximation of laws, the prediction of processes is the method by means of which these data and laws are obtained and the attitude of the people whose labor has secured them. ... What is the method of science? In essence it is this—the rejection *in toto* of all non-observational and non-experimental authority in the field of experience. ... When no evidence is produced [in favor of a pronouncement] other than personal dicta, past or present 'revelations' in dreams, or the 'voice of God', the scientist can pay no attention whatsoever, except to ask: How do they get that way?"

Karl Pearson presumably speaks for all science when he says, "The goal of science is clear—it is nothing short of the complete interpretation of the universe." And, "Science does much more than demand that it shall be left in undisturbed possession of what the theologian and metaphysician please to term its 'legitimate field'. It claims that the whole range of phenomena, mental as well as physical—the entire universe—is its field. It asserts that the scientific method is the sole gateway to the whole region of knowledge."

What Is Science?

Reflection on these quotations raises a series of puzzling questions, some of which ought to be answered by the serious theologian and scientist alike. Clifford and Huxley, and anyone who opposes them, ought to make clear what is *sufficient* evidence. Is evidence sufficient only when it is logically demonstrative? Would Clifford and

Huxley be satisfied with something less than demonstration, and if so, how much less? More fundamental is the plain question, What is evidence? Comte and Pearson assume that facts and classifications can be empirically discovered. But can they? Comte was certain that the positive character of knowledge, now that it has passed beyond the theological and metaphysical stages, will never again change. But if Comte is the father of sociology, it is one of his own sons, Sorokin, who is sure that it will change again and again. Further, must we hold with Karl Pearson that the judgments of science are absolute? Will a judgment or fact, once for all discovered, never be abandoned in favor of a more up-to-date fact or judgment? Do scientists never revise their conclusions? And very much more to the point, is the scientific method the sole gateway to the whole region of knowledge? What experiment or what evidence is sufficient to prove that science is the sole gateway to all knowledge that is yet to be obtained? If there is a God, is it absolutely necessary that his existence be discovered by some infinitely sensitive Geiger counters? If moral distinctions and normative principles exist—in particular, Carlson's principle that a scientist has no right to believe anything—must such principles be discovered through a microscope? And finally, and very generally, what is scientific method? One must seriously question not merely the desirability but the possibility of rejecting *in toto* all nonobservational and nonexperimental authority in science. In other words, What is science?

What Is A Fact?

The practical mind that loves facts and distrusts theory should acquire some patience and pause a while over the theory of facts. There may at first be reluctance to face the question, What is fact? Yet, if facts are unyielding absolutes, it ought not to prove too difficult to show what a fact is. Let us try.

Is it a fact that the Earth is round? In the Middle Ages the common people thought it was flat. Since then, evidence has accumulated (considerable evidence was known to astronomers during the

Middle Ages) and has been disseminated, until today everyone takes it as a fact that the Earth is round. But strictly, is it the Earth's roundness that is a fact, or is it the items of evidence that are facts on which the conclusion of the Earth's roundness rests? For example, the shadow of the Earth on the Moon during a lunar eclipse has a round edge: Perhaps this is a *fact,* and the roundness of the Earth is a *theory.* Of course, it is not a fact that the Earth is a sphere: It is flattened at the poles. But if it is not a fact that the Earth is perfectly round (spherical), what is the fact? Is it a fact that the Earth is an oblate spheroid? But this term embraces a variety of forms and proportions. Which form exactly is the absolute unchangeable fact?—though science does not pride itself on sticking to facts such as this.

Above, it was said that the shadow of the Earth in a lunar eclipse is a fact—on which the roundness of the Earth is erected as a theory. But is even the shadow a fact? Is it not rather the fact that a certain darkness on the Moon has a round edge, and is it not a theory that this darkness is the shadow of the Earth?

This type of analysis seems to lead to the conclusion that all, or at least many, alleged facts are theories developed out of simpler items of perception. The problem naturally arises whether there is any fact that is not a theory. Is there anything seen directly as what it is? No doubt many people in Atlantic City on a fine summer's day have seen an airplane high in the air pursuing an even course; and as they have watched the plane so high and so small, it has flapped its wings and dived to get a fish. Was it a fact that it was an airplane, or was this a theory about a small object in the sky? What is a fact?

How Long Is a Line?

There is one type of fact that seems to be preeminently scientific: It is the length of a line. When a scientist measures the boiling point of water, he measures a line—the length of mercury in a tube. When he measures the density of gold, he measures a line—the distance on a piece of steel between a scratch called zero and another scratch called, perhaps, nineteen. Similarly he measures another length to determine the amperes of an electric circuit. It may be that scientists never measure anything else than the lengths of lines; at least it is quite safe to say that no significant experiment can be completed without measuring a line. Therefore if science is to be understood, careful thought must be given to this exceedingly important step in experimentation. It has been shown that science is not a body of fixed truths, and if the length of a line turns out not to be a fact, the essential nature of science will have to be sought—not in its results—but in its methods. The experimental method, rather than the particular laws or facts discovered, is the important thing. And to understand the experimental method, an analysis of the process of measuring a length is as instructive as it is for determining whether or not science deals with facts.

Fact or not, the length of a line, be it mercury in a tube or the distance between scratches on a dial, is most difficult to ascertain. To put a ruler against the line and say, "nineteen," would be altogether unscientific. The scientist does of course put a ruler of some sort to the line and does read off nineteen spaces, or whatever it may happen to be; but he never supposes that this is the fact he wants. After he measures the distance between the two scratches on his bar of steel, he measures it again. And strange as it may seem, the length has changed. The lump of gold that a moment before weighed about nineteen units of the same volume of water now weighs less. When the scientist tries it a third time, the gold seems to have gained weight; that is, the line has become longer. The experiment is continued until the rigorous demands of science are satisfied, or the patience of the scientist is exhausted, and he finds himself with a list of numbers. Now it may be a fact (the empirical evidence seems to favor it) that the lump of gold, weighed these many times, is constantly changing; or the fact may be (not an impossibility) that the scientist's eyes blink so much that he cannot see the same length twice; or both of these may be facts. But instead of sticking to these facts, the scientists chooses to stick to the fact that he has a list of numbers.

These numbers he adds; the sum he divides by the number of

readings; and this gives him an arithmetical average, 19.3 for example. This new value, 19.3, does not occur, we may well suppose, in the original list. That list contained 19.29, 19.28, 19.31, 19.32, but never a 19.30. But if this is the case, could the arithmetic mean be the "real" length of the line, the fact itself? By what experimental procedure does one determine that the average is the sought-for fact and that none of the observed readings is? Or, further, would it not be justifiable for the scientist to choose the mode, or the median, instead of the arithmetic mean? Is it not a fact that the mode is the length—as much a fact at least as that the average is? Really, is it not more the fact, because the mode occurred several times in the list, while the mean has not occurred at all? Or, should we say that in this essential item of scientific procedure, science throws all the facts (observations) out the window and sticks to what is not a fact (the unobserved average)! Perhaps there is an aesthetic delight in averages that is not found in modes. Unless, therefore, some balance, some vernier, some scale shows our senses that averages are facts and that modes are not, can the scientist do anything but trust his aesthetic taste?

Further Complications

However, in any experiment that goes beyond a student's exercise, there is more to be considered. The scientist not only calculates the average, but he also takes the difference between each reading and the average, and calculates the average of these differences to construct a figure denoting variable error. The result of the previous example could be 19.3±.01. Suppose now that these repetitions of one measurement are a part of a much more complicated problem designed to determine a law of nature. The problem might be the determination of the law of gravity. As is known, the attraction of gravity, in the Newtonian theory, is directly proportional to the product of two masses and inversely proportional to the square of the distance between them. How could this law have been obtained by experimental procedures? It was not and could not have been obtained by measuring a series of lengths and (assuming unit masses) discovering that the value of the force equaled a fraction whose denominator was always the square of the distance. A length cannot be measured. If it could, the experimenter might have discovered that the force between the two masses, when they are a unit distance apart, was 100 units; he might then have measured the force when the two masses were two units apart and have discovered that it was 25 units; and a similar measurement at four units distance would have given the value of 6.25. The experimenter presumably would then have made a graph and indicated the values so obtained as points on the graph. Measuring four units on the x axis, he would have put a dot 6.25 units above it; and at two units on the x axis he would have put a dot 25 units above it; and so on. By plotting a curve through these points, the experimenter would have *discovered* the law of gravity. But as has been seen, the length of a line cannot be measured. The values for the forces therefore will not be numbers like 6.25, but something like 6.25±.0043. And since the same difficulty inheres in measuring the distances, the scientist will not have unit distances but other values with variable errors. When these values are transferred to a graph, they cannot be represented by points. On the x axis the scientist will have to measure off two units more or less, and on the y axis, 6.25 more or less. It will be necessary to indicate these measurements, not by points, but by rectangular areas. But, as an elementary account of curves would show, through a series of areas, an infinite number of curves may be passed. To be sure, there is also an infinite number of curves that cannot be drawn through these particular areas, and therefore the experimental material definitely rules out an infinite number of equations; but this truth is irrelevant to the present argument. The important thing is that areas allow the possibility of an infinite number of curves; that is, measurements with variable errors allow an infinite number of natural laws. The particular law that the scientist announces to the world is not a *discovery* forced on him by so-called facts; it is rather a choice from among an infinity of laws, all of which enjoy the same experimental basis.

Thus it is seen that the falsity of science derives directly from its ideal of accuracy. It may be a fact that gold is heavier than water, but it is not a scientific fact; it may be a fact that the longer and the farther a body falls, the faster it goes, but Galileo was not interested in this type of fact. The scientist wants mathematical accuracy; and when he cannot discover it, he makes it. Since he chooses his law from among an infinite number of equally possible laws, the probability that he has chosen the "true" law is one over infinity, i.e. zero; or, in plain English, the scientist has no chance of hitting upon the "real" laws of nature. No one doubts that scientific laws are useful: By them the atomic bomb was invented. The point of all this argument is that scientific laws are not *discovered* but are *chosen.*

Science Is Always False

Perhaps both points should be maintained. Not only are scientific laws nonempirical, they must indeed be false. Take for example the law of the pendulum. It states that the period of the swing is proportional to the square root of the pendulum's length. But when the scientific presuppositions of this law are examined, it will be found that the pendulum so described must have its weight concentrated at a point, its string must be tensionless, and there must be no friction on its axis. Since obviously no such pendulum ever existed, it follows that the law of the pendulum describes imaginary pendulums, and that real pendulums do not obey the law of physics. Note especially that the analysis does not separate pendulums under laboratory conditions from pendulums in living room clocks, and does not conclude that in the laboratory, but not in the living room, the laws of physics hold. The analysis shows that no physical pendulum, no matter how excellent the laboratory, satisfies the scientist's requirements. The scientist's world is (on pre-Heisenberg theory) perfectly mathematical, but the sense world is not.

Naturally a great many people, steeped in nineteenth-century scientific traditions, react violently to the idea that science is all false. Did we not make the atom bomb, they say? Does not vaccination prevent smallpox? Cannot we predict the position of Jupiter and an eclipse of the Sun? Verified prediction makes it forever ridiculous to attack science. This reaction is, of course, understandable, however irrational it may be. The argument has not "attacked" science at all; it has insisted that science is extremely useful—though by its own requirements it must be false. The aim nowhere has been to attack science; the aim is to show what science is.

How science can be useful though false is illustrated in a delightful textbook on inductive logic. Milk fever, the illustration goes, until late in the nineteenth century, was a disease frequently fatal to cows. A veterinarian proposed the theory that it was caused by bacteria in the cows' udders. The cure therefore was to disinfect the cow, which the veterinarian proceeded to do by injecting Lugol solution in each teat. The mortality under this treatment fell from a previous ninety percent to thirty. Does not this successful treatment prove that the bacteria were killed and that Lugol cured the disease? Unfortunately another veterinarian was caught without the Lugol solution one day, and he injected plain boiled water. The cow recovered. Had water killed the bacteria? What is worse, it was found later that air could be pumped into the cows' udders with equally beneficial results. The original science was wrong, but it cured the cows nonetheless.

A closer examination of the logic of verification should be made. In the example above, the first veterinarian probably argued: If bacteria cause milk fever, Lugol solution will cure; the disinfectant does cure it; therefore I have verified the hypothesis that bacteria cause milk fever. This argument, as would be explained in a course on deductive logic, is a fallacy. Its invalidity may perhaps be more clearly seen in an artificial example: If a student doggedly works through Plato's *Republic* in Greek, he will know the Greek language; this student knows Greek; therefore he has read Plato's *Republic*. This is the fallacy of asserting the consequent, and it is invalid whenever used. But it is precisely this fallacy that is used in every case of verification. If the law of gravitation is true, a freely falling body will have a constant acceleration, and the eclipse will begin at 2:58:03 p.m.; but freely falling bodies do have a constant acceleration and the eclipse did begin at 2:58:03 p.m.; therefore the law of gravitation is true. Or, if the periodic table of atomic weights is true, a new element of such and such a weight must exist; this new element has now been discovered; therefore the periodic table is verified. And, if I eat roast turkey and plum pudding, I lose my appetite; I have lost my appetite, therefore we had roast turkey for dinner. All these arguments are equally invalid. But sometimes there is an adverse reaction if it is claimed that verification never proves the truth of a scientific law. Is it worse to "attack" science, or to "murder" logic?

Gordon H. Clark
1952

F

KANT AND OLD TESTAMENT ETHICS

In current literature, and specifically in college textbooks, we meet frequent distortions of Christianity. One such is the subject of the present discussion. Two quotations from two textbooks by two well known American Professors set forth the distortion in question and furnish this article with an appropriate point of departure.

"Perhaps the best way to introduce [Immanuel] Kant is to conceive him as the last and most logical of the long line of Hebrew prophets and Christian Apostles."[1]

Consider also a second quotation. "Either then there is some way of defining a good end—an end which justifies the means—or else there must be a moral excellence that belongs to certain types of act irrespective of what they may lead to, if indeed they lead to aught in common. . . . The second interpretation is in the spirit of the decalogue. . . . This world, we might call it the Old Testament world, is then exactly the kind of world in which morality as Kant defines morality could and would exist."[2]

That some have had doubts as to the truth of the view given in the quotations is attested by the following footnote of the second writer. "This image of the Old Testament world is not of course supposed to be that of the ancient Hebrews. Rather does it repre-

[1] T.V. Smith, in *Readings in Ethics,* by Clark and Smith, 223.

[2] E.A. Singer, in *Modern Thinkers,* 132,137.

sent this world as reflected in the thought of a modern Christian community."[3]

Now whatever the force of this last admission may be, the two quotations strongly suggest a fundamental similarity between the ethics of Kant and of the Old Testament. Because of the footnote, however, this discussion needs to distinguish between the Testaments themselves and what that vague entity, a modern Christian community, might happen to think of those ancient documents. But both authors imply, and the second distinctly asserts, that common opinion makes Kant's strict morality essentially that of the Hebrew-Christian religion.

This opinion, permit me to repeat, seems to be a definitely mistaken one. And why those who express such an opinion without some qualification like that in the second author, are mistaken, admits of an easy psychological explanation. The modern Christian community is simply not Christian. The views of the intelligentsia artistically if sometimes flippantly expressed in dilettante magazines err through a profound unfamiliarity with the contents of the Old and New Testaments. The modern educated community is largely pagan, so largely in fact that the condition usually escapes notice. Owing to an educational system originated to preserve religious freedom, the victims of public instruction have been kept not so much free as ignorant. By means of a deliberate silence through the schools, a silence relieved occasionally only by a slur or a sarcasm, the great majority of college graduates go through life either with distorted views of the contents of Christianity or none at all— alternatives which in reality amount to the same thing. When asked in class the most authentic sources for the examination of early Christian thought, the instructor named certain twenty-seven books; the student then asked again if the Epistles of Paul had been included in the list. Yet this particular student (a Roman Catholic) knew more than another student who thought Christianity taught mainly that the universe was created in six periods of twenty-four hours. Aside from scholars who are both trained in research and

---

[3] Singer, 137.

have made this particular research, the educated people of the United States are not in general capable of deciding whether Kant is fundamentally similar to the Old Testament or not. Nor does their inability arise from any meagre acquaintance with Kant. If they were presented with the pamphlets of [Martin] Luther and [John] Eck, the *Institutes* of [John] Calvin or the Tridentine symbols, these writings would appear not so much untrue as unintelligible. In matters of religion these people are as advanced as high school pupils who think *hors d'oeuvres* means "out of work." It may, therefore, seem appropriate to show that any similarity between Kant's ethics and the Hebrew-Christian system is accidental and superficial.

There are two main views respecting the intent of the Old Testament which we must consider. One is that of the Jewish people both of Christ's day and, so far as I am informed, of to-day as well. The second is the Christian view. We anticipate little difficulty in showing that the Pharisees of the first century were not in harmony with the categorical imperative. For them, no one will deny, morality was the means of winning God's favor, of improving oneself until acceptable by God, in short of achieving salvation. Omniscient Jehovah knows and balances each fault against each good deed and if by observing the multitudinous regulations of the Pharisees, a man's good deeds exceed his evil ones, God accepts him as worthy of Heaven. Far from any suggestion that man should do his duty regardless of consequences, purely from the motive of vindicating an abstract formal duty, the Pharisees act deliberately for reward. Whether the reward be crudely or more intellectually conceived does not alter the matter. Any reward as a motive of action is inconsistent with Kant's theory.

Sometimes articles are written to show how primitive the Hebrews, or more strictly the Old Testament is in making fear of punishment so prominent in moral exhortation. Kant, whose position is sounder, higher, more ethical, would never, or ought never, to avoid evil through fear of punishment. With perhaps the exception of some obvious exaggerations, this attack on the Old Testament is far more accurate historically than the view we are here opposing. There is no need to make this article appear scholarly by quoting the penalties attached to infractions of the Mosaic code. Occasionally, through the lack of historical perspective, as in the case of eye for eye and tooth for tooth, these laws are understood more as vicious savagery than as an alleviation of the customary eye for an insult and a life for an eye; nevertheless the penalties, both civil and religious, are enunciated very explicitly. Likewise there are numerous promises to those who will honor father and mother, who will pay the tithe or who have the faith of Abraham. Nor, in this respect at least, can there be drawn any antithesis between the Law and the Prophets. The Prophets protest against violating the law by means of evasive technicalities, they inveigh against a self-complacency in obeying parts of the law and not other more important parts, but they never annul the rewards and punishments, nor preach duty for duty's sake. Amos in particular is singled out as having attained to high ethical standards of social justice. But his very first verses give warning of punishment in a tone indiscernible from the thunder of Mount Sinai. These facts, it seems reasonable to conclude, suffice to show that both the writers of the Old Testament and the Pharisees of Christ's day do not agree with any system which removed reward and punishment as motives toward morality.

But, it is maintained, Jesus attacked the Pharisaic interpretation of the Old Testament. He objects to their praying on the street corners to be seen of men, adding pointedly—they have their reward. Does his attack therefore apply to the point in question? Did he add some new spiritual principle abrogating the reward and punishment morality? No one can object to referring to the Sermon on the Mount as an important piece of evidence. Some members of the modern Christian community have placed this sermon, especially its specifically moral injunctions, in a position more systematically basic than sound scholarship would show it deserved. By making Jesus principally if not solely an ethical preacher, they have reversed the relation that obtains in the New Testament between ethics and theology. Yet on an ethical question, the Sermon on the Mount demands appeal. Its opening words are: "Blessed are the poor in spirit, for theirs is the kingdom of heaven." Blessing and reward begin the Sermon; rains, floods, winds, and destruction end it. Can then anyone seriously maintain that Jesus preaches a categorical imperative in the Kantian sense? "For if ye love them which love you, what reward have ye? Take heed that ye do not your righteousness before men, otherwise ye have no reward of your Father. Let not thy left hand know what thy right hand doeth, and thy Father shall recompense thee." Not less than three times in the sixth chapter of Matthew is the reward mentioned. In other discourses punishment is as clearly stated as reward. "Depart from me ye cursed into everlasting fire prepared for the devil and his angels. And these shall go away into everlasting punishment but the righteous into life eternal."

We have no intention of minimizing the differences between the Pharisees and Jesus. They held thoroughly inconsistent views respecting the sense of the Old Testament. They differed radically on the effective power of human morality with God, but neither obscured, it is quite permissible to say both emphasized reward and punishment. If Jesus objected to the Pharisees, it was not because they wanted a reward but because of the measly reward they wanted. Perhaps then it was the Apostles who changed Jesus' teaching in a Kantian direction.

Peter on the day of Pentecost testified and exhorted with many words, "Save yourselves from this untoward generation." At the Beautiful Gate he declares, "Repent so that there may come seasons of refreshing." Paul in 2 Thessalonians 1 asserts, "It is a righteous thing with God to recompense tribulation to them that trouble you." Or should we proceed to quote the Apocalypse? Indeed Christianity must be a strange thing to draw upon itself the attacks of those who consider Heaven and Hell a barbarous philosophy and at the same time to be understood as teaching duty for duty's sake.

This confusion results from assuming that modern communities are Christian. Scholarly opinion is still in process of recuperating from the effects of nineteenth century criticism. Historical investigations are showing that certain popular conceptions of the God of the early Christians derive more from Kant than from the early Christians. The God of the New Testament strikes Ananias and Sapphira dead for fraud. He is indeed a God who so loved the world that he gave his only begotten Son, but he is also a God who re-veals his wrath from Heaven against all ungodliness of men who suppress the truth in unrighteousness. At the present moment there are two classes of scholars who have seen something of the Chris-tian genius. First are those who definitely and consciously oppose it. Among others we may cite the example of George Santayana in *Winds of Doctrine*. This distinguished gentleman has some pecu-liar notions about Christianity; he thinks for example, that the uni-verse was created for the glory of man *(Winds of Doctrine,* 45, and *Genteel Tradition at Bay,* 42) but for all of that he sees clearly that modernism is not Christian. He judges modernists to be in a state of "fundamental apostasy from Christianity," "worship[ing] noth-ing and acknowledge[ing] authority in nothing save in their own spirit." He accuses the modernist who thinks he is Christian of "an inexplicable ignorance of history, of theology and of the world," and of substituting a theory which "steals empirical reality away from the last judgment, from hell and from heaven." Santayana may have some queer views on the nature of Christianity, but the views of our modern Christian community are still queerer.

The second class of scholars who grasp the essence of Chris-tianity is that small group which definitely and consciously accepts it. More and more is it being seen that the absolute anti-Christian radicals and the ultra-conservative Evangelicals are historically accurate, while the third class, the "modernists," are befogged in a cloud of subjective mysticism. This is a mere modern sentiment; the communities, to which the influence of Kant has finally seeped, insistently argue that the term *Christian* has noble connotations and therefore, refined and cultured as they know themselves to be, they must naturally be Christian. In order to discover what Christian thought is, therefore, it is no longer necessary to study the New Testament or make erudite investigations into ancient centuries; one needs only to express his own fine ideals and Christianity is thereby defined. Mysticism saves one so much trouble, you know.

This attitude, however, comes from Kant through [Albrecht] Ritschl. These are the men who in separating scientific truth from value judgments, have led, consistently or inconsistently, to the discarding of historical in favor of psychological investigation in religious matters. These men attempted to enclose intellect and religion in separate pigeon-holes so that neither should disturb the other. Yet such a separation is a complete reversal of the Christian world-view. Now, while this modern development may be much nearer the truth and the Testaments largely nonsense, as is usually assumed without much research, this is just one more reason for not confounding Kant's morality with that of the Old Testament.

The Hebrew-Christian system is more likely to cut the knot than follow the subtle wisdom of Kant. If we have no reason to believe there is a God, why should we act as though there were one? The early Christians were more empirically minded than the modern development would lead one to believe. John in his first epistle insists on the testimony of ears, eyes and hands. Paul in his defense before King Agrippa requests consideration of evidence, "for this thing was not done in a corner." The Christian preacher demands faith to be sure, but the faith he demands is a belief based on evidence. Those who reject Christianity act unwisely in refusing to engage in archaeological argument to demonstrate the mythical character of the Testaments. Such a demonstration would be far more convincing and presumably more scholarly than the actual publications of the day.

There still remains the question whether Kant and his followers, now shown to be at variance with Christianity, have provided a philosophically more acceptable ethic. It is doubtful. Any ethic to prove acceptable must, at least in my opinion, provide room for one principle among others, which Kant would be sure to deny, viz. each individual should always seek his own personal good. Such a principle is usually designated egoistic, and egoism usually carries unpleasant connotations. Yet when unnecessary implications are avoided and misunderstandings removed, it is my opinion that even apart from any discussion of Christianity, only some form of egoism can withstand criticism. A universalism, like [Jeremy] Bentham's for instance, finds embarrassment in considering the possible incompatibility of an individual's good with the good of the community. Kant, representing a different system, is forced to resort to elements discordant with the rest of his philosophy when he considers the possible conflict between an individual's good and the same individual's duty. It is true Kant attempts to harmonize duty and good by providing a *Deus ex machina* to reward duty, but he makes hope of that reward immoral.

Christ, on the other hand, did not think it immoral to seek one's own good. If you judge that Hebrews 12:2, "who for the joy that was set before him endured the cross," does not warrant any conclusion as to the nature of Christ's motives in undertaking the work of redemption, still we think we can insist that both Christ and the Apostles made abundant use of hope and fear in appealing for converts. So if anyone reproach Christianity as being egoistic and based on fear, partially, ask the objector if fear and self-interest are or are not worthy motives for preferring orange juice to carbolic acid for breakfast. The Bible appeals directly to fear and self-interest; it teaches that absolute destruction awaits him who rejects Christ; and it also teaches that although the Christian may have temporary tribulation, he ultimately loses nothing but gains everything in accepting Christ. Now this is what egoism means, and Kant would have none of it. Unfortunately, however, egoism is sometimes regarded as countenancing sharp practices and shady morality. Yet it requires but little reflection to conclude that sharp practices do not pay in the long run. Honesty and all other forms of virtue are the best policy. Egoism when correctly understood cannot in the least sanction violation of conscience. In this relation no better reference can be made than to a paragraph from the good Bishop Butler. "Conscience and self-love, if we understand our true happiness, always lead us the same way. Duty and interest are perfectly coincident; for the most part in this world, but entirely and in every instance in the future and the whole."

If we follow Bishop Butler and many others who have held that egoism does not counsel shady actions, that virtue is the best policy precisely because it is an indispensable means to our end, we are ready to consider the position assigned in this scheme to the good of others, for egoism in general and Christianity in particular have been attacked as selfish.

Without a Prayer: Ayn Rand and the Close of Her System

This is not quite the same problem as that usually raised about the compatibility of the good of all people. An egoist, Christian or not, will find quite a little difficulty in proving that the good of one individual harmonizes with the good of all other individuals. As a matter of fact the Christian might well conclude that had Judas done what was best for him, it would be too bad for us. Apparently, then, the good of some people is incompatible with the good of others. But whether we do accept this conclusion or not, that the good of two people may under given conditions conflict, it does not follow that egoism teaches selfishness. And yet Christianity has been assailed as selfish. That one must save his own soul first, and only afterwards turn his attention to others, and that his helping others reacts again to benefit himself, Hastings Rashdall for example, frankly considers "nauseous." To me, however, the attempt to help others before attending to one's own condition is a case of the blind leading the blind. Nor have I been able to find anything disgusting in regarding one's own development as a motive in missionary activity. We sing about stars in our crown, we speak of souls for our hire. If, then, I may be an instrument of effectual calling in God's hands, and if such instrumentality brings a blessing, I can see no good reason for denying that that blessing may properly be a part of the evangelistic motive.

Now, to bring this discussion to an end and perhaps to a conclusion as well, we should say that if portions of the modern Christian community regard Kant as the last of the prophets, a polite acquaintance with the Bible would remedy their misapprehension. And second, when our opponents claim that Christianity is a selfish soul-saving, egoistic religion, we should advise Christians not to be apologetic in the colloquial sense of the word but to be apologetic in the technical sense, and, with the aid of oranges and carbolic acid, follow the examples of Christ and the Apostles in holding out to them the hope of Heaven and the fear of Hell as legitimate motives for availing themselves of Christ's gracious redemption.

Gordon H. Clark
1935

G

CHRIST AND CIVILIZATION

This December 25 more than a billion people will celebrate the birth of Jesus Christ. The celebration is doubly ironic, for the date is not his birthday, and many celebrants have forgotten—or perhaps have never learned—the meaning of his birth. One of the most enthusiastic celebrants of Christmas I have known was an atheist. She loved the beautiful decorations, the luscious smells, the joyful songs, the bounteous food and drink, the smiling faces of children, the gifts, and the fleeting feeling of goodwill. She, like many others, was a devotee of Christmas, the holiday, but not of Christ, the man.

This is a tragedy of eternal proportions, for the work of Christ—his birth, life, death, and resurrection—is the most important event in the history of mankind. Christ's life is the point from which we date all of world history, and it is impossible to understand Western civilization, especially the United States, without understanding Christianity.

It has been 2,000 years since Jesus was born, and since that time the world has changed immensely. Jesus, born and reared in small towns in Judea, one of the outlying provinces of the Roman Empire, lived only 33 years—a young man by modern standards, and taught only three years—a short career—before he was tortured and executed by a local mob and the Roman government. Had he been an ordinary man, it would all have ended there. No one would have noticed. At best he would have been another statistic in the long annals of Roman cruelty. But Jesus was far from ordinary; he was and is the second person of the Trinity, the *Logos*, the Logic and Wisdom of God incarnate. Three days after his crucifixion, he walked out of his guarded tomb, just as he had predicted. The worst the Empire could do had failed. Jesus was alive.

About 500 years earlier and a few hundred miles to the east, King Nebuchadnezzar of the great empire of Babylonia had had a dream in which he saw "a great image whose splendor was excellent." The image stood before the King, and "its form was awesome." The image's head was of "fine gold, its chest and arms of silver, its belly and thighs of bronze, its legs of iron, its feet partly of iron and partly of clay." The King watched "while a stone . . . cut out without hands . . . struck the image on its feet of iron and clay, and broke them in pieces. The iron, the clay, the bronze, the silver, and the gold were crushed together, and became like chaff from the summer threshing floors; the wind carried them away so that no trace of them was found. And the stone that struck the image became a great mountain and filled the whole Earth."[1]

In this way God, through Daniel, foretold the coming of Christ. He was the stone that would crush the great image into dust and blow it away, and the image was the empires and rulers of the world. For the past two thousand years the stone has been growing, sometimes imperceptibly, sometimes rapidly, always inexorably. The spread of Christianity has profoundly changed society, its institutions, its beliefs, and its culture. What has emerged is nothing less than a new civilization.

The World Before Christ

Americans sometimes entertain a romantic and idealized view of ancient Greece and Rome as peaceful, pleasant, and free societies. We see the statuary and the ruins, we hear the philosophers discussed, and we read the exploits of the Caesars. Athens, we are

---

[1] Daniel 2.

told, was a model of enlightenment and democracy, and Rome was a model of justice and law. It is largely to Greece and Rome, to their philosophers and statesmen, so the conventional story goes, that we owe our freedom, our civilization, and our prosperity.

The *World Book Encyclopedia* informs its readers that "The principles that bound the Roman Empire together—justice, tolerance, and a desire for peace—influenced countless generations." But the very next sentence—so startling in contrast to the first—is closer to the truth: "Roman cruelty and greed caused great misery, and the use of force brought hardship and death."[2] Rome was an empire of violence, not justice; it was held together by the force of the feared Roman legions. It tolerated no disobedience, and peace was a rare event. Even at its best—the Pax Romana during the first and second centuries of the Christian era—the Empire was, in Livy's words, "rich in catastrophe, fearful in its battles, fertile in mutinies, bloody even in peace."[3] The debt that we owe to Greece and Rome has been exaggerated. To understand the impact of the coming of Christ, one must have a more accurate understanding of the classical world.

Ancient Religions

The religions of Rome and Greece were everywhere. On Paul's arrival in Athens he found a city "given over to idols."[4] Dreams, omens, ghosts, apparitions, and the "evil eye" were both feared as sources of harm and sought as sources of guidance. Astrology was a science and part of high culture, enjoying the respect psycho-

---

[2] "The Roman Empire," 16:380-381.

[3] The ancient world was one "in which a large part of the labor force worked under various forms of non-economic compulsion, in which for a long period and over wide stretches of territory gladiatorial combats to the death provided the most popular form of public entertainment for the elites and the masses alike, in which brigandage and piracy and reprisals were often encouraged and even practiced by 'civilized' governments" (M.I. Finley, *Ancient History* [New York: Penguin Books, 1987], 70-71).

[4] Acts 17:16.

analysis and psychiatry do today. Idols and images were everywhere. Animal sacrifice was a regular part of religious worship, and festivals and holidays—by one count 109 days each year were holidays in Rome—were frequent. Temple prostitution was commonplace. The city of Corinth, a center of religious devotion, became synonymous with sexual immorality. To "corinthianize" was to engage in the most perverted and debauched sexual practices. In the pagan culture of Rome, homosexuality was commonplace and accepted.

The Greek and Roman gods and goddesses were men and women larger than life. They fought, they schemed, they lied, they got drunk, they raped, and they committed incest. The Romans worshiped twelve major gods and goddesses and thousands of lesser gods, which had arisen from the animism of early Rome. There were gods for war, fertility, love, harvest, travel, doors, and so forth. Each god and goddess had his or her own sphere of influence; the devout Roman did not worship one god to the exclusion of others, but worshiped all as the circumstances demanded. Prayers and pilgrimages to shrines and temples were a common part of life in the ancient world. Rome was a very religious society.

Roman and Greek religions were very different from Christianity, not only in their polytheism, but in the fact that the pagan religions did not emphasize learning, understanding, and teaching: They had no sermons, no books to be studied, no doctrine to believe.

"The chief objects of pagan religions were to foretell the future [through the study of animal entrails and later the questioning of oracles], to explain the universe, to avert calamity, [and] to obtain the assistance of the gods. They contained no instruments of moral teaching analogous to our institution of preaching, or to the moral preparation for the reception of the sacrament, or to confession, or to the reading of the Bible, or to religious education, or to united prayer for spiritual benefits."[5]

[5] W. E. H. Lecky, *History of European Morals* (London: Watts and Company, 1946 [1869]), II:1.

Those things, to the extent they were done in Rome, were functions of the philosophers, who were both an elite and largely unconnected with the religious cult.

Christianity, by contrast, made theological and moral teaching central and available to all, not just to the aristocratic classes thought to be capable of virtue. "Under its [Christianity's] influence doctrines concerning the nature of God, the immortality of the soul, and the duties of man, which the noblest intellects of antiquity could barely grasp, have become the truisms of the village school, the proverbs of the cottage and of the alley."[6]

Because of the variety of gods in Rome, some historians have mistakenly concluded that Rome enjoyed religious liberty. But the command of the Twelve Tables (*c.* 450 B.C.), as well as the persecution of religious dissenters, makes it clear that religious liberty was not a feature of Roman society: "Let no one have gods on his own, neither new ones nor strange ones, but only those instituted by the State." In the second century after Christ, the pagan jurist Julius Paulus reported a contemporary legal decree: "Of those people who introduce new religions with unknown customs or methods by which the minds of men could be disturbed, those of the upper classes shall be deported, those of the lower classes shall be put to death." The only religions permitted in Rome were those licensed and approved by the State.

Both the Greek poleis and the Roman Empire were totalitarian church-states. Socrates was executed for being an atheist, that is, for not believing in the gods of the polis. Many others suffered the same fate. A letter that Pliny the Younger, Special High Commissioner to the provinces of Bithynia and Pontus, wrote to Trajan the Emperor in A.D. 111 illustrates both Rome's treatment of religious dissenters and its lack of a justice system:

> This is the plan which I have adopted in the case of those Christians who have been brought before me. I ask them whether they are Christians; if they say yes, then I

---

[6] Lecky. 11:2.

repeat the question a second and a third time, warning them of the penalties it entails, and if they still persist, I order them to be taken away to prison. For I do not doubt, whatever the character of the crime may be which they confess, their pertinacity and inflexible obstinacy certainly ought to be punished. . . .

In Rome, pertinacity was a crime punishable by indefinite incarceration. Pliny explained what his subjects were required to do in order to regain their freedom:

Those who denied that they were or had been Christians and called upon the gods in the usual formula, reciting the words after me, those who offered incense and wine before your [the Emperor's] image, which I had given orders to be brought forward for this purpose, together with the statues of the deities—all such I considered should be discharged, especially as they cursed the name of Christ, which, it is said, those who are really Christians cannot be induced to do.

In Rome one could escape punishment by worshiping the Emperor and the gods. In a case in which some persons had anonymously accused their neighbors of being Christians, Pliny

thought it the more necessary . . . to find out what truth there was in these statements [of accusation] by submitting two women, who were called deaconesses, to the torture. . . . Many persons of all ages, and of both sexes alike, are being brought into peril of their lives by their accusers, and the process [of inquisition and punishment] will go on. For the contagion of this superstition has spread not only through the free cities, but into the villages and rural districts, and yet it seems to me that it can be checked and set right. It is beyond doubt that the [pagan] temples, which have been almost deserted, are beginning again to be thronged with worshippers, that the sacred rites which for a long time have been allowed to lapse are now being renewed, and that the food of the sacrificial victims is once more finding a sale.[7]

Pliny was pleased to report that his methods of torture and imprisonment were encouraging people to worship the gods, and that business was booming.

In his letter to Trajan, Pliny emphasized that worshiping the Emperor was the way to avoid punishment. At the time of Christ, the imperial cult was the cult that unified Rome. Tiberius succeeded Augustus as Emperor in A.D. 14. Here are a few excerpts from a letter Tiberius sent to the magistrate of the city of Gytheon, instructing him in the proper rituals of the imperial cult:

> Tiberius Caesar Augustus, son of the god Augustus, pontifex maximus. . . . He should place an image of the god Augustus Caesar the father on the first [chair], one of Julia Augusta on the second from the right, and one of Tiberius Augustus on the third. . . . Let a table [for sacrifices] be set by him in the middle of the theater and an incense burner be placed there, and let the representatives and all magistrates offer sacrifices. . . . Let him conduct the festival on the first day in honor of the god Augustus the Savior and Liberator, son of the god Caesar. . . .[8]

The worship of the State, in the person of the divine Emperor, was the core of pagan society at the time of Christ.

War and Peace

The pagan world was not peaceful. Livy reports that the Roman Republic was at peace only twice in its entire history, once at the

---

[7] Ramsay MacMullen and Eugene N. Lane, editors, *Paganism and Christianity 100-425 C.E.* (Minneapolis: Fortress Press, 1992), 164-165.

[8] MacMullen and Lane, 74-75.

end of the First Punic War in the mid-third century B.C. and once in 30 B.C. after Augustus' defeat of Antony and Cleopatra. Athens, usually considered one of the most peaceful of the Greek city-states, was at war more than two years out of every three between the Persian Wars and 338 B.C., when Philip of Macedon was defeated. The following three centuries were even worse. Athens never enjoyed ten consecutive years of peace.

War was a way of life in the ancient world. In the opening pages of the *Laws,* Plato has Clinias say that "what most men call peace is merely an appearance; in reality all cities are by nature in a permanent state of undeclared war against all other cities." In his dialogues Plato describes a sanitized Athens of intellectuals discoursing and discussing philosophical questions, strolling about the city, eating and drinking from house to house.

"Yet for most of the time which Plato describes, Athens was fighting a long and bloody war in which at least half the population died, many of them from a particularly horrifying plague which scarred even those who survived it, and which was partly the consequence of the unsanitary conditions in which vast numbers of citizens were camped, at first in the heat of summer and later all year, on every available space of open or sacred land within the city walls."[9]

As for Rome, "In the half century of the Hannibalic and Macedonian Wars, ten percent and often more of all adult Italian males were at war year by year, a ratio that rose during the wars of the first century B.C. to one in every three males." Finley traces the prevalence of warfare in the ancient world to pagan religion: "Neither the enormously powerful Roman Mars nor the weaker Greek Ares received the slightest competition from the minor divinities of peace. It was always assumed that divine support was available for a war. . . . [T]he gods through their oracles and signs [never] recommended peace for its own sake. . . ."[10] The Pax Romana dur-

---

[9] Oswyn Murray, "Life and Society in Classical Greece," *The Oxford History of the Classical World* (New York: Oxford University Press, 1986), 205.

[10] Finley, 68.

ing the first two centuries of the Christian era, although an improvement from earlier centuries, was punctuated by wars on the Empire's frontiers and the destruction of Jerusalem in A.D. 70.

Economics, Slavery, and Work

At the time of Christ, the population of Roman Italy comprised five to six million free citizens and one to two million slaves. Many slaves worked the mines of the Roman Empire, and they were sometimes forced to live below ground until they died. Slaves were forbidden to marry, and the power of masters over their slaves was absolute. The castes of Roman society—slaves, plebeians, notables, and nobles—were not as rigid at the time of Christ as they had been in earlier centuries, but Roman society remained radically unequal.

The Empire's military conquests resulted in the influx of hundreds of thousands of slaves to Rome. These slaves were used not only for work, but for entertainment as well in the gladiatorial contests that both nobles and plebeians loved to attend. The enthusiasm of the Romans for gladiatorial gore both produced and reflected a savage delight in the infliction of pain. Thousands of slaves died entertaining the Romans. The gladiatorial "games" were part of the official celebration of the Emperor in every large city.

Apart from the gladiatorial system, "numerous acts of the most odious barbarity were committed: . . . Flaminius ordering a slave to be killed to gratify, by the spectacle, the curiosity of a guest; . . . Vedius Pollo feeding his fish on the flesh of slaves; . . . Augustus sentencing a slave, who had killed and eaten a favorite quail, to crucifixion. . . . Old and infirm slaves were constantly exposed to perish on an island of the Tiber."[11]

Slavery was not only the ubiquitous practice of the pagan world, it was the theory as well. The best of the Greek philosophers, Plato and Aristotle, defended slavery, for slaves were naturally inferior beings. The treatment of slaves, children, and women reflected the

---

[11] Lecky, I:127.

judgment of Aristotle that "the deliberative faculty is not present at all in the slave, in the female it is inoperative, in the child unde-veloped." The Christian notion that all men are created in the im-age of God, and that the image of God is rationality, was foreign to the pagan philosophers and societies.

In any society in which slavery plays a major role, idleness is a virtue. So it was in Rome. The Romans held labor in contempt and scorned those who worked with their hands. The workingman was base and a social inferior. All freedmen were artisans and shop-keepers; most shopkeepers and artisans were freedmen; and all were despised. "No one," Aristotle wrote, "who leads the life of a worker or laborer can practice virtue." The eloquent Demosthenes, defend-ing himself before an Athenian jury, presented his argument this way: "I am worth more than Eschinus [the plaintiff] and I am bet-ter born than he; I do not wish to seem to insult poverty, but I am bound to say that it was my lot as a child to attend good schools and to have had sufficient wealth that I was not forced by need to engage in shameful labors. Whereas you, Eschinus, it was your lot as a child to sweep, as might a slave, the classroom in which your father served as teacher."

Demosthenes easily won his case.

Seneca, the tutor and later the victim of Nero, wrote that "The common arts, the sordid arts, are according to the philosopher Posidonius those practiced by manual laborers, who spend all their time earning their living. There is no beauty in such occupations, which bear little resemblance to the Good." Cicero believed that "wage labor is sordid and unworthy of a free man, for wages are the price of labor and not of some art; craft labor is sordid, as is the business of retailing."

Rome's control over the economy was hampered by the primi-tiveness of the economy. But wherever economic activity could be controlled, the worldly philosophers and statesmen believed the State had the right to do it. A basic feature of the constitution of Sparta was complete control of economic activity. The silver mines of Laurium were owned by Athens. *Economics,* probably written in the third century before Christ and incorrectly attributed to

Aristotle, recounts how rulers filled their coffers by robbery and exploitation of their people. The book assumes that every sort of private property is at the disposal of the State. Hasebroek, writing in *Trade and Politics in Ancient Greece,* reports that the control of economic activity in the poleis was tyrannical.

As for Rome, "wholesale uncompensated confiscation of private estates and peasant farms to provide bonuses for soldiers was not an uncommon practice. . . . Eventually all generations of workers—oil-suppliers, butchers, fish handlers, bakers, transport and mine workers, and minor government officials—were frozen in their occupations to stabilize taxes and balance the budget."[12] For the pagans, statecraft was soulcraft. Fustel de Coulanges concludes that "The ancients, therefore, knew neither liberty in private life, liberty in education, nor religious liberty."[13]

Life and Death

In the ancient world abortion, the exposure of infants, infanticide, and suicide were common and legal. At the coming of Christ, the Roman governor in Judea, Herod the Great, in an attempt to murder Jesus, ordered that all the male infants in Bethlehem and the region surrounding it, from two years old and younger, be put to death.

The head of the Roman family had the power of life and death—*patria potestas*—over his children and slaves. At birth, the midwife would place the newborn on the ground, where he would remain unless the father took the child and raised him from the Earth. If the father did not raise the child, he—or more likely she—was left to die in some public place. The pagans exposed their children because they were poor, ambitious, or concerned about their "quality of life": "so as not to see them [the infants] corrupted by a mediocre education that would leave them unfit for rank and quality"

---

[12] E. G. Weltin, *Athens and Jerusalem* (Atlanta: Scholars Press, 1987), 34.

[13] *The Ancient City* (Garden City: Doubleday, n.d. [1901]), 297.

—to quote Plutarch. The early Christians rescued thousands of children abandoned by the pagans. Thousands were also rescued by pagans, who would raise them to be slaves and prostitutes. If infants were born with defects, they were frequently killed, rather than exposed. Infanticide was not merely the practice of the pagans, it was their doctrine as well: Plato and Aristotle endorsed infanticide, and Seneca wrote: "What is good must be set apart from what is good for nothing."

The contrast between paganism and Christianity is clearest in these matters of life and death. In his *History of European Morals,* Lecky writes: "The first aspect in which Christianity presented itself to the world was as a declaration of the fraternity of men in Christ. Considered as immortal beings, destined for the extremes of happiness or of misery, and united to one another by a special community of redemption, the first and most manifest duty of a Christian man was to look on his fellowman as sacred beings, and from this notion grew up the eminently Christian idea of the sanctity of all human life. . . ."

It is not the laws of nature that determine behavior or ethics, for

> nature does not tell man that it is wrong to slay without provocation his fellowman. . . . [I]t is an historical fact beyond all dispute that refined, and even moral, societies have existed in which the slaughter of men of some particular class or nation has been regarded with no more compunction than the slaughter of animals in the chase. The early Greeks, in their dealings with the barbarians; the Romans, in their dealings with gladiators, and in some periods of their history with slaves; the Spaniards in their dealings with Indians; nearly all colonists removed from European supervision, in their dealings with an inferior race; and an immense proportion of the nations of antiquity, in their dealings with newborn infants—all have displayed this complete and absolute callousness. . . .

320

Rather than the laws of nature, it was the teaching of the Bible that improved ancient culture:

> Now it was one of the most important services of Christianity that, besides quickening greatly our benevolent affections, it definitely and dogmatically asserted the sinfulness of all destruction of human life as a matter of amusement or of simple convenience, and thereby formed a new standard, higher than any which existed in the world.
>
> The influence of Christianity in this respect began with the very earliest stage of human life. The practice of abortion was one to which few persons in antiquity attached any deep feeling of condemnation. . . . In Greece, Aristotle not only countenanced the practice, but even desired that it should be enforced by law when population had exceeded certain assigned limits. No law in Greece, or in the Roman Republic, or during the greater part of the Empire, condemned it. . . . A long chain of writers, both pagan and Christian, represent the practice as avowed and almost universal. They describe it as resulting, not simply from licentiousness or from poverty, but even from so slight a motive as vanity, which made mothers shrink from the disfigurement of childbirth. . . . They assure us that the frequency of the crime was such that it gave rise to a regular profession.
>
> If we pass to the next stage of human life, that of the new-born infant, we find ourselves in [the] presence of that practice of infanticide which was one of the deepest stains of the ancient civilization. . . . Infanticide . . . was almost universally admitted among the Greeks, being sanctioned, and in some cases enjoined, upon what we should now call "the greatest happiness principle," by the ideal legislations of Plato and Aristotle, and by the actual legislations of Lycurgus and Solon.[14]

[14] Lecky, II:9–11.

But it was not only public violence that was condoned and encouraged at the time of Christ; suicide was also a virtue: "Suicide was accepted, even admired. The courage of the man who decides to end his suffering and accept eternal rest was extolled by the philosophers, for suicide proved the truth of the philosophical notion that what matters is the quality and not the quantity of time that one lives."[15]

Law and Government

Rome is commonly supposed to have given us our system of justice, but the law of Rome at the time of Christ was quite unjust: "In a society as unequal and inegalitarian as the Roman, it is obvious that formal rights, however clear, had no reality, and that a weak man had little to gain by going to court. . . ."[16]

Veyne gives this example of Roman law:

Suppose that all I own in the world is a small farm. . . . a powerful neighbor covets my property. Leading an army of slaves, he invades my land, kills those of my slaves who try to defend me, beats me with clubs, drives me from my land, and seizes my farm. What can I do? A modern citizen might say, go to court . . . to obtain justice and persuade the authorities to restore my property. . . .

For one thing, the aggression against me by my powerful neighbor would have been considered a strictly civil offense; it would not have been covered by the penal code. It would have been up to me, as plaintiff, to see to it that the defendant appeared in court. In other words, I would have had to snatch the defendant from the midst of his private army, arrest him, and hold him in chains in my private prison until the day of judgment. Had this been beyond my power, the case would never have been heard. . . .

---

[15] Murray, 229.

[16] Paul Veyne, "The Roman Empire," A *History of Private Life* (Cambridge: Harvard University Press, 1987), 166.

If, however, the victim did succeed in raising an army, capturing his enemy, bringing him to trial, and winning,

> it then would have been up to me to enforce that judgment, if I could. . . . [A] judge could not sentence a defendant simply to restore what he had taken. Leaving my farm to its fate, the judge would authorize me to seize my adversary's chattels real and personal and sell them at auction, keeping a sum equal to the value placed on my farm by the court . . . and returning the surplus to my enemy. Who would have considered recourse to a system of justice so little interested in punishing social transgressions?

But the systemic injustice of the Roman legal system was compounded by its systematic corruption:

> A Roman noble (or even a mere notable) [had] more in common with [a] "godfather" than with a modern technocrat. Getting rich through public service . . . never stood in the way of taking public service for one's ideal. . . .
> The honest functionary is a peculiarity of modern Western nations. In Rome every superior stole from his subordinates. The same was true in the Turkish and Chinese empires, where baksheesh was the general rule. . . . Every public function was a racket, those in charge "put the squeeze" on their subordinates, and all together exploited the populace. This was true during the period of Rome's greatness as well as during the period of its decline. . . . Even the least important public positions . . . , such as apparitor or clerk of the courts, were sold by their incumbents to aspiring candidates, because every position carried with it a guaranteed income in the form of bribes. . . . Ancient bureaucracy was nothing like our bureaucracy. For millennia sovereigns relied on racketeers to extort taxes and control their subjects.[17]

[17] Veyne, 167, 97-98, I(X).

Even the renowned Roman legions operated this way. Tacitus tells us that

> Soldiers traditionally bribed their officers for exemption from service, and nearly a quarter of the personnel of every regiment could be found idling about the countryside or even lounging around the barracks, provided their officer had received his kickback. ... Soldiers got the money they needed from theft and banditry or by doing the chores of slaves. If a soldier happened to be a little richer than the rest, his officer beat him and heaped duties upon him until he paid up and received dispensation.

Cicero, himself a senator, wrote that the "senatorial way to get rich" was to plunder the provinces under one's jurisdiction. Cicero prided himself on his honesty: After governing a province for a year, he was making the equivalent of a million dollars per year, a sum considered quite small.

The World After Christ

Christ was born within this pagan culture. But his kingdom, as he explained later, while it was in this world, was not of it.[18] It found its source, its authority, and its principles elsewhere. Instead of the prevailing polytheism of Greece and Rome he taught monotheism: "I and my Father are one."[19] Instead of the sinful and limited gods of paganism, Christ taught the holy and transcendent God, creator of Heaven and Earth, ruler of all things. Instead of the pagan gods whose primary pastimes were violence, sexual immorality, and indolence, he taught a rational God who works: "My Father works even until now, and I work."[20] He reiterated and explained the Ten Commandments with their condemnations of idolatry, of the use of

[18] John 18:36.

[19] John 10:30.

[20] John 5:17.

images and statuary in worship, of profanity, of disrespect for parents and the Lord's Day, of idleness, of murder, of sexual immorality, of theft, of lying, and of covetousness.[21]

More important than the law, Christ saved his people by enduring their just punishment in their place. His work earned for his people the divine gifts of belief, justification, obedience, and everlasting life. Instead of the pagan notion that if men are to have truth, they must discover it on their own power, he taught that God graciously reveals truth to men, and that the revealed truth is written so that all, not just the aristocratic or priestly few, might know.

Against the totalitarianism of the pagan world empires, Christ taught the limitation of state power and the separation of church and state: "Render therefore to Caesar the things that are Caesar's, and to God the things that are God's."[22] Neither Caesar nor any other mere man was Pontifex Maximus, the bridge between Heaven and Earth. Christ himself is the only way, the only truth, and the only life, the sole mediator between God and man. He explicitly challenged the political regimes of the pagans: "You know that the rulers of the Gentiles lord it over them, and those who are great exercise dominion over them. Yet it shall not be so among you; but whoever desires to become great among you, let him be your servant."[23] Christ demanded that rulers serve, not control, their people. He outlined a limited role for civil government, not as the shaper of souls, as in pagan philosophies, but simply as the punisher of criminals. He founded a church whose government is republican, whose leaders are elected by the people, and whose constitution is written. Inspired by his words, the American Founders made their plans for a new Republic, a government of the people, by the people, and for the people.[24]

---

[21] Matthew 5–7.

[22] Matthew 22:21.

[23] Matthew 22:20.

[24] The words are, of course, Lincoln's, but he got them from John Wyclif, who wrote of his English translation of the Bible: "This Bible is for the government of the people, by the people, and for the people."

The early Christians, condemned by learned pagans[25] such as Celsus and Porphyry as stupid, foolish, and superstitious, were not killed for their stupidity, but because they rejected the highest value of pagan society: worship of the totalitarian state. The Christians rejected Aristotle ("The State is the highest of all. . . . Citizens belong to the State. . . .") and followed Christ. Christ, in dying for the salvation of individual men, exalted both the individual and God. God is eternal and men are immortal; nations and rulers pass away. No earthly city, including Rome, is eternal; only individual men are immortal.

Christ taught that man is a creature of God and the lord of creation. Man's ancestry is not animal, but divine, and the Earth was made for man. Individual men are immortal; what they believe and do on Earth will have eternal consequences. After death, they do not descend into the shadowlands, limbo, or purgatory, but are required to give an account of their lives to their maker and judge. All men are equal before God and his law, and each man will be judged individually. The classes of pagan society—the nobles, the proletariat, the slaves, the citizens, the men, the women, the barbarians—mean nothing to God. In the new Christian faith, "There is neither Jew nor Greek, there is neither slave nor free, there is neither male nor female; for you are all one in Christ Jesus."[26]

Christ's rule was to be extended by persuasion not coercion[27]— it is to be an empire of ideas, not violence—and it has taken centuries for Christian ideas to be believed and absorbed into practice.

---

[25] It is an odd fact that there are so few references to Christianity among the extant writings of the pagan scholars and philosophers. It is almost as if they did not see the coming of Christianity, just as they were unaware of the coming of Christ. Perhaps it was because Christ was a Jew and the son of a carpenter, and Christianity was not a movement of the aristocratic classes, but of the scorned business, worker, and slave classes.

[26] Galatians 3:28.

[27] "Go therefore and make disciples of all nations, baptizing them in the name of the Father and of the Son and of the Holy Spirit, teaching them to observe all things that I have commanded you . . ." (Matthew 28:19-20).

As the anguished cries of Friedrich Nietzsche in the nineteenth century so clearly indicate, that absorption of ideas has been widespread, though far from complete.

The Impact of Christianity

Harold Berman has outlined the effect of the growth of Christianity on society:

> Under the influence of Christianity, the Roman law of the postclassical period reformed family law, giving the wife a position of greater equality before the law, requiring mutual consent of both spouses for the validity of a marriage, making divorce more difficult ..., and abolishing the father's power of life or death over his children; reformed the law of slavery, giving a slave the right to appeal to a magistrate if his master abused his powers and even, in some cases, the right to freedom if the master exercised cruelty, multiplying modes of manumission of slaves, and permitting slaves to acquire rights by kinship with freemen; and introduced a concept of equity into legal rights and duties generally, thereby tempering the strictness of general prescriptions.[28]

Even the codifications of Roman law were due to the belief that "Christianity required that the law be systematized as a necessary step in its humanization."

Christianity had the same effect on the barbarians who entered Rome in A.D. 410:

> The rulers of the Germanic, Slavic, and other peoples of Europe during roughly the same era (from the fifth to the tenth centuries) presided over a legal regime consisting chiefly of primitive tribal customs and rules of the blood

---

[28] Harold Berman, *The Interaction of Law and Religion* (London: SCM Press, 1974), 53.

feud. It is more than coincidence that the rulers of many of the major tribal peoples, from Anglo-Saxon England to Kievan Russia, after their conversion to Christianity, promulgated written collections of tribal laws and introduced various reforms. . . . The Laws of Alfred (about A.D. 890) start with a recitation of the Ten Commandments and excerpts from the Mosaic law. . . .

The Christian Reformation

It was not until the Christian Reformation in the sixteenth century that the teachings of Christ largely freed themselves from the melange of pagan and Christian philosophy, theology, and law that prevailed during the Middle Ages. Martin Luther's courageous rejection of ecclesiastical tradition and authority in the name of revelation and reason laid the theological foundation for the emergence of religious freedom in the modern world. In time, religious freedom yielded the fruit of political, civil, and economic freedom.

Berman argues that

the key to the renewal of law in the West from the sixteenth century on was the Protestant concept of the power of the individual, by God's grace, to change nature and to create new social relations through the exercise of his will. The Protestant concept of the individual will became central to the development of the modern law of property and contract. Nature became property. Economic relations became contract. . . . The property and contract rights so created were held to be sacred and inviolable, so long as they did not contravene conscience [informed by Scripture]. . . . And so the secularization of the state, in the restricted sense of the removal of ecclesiastical controls from it, was accompanied by a spiritualization, and even a sanctification, of property and contract.[29]

---

[29] Berman, 64–65.

Christ and Civilization

After Luther came John Calvin:

> Calvinism has also had profound effects upon the de-
> velopment of Western law, and especially upon American
> law. The Puritans carried forward the Lutheran concept of
> the sanctity of individual conscience and also, in law, the
> sanctity of individual will as reflected in property and con-
> tract rights. .... [S]eventeenth century Puritans, including
> men like [John] Hampden, [John] Lilburne, [Walter] Udall,
> William Penn and others, by their disobedience to English
> law, laid the foundations for the English and American law
> of civil rights and civil liberties as expressed in our respec-
> tive constitutions: freedom of speech and press, free exer-
> cise of religion, the privilege against self-incrimination, the
> independence of the jury from judicial dictation, the right
> not to be imprisoned without cause, and many other such
> rights and freedoms. We also owe to Calvinist congrega-
> tionalism the religious basis of our concepts of social con-
> tract and government by consent of the governed.[30]

Our political, social, and economic debt to Greece and Rome
has been exaggerated; our debt to Christianity has been ignored.

Judea Against Rome

Despite the progress made in Europe and America since the sixteenth century, a resurgence of paganism now threatens Western
civilization. Among modern philosophers it is the nineteenth-century pagan Friedrich Nietzsche who has best understood the "re-
valuation of all values" that Christianity achieved. Christianity
overthrew the "aristocratic values" of Greece and Rome and established a new set of values. In his *Genealogy of Morals* Nietzsche
wrote:

> The symbol of this struggle, inscribed in letters legible
> across all human history, is "Rome against Judea, Judea

[30] Berman, 66-67.

against Rome." There has hitherto been no greater event than *this* struggle, *this* question, *this* deadly contradiction. . . . One has the right to link the salvation and future of the human race with the unconditional dominance of aristocratic values, Roman values. . . . The Romans were the strong and noble, and nobody stronger and nobler has yet existed on Earth or even been dreamed of.[31]

Nietzsche longed, not only for the values of the noble Greeks and Romans, but for their gods as well:

[T]he conception of gods in itself need not lead to the degradation of the imagination . . . [for] there are nobler uses for the invention of gods than for the self-crucifixion and self-violation of man in which Europe over the past millennia achieved its distinctive mastery—that is fortunately revealed even by a mere glance at the Greek gods, those reflections of noble and aristocratic men, in whom the animal in man felt deified and did not lacerate itself, did not rage against itself.[32]

Nietzsche denied that man was lord of the creation: "We no longer derive man from 'the spirit' or 'the deity'; we have placed him back among the animals. . . . Man is by no means the crown of creation; every living being stands beside him on the same level of perfection."[33] Anticipating the neopagan environmental movement of the twentieth century, Nietzsche declared: "Our whole attitude toward nature, the way we violate her with the aid of machines and

[31] First Essay, section 16.

[32] Second Essay. section 23.

[33] *The Antichrist,* section 14. One might contrast Nietzsche with John Calvin, who wrote: "Men themselves . . . are the most illustrious ornament and glory of the Earth. If they should fail, the Earth would exhibit a scene of desolation and solitude, not less hideous than if God should despoil it of all its other riches" (*Commentary* on Psalm 24).

the heedless inventiveness of our technicians and engineers, is hubris. . . ."[34]

But Nietzsche's aristocratic paganism did not merely herald the environmental movement; it was an omen of the catastrophic eruption of political and economic paganism in the twentieth century. Nietzsche decried "the poison of the doctrine of 'equal rights for all. . . .' 'Immortality,' conceded to every Peter and Paul," he rasped, "has so far been the greatest, the most malignant, attempt to assassinate noble humanity."[35]

Nietzsche praised the values of Rome: "What is good? Everything that heightens the feeling of power in man, the will to power, power itself. What is bad? Everything that is born of weakness. What is happiness? The feeling that power is growing, that resistance is overcome. Not contentedness, but more power; not peace, but war; not virtue, but fitness. . . ." He welcomed "all signs that a more manly, a warlike, age is about to begin, an age which above all, will give honor to valor once again."[36]

Before he finally went insane, Nietzsche called himself the Antichrist, for he despised Christianity, its "slave morality," and its civilization. For the past century paganism has been resurgent, but it will end: Christ will continue to crush world empires, and of his government, peace, and liberty there shall be no end.

[34] *The Genealogy of Morals,* Third Essay, section 9.

[35] *The Antichrist,* section 43.

[36] *The Gay Science,* 283.

H

AN INTRODUCTION TO
GORDON H. CLARK

Who Is Gordon Clark?

Carl Henry thinks he is "one of the profoundest evangelical Protestant philosophers of our time." Ronald Nash has praised him as "one of the greatest Christian thinkers of our century." He is a prolific author—having written more than 40 books during his long academic career. His philosophy is the most consistently Christian philosophy yet published, yet few seminary and college students hear his name even mentioned in their classes, much less are required to read his books. If I might draw a comparison, it is as though students in the mid-sixteenth century never heard their teachers mention Martin Luther or John Calvin. There has been a great educational and ecclesiastical blackout. Both churches and educators have gone out of their way to avoid Clark. They have cheated a generation of students and churchgoers. As students of philosophy at the end of the twentieth century, you ought not consider yourself well educated until you are familiar with the philosophy of Gordon Haddon Clark.

A Brief Biography

Clark's life was one of controversy—theological and philosophical. He was a brilliant mind, and his philosophy continues to be a challenge to the prevailing notions of our day. It is his philosophy that makes his biography both interesting and important, for his battles were intellectual battles.

Clark was a Presbyterian minister, and his father was a Presbyterian minister before him. Born in urban Philadelphia in the summer of 1902, he died in rural Colorado in the spring of 1985. Clark was educated at the University of Pennsylvania and the Sorbonne. His undergraduate degree was in French; his graduate work was in ancient philosophy. He wrote his doctoral dissertation on Aristotle. He quickly earned the respect of fellow professional philosophers by publishing a series of articles in academic journals, translating and editing philosophical texts from the Greek, and editing two standard texts, *Readings in Ethics* and *Selections from Hellenistic Philosophy*. He taught at the University of Pennsylvania, Reformed Episcopal Seminary, Wheaton College, Butler University, Covenant College, and Sangre de Cristo Seminary. Over the course of his 60-year teaching career, he wrote more than 40 books, including a history of philosophy, *Thales to Dewey*, which remains the best one-volume history of philosophy in English. He also lectured widely, pastored a church, raised a family, and played chess. For the past 15 years I have been the publisher of his books and essays. More of his books are in print today than at any time during his life on Earth, yet few students know anything about him.

Throughout his life Clark was enmeshed in controversy: first, as a young man in the old Presbyterian Church of Benjamin Warfield and J. Gresham Machen, where as a ruling elder at age 27 he first fought the modernists and then helped Machen organize the Presbyterian Church of America, later known as the Orthodox Presbyterian Church. Those ecclesiastical activities cost Clark the chairmanship of the Department of Philosophy at the University of Pennsylvania.

Clark's second major controversy was at Wheaton College in Illinois, where he taught from 1936 to 1943 after leaving the University of Pennsylvania. There his Calvinism brought him into conflict with the Arminianism of some faculty members and the administration, and he was forced to resign in 1943. Wheaton College has never been the same since, declining into a sort of vague, lukewarm, and trendy neo-evangelicalism and modernism.

From 1945 to 1973 Clark was Chairman of the Department of Philosophy at Butler University in Indianapolis, where he enjoyed relative academic peace and freedom. But within his denomination, the Orthodox Presbyterian Church, a third major controversy arose, and there was no peace.

In 1944, at age 43, Clark was ordained a teaching elder by the Presbytery of Philadelphia. His ordination was quickly challenged by a faction led by Cornelius Van Til and composed largely of the faculty of Westminster Seminary. The battle over Clark's ordination, which became known as the Clark-Van Til controversy, raged for years. Clark was finally vindicated by the General Assembly of the Orthodox Presbyterian Church. His ordination stood; the effort to defrock him had failed. Yet this failure of the Vantilians to defrock Clark has been falsified by at least one biographer of Van Til, the late William White, and that falsification of history has become the stock in trade of some proponents of Van Til and Westminster Seminary.

Unfortunately, the defeat of the Van Til/Westminster Seminary faction did not end the matter. Those who had unsuccessfully targeted Clark for removal next leveled similar charges against one of Clark's defenders. At that point, rather than spend another three years fighting a faction that had already been defeated once, Clark's defenders left the Orthodox Presbyterian Church, and Clark reluctantly went with them. Years later he told me that he would have liked to stay in the OPC, but felt a sense of loyalty to those who had defended him. After he left, the Vantilians had no serious intellectual opposition within the Orthodox Presbyterian Church.

Clark entered the United Presbyterian Church—not the large denomination, which was not called the United Presbyterian Church at that time—but a small, more conservative, denomination. There he fought another battle about both doctrine and church property. When the United Presbyterian denomination joined the mainline church in the 1950s, Clark left that church and joined the Reformed

Presbyterian Church, which later merged with the Evangelical Synod to form the RPCES. He remained a part of that church until it merged with the PCA in 1983. Clark refused to join the PCA on doctrinal grounds, and for about a year he *was* the RPCES. Some months before his death in April 1985 he affiliated with Covenant Presbytery.

During his lifetime Clark never settled on a name for his philosophy. At times he called it *presuppositionalism;* at other times *dogmatism;* at still other times *Christian rationalism or Christian intellectualism.* None of these names, I fear, catches the correct meaning. Let me explain why: Every philosophy, as I will explain in a moment, has presuppositions; some philosophers just won't admit it. All philosophies, for the same reason, are dogmatic, though some pretend to be open-minded. And the phrase "Christian rationalism" is an awkward and misleading way of describing Clark's views, since Clark refutes rationalism in his books. Nevertheless, one can see why Clark used the terms: *Presuppositionalism* was the term he used to distinguish his views from evidentialism; *dogmatism* was the term he used to distinguish his views from both evidentialism and rationalism; and *rationalism* and *intellectualism* were the terms he used to distinguish his views from religious irrationalism and anti-intellectualism. Clark, of course, always maintained that his philosophy was Christianity, rightly understood. But since there are so many views claiming to be Christianity, it is useful to name Clark's philosophy and thus easily distinguish it from the rest.

Therefore, I would like to begin my talk this evening by naming his philosophy—and rather than calling it Dogmatic Presuppositional Rationalism, or Rational Dogmatic Presuppositionalism, or Presuppositional Rational Dogmatism—rather than letting its title be determined by its theological opposite—I shall give it a name that discloses what it stands for: *Scripturalism.* It avoids all the defects of the other names, and it names what makes Clark's philosophy unique: an uncompromising devotion to Scripture alone. Clark did not try to combine secular and Christian notions, but to derive all of his ideas from the Bible alone. He was intransigent in his devotion to Scripture: All our thoughts—there are no exceptions—are to be brought into conformity to Scripture, for all the treasures of wisdom and knowledge are contained in Scripture. Scripturalism is the logically consistent application of Christian—that is, Scriptural—ideas to all fields of thought. One day, God willing, it will not be necessary to call this philosophy Scripturalism, for it will prevail under its original and most appropriate name, *Christianity.*

The Philosophy of Scripturalism

If I was to summarize Clark's philosophy of Scripturalism, I would say something like this:

1. Epistemology: Propositional Revelation
2. Soteriology: Faith Alone
3. Metaphysics: Theism
4. Ethics: Divine Law
5. Politics: Constitutional Republic

Translating those ideas into more familiar language, we might say:

1. Epistemology: The Bible tells me so.
2. Soteriology: Believe on the Lord Jesus Christ and you shall be saved.
3. Metaphysics: In him we live and move and have our being.
4. Ethics: We ought to obey God rather than men.
5. Politics: Proclaim liberty throughout the land.

Clark developed this philosophy in more than 40 books, many of which were published during his lifetime, most of which are now in print, and a few of which have not been published yet. Let us first consider the foundational branch of philosophy, epistemology, the theory of knowledge.

Epistemology

Scripturalism holds that truth is revealed by God. Christianity is

338

propositional truth revealed by God, propositions which have been written in the 66 books we call the Bible. Revelation is the starting point of Christianity, its axiom. The axiom, the first principle, of Christianity is this: "The Bible alone is the Word of God."

I must interject a few words here about axioms, for some persons, as I mentioned a few paragraphs ago, insist that they do not have any. That is like saying one does not speak prose. Any system of thought, whether it be called philosophy or theology or geometry, must begin somewhere. Even empiricism or evidentialism begins with axioms. That beginning, by definition, is just that, a beginning. Nothing comes before it. It is an axiom, a first principle. That means that those who start with sensation rather than revelation, in a misguided effort to avoid axioms, have not avoided axioms at all: They have merely traded the Christian axiom for a secular axiom. They have exchanged infallible propositional revelation, their birthright as Christians, for fallible sense experience. All empiricists, let me emphasize, since it sounds paradoxical to those accustomed to thinking otherwise, are presuppositionalists: They presuppose the reliability of sensation. They do not presuppose the reliability of revelation. That is something they attempt to prove. Such an attempt is doomed.

Thomas Aquinas, the great thirteenth-century Roman Catholic theologian, tried to combine two axioms in his system: the secular axiom of sense experience, which he obtained from Aristotle, and the Christian axiom of revelation, which he obtained from the Bible. His synthesis was unsuccessful. The subsequent career of western philosophy is the story of the collapse of Thomas' unstable Aristotelian-Christian condominium. Today the dominant form of epistemology in putatively Christian circles, both Roman Catholic and Protestant, is empiricism. Apparently today's theologians have learned little from Thomas' failure. If Thomas Aquinas failed, one doubts that Norman Geisler or R. C. Sproul can succeed.

The lesson of the failure of Thomism was not lost on Clark. Clark did not accept sensation as his axiom. He denied that sense experience furnishes us with knowledge at all. Clark understood the necessity of refuting all competing axioms, including the axiom

337

of sensation. His method was to eliminate all intellectual opposition to Christianity at its root. In his books—such as *A Christian View of Men and Things, Thales to Dewey, Religion, Reason, and Revelation,* and *Three Types of Religious Philosophy*—he pointed out the problems, failures, deceptions, and logical fallacies involved in believing that sense experience provides us with truth.

Clark's consistently Christian rejection of sense experience as the way to truth has many consequences, one of which is that the traditional proofs for the existence of God are all logical fallacies. David Hume and Immanuel Kant were right: Sensation cannot prove God, not merely because God cannot be sensed or validly inferred from sensation, but because no knowledge at all can be validly inferred from sensation. The arguments for the existence of God fail because both the axiom and method are wrong—the axiom of sensation and the method of induction—not because God is a fairy tale. The correct Christian axiom is not sensation, but revelation. The correct Christian method is deduction, not induction.

Another implication of the axiom of revelation is that those historians of thought who divide epistemologies into two types of philosophy, empiricist and rationalist, as though there were only two possible choices—sensation or logic—are ignoring the Christian philosophy, Scripturalism. There are not only two general views in epistemology; there are at least three, and we must be careful not to omit Christianity from consideration simply by the scheme we choose for studying philosophy.

Another implication of the axiom of revelation is this: Rather than accepting the secular view that man discovers truth on his own power using his own resources, Clark asserted that truth is a gift of God, who graciously reveals it to men. Clark's epistemology is consistent with his soteriology: Just as men do not attain salvation themselves, on their own power, but are saved by divine grace, so men do not gain knowledge on their own power, but receive knowledge as a gift from God. Truth is a gift from God. Man can do nothing apart from the will of God, and man can know nothing part from the revelation of God. Clark's epistemology is a Reformed epistemology. All other epistemologies are inconsistent and

338

derived from secular premises. No starting point, no proposition, no experience, no observation, can be more truthful than a word from God: "Because he could swear by no greater, he swore by himself," the author of Hebrews says. If we are to be saved, we must be saved by the words that come out of the mouth of God, words whose truth and authority are derived from God alone.

Scripturalism does not mean, as some have objected, that we can know only the propositions of the Bible. We can know their logical implications as well. The Westminster Confession of Faith, which is a Scripturalist document, says that "The authority of the holy Scripture, for which it ought to be believed and obeyed, depends not upon the testimony of any man or church, but *wholly* upon God (who is Truth itself), the author thereof; and therefore it is to be received, *because it is the word of God"* (emphasis added). By these words, and by the fact that the Confession begins with the doctrine of Scripture, not with the doctrine of God, and certainly not with proofs for the existence of God, the Confession shows itself to be a Scripturalist document.

Continuing with the idea of logical deduction, the Confession says: "The whole counsel of God, concerning all things necessary for his own glory, man's salvation, faith, and life, is either expressly set down in scripture, or by good and necessary consequence may be deduced from scripture: unto which nothing at any time is to be added, whether by new revelations of the Spirit or traditions of men."

Notice the claim of the Confession: "The *whole* counsel of God" is either expressly set down in Scripture or may be deduced from it. *Everything* we need for faith and life is found in the propositions of the Bible, either explicitly or implicitly. *Nothing* is to be added to the revelation at any time. Only logical deduction from the propositions of Scripture is permitted. No synthesis, no combination with secular ideas is either necessary or permissible.

Logic—reasoning by good and necessary consequence—is not a secular principle not found in Scripture and added to the Scriptural axiom; it is contained in the axiom itself. The first verse of John's Gospel may be translated, "In the beginning was the Logic, and the Logic was with God and the Logic was God." Every word of the Bible, from *bereshith* in Genesis 1:1 to *Amen* in Revelation 22:21, exemplifies the law of contradiction. "In the beginning" means in the beginning, not a hundred years or even one second after the beginning. "Amen" expresses agreement, not dissent. The laws of logic are embedded in every word of Scripture. Only deductive inference is valid, and deductive inference—using the laws of logic—is the principal tool of hermeneutics. Sound exegesis of Scripture is making valid deductions from the statements of Scripture. If your pastor is not making valid deductions from Scripture in his sermons, then he is not preaching God's Word. It is in the conclusions of such arguments, as well as in the Biblical statements themselves, that our knowledge consists.

Some will object, "But don't we know that we are in this room, or that 2 plus 2 equals four, or that grass is green?" To answer that objection, we must define the words "know" and "knowledge."

There are three sorts of cognitive states: knowledge, opinion, ignorance. Ignorance is simply the lack of ideas. Complete ignorance is the state of mind that empiricists say we are born with: We are all born with blank minds, *tabula rasa,* to use John Locke's phrase. (Incidentally, a *tabula rasa* mind—a blank mind—is an impossibility. A consciousness conscious of nothing is a contradiction in terms. Empiricism rests on a contradiction.) At the other extreme from ignorance is knowledge. Knowledge is not simply possessing thoughts or ideas, as some think. Knowledge is possessing true ideas and knowing them to be true. Knowledge is, by definition, knowledge of the truth. We do not say that a person "knows" that 2 plus 2 is 5. We may say he thinks it, but he does not know it. It would be better to say that he opines it.

Now, most of what we colloquially call knowledge is actually opinion: We "know" that we are in Pennsylvania; we "know" that Clinton—either Bill or Hillary—is President of the United States, and so forth. Opinions can be true or false; we just don't know which. History, except for revealed history, is opinion. Science is opinion. Archaeology is opinion. John Calvin said, "I call that knowledge, not what is innate in man, nor what is by diligence acquired, but what is revealed to us in the Law and the Prophets." Knowledge is true opinion with an account, that is, a demonstration of its truth.

It may very well be that William Clinton is President of the United States, but I do not know how to prove it, nor, I suspect, do you. In truth, I do not know that he is President, I opine it. I can offer no valid argument based on a true axiom to prove his presidency. I can, however, prove that Jesus Christ rose from the dead.

That information is revealed to me, not by the daily newspaper or the evening news, but by the infallible Word of God. The resurrection of Christ is deduced by good and necessary consequence from the axiom of revelation.

Any view of knowledge that makes no distinction between the cognitive standing of Biblical propositions and statements found in the daily paper does three things: First, it equivocates by applying one word, "knowledge," to two quite different sorts of statements: statements infallibly revealed by the God who can neither lie nor make a mistake, and statements made by men who both lie and make mistakes; second, by its empiricism, it actually makes the Biblical statements less reliable than those in the daily paper, for statements in the paper are subject to empirical investigation and Biblical statements are not; and third, it thereby undermines Christianity.

Revelation is our only source of truth and knowledge. Neither science, nor history, nor archaeology, nor philosophy can furnish us with truth. Scripturalism takes seriously Paul's warning to the Colossians: "Beware lest anyone cheat you through philosophy and empty deceit, according to the tradition of men, according to the basic principles of the world, and not according to Christ. For in him dwells all the fullness of the Godhead bodily, and you are complete in him. . . ."

One naive objection to the axiom of revelation crops up repeatedly: Don't I have to read the Bible? Don't I have to know that I have a book in my hands and that that book is the Bible? Don't I have to rely on the senses to obtain revelation?

First, this objection begs the epistemological question, How does one know? by assuming that one knows by means of the senses.

341

But that is the conclusion that must be proved. The proper response to these questions is another series of questions: How do you know you have a book in your hands? How do you know that you are reading it? What is sensation? What are perceptions? What is abstraction? And so forth. The naive question—Don't you have to read the Bible?—assumes that empiricism is true. It ignores all the arguments demonstrating the impossibility of empiricism. An acceptable account of epistemology, however, must begin at the beginning, not in the middle. Few philosophers, however, want to start at the beginning.

But there is another confusion in this question: It assumes that revelation is not a distinct means of gaining knowledge, but that even revealed information has to be derived from the senses. A conversation between Peter and Christ will indicate how far this assumption is from the Scriptural view of epistemology:

"He said to them, 'But who do you say that I am?'"

"And Simon Peter answered and said, 'You are the Christ the Son of the living God.'"

"Jesus answered and said to him, 'Blessed are you, Simon Bar-Jonah, for flesh and blood has not revealed this to you, but my Father who is in Heaven.' "

Presumably Peter had "heard" with his ears and "seen" with his eyes, but Christ says that his knowledge did not come by flesh and blood—it did not come by the senses; it came by revelation from the Father. That is why Christ forbids Christians to be called teacher, " 'for one is your Teacher, the Christ' " (Matthew 23). It is in God, not matter, that we live and move, and have our being.

Soteriology

Soteriology, the doctrine of salvation, is a branch of epistemology, the theory of knowledge. Soteriology is not a branch of metaphysics, for men are not deified when they are saved; saved men, even in Heaven, remain temporal and limited creatures. Only God is eternal; only God is omniscient; only God is omnipresent.

Nor is soteriology a branch of ethics, for men are not saved by works. We are saved in spite of our works, not because of them.

Nor is soteriology a branch of politics, for the notion that salvation, either temporal or eternal, can be achieved by political means is an illusion. Attempts to immanentize the eschaton have brought nothing but blood and death to Earth.

Salvation is by faith alone. Faith is belief of the truth. Truth is revealed by God. Faith, the act of believing, is a gift of God. "By his knowledge, my righteous servant shall justify many."

Clark's view of salvation, reflected in the Westminster Confession's chapter on Justification, is at odds with most of what passes for Christianity today. Popular Christianity decries knowledge. Clark points out that Peter says that we have received everything we need for life and godliness through knowledge. James says we are regenerated by the Word of Truth. Paul says we are justified through belief of the truth. Christ says we are sanctified by truth.

There are three popular theories of sanctification today: sanctification by works, sanctification by emotions, sanctification by sacraments. The first, sanctification by works, is sometimes expressed by those who claim to be Reformed or Calvinist: They teach that we are justified by faith, but we are sanctified by works. Calvin held no such view, and the Westminster Confession refutes it. The second view, sanctification by emotions, is the view of the pentecostal, charismatic, and holiness groups. The third view, sanctification by sacraments, is held by Roman Catholic and other churches that believe in the magical power of sacraments to regenerate or sanctify. But just as we are regenerated by truth alone, and justified through belief of the truth alone, we are sanctified by truth alone as well.

Metaphysics

Let us turn briefly to metaphysics. Clark wrote relatively little on the subject of metaphysics in the philosophical sense. Clark was, obviously, a theist. God, revealed in the Bible, is spirit and truth. Since truth always comes in propositions, the mind of God, that is,

God himself, is propositional. Clark wrote a book called *The Johannine Logos,* in which he explained how Christ could identify himself with his words: "I am the truth." "I am the life." "The words that I speak to you are truth and life." Clark, like Augustine, was accused of "reducing" God to a proposition. Rather than fleeing from such an accusation, Clark astonished some of his readers by insisting that persons are indeed propositions. Some have been so confused by his statement that they think he said that propositions are persons, and so they wonder whether a declarative sentence, The cat is black, is really a person.

Knowledge is knowledge of the truth, and truth is unchanging. Truth is eternal. We know David was King of Israel and that Jesus rose from the dead, not because we saw them, but because those truths have been revealed to us by God. They are knowledge because they are revealed as truth. Because we all live and move and have our being in God, both thought and communication are possible. Communication is not based on having the same sensations, as empiricists think, but on having the same ideas. We can never have the same sensations as another person—you cannot have my toothache, and I cannot see your color blue—but we can both think that justification is by faith alone. Empiricism, which promises us an objective reality—the reality it calls matter—delivers only solipsism. In the material world the empiricists describe, each of us—if indeed you are more than one of my headaches—is shut inside our own sensations, and there is no escape. Science, however, is an attempt to escape the solipsism of sensation.

Those Christians who put their trust in science as the key to understanding the material universe should be embarrassed by the fact that science never discovers truth. One of the insuperable problems of science is the fallacy of induction; indeed, induction is an insuperable problem for all forms of empiricism. The problem is simply this: Induction, arguing from the particular to the general, is always a fallacy. No matter how many white swans one observes, one never has sufficient reason to say all swans are white. There is another fatal fallacy in the scientific method as well: asserting the consequent. Bertrand Russell put the matter this way:

344

"All inductive arguments in the last resort reduce themselves to the following form: 'If this is true, that is true: now that is true, therefore this is true.' This argument is, of course, formally fallacious. [It is the fallacy of asserting the consequent.] Suppose I were to say: 'If bread is a stone and stones are nourishing, then this bread will nourish me; now this bread does nourish me; therefore it is a stone and stones are nourishing.' If I were to advance such an argument, I should certainly be thought foolish, *yet it would not be fundamentally different from the argument upon which all scientific laws are based"* (emphasis added).

Recognizing that the problem of induction is insoluble, and that asserting the consequent is a logical fallacy, philosophers of science in the twentieth century, in an effort to justify science, developed the notion that science does not rely on induction at all. Instead, it consists of conjectures and refutations. That is the title of a book by Karl Popper, one of the leading philosophers of science in this century. But in their attempt to save science from epistemological disgrace, the philosophers of science had to abandon any claim to knowledge: Science is nothing but conjectures and refutations of conjectures. Popper wrote:

"First, although in science we do our best to find the truth, we are conscious of the fact that we can *never* be sure whether we have got it. . . . [W]e know that our scientific theories *always* remain hypotheses. . . . [I]n science there is *no* 'knowledge' in the sense in which Plato and Aristotle understood the word, in the sense which implies finality; in science, we *never* have sufficient reason for the belief that we have attained the truth. . . . Einstein declared that his theory was *false:* he said that it would be a better approximation to the truth than Newton's, but he gave reasons why he would not, even if all predictions came out right, regard it as a true theory. . . . Our attempts to see and to find the truth are not final, but open to improvement; . . . our knowledge, our doctrine is conjectural; . . . it consists of guesses, of hypotheses, rather than of final and certain truth."

Those theologians who accept observation and science as the basis for arguing for the truth of Christianity are attempting the impossible. Science cannot funish us with truth about the material universe that it purports to describe, let alone truth about God. The empirical world view, which begins with a metaphysics of matter, knowledge of which we obtain from sensation, cannot furnish us with knowledge at all. In *him*—not in matter–we live and move and have our being.

Ethics

Clark's ethical philosophy is also derived from the axiom of revelation. The distinction between right and wrong depends entirely upon the commands of God. There is no natural law that makes some actions right and others wrong. In the words of the Shorter Catechism, sin is any want of conformity to or transgression of the law of God. Were there no law or God, there would be no right or wrong.

This may be seen very clearly in God's command to Adam not to eat the fruit of the tree of knowledge of good and evil. Only the command of God made eating the fruit sin. It may also be seen in God's command to Abraham to sacrifice Isaac. God's command alone made the sacrifice right, and Abraham hastened to obey. Strange as it may sound to modern ears used to hearing so much about the right to life, or the right to decent housing, or the right to choose, the Bible says that natural rights and wrongs do not exist: Only God's commands make some things right and other things wrong.

In the Old Testament, it was a sin for the Jews to eat pork. Today, we can all enjoy bacon and eggs for breakfast, although theonomists, reconstructionists, and judaizers may choke. And it may bother some who are not theonomists to learn that God might have made the killing of a human being or the taking of property a virtue, not a sin. That is one of the lessons of the command to Abraham. But in fact God made killing an innocent man a sin. In this world God commands, "You shall not murder." What makes murder wrong is not some presumed or pre-existing right to life, but the divine command itself.

If we possessed rights because we are men—if our rights were natural and inalienable—then God himself would have to respect them. But God is sovereign. He is free to do with his creatures as he sees fit. One need read only Isaiah 40. So we do not have natural rights. That is good, for natural and inalienable rights are logically incompatible with punishment of any sort. Fines, for example, violate the inalienable right to property. Imprisonment violates the inalienable right to liberty. Execution violates the inalienable right to life. Natural right theory is logically incoherent at its foundation. Natural rights are logically incompatible with justice. The Biblical idea is not natural rights, but imputed rights. Only imputed rights, not intrinsic rights—natural and inalienable rights— are compatible with liberty and justice. And those rights are imputed by God.

Furthermore, Clark demonstrates, all attempts to base ethics on some foundation other than revelation fail. Natural law is a failure, as David Hume so obligingly pointed out, because "oughts" cannot be derived from "ises." In more formal language, the conclusion of an argument can contain no terms that are not found in its premise. Natural lawyers, who begin their arguments with statements about man and the universe, statements in the indicative mood, cannot end their arguments with statements in the imperative mood.

The major ethical theory competing with natural law theory today is utilitarianism. Utilitarianism tells us that the moral action is one which results in the greatest good for the greatest number. It furnishes an elaborate method for calculating the effects of choices. Unfortunately, utilitarianism is also a failure, for it not only commits the naturalistic fallacy of the natural lawyers, it requires a calculus that cannot be executed as well. We cannot know what is the greatest good for the greatest number.

The only logical basis for ethics is the revealed commands of God. They furnish us not only with the basic distinction between right and wrong, but with detailed instructions and practical examples of right and wrong. They actually assist us in living our daily lives. Secular attempts to provide an ethical system fail on both counts.

Politics

Clark did not write a great deal about politics either, but it is clear from what he did write that he grounded his political theory on revelation, not on natural law, nor on the consent of the governed, nor on the exercise of mere force.

In a long chapter in *A Christian View of Men and Things,* he argues that attempts to base a theory of politics on secular axioms result in either anarchy or totalitarianism. He argues that only Christianity, which grounds the legitimate powers of government not in the consent of the governed but in the delegation of power by God, avoids the twin evils of anarchy and totalitarianism.

Government has a legitimate role in society: the punishment of evildoers, as Paul put it in Romans 13. Education, welfare, housing, parks, retirement income, health care, the exploration of space, and most of the thousands of other programs in which government is involved today are illegitimate. The fact that government is involved in all these activities is a primary reason why government is not doing its one legitimate job well: Crime is rising, and the criminal justice system is a growing threat to freedom. People are tried twice for the same crime, their property is taken without due process of law or just compensation, innocent persons are punished and guilty persons released.

Clark believed that the Bible teaches a distinctly limited role for government. The current activities of many Christians in politics would have been foreign to his thinking. The Biblical goal is not a large bureaucracy staffed by Christians, but virtually no bureaucracy. There should be no Christian Department of Education, no Christian Housing Department, no Christian Agriculture Department, simply because there should be no Departments of Education, Housing, and Agriculture, period. We do not need and should oppose a Christian Bureau of Alcohol, Tobacco, and Firearms or a Christian Internal Revenue Service. So-called evangelical Christians are engaged in a pursuit of political power that makes their activities almost indistinguishable from the activities of the social gospelers in the early and mid-twentieth century. This sort of political action has nothing to do with Scripture.

An Introduction to Gordon H. Clark

The System

Each of the parts of this philosophical system—epistemology, soteriology, metaphysics, ethics, and politics—is important, and the ideas gain strength from being arranged in a logical system. In such a system, where propositions are logically dependent on or logically imply other propositions, each part mutually reinforces the others. Historically—though not in this decadent century—Calvinists have been criticized for being too logical. But if we are to be transformed by the renewing of our minds, if we are to bring all our thoughts into conformity with Christ, we must learn to think as Christ does, logically and systematically.

Gordon Clark elaborated a complete philosophical system that proceeds by rigorous deduction from one axiom to thousands of theorems. Each of the theorems fits into the whole system. If you accept one of the theorems, you must, on pain of contradiction, accept the whole. But many leaders in the professing church feel no pain, and some even glory in contradiction. They are utterly confused and are thwarting the advance of the kingdom of God.

Scripturalism—Christianity—is a whole view of things thought out together. It engages non-Christian philosophies on every field of intellectual endeavor. It furnishes a coherent theory of knowledge, an infallible salvation, a refutation of science, a theory of the world, a coherent and practical system of ethics, and the principles required for political liberty and justice. No other philosophy does. All parts of the system can be further developed; some parts have been barely touched at all. It is my hope and prayer that the philosophy of Scripturalism will conquer the Christian world in the next century. If it does not, if the church continues to decline in confusion and unbelief, at least a few Christians can take refuge in the impregnable intellectual fortress that God has given us in his Word. May you be among those few.

BIBLIOGRAPHY

Annas, Julia and Jonathan Barnes. *The Modes of Scepticism: Ancient Texts and Modern Interpretations.* Cambridge University Press, 1985.

Augustine, Aurelius and Gordon H. Clark, *De Magistro and Lord God of Truth.* The Trinity Foundation, 1994.

Baker, James T. *Ayn Rand.* Twayne Publishers, 1987.

Barnes, Hazel. *An Existentialist Ethics.* Alfred A. Knopf, 1967.

Becker, Carl L. *The Heavenly City of the Eighteenth-Century Philosophers.* Yale University Press, 1965 [1932].

Binswanger, Harry, editor. *The Ayn Rand Lexicon: Objectivism from A to Z.* New American Library, 1986.

Blanshard, Brand. *The Nature of Thought.* Two volumes. George Allen and Unwin, 1939.

Branden, Barbara. "Ayn Rand and Her Movement" [interview]. *Liberty,* 1991 [January 1990].

———. *The Passion of Ayn Rand.* Doubleday, 1986.

Branden, Nathaniel. *Judgment Day: My Years with Ayn Rand.* Houghton Mifflin, 1989.

———. *The Psychology of Self-Esteem.* Bantam, 1971 [1969].

Branden, Nathaniel and Barbara. *In Answer to Ayn Rand.* Nathaniel Branden Institute, 1968.

———. *Who Is Ayn Rand?* Paperback Library, 1967 [1962].

Bredvold, Louis I. *The Brave New World of the Enlightenment.* University of Michigan Press, 1961.

Chambers, Whittaker. "Big Sister Is Watching You" [review of *Atlas Shrugged*]. *National Review,* December 28, 1957, 594-596.

Bibliography

Childs, Roy A. "Ayn Rand, Objectivism and All That" [interview]. *Liberty*, April 1993, 31-42, 46.

Clark, Gordon H. *Behaviorism and Christianity*. The Trinity Foundation, 1982.

——. *A Christian Philosophy of Education*. The Trinity Foundation, 1988 [1946].

——. *A Christian View of Men and Things*. The Trinity Foundation, 1990 [1952].

——. *Essays on Ethics and Politics*. John W. Robbins, editor. The Trinity Foundation, 1992.

——. *God's Hammer: The Bible and Its Critics*. John W. Robbins, editor. The Trinity Foundation, 1995 [1982].

——. *Historiography Secular and Religious*. The Trinity Foundation, 1993 [1971].

——. *In Defense of Theology*. Mott Media, 1984

——. *An Introduction to Christian Philosophy*. The Trinity Foundation, 1993.

——. *Language and Theology*. The Trinity Foundation, 1993 [1980].

——. *Logic*. The Trinity Foundation, 1988 [1985].

——. *The Philosophy of Science and Belief in God*. The Trinity Foundation, 1996 [1964].

——. *Religion, Reason, and Revelation*. The Trinity Foundation, 1995 [1961].

——. *Thales to Dewey: A History of Philosophy*. The Trinity Foundation, 1989 [1957].

——. *Three Types of Religious Philosophy*. The Trinity Foundation, 1989 [1973].

Copleston, Frederick. *A History of Philosophy*. Doubleday, 1962 [1946].

Davis, R. W., editor. *The Origins of Modern Freedom in the West*. Stanford University Press, 1995.

Den Uyl, Douglas J. and Douglas B. Rasmussen. *The Philosophic Thought of Ayn Rand*. University of Illinois Press, 1986 [1984].

Efron, Robert. "The Conditioned Reflex: A Meaningless Concept." The Objectivist, n.d.

Ellis, Albert. *Is Objectivism a Religion?* Lyle Stuart, 1968.

Engels, Friedrich. *Anti-Duhring*. International Publishers, 1970 [1939, 1878].

Fallows, James. "What the Left Can Learn from Ayn Rand." *The Washington Monthly*, May 1975, 54-59.

Feuer, Lewis S., editor. *Marx and Engels: Basic Writings on Politics and Philosophy*. Doubleday, 1959.

Feuerbach, Ludwig. *Essence of Christianity*.

———. *Lectures on Religion*.

Fischer, David Hackett. *Historians' Fallacies: Toward a Logic of Historical Thought*. Harper and Row, 1970.

Gay, Peter. *The Enlightenment: An Interpretation*. Two volumes. W. W. Norton, 1977 [1966].

———. *The Enlightenment: The Rise of Modern Paganism*. W. W. Norton, 1977 [1966].

Gilovich, Thomas. *How We Know What Isn't So: The Fallibility of Human Reason in Everyday Life*. The Free Press, 1991.

Gladstein, Mimi Reisel. *The Ayn Rand Companion*. Greenwood Press, 1984.

Goldberg, Bruce. "Ayn Rand's *For the New Intellectual*." *New Individualist Review*, November 1961.

Greenberg, Sid. *Ayn Rand and Alienation: The Platonic Idealism of the Objectivist Ethics and a Rational Alternative*. Sid Greenberg, 1977.

Hamel, Virginia L. L. *In Defense of Ayn Rand*. New Beacon Publications, 1990.

Historic and Scenic Tour of The Kensico Cemetery.

Hospers, John. "Conversations with Ayn Rand" [interview]. *Liberty,* September 1990, 42-52.

James, William. *Radical Empiricism* and *A Pluralistic Universe*. Ralph Barton Perry, editor. Dutton, 1971.

Jaeger, Werner. *Aristotle: Fundamentals of the History of His Development*. Second edition. Oxford at the Clarendon Press, 1968 [1934].

Jeans, James. *Physics and Philosophy*. Dover, 1981 [1943].

Jones, W. T. *A History of Philosophy*. Harcourt, Brace and World, 1952.

Kelley, David. *The Evidence of the Senses*. Louisiana State University Press, 1986.

Kline, Morris. *Mathematics and the Search for Knowledge*. Oxford University Press, 1985.

Lakatos, Imre and Alan Musgrave, editors. *Criticism and the Growth of Knowledge*. Cambridge University Press, 1974 [1970].

Lenin, V. I. *Materialism and Empirio-Criticism*. Foreign Languages Publishing House, 1952.

Lepanto, Paul. *Return to Reason*. Exposition Press, 1971.

Marx, Karl and Friedrich Engels. *The German Ideology*. International

Bibliography

Publishers, 1968 [1947].

——. *On Religion*. Schocken Books, 1964 [1957].

McLellan, David. *Marxism and Religion*. Harper and Row, 1987.

Merrill, Ronald E. *The Ideas of Ayn Rand*. Open Court, 1991.

Morick, Harold, editor. *Challenges to Empiricism*. Hackett, 1980.

Nozick, Robert. *Anarchy, State and Utopia*. Basic Books, 1974.

O'Neill, William F. *With Charity Toward None: An Analysis of Ayn Rand's Philosophy*. Philosophical Library, 1971.

Peikoff, Leonard. "The Analytic-Synthetic Dichotomy." The Objectivist, 1967.

——. editor. *The Early Ayn Rand: A Selection from Her Unpublished Fiction*. New American Library, 1984.

——. "An Examination Study-Guide to the Ethics of Objectivism." NBI Press, 1967.

——. *Objectivism: The Philosophy of Ayn Rand*. Dutton, 1991.

——. *The Ominous Parallels*. Stein and Day, 1982.

Popper, Karl. *Conjectures and Refutations: The Growth of Scientific Knowledge*. Harper and Row, 1968 [1963].

——. *Popper Selections*. David Miller, editor. Princeton University Press, 1985.

——. *Unended Quest: An Intellectual Autobiography*. Open Court, 1982 [1974].

Rand, Ayn. *Anthem*. New American Library, no date [1946, 1937].

——. *Atlas Shrugged*. Random House, 1957.

——. *The Ayn Rand Column*. Second Renaissance Books, 1991.

——. *The Ayn Rand Letter, Volumes 1-4, 1971-1976*. Second Renaissance Books, no date [1990].

——. *Capitalism: The Unknown Ideal*. New American Library, 1967.

——. "Comment!" Merkle Press [for the National Broadcasting Company]. Television interview transcript, May 2, 1971.

——. *The Early Ayn Rand*. Leonard Peikoff, editor. New American Library, 1984 [1926-1938].

——. "Faith and Force: The Destroyers of the Modern World." The Objectivist, 1960.

——. *For the New Intellectual*. Random House, 1961.

——. *The Fountainhead*. Bobbs-Merrill, 1978 [1943].

——. "The Intellectual Bankruptcy of Our Age." The Objectivist, 1961

——. *Introduction to Objectivist Epistemology*. The Objectivist, 1967.

——. *Introduction to Objectivist Epistemology*. Harry Binswanger and

Leonard Peikoff, editors. Second edition. Penguin, 1990 [1979].

———. *Letters of Ayn Rand.* Michael S. Berliner, editor. Dutton, 1995.

———. *The New Left: The Anti-Industrial Revolution.* New American Library, 1971.

———. *Night of January 16th.* New American Library, 1971 [1933].

———. "Notes on the History of American Free Enterprise."

———. *The Objectivist, 1966-1968.* The Objectivist, 1968.

———. *The Objectivist Newsletter, Volume 1-4, 1962-1965.* The Objectivist, 1967.

———. *Philosophy: Who Needs It?* Bobbs-Merrill, 1982.

———. *The Romantic Manifesto.* New American Library, 1971.

———. "Textbook of Americanism." Nathaniel Branden Institute, no date [1946].

———. *The Virtue of Selfishness.* New American Library, 1964.

———. *The Voice of Reason.* Leonard Peikoff, editor. New American Library, 1989.

———. *We the Living.* Random House, 1959 [1936].

Rivlin, Robert and Karen Gravelle. *Deciphering the Senses.* Simon and Schuster, 1984.

Rothbard, Murray. *The Sociology of the Ayn Rand Cult.* Unpublished manuscript, no date.

Sciabarra, Chris Matthew. *Ayn Rand The Russian Radical.* Pennsylvania State University Press, 1995.

Sextus Empiricus: *Selections from the Major Writings on Scepticism, Man and God.* Philip P. Hallie, editor. Hackett, 1985 [1968].

Sowell, Thomas. *Marxism: Philosophy and Economics.* William Morrow and Company, 1985.

Steele, David Ramsay. "Peikoff's *Objectivism*: An Autopsy" [review of *Objectivism: The Philosophy of Ayn Rand*], *Liberty*, January 1992, 60-68.

Tawney, R.H. *Religion and the Rise of Capitalism.* New American Library, 1963 [1926].

Taylor, Stephen E. "Is Ayn Rand Really Selfish . . . Or Only Confused?" *Journal of Thought*, January 1969, 12-27.

Tuccille, Jerome. *It Usually Begins with Ayn Rand.* Stein and Day, 1971.

Weber, Max. *The Protestant Ethic and the Spirit of Capitalism.* Charles Scribner's Sons, 1958 [1904/5].

Windelband, Wilhelm. *A History of Philosophy.* Harper and Row, 1958 [1901].

INDEX

Abelard, 277
ability and responsibility, 115
Abolition of Man, The (Lewis), 142
abortion, 205-207, 212, 319, 321
Abraham, 289, 303, 346
absolute(s), 32, 81
abstraction, 27, 32, 58, 60, 62,
    64-65, 68-72, 82, 93-94, 164-
    165, 216, 222-223, 269, 274,
    286, 342
Academy, Plato's, xvii
accuracy, 239, 273, 296
action(s), 102, 145, 166-167, 175-
    176, 182-184, 186, 234
Acts 17:16, 311; 17:28, 224
actuality/potentiality, 206
Adam, 136, 286-288, 346
Adams, Jay, 114
adultery, 187, 225, 253
Aeschylus, 135; *Works:*
    Prometheus Bound, 135
aesthetics, 61, 295
aggression, 188, 322; *see also*
    force
agnosticism, 137-138, 273

Agriculture Department, 348
Agrippa, King, 306
Alamo, xvii
Alfred, King, 328
algebra, 246-248
alternatives, 159
altruism, xiii, 9, 14, 20, 89, 111
"Altruism as Appeasement"
    (Rand), 100
Amen, 340
America, 329
American Association for the
    Advancement of Science, 291
Amos, 303
amusement, 321
"Analytic-Synthetic Dichotomy,
    The" (Peikoff), 39, 70, 72, 95,
    98
Ananias, 304
anarchism/anarchy, 19, 181, 196,
    198-200, 203, 214, 216, 218-
    219, 348
Anaxagoras, 262
Ancient City, The (Coulanges),
    319

Ancient History (Finley), 311
Andrei, 152, 155
animal(s), 27, 41, 66, 71, 159-
161, 163, 165, 286, 320, 326,
330
animal rights, 212-214
animism, 312
Anselm, 111; *Works: Cur Deus
Homo,* 288
Answer to Ayn Rand (Robbins),
xvi, 3, 118
Anthem (Rand), 11, 23, 128,
130-136, 198
Anti-Dühring (Engels), 81
anthropology, 128
Antichrist, 331
Antichrist, The (Nietzsche), 330-
331
Antony, 316
anxiety, 114
apagogic method, 18-19
Apocalypse, 304; *see also*
Revelation, book of
Apocrypha, 1
"Apologetics" (Clark), 77
apostasy, 305
apostles, 300, 304, 307-308
apparitions, 311
appearance(s), 139, 264-267
approximations vs. knowledge,
48, 52
archaeology, 306, 341
Ares, 316
argument from intimidation,
fallacy of, 111
arguments, xiii
Aristotle, xiv, 8, 13-14, 16, 22,
31-32, 35, 44-45, 53, 58, 61,
64, 71, 78-80, 82, 92-94, 104,

109, 111, 116-117, 180, 194,
198, 204-206, 209, 211-212,
214, 223-224, 231, 236, 238,
251-252, 259-260, 263, 265,
281-282, 284, 317-319, 320-
321, 326, 333, 337, 345;
Works: De Anima, 263;
Physics, 117; *Politics,* 208
Aristotle (Randall), 263
arithmetic, 150, 277, 287
Arminianism, 333
army, 198
arrest, 187, 198
arsenic, 156
artisans, 318
asserting the consequent, fallacy
of, 55-56, 221, 288, 298, 344-
345
assumptions, 13, 56; *see also*
axioms, presuppositions
astrology, 311
atheism, xiii, 17, 108-109, 127,
130, 132, 236
Athens, 212, 310-311, 316
Athens and Jerusalem (Weltin),
319
Atlas Shrugged (Rand), xiv, 6-8,
10-11, 13, 23-26, 30, 36, 84-
85, 87, 112-113, 116, 120-
121, 123-124, 126-127, 136,
138, 141, 145, 147-148, 152-
154, 165, 167-168, 172-173,
177, 179, 184, 189, 195, 199-
200, 215, 220, 229
atomic bomb, 290, 297
atoms, ix, 21, 34, 45, 88-89, 121,
169
Atonement, 97, 286
attention, 273

Attila, 105, 111, 201
Augsburg Confession, 285
Augusta, Julia, 315
Augustine, Aurelius, 34, 73, 124,
    176, 217, 273, 280, 344;
    Works: De Magistro, 73
Augustus, Emperor, 315-317
Aurelius, Emperor Marcus, 173;
    Works: Meditations, 173
authority, 292, 339
Autobiography (Franklin), 145
automatic knowledge, 158
autonomy, 10, 18
average(s), 50, 52, 55, 295
axiom(s), 13, 16, 18, 22, 36, 64,
    72-73, 82-83, 87, 93, 120,
    148-149, 177, 203, 217, 219,
    221-222, 233-235, 278, 285,
    337-338, 349
axiomatic concepts, 44, 72, 77,
    81-94, 234, 248-249; *see also*
    consciousness, existence
Ayn Rand Column, The (Rand), 6
Ayn Rand Institute, 7
Ayn Rand Lexicon, The
    (Binswanger), 7, 41, 43, 73,
    101, 119, 207-209
Ayn Rand The Russian Radical
    (Sciabarra), 129

Babel, 136, 218
babies, 205-209; *see also*
    abortion, infanticide
Babylon, 284, 287
Babylonia, 310
Bacon, Francis, 54, 109, 140
bacteria, 213
bad, 331; *see also* evil, good
baksheesh, 323

Bakunin, Michael, 199
banditry, 324
barbarians, 327
baseball, 179
"Basic Principles of Objecti-
    vism, The" (Branden), 3
Beach Boys, 259
Beethoven, Ludwig van, 258;
    Works: Ninth Symphony, 258
behavior, 166, 320
behaviorism, 236
Behaviorism and Christianity
    (Clark), 140
being, 64, 86-87, 122; *see also*
    existence
Belgic Confession, 285
belief, 49, 260, 336; *see also*
    faith
benevolent universe, 118
Bentham, Jeremy, 306
bereshith, 340
Berkeley, George, 42-43, 62,
    270; *Works: A Treatise
    Concerning the Principles of
    Human Knowledge,* 43
Berliner, Michael, 7
Berman, Harold, 183, 327-329;
    *Works: The Interaction of
    Law and Religion,* 327; *Law
    and Revolution,* 183
Bernard, 277, 281
Bethlehem, 319
Beyond Good and Evil
    (Nietzsche), 6, 14, 108, 131,
    147
Bible, xii, xv, xvi, 4, 22, 81, 102,
    109-111, 127, 132-133, 142,
    168, 177-178, 195, 203-204,
    217, 219-221, 225, 233, 251,

253, 278, 282-286, 307, 312,
325, 335, 337, 339, 343
bibliolatry, 283
Binswanger, Harry, 7, 38, 208;
*Works: The Ayn Rand
Lexicon,* 7, 41, 43, 73, 101,
119, 207-209
biocentric psychology, 9
Bithinia, 313
blackmail, 187
blanking out, xvi, 119; *see also*
faking reality
Blanshard, Brand, 8, 47, 61, 64-
65, 76, 121; *Works: The
Nature of Thought,* 8, 47, 61,
64-65, 76
blood feud, 327-328
Blumenthal, Joan, 41-42
Bobgan, Martin and Deirdre, 114
body, 90, 286
Book of Mormon, 1
books, 312
Boole, George, 277
Bottomore, 17; *Works,: Early
Writings of Karl Marx,* 17
bourgeoisie, 192
brain, 39-40, 46, 56, 63, 77, 137,
141, 160, 164, 236, 242, 259
Branden, Barbara, x, 2, 5, 26,
28, 110-111, 220; *Works: The
Passion of Ayn Rand,* x, 26,
42; *Who Is Ayn Rand?* 2, 10,
21, 26, 100, 110, 127, 215
Branden, Nathaniel, 2, 3, 26, 29,
33, 40, 48-49, 66, 96-99, 100-
102, 105, 108-110, 115, 117,
121-122, 127, 138-139, 162,
166, 171, 173, 203, 275;
Works: "Common Fallacies

About Capitalism," 203;
"Mental Health versus
Mysticism and Self-sacrifice,"
8; *Who Is Ayn Rand?* 2, 10,
21, 26, 100, 110, 127, 215
breach of contract, 187
bribes, 323
Bridgman, Percy, 257
budget of Roman Empire, 319
Bultmann, Rudolf, 28
Bureau of Alcohol, Tobacco, and
Firearms, 348
Bureau of Standards, 49
bureaucracy, 322, 348
Butler, Bishop, 307
Butler University, 333, 334
Byteon, 315

Caesar, 204, 310, 325
Cain, 135
calculus, 150
calling, 308
Calvin, John, 109, 183, 302,
329-330, 332, 340, 343;
*Works: Institutes of the
Christian Religion,* 302
Calvinism, 230-231, 277, 333,
343, 349
Calvinists, 97, 283
canon of Objectivism, 1-5
capital punishment, 196, 225; *see
also* execution, punishment
capitalism, xiii, 10, 26, 180, 181
Capitalism: The Unknown Ideal
(Rand), 6, 23, 86, 100, 134,
138, 180-188, 193, 195-196,
203, 212, 225
Carlson, A. J., 291; *Works:*
"Science and the

Supernatural," 291
Case for Gold, The (Paul), 132
Cassirer, Ernst, 11, 12, 15, 115;
    Works: The Philosophy of the
    Enlightenment, 11, 12, 15,
    115
castes, 317
categorical imperative, 302, 304
categories, 63, 81-83, 91, 285
cathedrals, 20
cattle, 264
causality/causation, 98, 102-104,
    115, 122, 169, 176
cells, 213
Celsus, 326
censorship, 176
certainty, 106
change, 49, 103
chaos, 40, 46
charismatic movement, 343
Charnock, Stephen, 279, 281,
    285; *Works: The Existence*
    and Attributes of God, 279
child neglect, 187
children, 66, 80, 205, 208, 212,
    225, 317
Childs, Roy A., 4
China, 284
choice(s), 56, 99, 145, 148-149,
    155, 159, 166, 170, 177, 216,
    254, 296
"Christ and Civilization"
    (Robbins), 212, 309-331
Christian View of Men and
    Things, A (Clark), 194, 203,
    222, 338, 348
Christianity, xii, xv-xvi, 1, 4, 18,
    20, 28, 49, 90, 97, 101, 109,
    112-115, 123-124, 127, 142,

178-179, 182-183, 203, 211,
    218-222, 225, 253, 290-291,
    300-301, 305-306, 309-331,
    345, 348-349
Christianity: The Unknown
    Ideal, xvi
Christmas, 309
church, xv; and state, 325
Churchill, Winston, 284
Cicero, 318, 324
civil disobedience, 225
civil rights, 329
civilization, 290, 309-331
clams, 265
Clark, Gordon Haddon, xvi, 10,
    18, 20, 24-25, 35, 44-45, 47,
    49, 52, 62, 64, 77, 87, 89-90,
    92, 97, 101, 104, 109, 140,
    142, 178, 180, 194, 203, 221-
    223, 226, 236, 332-349;
    Works: "Apologetics," 77;
    Behaviorism and Christianity,
    140; *A Christian View of Men*
    and Things, 194, 203, 222,
    338, 348; *Essays on Ethics*
    and Politics, 20; "The Ethics
    of Abortion," 209; *God's*
    Hammer: The Bible and Its
    Critics, 97, 178; *An*
    Introduction to Christian
    Philosophy, 4, 45, 104, 194,
    203; *The Johannine Logos,*
    344; *Karl Barth's Theological*
    Method, 18; *The Philosophy*
    of Gordon H. Clark, 35, 62,
    82, 87, 109; *The Philosophy*
    of Science and Belief in God,
    49, 52, 221; *Readings in*
    Ethics, 333; *Religion, Reason*

and Revelation, 101, 338;
Selections from Hellenistic Philosophy, 333; "Special Divine Revelation as Rational," 97, 178; *Thales to Dewey,* 64, 142, 180, 338; *Three Types of Religious Philosophy,* 47, 89-90, 221, 223, 226, 338; *William James and John Dewey,* 151, 236
classification, 44
Cleopatra, 316
Clifford, W. K., 290-291
Clinias, 316
Clinton, Bill, 340-341; Hillary, 340
clothing, 169
cocaine, 146, 156
coercion, 326
cognition, 28, 67, 156-157, 161, 170, 264
collectivism, 10
color(s), 62-63, 241, 245, 268, 271, 275
color blindness, 240
Colossians, 341; 3:10, 286
Columbus, 256
commands, 151, 347
Comment!, 11
"Common Fallacies About Capitalism" (Branden), 203
common sense, 50
communication, 14, 16, 27, 344
Communism, 111, 194, 224
Communist Manifesto, The (Marx and Engels), 117
Communists, 36, 137, 192, 209
competing governments, 202
"Comprachicos, The" (Rand),
101
Comte, Auguste, 292
concept(s), 31, 41-42, 47-48, 57, 66, 77-78, 80, 82, 164, 222, 224, 234, 238, 245-247, 250-251, 260, 273-274; *see also* universals
concept formation, 56-57, 242-246
conception, 208
conceptual common denominator, 63, 69, 91
concretes, 71, 243; *see also* existents, things
conditioning, 141
conduct, 252
conflict of interests, 308
confusion, 233
congregationalism, 329
Congressional law, 183-184
conjecture, science as, 54, 251, 345
Conjectures and Refutations (Popper), 54, 122
conscience, 307, 328-329
consciousness, 21, 30, 37, 39, 45, 61, 83-84, 90-93, 101, 121, 123, 131, 172, 236-238, 241, 250, 262
consent, 185
consent of the governed, 193-194, 200, 329, 348
"Conservatism: An Obituary" (Rand), 195
conservatives, 10, 16, 198
consistency, 222
conspiracy, 187
constitutionalism, 336
Constitutionalism and

Index

Resistance in the Sixteenth Century (Franklin, ed.), 183
constructs, 48, 52
Contemporary Evangelical Thought (Henry, ed.), 77
contract, 187, 201, 328-329
contradictions, 19, 349
Contribution to the Critique of Hegel's Philosophy of Right (Marx), 133
convenience, 321
"Conversations with Ayn Rand," 5
converse, fallacy of, 188
Corinth, 312
Corinthians, 283
1 Corinthians 7:40, 283; 11:7, 286; 13:12, 125; 15:15-18, 284
corn, 265
correspondence, 41, 250, 261-262
corroboration, 54
corruption, 323-324
courts, 198
covetousness, 253, 325
creation, 116, 135, 141, 164, 278-279, 286, 305, 324, 326, 330
creativeness, 136
crime, 187-189, 200, 325, 348
Critique of Practical Reason (Kant), 133, 137, 169
Crockett, Davy, xvii; *Works:* "Not Yours to Give," xvii
crows, 66-68
crucifixion, 317
cruelty, 311
Crusoe, Robinson, 186

Cur Deus Homo (Anselm), 288
customs, 327
Cyrenaics, 159

Danagger, Ken, 125
Daniel 2, 310
Danneskjold, Ragnar, 124
Darwin, Charles, 224, 230; *Works: The Origin of Species,* 224, 230
data, 51, 76, 80, 238, 249, 259
David, King, 284, 287, 344
Davis, R. W., 183; *Works: The Origins of Modern Freedom in the West,* 183
Dawn, The (Nietzsche), 98
De Anima (Aristotle), 263
de Coulanges, Fustel, 319; *Works: The Ancient City,* 319
De Magistro (Augustine), 73
death, 147, 156, 319-322
debate, 13
deception, 239
Deciphering the Senses (Rivlin and Gravelle), 38
Declaration of the Rights of Man, 203
deduction, 208, 235, 339-340, 349
defense, 169
definition(s), 39, 53, 56-59, 72-75, 78-81, 94, 127, 145-147, 164, 222, 230, 234, 248-251
deism, 115, 203
demiurge, 22, 278
democracy, 311
Democritus, 236
demons, 125
demonstration, 111, 292; *see*

also proof
Demosthenes, 318
Den Uyl, Douglas, 150, 155-156; *Works:* "Nozick on the Randian Argument," 155; *The Philosophic Thought of Ayn Rand,* 150
Department of Education, 348
depravity, 194, 253; *see also* total depravity
Descartes, René, 13-14, 87, 109, 120, 217, 257, 261
desires, 171
detention, 187
determinism, 96, 99, 102, 122, 139, 161, 165-172, 238
Deus, 288
Deus sive natura, 285
devil, 304
Dewey, John, 25, 236
Dialectical Materialism (Wette), 141
Dialectics of Nature (Engels), 130
diaphanous perception, 262-263, 276
diet, 169
Dietzgen, 118
Difference Between the Nature Philosophy of Democritus and the Nature Philosophy of Empiricus, The (Marx), 135
differentiation, 39, 44, 86, 164, 246, 248
digestion, 264
distortion, 239, 242
divine law, 84, 183, 288, 336; *see also* law of God, Ten Commandments

division of power, 193
divorce, 225, 327
doctrine, 13
Dodgson, Luttwidge, 274
dogmatism, 335
dogs, 148
Dooyeweerd, Herman, 11, 13, 16, 18; *Works: A New Critique of Theoretical Thought,* 16; *In the Twilight of Western Thought,* 11, 13
double jeopardy, 348
dreams, 34, 87, 89, 233, 261, 291, 311
drives, 153
drugs, 185
due process, 348
duress, 255
duty, 20, 302-309

Early Ayn Rand, The (Rand), 3, 5-6
Early Writings, The (Marx), 17, 37, 134-135
Earth, xiv, xvi, 48-49, 292-293
Ebola virus, 148
Eck, John, 302
eclipse, 298
economics, 254
Economics (pseudo-Aristotle), 318
education, 141, 218-219, 312, 319, 348
egoism, xiii, 154, 306-308
Egypt, 211
Einstein, Albert, 53, 90, 345
Eire, Carlos M. N., 183; *Works: War Against the Idols,* 183
election, 97, 123

element, 299
elimination, 207
Ellis, Albert, 20
Ellis, Edward, xvii; *Works:* "Not
  Yours To Give," xvii
Elohim, 288
eloquence, 154
embezzlement, 187
embryo, 206, 208, 213
*Emergence, of Liberty in the
  Modern World, The* (Kelley),
  183
emotion(s), 28, 127, 152, 158,
  171, 206, 343; *see also*
  feelings
empiricism, xiii, 24, 29-35, 218-
  219, 223, 243, 260, 273, 337,
  340, 342
employers, 192
encounter(s), 78, 91
encyclicals, 1
energy, 37, 43, 120, 123, 257-
  259, 269-270
Engels, Friedrich, 17, 36, 81,
  117, 130, 137, 141, 203, 219-
  221; *Works: Anti-Dühring,*
  81; *Dialectics of Nature,* 130;
  The German Ideology, 219;
  Marx and Engels on Religion,
  130, 133, 135, 137, 221;
  *Social-ism: Utopian and
  Scientific,* 17, 117, 203, 220-
  221
engineering, 54
England, 328
enlightenment, 311
Enlightenment, 11, 114-115, 195
*Enquiry Concerning Human
  Understanding, An* (Hume),

88
entertainment, 317
entity/entities, 38, 43-45, 58-59,
  64-66, 73, 92, 103, 160, 275
environmentalism, 134, 224,
  330-331
Ephesians 1:8, 279
epistemology, xiii, 5, 10, 13-14,
  18, 21-23, 25-107, 142, 148,
  156-157, 160, 165, 180, 214,
  216, 219, 241, 243, 246, 254-
  255, 266, 281, 336-342, 349
equal rights, 331
equality, 62
equity, 327
equivocation, 12
error, 255, 295
Eschinus, 318
Essays on Ethics and Politics
  (Clark), 20
essence(s), 21, 73, 78-81, 93,
  163
Essence of Christianity
  (Feuerbach), 123, 125, 127-
  128
ethics, xiii, 9, 19, 22-23, 26,
  106, 115, 119-120, 123, 127-
  128, 132, 139, 142, 144-179,
  180-181, 216, 219, 225, 231,
  235-236, 303, 320, 336, 346-
  347, 349
"Ethics of Abortion, The"
  (Clark), 209
"Ethics of Emergencies, The"
  (Rand), 178
eugenics, 141
Europe, 329
euthanasia, 211-212
evaluation, 156-157, 161

Eve, 135-136
evidence, 74, 260, 290-292
Evidence of the Senses, The
(Kelley), 37, 38, 255-276
evidentialism, 335, 337
evil, 147, 151, 156, 158, 161,
172, 175-177, 189, 225
evil eye, 311
evolution, 20, 130, 230
exaltation, 128
"Examination Study Guide to the
Ethics of Objectivism, An"
(Peikoff), 7
execution, 192; *see also* capital
punishment
existence, 21, 44, 64, 76, 83-84,
87-88, 90-93, 118-120, 123,
131, 149, 163, 233-235, 237;
see also being
*Existence and Attributes of God,
The* (Charnock), 279
Existentialism, 11, 129, 163
existents, 57, 63, 73, 88, 92; *see
also* individuals, things
Exodus 33:19, 124
experience, 32, 35, 47, 78, 83,
88, 104, 170, 218, 221, 239,
246, 248, 274, 288, 291, 339
experimentation, 49-52, 291-294
exposure, of infants, 317, 319
extension, 270
extortion, 210
extrasensory perception, 36
"Extremism: or the Art of
Smearing" (Rand), 100

fact(s), 48, 52, 77, 81-82, 92, 98,
170, 194, 208, 234, 250, 257,
261, 263, 265-266, 268-269,
291-293, 296
failure, 119
faith, xii, 1, 8, 14, 16, 22, 28-29,
33, 40, 108-109, 157, 179,
222, 230, 303, 306, 336, 339,
343-344
"Faith and Force" (Rand), 14-16,
179
Faith and Freedom (Hart), 183
faking reality, 119, 191, 252
Fall, 136
fallacy, argument from
intimidation, 111; asserting
the consequent, 55-56, 221,
288, 298, 344-345; converse,
188; frozen abstraction, 9;
genetic, 98, 162; naturalistic,
347; pathetic, 118, 158; self-
exclusion, 97; stolen concept,
33, 130, 157, 162, 196-197,
203
family, 208, 327
fascism, 194
Faust (Goethe), 289
fear, 111, 307
federalism, 193
feeling(s), 20, 28-29, 32, 91, 96,
170-171, 195
Feigl, Herbert, 12; *Works:
Logical Empiricism,* 13
festivals, 312
Feuerbach, Ludwig, 36-37, 116,
123, 125, 127-128, 131, 140-
141, 152-153; *Works: Essence
of Christianity,* 123, 125, 127-
128; *Lectures on the Essence
of Religion,* 116-117, 131,
141, 153
fiction, xiv

fideism, 137
figure, 64-65, 69
Filmer, Robert, 194
fines, 192, 347
Finley, M. I., 311, 316; *Works:*
    Ancient History, 311
first cause, 117-118, 139-140,
    162-163
Flaminius, 317
flavor(s), 269
Fletcher, Joseph, 253
focus, 98, 162, 167, 170
For the New Intellectual (Rand),
    6-7, 16, 21, 41, 66, 89, 105,
    111, 201
force, 14-17, 185, 187-188, 195,
    197, 202, 204, 311, 348;
    initiation of, 186-193; *see
    also* coercion
forces, xii, 258
forfeiture, 173, 203-205
form(s), platonic, peikoffian, and
    kellian, 22, 46, 63, 83-84,
    237, 241, 263, 267, 269-270,
    276
Fountainhead, The (Rand), xi,
    11, 23, 127, 152
Françon, Dominique, 152
Franklin, Benjamin, 145; *Works:*
    Autobiography, 145
Franklin, Julius, 185; *Works:*
    *Constitutionalism and
    Resistance in the Sixteenth
    Century,* 185
fraud, 187, 210
free will, 98-102, 115, 138, 165-
    172, 195
freedom, 10, 24, 133, 139-140,
    153, 180-214, 311; of press,

329; of speech, 329
French Confession of 1559, 285
French Revolution, 17, 203
frozen abstraction, fallacy of, 9
Führer, 229
fundamentalism, 283

Gaea, 134, 136
gain, 190
Galatians 3:28, 326
Galileo, 297
Gall, John, 152
Galt, John, xii, xiv, 13, 49, 52,
    112-113, 124-126, 136, 147,
    152, 154-155, 168, 177
Galt's Gulch, 124, 199
gambling, 201
Gay Science, The (Nietzsche),
    331
Geisler, Norman, 337
Genealogy of Morals, The
    (Nietzsche), 329-330
Genesis, 134; 1:1, 340; 5:1, 286;
    9:6, 286
genetic fallacy, 98, 162
genius, ix
Genteel Tradition At Bay, The
    (Santayana), 305
Gentiles, 325
geometry, 249, 337
German Ideology, The (Marx),
    219
germs, 220
ghosts, 311
gladiatorial contests, 311, 317
goals, 146, 150, 159, 174
God, 1, 22, 49, 85-87, 89, 98,
    106, 109, 110-111, 113, 116,
    118, 121, 124, 132, 136, 140-

142, 144, 163-164, 169, 179, 183, 194, 203, 217-221, 224, 226, 230, 233, 236-237, 253, 277-289, 291-292, 304-306, 310, 313, 326, 330, 338, 341-342, 346; attributes of, 118; God the Father, 304, 324, 326; God the Holy Spirit, 229, 283, 296, 309, 326; law of, 219; God the Son, 287, 305, 326; *see also* Jesus Christ
God's Hammer: The Bible and Its Critics (Clark), 97, 178
godfather, 323
gods, 125, 134-135, 137, 140, 143, 152, 211, 312, 314, 316, 330
Goering, Herman, 229
Goethe, Johann Wolfgang von, 289; *Works: Faust,* 289
Gomorrah, 127
good, 147, 151, 156, 158, 161, 172, 175-177, 225, 231, 252, 331; *see also* bad, evil
government, xiii, 19, 180-214, 219, 224, 322-324
grace, 328, 338
grants, 190
Gravelle, Karen, 38; *Works: Deciphering the Senses,* 38
gravity, 51
greatest happiness principle, 321
Greece, 211-212, 310-331
greed, 311
Greek, 298
Green, T. H., 61; *Works: Introduction to Hume,* 61
Ground of Being, 22

guesses, 54, 345
guilt, 111

habeas corpus, 329
Haeckel, Ernst, 230
hallucination(s), 42, 87, 233, 240, 272-273
Hampden, John, 329
Hannibalic Wars, 316
happiness, 331
"Happy Birthday," 258
Hart, Benjamin, 183; *Works: Faith and Freedom,* 183
Hasebroek, 319; *Works: Trade, and Politics in Ancient Greece,* 319
hatred, 62
health, 146
health care, 348
heat, 269
Heaven, xii, 48, 125, 278, 302, 304-305, 308, 324, 342
Hebrews, 302, 339; 1:3, 286; 2:6-8, 286; 12:2, 307
hedonism, 19, 157, 159, 174, 216, 225
Hegel, G. W. F., 4, 12-14, 64, 78, 82-83, 86-87, 91-92, 109, 120, 122, 217, 231, 236
Heisenberg, Werner, 90, 297
Hell, 304-305, 308
Henry, Carl F. H., 77, 332; *Works: Contemporary Evangelical Thought,* 77
Henry, Patrick, 187
hermeneutics, 340
Herod the Great, King, 319
heroin, 125
heroism, ix

heterosexuality, 225
hierarchies, 20
Hinduism, 272
historicism, 11
historiography, 219
history, xiv, 134, 258, 287-288,
341
History of Private Life, A, 322
History of European Morals, A
(Lecky), 312, 320
Hitler, Adolf, 177, 229
Hobbes, Thomas, 13-14, 236
Holbach, Baron, 173
holidays, 312
Hollywood, 11
Holy Spirit, 229, 326; *see also*
God
homicide, 137
homosexuality, 20, 225, 312
honesty, 307
Hospers, John, 5, 230
housing, 346, 348
Hugo, Victor, 289
human action, 254
humanism, 8-9, 17, 135-137
humanitarianism, 178
Hume, David, 12-14, 61, 88,
102-103, 105, 109, 115, 144-
146, 216, 221, 259, 262, 285,
338, 347; *Works: An Enquiry
Concerning Human
Understanding,* 88; *A Treatise
of Human Nature,* 144
Huxley, T. H., 290-292

ideals, 305
Ideas/Idealism, xi-xii, xiv, 121,
224, 237, 246, 259-260, 265,
269, 278, 326

Ideas of Ayn Rand, The (Merrill),
127, 178
identity/identities, 44-45, 47, 83-
84, 90-93
idiots, 209
idleness, 318, 325
idolatry, 224, 311-312, 324
ignorance, 111, 195, 340
illusions, 233, 261
image(s)/imagery, 36, 46, 88,
105, 162, 223, 237, 239, 259,
272, 312, 325
image of God, 140, 142, 286,
318
imbeciles, 209
immorality, of God, 111
immortality, 313, 331
immutability, 121
imperative mood, 347
implicit concepts, 42, 44-45, 76-
77, 243-244
implicit knowledge, 77
implicit propositions, 244
imprisonment, 192, 347
imputed rights, 347
incentives, 171
indicative mood, 347
individual/individualism, 10,
179, 182, 194, 198, 216, 224,
326, 328-329
individuals, 44-45, 57, 64; *see
also* existents, things
individuation, 46
induction, 55-56, 208, 235, 298,
338, 344-345
Industrial Revolution, 208
industry, 208
infallibility, 255-256; of brain,
41; of senses, 41-42, 78

infanticide, 209, 211-212, 319-321
infants, 209
inference, 272, 277
infinite regress, 116
information, 256
injunction, 187
innate ideas, 76, 226, 244, 246
innate knowledge, 168
innocence, 253
Innocent III, pope, 283
inquisition, 314
inspiration, 1, 283-284
instinct, 29, 168
Institute for Objectivist Studies, 7
Institutes of the Christian Religion (Calvin), 302
insurance, 201
integration, 39, 44, 86, 121, 164, 167, 248, 250, 261
integrity, 253
intellect, 10, 306
intellection, 101
"Intellectual Bankruptcy of Our Age, The" (Rand), 10
intellectualism, 280, 335
intelligence, 229-230
Interaction of Law and Religion, The (Berman), 327
Internal Revenue Service, 348
Introduction to Christian Philosophy, An (Clark), 194, 203
Introduction to Hume (Green), 61
Introduction to Objectivist Epistemology (Rand), 6-7, 21, 26, 30-31, 33-34, 38-107, 123, 132, 157, 160, 162, 164,

197, 234, 254, 264
introspection, 67, 167, 237
intuition, 29
invention(s), 48, 52, 57
irrationalism, xvi, 287, 335
irrationality, 172, 289
is/ought, 144-145, 148, 196, 216, 347
Isaac, 289, 346
Isaiah 40, 347
Israel, xii, 194, 284, 287, 344

Jacob, 289
James, 343; 3:9, 286
James, William, 46; *Works: Principles of Psychology,* 46
Jefferson, Thomas, 194
Jerusalem, 317
Jesus Christ, xii, 24, 84, 124-126, 179, 204, 287, 302, 304, 307-331, 336, 341, 344, 349; *see also* God
Jews, xii, 17, 20, 177, 346
Johannine Logos, The (Clark), 344
John, Gospel of, 133, 246, 280, 282, 286, 289, 339; 1:1, 181, 289; 5:17, 324; 10:24-29, 124; 10:30, 324; 17, 124; 17:3, 277; 18:36, 324
1 John, 306; 5:6, 277
John Paul, pope, xv
joy, 136
Judaism, xii, 20
judaizers, 346
Judas, 308, 319
Judea, 309, 329
judgment, 271-275, 292
Judgment Day (Branden), 5

Index

Jupiter, 297-298
jury, 329
justice, 34, 43, 62, 113, 180-214, 245, 311, 322, 347, 349
justification, 325, 344

Kant, Immanuel, 4, 13-14, 20, 46, 115, 120, 131-133, 139, 168-170, 177-179, 211, 231, 238, 242, 263-264, 267, 300-308, 338; *Works: Critique of Practical Reason,* 133, 137, 139, 169; *Political Writings,* 169; *Religion Within the Limits of Pure Reason,* 133
"Kant and Old Testament Ethics" (Clark), 20
Kelley, David, xii, 4, 7, 37-38, 255-276; *Works: The Evidence of the Senses,* 255-276
Kelley, Douglas, 183; *Works: The Emergence of Liberty in the Modern World,* 183
Kensico Cemetery, 11
kidnappers, 148
Kierkegaard, Sören, 28
King, J. Charles, 150; *Works:* "Life and the Theory of Value: The Randian Argument Reconsidered," 150
King, Martin Luther, xv, I
Klingons, 233
knowing how, 256
knowledge, 3, 8, 21, 26, 31, 34-35, 48, 53, 61, 96, 100, 102, 160, 164, 216, 220, 233, 254, 263, 267, 275, 291-292, 338, 340-341, 344
Koran, 1

Kuhn, Thomas, 80; *Works: The Structure of Scientific Revolutions,* 80
kulaks, 177

L'homme machine (Lamettrie), 15
labor, 134, 136, 318
Lamettrie, 15; *Works: L'homme machine,* 15
Lane, Eugene N., 315; *Works: Paganism and Christianity,* 315
language, 59, 219, 243, 287-288
LaPlace, Marquis de, 53
Laslett, Peter, 205
law(s), 100, 194, 199, 311, 322-324, 328; of causality, 102-103; of contradiction, 19, 99, 102, 104, 226, 234, 281-282, 284-285, 287-288, 340; of excluded middle, 104; of God, 115, 204, 346; of gravity, 235, 295-296, 298-299; of identity, 102, 104, 183-184, 189, 288; of nature, 194, 197, 295, 320-321; of pendulum, 298; of physics, 51, 291, 297; of thought, 104
Law and the Prophets, The, 303, 340
Law and Revolution (Berman), 183
lawlessness, 181
Laws (Plato), 316
laziness, xiii
Lecky, W. E. H., 312-313, 320; *Works: A History of European Morals,* 312, 320

lectures, 3, 7
*Lectures on the Essence of
Religion* (Feuerbach), 116-
117, 131, 141, 153
length, 50, 60, 63, 243, 293-296
Lenin, V. I., 17, 36-37, 81, 85-
86, 118, 120, 137-138, 141;
*Works: Materialism and
Empirio-criticism,* 17, 36-37,
81, 85, 118, 120, 137-138, 141
Lessing, 217
"Letter from Birmingham Jail"
(King), 1
Letters of Ayn Rand, xi-xii, xv-
xvi, 6, 78, 152, 179, 230
Lewis, C. S., 142; *Works: The
Abolition of Man,* 142
libel, 187
liberals, 10, 16
Libertarian Review, 3
liberty, 100, 192, 319, 336, 347,
349; *see also* freedom
Liberty, 5
licentiousness, 321
life, 75, 120, 147, 153, 160, 319-
322, 347
"Life and Society in Classical
Greece" (Murray), 316
"Life and the Theory of Value:
The Randian Argument
Reconsidered" (King), 150
Lilburne, John, 329
limbo, 326
Lincoln, Abraham, 325
litigation, 188
Livy, 311, 315
Locke, John, 31, 35, 109, 173,
193-194, 205, 258-259, 340;
Works: Treatise of Civil

Government, 174, 205
locomotion, 206
logic, xiii-xiv, 10, 12, 23, 53, 67,
98-100, 104, 109, 118, 171,
173, 186, 214, 219, 221, 225-
226, 246, 260-261, 265, 277-
289, 299, 310, 338-340
Logic (Sigwart), 62
"Logic and Mysticism"
(Branden), 3
Logical Empiricism (Feigl), 13
logical positivism, 73
Logos, 246, 280, 289, 310
Lord's Day, 325
Lord's Prayer, 133
Los Angeles Times, 2
lottery, 201; *see also* gambling
love, 34, 43, 208
Lugol, 298
Luther, Martin, 109, 183, 230,
302, 328-329, 332
Lycurgus, 321
lying, 252, 325

Machen, J. Gresham, 333
machines, 119
MacMullen, Ramsay, 315;
*Works: Paganism and
Christianity,* 315
Madison, James, 183
Magna Carta, 204
malice, 195
man, ix, 8, 15, 26, 60, 70, 74-75,
94, 102, 113, 123, 130-133,
135, 138-142, 161, 163, 168,
172-176, 186, 204-209, 224,
251-254, 278, 281, 286-287
mannishness of man, 205-209
"Man's Rights" (Rand), 181

manumission, 327
marriage, 225, 327
Marx, Karl, xii, 17, 36-37, 117,
133-135, 199, 218-219, 229,
236, 316; *Works: The
Communist Manifesto,* 117;
*Contribution to the Critique
of Hegel's Philosophy of
Right,* 133; *The Difference
between the Nature,
Philosophy of Democritus and
the Nature Philosophy of
Empiricus,* 135; *Early
Writings,* 17, 37, 134-135;
The German Ideology, 219;
Marx and Engels on Religion,
130, 133, 135, 137, 221;
Selected Correspondence, 199
Marxism, 10, 17
materialism, 37, 86, 89, 116-117,
174, 203, 218, 233, 236-237,
257, 283
*Materialism and Empirio-
Criticism* (Lenin), 17, 36-37,
81, 85, 118, 137-138, 141
mathematics, 47, 50, 53, 242, 289
matter, ix, 19, 43, 85-86, 89-90,
117-121, 123, 137-138, 140,
147, 169, 216, 219, 233, 258,
344, 346
Matthew, 304; 5-7, 325; 11:27,
124; 22:20, 325; 22:21, 325;
23, 342; 25:21, 23, 126;
25:40-42, 125; 28:19-20, 326
mean, 50-51, 295
meaning, 73, 79-80, 89
measurement, 47-52, 244-245,
294
mechanism, 29-30, 61, 101, 122-
123, 134, 140, 169, 174, 257
median, 50, 295
Meditations (Aurelius), 173
memory, 46, 195, 271
"Mental Health versus
Mysticism and Self-sacrifice"
(Branden), 8
Merrill, Ronald E., 27, 127, 209;
*Works: The Ideas of Ayn
Rand,* 27, 127, 178
Messiah, xii, 24, 125-126, 231
meta-ethics, 146, 154
metaphysics, xiii, 14, 19, 21-23,
26, 37, 73, 81, 83, 87, 97,
106, 115, 123, 180-214, 216,
241, 336, 342-346, 349
"Metaphysics in Marble"
(Sures), 211
method, 21, 26
Middle Ages, 292-293, 328
milk fever, 298
mind(s), 39, 46, 56, 62, 77, 87,
90, 104-105, 137, 212, 263,
266, 268-269
mind-body dichotomy, 98
miracles, 20
mirages, 89
Mises, Ludwig von, 194, 254
misprision, 187
misrepresentation, 187
mistakes, 215
MIT, 127
mode, 50, 295
Modern Thinkers (Singer), 300
modernism, 305, 334
molecules, 45
monarchy, 230
monogamy, 225
monopoly, 193, 197, 202

monotheism, 324
moral law, 112, 169, 182, 236
morality, 100, 113, 131, 136,
 160, 229
Morgan, Edmund S., 183;
 *Works: Puritan Political
 Ideas,* 183
morons, 209
mortality, xvi
Moses, 282-283
Mother Teresa, xv
motion(s), 102
motives, 171
Mt. Blanc, 45
Mount Olympus, 45
Mount Sinai, 303
Mulligan, Midas, 200
murder, 106, 148, 178, 187, 209,
 236, 253, 325, 346
Murray, Oswyn, 211-212, 316;
 Works: "Life and Society in
 Classical Greece," 212, 316
music, 288
mutability, 55
"My Thirty Years with Ayn
 Rand" (Peikoff), 20-21
mysticism/mystics, 9, 11, 13-15,
 33, 36-37, 41, 85, 89, 106,
 109, 111, 127-128, 138, 210-
 211, 248, 305
Mysticism and Logic (Russell), x
myths, 220

Nash, Ronald, 332
Nathaniel Branden Institute, 7
National Socialism, 210, 224,
 229-231
natura, 285
natural law(s), 169, 235-236,

238-239, 247, 296, 346, 348
natural rights, 181, 346-347
natural selection, 122
naturalism, 140, 151; *see also*
 atheism
naturalistic fallacy, 347
nature, 37, 49, 51, 55, 86, 104,
 113, 116, 119-122, 134-135,
 137-139, 141-142, 149, 164,
 168-169, 173, 178, 195, 205-
 206, 236, 279, 328, 330
"Nature of Government, The"
 (Rand), 181, 187
"Nature of Reason, The"
 (Branden), 3
Nature of Thought, The
 (Blanshard), 8, 47, 61, 64-65,
 76
navigation, 54
Nebuchadnezzar, 310
necessity, 99-100
need(s), 146, 149, 153, 196, 216,
 254
neighbors, 195
neo-evangelicalism, 334
Nero, 318
nervous system, 258-259, 268
*New Critique of Theoretical
 Thought, A* (Dooyeweerd), 16
*New Left: The Anti-Industrial
 Revolution, The* (Rand), 6, 23,
 29, 40, 61, 101, 119, 164, 204
New Testament, 1, 280, 304
Newton, Isaac, 43, 345
Nietzsche, Friedrich, 6, 14, 98,
 104, 108, 111-112, 131, 147,
 179, 327, 329-331; *Works:
 The Antichrist,* 330-331;
 Beyond Good and Evil, 6, 14,

108, 131, 147; *The Dawn,* 98;
The Gay Science, 331; *The
Genealogy of Morals,* 329-
331; *Twilight of the Idols,* 179
Night of January 16 (Rand), 6
nihilism, 218
1984 (Orwell), 214
Ninth Symphony (Beethoven),
258
nominalism, 243
non-propositional truth, 91
"Not Yours to Give" (Crockett),
xvii
nothing, 64, 122
noumenal, 170
noumenon, 139
"Nozick on the Randian
Argument" (den Uyl and
Rasmussen), 155
numbers, 67

O'Connor, Charles Francis, 11,
84
O'Hair, Madalyn Murray, 109
O'Neill, William F., 145; *Works:
With Charity Toward None,*
145
oath (Objectivist), 154
objective reality, 26, 57, 87, 89-
90, 105-106, 118-120, 131,
137-138, 208, 233, 240-242,
262, 264, 344
*Objectivism: The Philosophy of
Ayn Rand* (Peikoff), 3, 7, 20,
138
Objectivist, The, 1-2, 7-8, 46, 66,
68, 98, 100, 102-103, 105,
114, 122, 125, 127, 136, 139,
142, 166, 170-172, 179, 191,

199, 206, 208, 211, 214
"Objectivist Ethics, The"
(Rand), 145, 149
Objectivist Forum, The, 207
"Objectivist Meta-ethics, The"
(Peikoff), 3
Objectivist Newsletter, The, 2,
15, 17, 26-29, 33, 35, 40, 96-
97, 106, 108-109, 115, 117,
121, 139-140, 157-159, 162-
163, 166-167, 170, 173, 216,
220, 263
objectivity, 52
observation(s), 44, 51, 78, 104,
233, 249-250, 288, 291, 295,
339, 345
occultism, 37
odor(s), 269
Old Testament, 1, 126, 278, 300-
308, 346
omens, 311
Ominous Parallels, The
(Peikoff), 214, 229-231, 236
omnipresence, 342
omniscience, 251, 278-279, 342
one, 245
open-ended concepts, 74-76, 81,
94-95
opinion, 53, 251, 256, 340
oracles, 316
order of being, 26
order of knowing, 27
ordination, 194
Origin of Species, The (Darwin),
224, 230
original sin, 113-115, 136, 220
*Origins of Modern Freedom in
the West, The* (Davis), 183
Orthodox Presbyterian Church,

333-334

Orwell, George, 214; *Works: 1984,* 214

ostensive definition, 72-73, 88-89, 234, 249

other minds, 84

ought/is, 144-145, 148, 196, 216, 347

Oxford English Dictionary, 128

Oxford History of the Classical World, 212, 316

paganism, 142, 231, 309-331

Paganism and Christianity (MacMullen and Lane), 315

pain, 119, 156-159

pantheism, 134, 224

parents, 193, 206, 325

parks, 348

Parmenides, 64, 78, 86-87, 217

Parmenides (Plato), 224

Parousia, 124

Pascal, Blaise, 56, 215, 225; *Works: Pensées,* 215

Passion of Ayn Rand, The (Branden), x, 26, 42

pathetic fallacy, 118, 158

patria potestas, 319, 327

Paul, 164, 283, 301, 304, 306, 311, 341, 343, 348

Paul, Ron, 231

Paulus, Julius, 313

Pax Romana, 311, 316-317

peace, 180-214, 311

Pearson, Karl, 291-292

Peikoff, Leonard, xvii, 1, 2, 4-5, 7, 21, 32, 38, 43, 70, 72-73, 82, 95, 98, 101, 118-119, 129, 157, 159, 210-211, 214, 255,

264; *Works:* "The Analytic-Synthetic Dichotomy," 39, 70, 72, 95, 98; "My Thirty Years with Ayn Rand," 20-21; *Objectivism,* 82; *The Ominous Parallels,* 214, 229-231; *Philosophy of Objectivism,* 73, 101

Pelagius, 176, 195

Penn, William, 329

Pensées (Pascal), 215

Pentecost, 304

percept(s)/perception, 27, 31, 34-35, 39, 45-46, 56, 58, 67, 77, 82, 88, 91, 160, 220-222, 234-235, 238-242, 245, 254, 257-259, 261, 264-266, 269-272, 274-276, 293, 342

perfection, 253

periodic table, 299

perjury, 187

persecution, 313

Persian Wars, 316

person(s), 19, 102, 207, 224, 344

Personalist, The, 155

personality, 281

perspective, 266

perspicuity, 284

persuasion, 15, 326

Peter, 304, 342-343

Pharisees, 231, 302-304

phenomenal, 170

phenomenalism, 35, 260

phenomenon, 139

Philip of Macedon, 316

Philippians 2:5, 283

Philo, 278, 280-281

philosophers, 6

Philosophic Thought of Ayn

Rand, The (den Uyl and Rasmussen), 150
philosophy, xv, 9, 22, 132, 217-219, 236, 328, 337, 341
Philosophy of the Enlightenment, The (Cassirer), 11-12, 15, 115
Philosophy of Gordon H. Clark, The (Clark), 35, 87, 92
Philosophy of Objectivism (Peikoff), 73, 101, 119
Philosophy of Science and Belief in God, The (Clark), 52, 221
Philosophy: Who Needs It? (Rand), 3-4, 6, 67, 207
physical objects, 263, 265, 267, 269, 271
physics, 43, 49-50, 52, 122, 142, 241
Physics (Aristotle), 117
physiology, 266, 268
pietists, 286
pilgrimages, 312
piracy, 311
plants, 159, 161, 165, 213
Plato, xvii, 4, 13-14, 53, 78-80, 83, 91, 93-94, 194, 211, 217, 224, 231, 236, 238, 251-252, 256-257, 278, 298, 316-317, 320-321, 345; *Works: Parmenides,* 224; *Republic, 298*
pleasure, 119, 156-159, 201
Pliny the Younger, 313-315
Plotinus, 284
Plutarch, 320
polio, 148
Political Sermons of the American Founding Era (Sandoz), 183

Political Thought of Sir Robert Filmer, The (Robbins), 194
Political Writings (Kant), 169
politics, 19, 22, 26, 106, 132, 173-174, 178, 180-214, 216, 336, 343, 348-349
Politics (Aristotle), 208
Pollo, Vedus, 317
Pollock, Channing, xii
pollution, 187
polygamy, 225
polytheism, 142, 312, 324
pontifex maximus, 315, 325
Pontus, 313
pope, 229, 283
Popper, Karl, 52-54, 122, 256-257, 345; *Works: Conjectures and Refutations,* 54, 122; *Popper Selections,* 53; "The Problem of Demarcation," 53; "Two Kinds of Definitions," 53
pork, 346
Porphyry, 326
Posidonius, 318
post hoc ergo propter hoc, 103
potentiality/actuality, 206
poverty, 318, 320
power, 153
pragmatism, 220
prayers, 312
predestination, xii, 124, 168; *see also* determinism
prediction, 291, 298, 345
prejudice, 195
Presbyterian Church of America, 333
presupposition(s), 8, 10, 13, 16, 18-19, 35, 180, 203, 282, 285,

297, 335; *see also* axioms
pride, 27
primacy, of consciousness, 85,
120; of existence, 85-86, 109,
120; of will, 130, 132
Prime Mover, 22
principles, 225, 233, 252
Principles of Psychology
(James), 46
probability, 53-54
"Problem of Demarcation, The"
(Popper), 53
production, 202
profanity, 325
profit, 20, 145, 190
Prometheus, 134-136
Prometheus Bound (Aeschylus),
135
proof, 53, 84, 109, 234-235, 338;
for God, 115-119
propaganda, 141
proper names, 165
property, xiii, 191-192, 319, 322,
328-329, 346-348
prophets, 288, 300, 308
proposition(s), 31, 47, 49, 77-78,
82, 92, 144, 151, 224, 260,
271-272, 274, 280, 288, 290,
341, 344, 349
prose, 337
prosperity, 311
prostitution, 146, 312, 320
Protagoras, 131, 236, 241, 266
Protestantism, 20, 284, 337
Psalm 8, 286; 24, 330; 31:5, 277;
33:12, 124; 147:5, 279
psychiatry, 114, 312
psychoanalysis, 114
psychology, 9, 98, 114, 141, 219,

311-312
Psychology of Self-Esteem, The
(Branden), 9
Punic Wars, 316
punishment, 106, 148, 187, 189,
192-193, 200, 204, 224, 302-
303, 314, 348
purgatory, 326
Puritan Political Ideas
(Morgan), 183
Puritans, 124, 329
purpose, xiii

qualia, 269
qualities, 266-270
quarks, 45

Randall, John Herman, 262;
Works: Aristotle, 263
Rand's razor, 95
Ranke, Leopold von, 183
rapists, 148
Rashdall, Hastings, 308
Rasmussen, Douglas, 150, 155-
156: *Works:* "Nozick on the
Randian Argument," 155; *The
Philosophic Thought of Ayn
Rand,* 150
ratiocination, 12
rationalism, 288, 335
rationality, 73, 286
reactions, 271
Readings in Ethics (Clark and
Smith), 300, 333
Reagan, Ronald, xvii
realism, 259-260, 267-268, 271-
272
reality, 14-15, 17, 27, 31, 34-35,
41, 81, 87, 102, 119, 121,

132, 179, 221, 239, 257, 261, 265-266, 275; *see also* objective reality
Rearden, Henry, 124
reason, 6-24, 26-27, 67, 94-97, 108-109, 113, 136, 140, 144, 149, 165, 168, 171-172, 177, 205, 211-212, 220, 230, 277, 281, 286-287, 328
reconstructionists, 346
Red Pawn (Rand), 11
redemption, 307-308, 320
redistribution, 190-192
reduction, 249-250
Reformation, 109, 283, 328
Reformed Presbyterian Church, 334
regulation, 181
Regulative Idea, 22
relationships, 57-58
relativism, 32, 266, 276
relativity, 267, 270
religion(s), 8, 17, 127-128, 229, 291, 306
Religion, Reason and Revelation (Clark), 101, 338
Religion Within the Limits of Pure Reason (Kant), 133
religious freedom, 301, 313, 319, 328-329
Renaissance, 22, 109
representationalism, 222-223, 259, 269
reproduction, 207
Republic (Plato), 298
respiration, 207
responsibility, 115, 166
restitution, 190-192
resurrection, 284, 288, 341, 344

retailing, 318
retaliation, 188, 192-193
retirement, 348
revelation, 29, 97, 109, 133, 142, 203, 217-219, 221, 223, 258, 278, 282, 328, 336-342, 346, 348
Revelation, book of, 81; 22:21, 340
reverence, 128; for life, 214
reward, 303-304, 307
rhetoric, xiv, 23, 152, 154, 171-172, 175, 177, 186, 190, 214
right, 187, 347; to life, 346; *see also* natural rights
rites, 20, 315
Ritschl, Albrecht, 305
Rivlin, Robert, 38; *Works: Deciphering the Senses,* 38
Roark, Howard, xii
robbery, 319
Robbins, John, 194; *Works: The Political Thought of Sir Robert Filmer,* 194
robot, 149-150
Roman Catholicism, 20, 109, 185, 208, 229-230, 337, 343
Roman Empire, 309-331
"Roman Empire, The" (Veyne), 322
Romans 1:17, 279; 1:18, 22; 4:2, 284; 5:13, 284; 8:28-30, 124; 9:10-24, 124; 13, 248
Romantic Manifesto, The (Rand), 6, 38, 40, 61, 132
romanticism, 208
Rome, 212, 309-331
Rosenbaum, Alissa Zinovievna, xvii, 11

Rothbard, Murray, 230-231
Rousseau, Jean-Jacques, 115, 180, 194
Royalists, 203
rules, 48, 52, 199, 252-253
Russell, Bertrand, x, 55-56, 230, 277, 344-345; *Works: Mysticism and Logic,* x; *Why I Am Not a Christian,* 55
Russia, xvii
Russian Orthodoxy, xvi

sacraments, 343
sacred, 128
sacrifice, 179, 230; animal, 312
saints, 124
salvation, 302, 338, 342, 349
1 Samuel, 282; 2:3, 279
sanctification, 286, 343
Sandoz, Ellis, 183; *Works: Political Sermons of the American Founding Era,* 183
Santayana, George, 305; *Works: Genteel Tradition at Bay,* 305; *Winds of Doctrine,* 305
Sapphira, 304
scholarship, 230
scholarships, 190-192
Schuller, Robert, xv
Sciabarra, Chris, xvii, 1, 129; *Works: Ayn Rand The Russian Radical,* xvii, 129, 209
science, 9-10, 17, 25, 36-37, 47-56, 80-81, 89, 122, 142, 208, 219-221, 236, 242, 256-257, 270, 290-299, 340, 344, 346, 349; *see also* asserting the consequent, experimentation, induction, physics, scientific

method, scientific laws
Science, Politics, and Gnosticism (Voegelin), 135, 137
"Science and the Supernatural" (Carlson), 291
"Science and Truth" (Clark), 56
scientific laws, 50, 52, 55, 299, 345
scientific method, 52, 55-56, 290-299, 344
scientific theories, 53
Scotch Confession of 1560, 285
Scripturalism, 223, 335-342
Second Coming of Christ, 124
Selected Correspondence (Marx), 199
Selections from Hellenistic Philosophy (Clark), 333
self, 104-106
self-consistency, 97
self-defense, 187-188, 190, 192-193, 204
self-esteem, 114, 168-169
self-evidence, 235
self-exclusion, fallacy of, 97
self-incrimination, 329
self-interest, 11, 20, 26, 43, 199, 218, 307; *see also* egoism
self-love, 307
self-sacrifice, 152
selfishness, 154, 179, 308
Seneca, 318, 320
sensation(s), 17, 31-32, 36, 39-40, 45-47, 56, 72-77, 82, 85, 88, 105, 109, 137-138, 156, 158, 160-161, 174-175, 201, 216, 219, 222-223, 239, 242, 248, 261, 263, 265-266, 269,

273-274, 337, 342, 344; *see also* sense experience, sense organs, senses
sense experience, 12, 97, 106, 225
sense organs, 238, 240, 242
senses, 8-9, 15, 27-29, 31, 33, 35, 55, 67, 88, 104, 123, 156-157, 161, 165, 218, 257, 263, 270, 295, 341
separation of power, 193
Sermon on the Mount, 303
serpent, 135-136
services, 202
sex, 201, 325
Shakespeare, William, 84
sharp practices, 307
shopkeepers, 318
Shorter Catechism, 277, 346
shrines, 312
sight, 38
signs, 288
Sigwart, 62; *Works: Logic,* 62
similarity, 57, 71, 273
sin, 113, 139, 195, 346
Singer, Edgar A., 300-301; *Works: Modern Thinkers,* 300
situational ethics, 253
skepticism, 11, 19, 31-35, 97, 216-218, 257, 273
Skinner, B. F., 101, 236
slander, 187
slavery, 205, 211, 317-320, 327
sleeping, 258
smallpox, 297
smell, 241
Smith, T. V., 300; *Works: Readings in Ethics,* 300
social contract, 193, 329

social gospel, 348
social justice, 303
social security, 191
socialism, 16, 218
Socialism: Utopian and Scientific (Engels), 17, 117, 203, 220-221
society, 182-183
sociology, 292
Socrates, 313
Sodom, 127
sola Scriptura, 109
solipsism, 84, 87, 93, 223, 344
Solon, 321
sophists, 217
sorites, 284
Sorokin, Pitirim, 292
soteriology, 336, 338, 342-343
soul, 165, 237, 262, 286
soul-body dichotomy, 138
sound, 241, 269
sovereignty, 133, 203, 224
space, 270, 278, 348
Sparta, 318
"Special Divine Revelation as Rational" (Clark), 97, 178
speculation, 256
speech, 49
Spengler, Oswald, 180
spider, 95
Spinoza, Baruch, 12, 35, 109, 285
spirit, 165, 277
Sproul, R. C., 337
square roots, 89, 233
St. Petersburg, 11
Stalin, Joseph, 177
State, 194-195, 198-199, 224
state of nature, 205
statuary, 181, 325

stealing, 146, 253
Stirner, Max, 129; *Works: The Ego and His Own,* 129
stolen concept, fallacy of, 33, 130, 157, 162, 196-197, 203
Structure of Scientific Revolutions, The (Kuhn), 80-81
students, 191
subconscious, 28-29, 101
subjectivism, 15, 89, 137-138, 148, 241, 268, 273
subpoena, 187, 198
success, 119
suffering, 119
suicide, 150-156, 177, 185, 190, 211, 254, 319, 322
supreme being, 118
Sures, Mary Ann, 211; *Works:* "Metaphysics in Marble," 211
survival, 119, 147-148, 150-152, 154, 161, 164, 172-178, 184-185, 212, 230, 252
swans, 95
syllogism, 284, 287
symbolic logic, 277
system, x, xiii, 19, 26, 83, 102, 179, 217-218, 349
System Social (Holbach), 173
Szasz, Thomas, 114

tabula rasa, 28-31, 46, 57, 63, 76, 104, 164, 176, 244, 340
Tacitus, 324
Taggart, Cheryl, 152-155
Taggart, Dagny, 15, 124, 126
tapes, 3
taste, 29
taxes, 190, 198, 200-203, 319, 323

Te Deum, 288
technology, 119
television, 239
temples, 312
Ten Commandments, 112, 182, 324, 328
terrorists, 203
"Textbook of Americanism, A" (Rand), 183, 185-187, 189, 194
Thales to Dewey (Clark), 24-25, 142, 333, 338
theft, 191-192, 325
theism, 90, 290, 336
theology, 22, 108-143, 162, 165, 219, 224, 278, 303, 305, 328, 337
theonomists, 346
theory, 292, 345
Theos, 288
2 Thessalonians 1, 304
things, 57, 103, 160; *see also* existents, individuals
things-in-themselves, 241-242
Thirty-nine Articles, 285
Thomas Aquinas, 12, 16, 28, 31, 117, 259, 337
thought(s), ix, 13, 176, 344
thought thinking thought, 282
Three Types of Religious Philosophy (Clark), 47, 89-90, 221, 223, 226, 338
Tiberius, 315
1 Timothy 1:17, 279
tolerance, 311
Toohey, Ellsworth, 191
Torah, xii
torture, 314-315
total depravity, 113, 115

totalitarianism, 19, 37, 136, 180,
194, 196, 203-205, 211, 214,
231, 325, 348
touch, 38
*Trade and Politics in Ancient
Greece* (Hasebroek), 319
tradition, 339, 341
Trajan, Emperor, 313, 315
Treatise of Civil Government
(Locke), 174, 205
*Treatise Concerning the Prin-
ciples of Human Knowledge,
A* (Berkeley), 43
Treatise of Human Nature, A
(Hume), 144
tree of knowledge, 136
trees, 87
Trinity, 124, 285, 288, 310
Trinity Review, The, 209
truth, xiv, 15, 22, 24, 32, 43, 49,
53, 77-78, 97, 99-100, 102,
148, 218-219, 224, 226, 230-
231, 249-251, 255-256, 271-
272, 277, 279-280, 285, 287,
290-299, 305, 325, 336, 340,
343-346
Tuccille, Jerome, 10; *Works: It
Usually Begins with Ayn
Rand,* 10
Twelve Tables, 313
Twilight of the Idols (Nietzsche),
18, 179
"Two Kinds of Definitions"
(Popper), 53
*Two Treatises of Civil
Government* (Locke), 174

Udall, Walter, 329
unemployment compensation,

191
unicorns, 34, 87, 233
unit(s), 45, 47, 56, 67, 72-73,
92-93, 242, 251
universal(s), 31, 47, 57-58, 62,
65, 70, 72, 93, 236, 243, 251,
253-254
universe, 21-22, 45, 85, 98, 116,
118, 139, 169, 291, 301
University of Pennsylvania, 333
University of Petrograd, 4, 11
Urban, Wilbur Marshall, 8
urge, 29
utilitarianism, 347
utility, 148

vaccination, 297
validation, 235
validity of senses, 255
validity, 272
value judgments, 28, 158, 173-
174, 305
values, 28, 136, 144-179, 184,
189, 329-330
variable error, 51
verification, 221, 298-299
Veyne, Paul, 322-323; *Works:*
"The Roman Empire," 322
vice, 99, 144, 157
violence, 322, 326
virgin birth, 284
virtue(s), 27, 99, 144, 157, 179,
252, 307, 318
Virtue of Selfishness, The
(Rand), 6, 8-9, 15, 27-30, 111,
120, 129, 145, 146-179, 180-
181, 195, 198, 200-202, 213
viruses, 213
Voegelin, Eric, 135; *Works:*

Science, Politics, and Gnosticism, 135, 137
Voice of Reason, The (Peikoff), 6, 21
volition, 101, 113, 170
volitional consciousness, 26, 60-61, 68, 96-102, 130, 158, 161-165, 205, 233, 244
Voltaire, 115

wages, 318
war, 288, 290, 315-317, 331
War Against the Idols (Eire), 183
Warfield, Benjamin, 333
We, the Living (Rand), 11, 23, 152, 209-210
weakness, 311
wealth, 145
welfare state, 190-192, 348
Weltin, E.G., 319; *Works: Athens and Jerusalem,* 319
Westminster Confession, 1, 282, 285, 339, 343
Wette, 141; *Works: Dialectical Materialism,* 141
whim, 29, 206
whim-worshipers, 111
White, William, 334
Who Is Ayn Rand? (Branden), 2, 10, 21, 26, 100, 127, 215
Why I Am Not a Christian (Russell), 55
William James and John Dewey (Clark), 151, 236
Winds of Doctrine (Santayana), 305
wisdom, 246, 310
wish, xvii, 29
witch doctors, 11

With Charity Toward None (O'Neill), 145, 147
women, 20, 205, 212, 317
word(s), 59, 165, 243-244, 288, 344
work, xiii, 184-185, 212, 317-319
workers, 192, 319
works, 324, 343
World Book Encyclopedia, 311
worship, 127-128, 325
wrath, 305
Wright, Frank Lloyd, xii
wrong, 347
Wyclif, John, 325
Wynand, Gail, 152

zoology, 288

THE CRISIS OF OUR TIME

Historians have christened the thirteenth century the Age of Faith and termed the eighteenth century the Age of Reason. The twentieth century has been called many things: the Atomic Age, the Age of Inflation, the Age of the Tyrant, the Age of Aquarius. But it deserves one name more than the others: the Age of Irrationalism. Contemporary secular intellectuals are anti-intellectual. Contemporary philosophers are anti-philosophy. Contemporary theologians are anti-theology.

In past centuries, secular philosophers have generally believed that knowledge is possible to man. Consequently they expended a great deal of thought and effort trying to justify knowledge. In the twentieth century, however, the optimism of the secular philosophers has all but disappeared. They despair of knowledge.

Like their secular counterparts, the great theologians and doctors of the church taught that knowledge is possible to man. Yet the theologians of the twentieth century have repudiated that belief. They also despair of knowledge. This radical skepticism has filtered down from the philosophers and theologians and penetrated our entire culture, from television to music to literature. *The Christian in the twentieth century is confronted with an overwhelming cultural consensus–sometimes stated explicitly but most often implicitly: Man does not and cannot know anything truly.*

What does this have to do with Christianity? Simply this: If man can know nothing truly, man can truly know nothing. We cannot know that the Bible is the Word of God, that Christ died for his people, or that Christ is alive today at the right hand of the Father. Unless knowledge is possible, Christianity is nonsensical, for it claims to be knowledge. What is at stake in the twentieth century is not simply a single doctrine, such as the virgin birth, or the existence of Hell, as important as those doctrines may be, but the whole of Christianity itself. If knowledge is not possible to man, it is worse than silly to argue points of doctrine–it is insane.

The irrationalism of the present age is so thoroughgoing and pervasive that even the Remnant–the segment of the professing church that remains faithful–has accepted much of it, frequently without even being aware of what it was accepting. In some circles this irrationalism has become synonymous with piety and humility, and those who oppose it are denounced as rationalists–as though to be logical were a sin. Our contemporary anti-theologians make a contradiction and call it a Mystery. The faithful ask for truth and are given Paradox. If any balk at swallowing the absurdities of the anti-theologians, they are frequently marked as heretics or schismatics who seek to act independently of God.

There is no greater threat facing the true church of Christ at this moment than the irrationalism that now controls our entire culture. Totalitarianism, guilty of tens of millions of murders–including those of millions of Christians–is to be feared, but not nearly so much as the idea that we do not and cannot know the truth. Hedonism, the popular philosophy of America, is not to be feared so much as the belief that logic–that "mere human logic," to use the religious irrationalists' own phrase–is futile. The attacks on truth, on revelation, on the intellect, and on logic are renewed daily. But note well: The misologists–the haters of logic–use logic to demonstrate the futility of using logic. The anti-intellectuals construct intricate intellectual arguments to prove the insufficiency of the intellect. The anti-theologians use the revealed Word of God to show that there can be no revealed Word of God–or that if there could, it would remain impenetrable darkness and Mystery to our finite minds.

The Crisis of Our Time

Nonsense Has Come

Is it any wonder that the world is grasping at straws–the straws of experientialism, mysticism, and drugs? After all, if people are told that the Bible contains insoluble mysteries, then is not a flight into mysticism to be expected? On what grounds can it be condemned? Certainly not on logical grounds or Biblical grounds, if logic is futile and the Bible unintelligible. Moreover, if it cannot be condemned on logical or Biblical grounds, it cannot be condemned at all. If people are going to have a religion of the mysterious, they will not adopt Christianity: They will have a genuine mystery religion. "Those who call for Nonsense," C.S. Lewis once wrote, "will find that it comes." And that is precisely what has happened. The popularity of Eastern mysticism, of drugs, and of religious experience is the logical consequence of the irrationalism of the twentieth century. There can and will be no Christian reformation–and no reconstruction of society–unless and until the irrationalism of the age is totally repudiated by Christians.

The Church Defenseless

Yet how shall they do it? The spokesmen for Christianity have been fatally infected with irrationalism. The seminaries, which annually train thousands of men to teach millions of Christians, are the finishing schools of irrationalism, completing the job begun by the government schools and colleges. Some of the pulpits of the most conservative churches (we are not speaking of the apostate churches) are occupied by graduates of the anti-theological schools. These products of modern anti-theological education, when asked to give a reason for the hope that is in them, can generally respond with only the intellectual analogue of a shrug–a mumble about Mystery. They have not grasped–and therefore cannot teach those for whom they are responsible–the first truth: "And you shall know the truth." Many, in fact, explicitly deny it, saying that, at best, we possess only "pointers" to the truth, or something "similar" to the truth, a mere analogy. Is the impotence of the Christian church a puzzle? Is the fascination with pentecostalism and faith healing among members of conservative churches an enigma? Not when one understands the sort of studied nonsense that is purveyed in the name of God in the seminaries.

The Trinity Foundation

The creators of The Trinity Foundation firmly believe that theology is too important to be left to the licensed theologians–the graduates of the schools of theology. They have created The Trinity Foundation for the express purpose of teaching the faithful all that the Scriptures contain–not warmed over, baptized, secular philosophies. Each member of the board of directors of The Trinity Foundation has signed this oath: "I believe that the Bible alone and the Bible in its entirety is the Word of God and, therefore, inerrant in the autographs. I believe that the system of truth presented in the Bible is best summarized in the Westminster Confession of Faith. So help me God."

The ministry of The Trinity Foundation is the presentation of the system of truth taught in Scripture as clearly and as completely as possible. We do not regard obscurity as a virtue, nor confusion as a sign of spirituality. Confusion, like all error, is sin, and teaching that confusion is all that Christians can hope for is doubly sin.

The presentation of the truth of Scripture necessarily involves the rejection of error. The Foundation has exposed and will continue to expose the irrationalism of the twentieth century, whether its current spokesman be an existentialist philosopher or a professed Reformed theologian. We oppose anti-intellectualism, whether it be espoused by a neo-orthodox theologian or a fundamentalist evangelist. We reject misology, whether it be on the lips of a neo-evangelical or those of a Roman Catholic charismatic. To each error we bring the brilliant light of Scripture, proving all things, and holding fast to that which is true.

The Primacy of Theory

The ministry of The Trinity Foundation is not a "practical" ministry. If you are a pastor, we will not enlighten you on how to organize an ecumenical prayer meeting in your community or how to double church attendance in a year. If you are a homemaker, you will have to read elsewhere to find out how to become a total woman. If you are a businessman, we will not tell you how to develop a social conscience. The professing church is drowning in such "practical" advice.

The Trinity Foundation is unapologetically theoretical in its outlook, believing that theory without practice is dead, and that practice without theory is blind. The trouble with the professing church is not primarily in its practice, but in its theory. Christians do not know, and many do not even care to know, the doctrines of Scripture. Doctrine is intellectual, and Christians are generally anti-intellectual. Doctrine is ivory tower philosophy, and they scorn ivory towers. The ivory tower, however, is the control tower of a civilization. It is a fundamental, theoretical mistake of the practical men to think that they can be merely practical, for practice is always the practice of some theory. The relationship between theory and practice is the relationship between cause and effect. If a person believes correct theory, his practice will tend to be correct. The practice of contemporary Christians is immoral because it is the practice of false theories. It is a major theoretical mistake of the practical men to think that they can ignore the ivory towers of the philosophers and theologians as irrelevant to their lives. Every action that the "practical" men take is governed by the thinking that has occurred in some ivory tower—whether that tower be the British Museum; the Academy; a home in Basel, Switzerland; or a tent in Israel.

In Understanding Be Men

It is the first duty of the Christian to understand correct theory—correct doctrine—and thereby implement correct practice. This order—first theory, then practice—is both logical and Biblical. It is, for example, exhibited in Paul's epistle to the Romans, in which he spends the first eleven chapters expounding theory and the last five discussing practice. The contemporary teachers of Christians have not only reversed the order, they have inverted the Pauline emphasis on theory and practice. The virtually complete failure of the teachers of the professing church to instruct the faithful in correct doctrine is the cause of the misconduct and cultural impotence of Christians. The church's lack of power is the result of its lack of truth. The *Gospel* is the power of God, not religious experience or personal relationship. The church has no power because it has abandoned the Gospel, the good news, for a religion of experientialism. Twentieth-century American Christians are children carried about by every wind of doctrine, not knowing what they believe, or even if they believe anything for certain.

The chief purpose of The Trinity Foundation is to counteract the irrationalism of the age and to expose the errors of the teachers of the church. Our emphasis—on the Bible as the sole source of truth, on the primacy of the intellect, on the supreme importance of correct doctrine, and on the necessity for systematic and logical thinking—is almost unique in Christendom. To the extent that the church survives—and she will survive and flourish—it will be because of her increasing acceptance of these basic ideas and their logical implications.

We believe that the Trinity Foundation is filling a vacuum in Christendom. We are saying that Christianity is intellectually defensible—that, in fact, it is the only intellectually defensible system of thought. We are saying that God has made the wisdom of this world—whether that wisdom be called science, religion, philosophy, or common sense—foolishness. We are appealing to all Christians who have not conceded defeat in the intellectual battle with the world to join us in our efforts to raise a standard to which all men of sound mind can repair.

The love of truth, of God's Word, has all but disappeared in our time. We are committed to and pray for a great instauration. But though we may not see this reformation of Christendom in our lifetimes, we believe it is our duty to present the whole counsel of God because Christ has commanded it. The results of our teaching are in God's hands, not ours. Whatever those results, his Word is never taught in vain, but always accomplishes the result that he intended it to accomplish. Professor Gordon H. Clark has stated our view well:

The Crisis of Our Time

There have been times in the history of God's people, for example, in the days of Jeremiah, when refreshing grace and widespread revival were not to be expected: The time was one of chastisement. If this twentieth century is of a similar nature, individual Christians here and there can find comfort and strength in a study of God's Word. But if God has decreed happier days for us and if we may expect a world-shaking and genuine spiritual awakening, then it is the author's belief that a zeal for souls, however necessary, is not the sufficient condition. Have there not been devout saints in every age, numerous enough to carry on a revival? Twelve such persons are plenty. What distinguishes the arid ages from the period of the Reformation, when nations were moved as they had not been since Paul preached in Ephesus, Corinth, and Rome, is the latter's fullness of knowledge of God's Word. To echo an early Reformation thought, when the ploughman and the garage attendant know the Bible as well as the theologian does, and know it better than some contemporary theologians, then the desired awakening shall have already occurred.

In addition to publishing books, the Foundation publishes a monthly newsletter, *The Trinity Review.* Subscriptions to *The Review* are free to U.S. addresses; please write to the address below to become a subscriber. If you would like further information or would like to join us in our work, please let us know.

The Trinity Foundation is a non-profit foundation, tax exempt under section 501 (c)(3) of the Internal Revenue Code of 1954. You can help us disseminate the Word of God through your tax-deductible contributions to the Foundation.

John W. Robbins

INTELLECTUAL AMMUNITION

The Trinity Foundation is committed to the reformation of philosophy and theology along Biblical lines. We regard God's command to bring all our thoughts into conformity with Christ very seriously, and the books listed below are designed to accomplish that goal. They are written with two subordinate purposes: (1) to demolish all secular claims to knowledge; and (2) to build a system of truth based upon the Bible alone.

Philosophy

Ancient Philosophy, Gordon H. Clark $24.95

This book covers the thousand years from the Pre-Socratics to Plotinus. It represents some of the early work of Dr. Clark–the work that made his academic reputation. It is an excellent college text.

Behaviorism and Christianity, Gordon H. Clark $6.95

Behaviorism is a critique of both secular and religious behaviorists. It includes chapters on John Watson, Edgar S. Singer, Jr., Gilbert Ryle, B.F. Skinner, and Donald MacKay. Clark's refutation of behaviorism and his argument for a Christian doctrine of man are unanswerable.

A Christian Philosophy of Education $8.95
Gordon H. Clark
The first edition of this book was published in 1946. It sparked the contemporary interest in Christian schools. In the 1970s, Dr. Clark thoroughly revised and updated it, and it is needed now more than ever. Its chapters include: The Need for a World-View, The Christian World-View, The Alternative to Christian Theism, Neutrality, Ethics, The Christian Philosophy of Education, Academic Matters, and Kindergarten to University. Three appendices are included: The Relationship of Public Education to Christianity, A Protestant World-View, and Art and the Gospel.

A Christian View of Men and Things $10.95
Gordon H. Clark
No other book achieves what A Christian View *does: the presentation of Christianity as it applies to history, politics, ethics, science, religion, and epistemology. Clark's command of both worldly philosophy and Scripture is evident on every page, and the result is a breathtaking and invigorating challenge to the wisdom of this world.*

Clark Speaks From The Grave, Gordon H. Clark $3.95
Dr. Clark chides some of his critics for their failure to defend Christianity competently. Clark Speaks *is a stimulating and illuminating discussion of the errors of contemporary apologists.*

Education, Christianity, and the State $9.95
J. Gresham Machen
Machen was one of the foremost educators, theologians, and defenders of Christianity in the twentieth century. The author of numerous scholarly books, Machen saw clearly that if Christianity is to survive and flourish, a system of Christian schools must be established. This collection of essays captures his thoughts on education over nearly three decades.

Essays on Ethics and Politics, Gordon H. Clark $10.95

Clark's essays, written over the course of five decades, are a major statement of Christian ethics.

Gordon H. Clark: Personal Recollections $6.95
John W. Robbins, editor

Friends of Dr. Clark have written their recollections of the man. Contributors include family members, colleagues, students, and friends such as Harold Lindsell, Carl Henry, Ronald Nash, Dwight Zeller, and Mary Crumpacker. The book includes an extensive bibliography of Clark's work.

Historiography: Secular and Religious $13.95
Gordon H. Clark

In this masterful work, Clark applies his philosophy to the writing of history, examining all the major schools of historiography.

An Introduction to Christian Philosophy $8.95
Gordon H. Clark

In 1966 Clark delivered three lectures on philosophy at Wheaton College. In these lectures he criticizes secular philosophy and launches a philosophical revolution in the name of Christ.

Language and Theology, Gordon H. Clark $9.95

There are two main currents in twentieth-century philosophy— language philosophy and existentialism. Both are hostile to Christianity. Clark disposes of language philosophy in this brilliant critique of Bertrand Russell, Ludwig Wittgenstein, Rudolf Carnap, A.J. Ayer, Langdon Gilkey, and many others.

Logic, Gordon H. Clark $8.95

Written as a textbook for Christian schools, Logic *is another unique book from Clark's pen. His presentation of the laws of thought, which must be followed if Scripture is to be understood correctly, and which are found in Scripture itself, is both clear and thorough.* Logic *is an indispensable book for the thinking Christian.*

Intellectual Ammunition

Logic Workbook, Elihu Carranza $11.95
Designed to be used in conjunction with Clark's textbook Logic, *this* Workbook *contains hundreds of exercises and test questions on perforated pages for ease of use by students.*

Lord God of Truth, Concerning the Teacher $7.95
Gordon H. Clark and Aurelius Augustine
This essay by Clark summarizes many of the most telling arguments against empiricism and defends the Biblical teaching that we know God and truth immediately. The dialogue by Augustine is a refutation of empirical language philosophy.

The Philosophy of Science and Belief in God $8.95
Gordon H. Clark
In opposing the contemporary idolatry of science, Clark analyzes three major aspects of science: the problem of motion, Newtonian science, and modern theories of physics. His conclusion is that science, while it may be useful, is always false; and he demonstrates its falsity in numerous ways. Since science is always false, it can offer no objection to the Bible and Christianity.

Religion, Reason and Revelation $10.95
Gordon H. Clark
One of Clark's apologetical masterpieces, Religion, Reason and Revelation *has been praised for the clarity of its thought and language. It includes chapters on* Is Christianity a Religion? Faith and Reason, Inspiration and Language, Revelation and Morality, *and* God and Evil. *It is must reading for all serious Christians.*

Thales to Dewey: A History of Philosophy $27.95
Gordon H. Clark
This is the best one-volume history of philosophy in English.

Three Types of Religious Philosophy $6.95
Gordon H. Clark
In this book on apologetics, Clark examines empiricism, ration-

393

alism, dogmatism, and contemporary irrationalism, which does not rise to the level of philosophy. He offers a solution to the question, "How can Christianity be defended before the world?"

William James and John Dewey $8.95
Gordon H. Clark
  William James and John Dewey are two of the most influential philosophers America has produced. Their philosophies of instrumentalism and pragmatism are hostile to Christianity, and Clark demolishes their arguments.

Without a Prayer: Ayn Rand and the Close of Her System
John W. Robbins $27.95
  This is the only book-length critique of Rand's philosophy of Objectivism written by a Christian. Objectivism's epistemology, theology, ethics, and politics are discussed in detail. Appendixes include analyses of books by Leonard Peikoff and David Kelley, as well as several essays on Christianity and philosophy.

Theology

The Atonement, Gordon H. Clark $8.95
  In The Atonement, *Clark discusses the covenants, the virgin birth and incarnation, federal headship and representation, the relationship between God's sovereignty and justice, and much more. He analyzes traditional views of the atonement and criticizes them in the light of Scripture alone.*

The Biblical Doctrine of Man, Gordon H. Clark $6.95
  Is man soul and body or soul, spirit, and body? What is the image of God? Is Adam's sin imputed to his children? Is evolution true? Are men totally depraved? What is the heart? These are some of the questions discussed and answered from Scripture in this book.

The Clark–Van Til Controversy $7.95
Herman Hoeksema
This collection of essays by the founder of the Protestant Reformed Church–essays written at the time of the Clark–Van Til controversy–is one of the best commentaries on the events in print.

Cornelius Van Til: The Man and The Myth $2.45
John W. Robbins
The actual teachings of this eminent Philadelphia theologian have been obscured by the myths that surround him. This book penetrates those myths and criticizes Van Til's surprisingly unorthodox views of God and the Bible.

The Everlasting Righteousness, Horatius Bonar $8.95
Originally published in 1874, the language of Bonar's masterpiece on justification by faith alone has been updated and Americanized for easy reading and clear understanding. This is one of the best books ever written on justification.

Faith and Saving Faith, Gordon H. Clark $8.95
The views of the Roman Catholic church, John Calvin, Thomas Manton, John Owen, Charles Hodge, and B. B. Warfield are discussed in this book. Is the object of faith a person or a proposition? Is faith more than belief? Is belief more than thinking with assent, as Augustine said? In a world chaotic with differing views of faith, Clark clearly explains the Biblical view of faith and saving faith.

God and Evil, Gordon H. Clark $4.95
This volume is Chapter 5 of Religion, Reason and Revelation, *in which Clark presents his solution to the problem of evil.*

God's Hammer: The Bible and Its Critics $10.95
Gordon H. Clark
The starting point of Christianity, the doctrine on which all other doctrines depend, is "The Bible alone, and the Bible in its entirety, is the Word of God written, and therefore inerrant in the

autographs." Over the centuries the opponents of Christianity, with Satanic shrewdness, have concentrated their attacks on the truthfulness and completeness of the Bible. In the twentieth century the attack is not so much in the fields of history and archaeology as in philosophy. Clark's brilliant defense of the complete truthfulness of the Bible is captured in this collection of eleven major essays.

Guide to the Westminster Confession and Catechism
James E. Bordwine $13.95
This book contains the full text of both the Westminster Confession (both original and American versions) and the Larger Catechism. In addition, it offers a chapter-by-chapter summary of the Confession and a unique index to both the Confession and the Catechism.

The Holy Spirit, Gordon H. Clark $8.95
This discussion of the third person of the Trinity is both concise and exact. Clark includes chapters on the work of the Spirit, sanctification, and Pentecostalism. This book is part of his multivolume systematic theology that began appearing in print in 1985.

The Incarnation, Gordon H. Clark $8.95
Who is Christ? The attack on the incarnation in the nineteenth and twentieth centuries has been vigorous, but the orthodox response has been lame. Clark reconstructs the doctrine of the incarnation, building and improving upon the Chalcedonian definition.

In Defense of Theology, Gordon H. Clark $9.95
There are four groups to whom Clark addresses this book: average Christians who are uninterested in theology, atheists and agnostics, religious experientialists, and serious Christians. The vindication of the knowledge of God against the objections of three of these groups is the first step in theology.

The Johannine Logos, Gordon H. Clark $5.95
Clark analyzes the relationship between Christ, who is the truth, and the Bible. He explains why John used the same word to refer

to both Christ and his teaching. Chapters deal with the Prologue to John's Gospel, Logos and Rheemata, Truth, and Saving Faith.

Justification by Faith Alone, Charles Hodge $10.95

Charles Hodge of Princeton Seminary was the best American theologian of the nineteenth century. Here in one volume are his two major essays on justification. This book is essential in defending the faith.

Predestination, Gordon H. Clark $10.95

Clark thoroughly discusses one of the most controversial and pervasive doctrines of the Bible: that God is, quite literally, Almighty. Free will, the origin of evil, God's omniscience, creation, and the new birth are all presented within a Scriptural framework. The objections of those who do not believe in the Almighty God are considered and refuted. This edition also contains the text of the booklet, Predestination in the Old Testament.

Sanctification, Gordon H. Clark $8.95

In this book, which is part of Clark's multi-volume systematic theology, he discusses historical theories of sanctification, the sacraments, and the Biblical doctrine of sanctification.

Study Guide to the Westminster Confession $10.95
W. Gary Crampton

This Study Guide *may be used by individuals or classes. It contains a paragraph by paragraph summary of the Westminster Confession, and questions for the student to answer. Space for answers is provided. The* Guide *will be most beneficial when used in conjunction with Clark's* What Do Presbyterians Believe?

Today's Evangelism: Counterfeit or Genuine? $6.95
Gordon H. Clark

Clark compares the methods and messages of today's evangelists with Scripture, and finds that Christianity is on the wane because the Gospel has been distorted or lost. This is an extremely useful and enlightening book.

Without a Prayer: Ayn Rand and the Close of Her System

The Trinity, Gordon H. Clark $8.95
Apart from the doctrine of Scripture, no teaching of the Bible is more fundamental than the doctrine of God. Clark's defense of the orthodox doctrine of the Trinity is a principal portion of Clark's systematic theology. There are chapters on the deity of Christ, Augustine, the incomprehensibility of God, Bavinck and Van Til, and the Holy Spirit, among others.

What Calvin Says, W. Gary Crampton $7.95
This is both a readable and thorough introduction to the theology of John Calvin.

What Do Presbyterians Believe? Gordon H. Clark $10.95
This classic introduction to Christian doctrine has been republished. It is the best commentary on the Westminster Confession of Faith that has ever been written. A Study Guide *is now available for it.*

Commentaries on the New Testament

Colossians, Gordon H. Clark	$ 6.95
Ephesians, Gordon H. Clark	$ 8.95
First Corinthians, Gordon H. Clark	$10.95
First John, Gordon H. Clark	$10.95
First and Second Thessalonians, Gordon H. Clark	$ 5.95
New Heavens, New Earth (First and Second Peter) Gordon H. Clark	$10.95
The Pastoral Epistles (I and II Timothy and Titus) Gordon H. Clark	$ 9.95
Philippians, Gordon H. Clark	$ 9.95

All of Clark's commentaries are expository, not technical, and are written for the Christian layman. His purpose is to explain the text clearly and accurately so that the Word of God will be thoroughly known by every Christian.

The Trinity Library

We will send you one copy of each of the 49 books listed above for $350 (retail value: $485), postpaid to any address in the U. S. You may also order the books you want individually on the order blank on the next page. Because some of the books are in short supply, we must reserve the right to substitute others of equal or greater value in The Trinity Library. This special offer expires June 30, 2001.

ORDER FORM

Name _____

Address _____

_____

Please: ☐ add my name to the mailing list for *The Trinity Review.*
        I understand that there is no charge for the *Review* sent
        to a U.S. address.

        ☐ accept my tax deductible contribution of $ _____
        for the work of the Foundation.

        ☐ send me_____ copies of *Without a Prayer.* I enclose as
        payment $_____ .

        ☐ send me the Trinity Library of 49 books. I enclose
        US$350 as full payment.

        ☐ send me the following books. I enclose full payment
        in the amount of $_____ for them.

_____

_____

_____

_____

_____

Mail to:

The Trinity Foundation
Post Office Box 1666, Hobbs, New Mexico 88240
United States of America

Please add $5.00 for postage. For foreign orders, please enclose
20 percent of the total value of the books ordered. Thank you.
For quantity discounts, please write to The Foundation.

55